The History of American Women's Voluntary Organizations, 1810-1960

a guide to sources

G. K. Hall

WOMEN'S
STUDIES
Publications

Barbara Haber
Editor

The History of American Women's Voluntary Organizations, 1810-1960

a guide to sources

KAREN J. BLAIR

G.K.HALL &CO.
70 LINCOLN STREET, BOSTON, MASS.

Book production by Patricia D'Agostino
Copyediting supervised by Ara Salibian

Library of Congress Cataloging-in-Publication Data
Blair, Karen J.
      The history of American women's voluntary organizations, 1810-1960:
      a guide to sources / by Karen J. Blair.
         p.   cm. -- (women's studies publications)
      Bibliography: p.
      Includes index.
      ISBN 0-8161-8648-0
      1. Women--United States--Societies and clubs--History--19th
century--Bibliography. 2. Women--United States--Societies and
clubs--History--20th century--Bibliography. I. Title. II. Series:
G.K. Hall women's studies publications.
Z7964.U49B53 1988
[HQ1904]
016.3054'06'073--dc19   88-19946
                                        CIP

To Carol Ellen DuBois

Contents

The Author

Karen J. Blair, a historian, was trained at Mount Holyoke College and the State University of New York at Buffalo. She is a specialist in the field of American women's history and teaches in the Department of History, Central Washington University, Ellensburg, WA. She is the author of *The Clubwoman as Feminist: True Womanhood Redefined, 1868-1914* (1980) and editor of *Essays in Pacific Northwest Women's History* (1988). She has held fellowships from the Rockefeller Foundation, Haynes Foundation at the Huntington Library, the Moody Foundation at the Lyndon Baines Johnson Library, and the Newberry Library. She has held the Woodrow Wilson Doctoral Dissertation Fellowship in Women's History.

Introduction

Since the beginning of the nineteenth century, great numbers of American women have defied the dictum that "woman's place is in the home." As soon as they enjoyed some relief from domestic responsibilities, they began to devote leisure time to organizational life. Women faced criticisms that they were neglecting their homes and families, to which they were supposed to be single-mindedly devoted. They persisted, however, in asserting that they could take on a public role in addition to their domestic one. Soon, volunteers established a public voice that they did not enjoy in business, the professions, politics, or even in the educational arena. Generally, their associative efforts were connected to church and philanthropic projects in antebellum America. After the Civil War, when the rash of patriotic women's groups emerged, secular societies truly began to flourish. Until the Great Depression, women's organizations served as a singularly vital force for personal and political change. Clubs have continued to form, throughout the twentieth century, meeting the changing needs of women.

The typical woman who joined clubs was white, middle-class, married, and whose children had already entered school. However, clubs existed for other women as well. For single career women, the clubs and its members provided a family's warmth and companionship. For women of color, working women, for women of every political persuasion or no political feeling whatsoever, and for girls too, clubs developed to bring like-minded neighbors together. The many women who joined clubs exhibited a wide range of commitments in their organizational priorities: to themselves, by acquiring knowledge, skills and new experiences; to their sister members, by engaging in social, intellectual and political cooperation; to all women, by identifying problems and devising solutions for all women's political rights, conditions in the workplace, educational opportunities, and for their children; and to the larger society, by creating and supporting a wide variety of institutions from which everyone might benefit--including public libraries, parks, churches, and the World Court. In so far as these goals of women were systematically met by few other institutions in American history, clubs held a far more significant place in women's lives than men's clubs and organizations did for men, and they deserve far more serious attention from researchers than they have previously enjoyed. The contributions clubs made to women's lives is affirmed by the enthusiasm with which women participated in clubs. To the American landscape, clubs provided a multitude of services and facilities previously unavailable. In fact, the absence of such "amenities" as street lights, playgrounds, drinking fountains, little theaters, baby clinics, ambulances for soldiers, beds for children's hospitals, mission schools abroad--all initiated by women's organizations--would have rendered life more bleak and difficult, for them and for us.

I have located almost seven hundred published books and articles treating the history of women's organizations between the years 1810, when the club movement gained momentum, and 1960, the eve of the contemporary women's movement. Many of the most analytical studies have been written by historians and scholars in recent decades. In these, the documentation is strong. The most detailed works were often written by club members themselves, for a readership of their peers, full of anecdotes and the flavor of club life. The bulk of the organizations analyzed have fallen into thirteen basic categories. They are: benevolence (including charity, philanthropy), culture (arts, civics, mothers clubs, recreation), sororities (fraternal organizations, secret societies), peace, race, patriotic, religion (missionary), suffrage, temperance, work, youth (including scouts), politics, and miscellaneous (or studies which include discussion of several of the categories listed).

All groups included required of women both time and energy which they contributed voluntarily, to push forward an agreed-upon program. Thus, there is no mention of women who volunteered during World War II for military service, because they were paid for their labor. Neither have I included organizations devoted to improving the working conditions and wages of working women, such as trade unions, leaving the topic of women and work to another annotated bibliography. The only exceptions are these: the work of Women's Trade Union League, because so many of its members were volunteer activists rather than wage-earners; and the histories of professional women's clubs which emphasize social and civic activities, rather than members' career networking efforts. Nuns, whose calling is a full-time commitment, have not been included here. Nor have the utopian communal experiments of women, like the Woman's Commonwealth of Belton, Texas.

Many of the club-commissioned surveys were published only in limited editions and are now out-of-print. Students of this subject may have to order these titles through their college or university inter-library loan offices from distant repositories. I have not included works of fiction dealing with club life, with unpublished dissertations or master's theses, with sociological studies of patterns among volunteers in their clubs, with newspaper clippings, with biographies of clubwomen which ignore their club work and stress other aspects of their lives, or with collections of primary documents. No doubt intrepid researchers can supplement my list by scavenging in collections of primary sources for unheralded, unpublished manuscripts on the history of individual women's clubs, written by members, intended for members and forgotten in their archives.

I have hopes that my inclusion of descriptions of photographs in the published sources will hold value to scholars willing to evaluate non-written materials. Four categories describe the bulk of the images I have listed: individual portraits of clubwomen; formal group photographs; spontaneous snap-shots of clubwomen involved in their projects; and depictions of the fruits of their voluntary labor, as diverse as clubhouses they built, classes they sponsored, drinking fountains they paid for.

My sources are alphabetized by author, but the codes should enable researchers to locate quickly the sub-categories about which they are curious. Many works address the histories of several types of women's voluntary organizations and the multiple codes reflect that diversity.

Acknowledgments

To the students who so enthusiastically assisted me in retrieving materials; I am tremendously grateful--Karen Rundburg-Bunney, Mary Lou Laprade, Beth Draig, Susan Haymes, Margaret Amara, Elizabeth Guerin and Nancy Tuinstra. I wish to thank the Inter-Library Loan staff at the University of Washington for securing so cheerfully the bulk of the volumes annotated here. At Central Washington University, Mae Morey provided invaluable aid. Ruth Kirk, Anna McCausland, and Joan Ramos were a pleasure to work with. Janet Jenks also located some obscure materials. Marian Bolan has been a remarkable typist. Sharon Tighe was a careful indexer. To Central Washington University's Graduate School, I give thanks for a Faculty Research Grant to facilitate manuscript preparation. This volume is dedicated to Carol Ellen DuBois, a small thank you for her serious, generous and affable supervision of my doctoral dissertation and graduate career in American women's history.

Codes

b: benevolence, charity, philanthropy

c: culture, arts, civics, mother's clubs, recreation, and education

f: fraternity, sorority, secret society

i: peace

m: miscellaneous, several of the other categories

n: race

p: patriotic

r: religion, mission

s: suffrage

t: temperance

w: work

y: youth, scouts

z: politics

Bibliographic Sources

The most useful sources have been:

America: History and Life. Santa Barbara: ABC-Clio, 1964-.

HARRISON, CYNTHIA ELLEN. *Women in American History.* 2 vols. Santa Barbara: ABC-Clio, 1979, 1985.

Additional bibliographic aids include:

ARTHUR AND ELIZABETH SCHLESINGER LIBRARY ON THE HISTORY OF WOMEN IN AMERICA. *Book Catalog.* Vol. 8. Boston: G.K. Hall & Co., 1984.

BALLOU, PATRICIA K. *Women: A Bibliography of Bibliographies.* Boston: G.K. Hall & Co., 1980.

THE CENTER FOR THE AMERICAN WOMAN AND POLITICS. *Voluntary Participation among Women in the United States: A Selected Bibliography.* New Brunswick, N.J.: Rutgers University Press, 1976.

COUNCIL OF PLANNING LIBRARIANS. "The Changing Role of Women in America: A Selected Annotated Bibliography of

Reference Sources." *Women in American Society*, No. 931 (Dec. 1975).

Gerritson Collection of Women's History: A Bibliographic Guide to the Microfilm Collection. Glen Rock, N.J.: Microfilming Corporation of America, 1977.

HABER, BARBARA. *Women in America: A Guide to Books, 1963-1975*. Boston: G.K. Hall & Co., 1978.

JACOBS, SUE-ELLEN. *Women in Perspective: A Guide for Cross-Cultural Studies*. Urbana: University of Illinois Press, 1974.

KING, JUDITH D. *Women: A Select Bibliography of Books*. Allendale, Mich.: Grand Valley State College Library, 1974.

KRICHMAR, ALBERT. *The Women's Rights Movement in the United States, 1848-1970: A Bibliography and Sourcebook*. Metuchen, N.J.: Scarecrow Press, 1972.

LERNER, GERDA. *Bibliography in the History of American Women*. Bronxville, N.Y.: Sarah Lawrence College, 1978.

RITCHIE, MAUREEN, comp. *Women's Studies: A Checklist of Bibliographies*. London: Manrell, 1980.

SALZER, ELIZABETH, and HANNAH APPLEBAUM. *A Selected Bibliography of Books on Women in the Libraries of the State University of New York at Albany*. New York: University Library, 1972.

SEARING, SUSAN E. *Introduction to Library Research in Women's Studies*. Boulder, Colo.: Westview Press, 1985.

SMITH, CONSTANCE, and ANNE FREEDMAN. *Voluntary Associations: Perspectives on the Literature*. Cambridge, Mass.: Harvard University Press, 1972.

STANWICK, KATHY, and CHRISTINE LI. *The Political Participation of Women in the United States: A Selected Bibliography, 1950-1976*. Metuchen, N.J.: Scarecrow Press, 1977.

STEINMAN, ESTHER.　　Women's Studies:　*A Recommended Core Bibliography*. Littleton, Colo.: Libraries Unlimited, 1979.

Women's Studies Abstracts. Rush, N.Y.: Rush Publishing, 1972-86.

The History of American Women's Voluntary Organizations, 1810-1960

1   *s ABBOTT, VIRGINIA CLARK. *The History of Women Suffrage and the League of Women Voters in Cuyahoga County, 1911-1945.* Cleveland, Ohio: the organization, 1945. 178 pp. Bib.

Despite its title, this history begins with the origins of the women's suffrage movement at the 1848 Seneca Falls Conference in New York State. It surveys the roots of the women's rights movement in Ohio with Lucy Stone's stellar career at Oberlin College in 1847, the Salem Woman's Rights Convention of 1850, the efforts of the eight Newbury Woman's Political Suffrage Club members to cast "illegal" votes for the Ohio governor in 1871, and the formation in Cleveland of a branch of the American Woman Suffrage Association by Julia Ward Howe of Boston in 1869. In a chatty writing style, rich with anecdotes, the author describes the 1869 founding of the Cuyahoga County Woman's Suffrage Association. Details are lively for the decade of suffrage activity prior to the passage of the women's suffrage amendment to the federal Constitution in 1920; a 1912 campaign to alter the Ohio constitution via a constitutional convention with a parade in the city of Columbus and opposition by the whiskey lobby and antisuffragists; fund-raising efforts through parties and pageants; a second parade in 1914 including "Negro" women marchers; efforts to enlist more Ohio women in the suffrage struggle; plain bitterness toward the militant National Woman's party supporters. War service during World War I, in the form of purchase of Liberty Loans, is proudly described. The twenty-five-year history of the League of Woman Voters in Cuyahoga County, Ohio, receives ample scrutiny, with its founding in 1920 and its hosting in Cleveland of the national conference in the following year, where President Carrie Chapman Catt unveiled her world disarmament plan. Among the specific programs supported by this branch in its decade were support for Florence Allen for judge of the common pleas court, citizenship schools to inform Americans of governmental organization, the World Court, protective legislation rather than an equal rights amendment, participation in the Woman's Council for the Prevention of War and the Pan-Pacific Conference, the Bing school attendance law, child labor restrictions, and a new Cleveland city charter. In 1928, the group succeeded in its goal to prevent the adoption of the Davis amendment and secure a city-manager plan. In the 1930s, the group supported Social Security, Civil Service, modernization of the food and drug laws, world disarmament, the welfare of children, mental health laws, and public meetings for voters to meet candidates.

2   *r ABERNATHY, MOLLIE C. (DAVIS). "Southern Women, Social Reconstruction, and the Church in the 1920's." *Louisiana Studies* 13 (Winter 1974): 289-312. Notes.

The author asserts that the evolution of women's organizations in the South was a decade behind that in the West and the East, and claims that southern churches share the blame for retarding women's progress. Baptists and Methodists, especially, retained a conservative outlook and defined women's roles as caretakers for home and family. World War I served as a catalyst for southern women and presented many of them with the opportunity to engage in volunteer work. Exploring southern social feminists of the 1920s, Abernathy finds radicals atypical of southern women but nevertheless visible and important in drawing on church resources to combat racism. She cites the 1920 Methodist women who created a Commission on Racial Relationships which united white and black women to publicize the menace of lynching. She also discusses the Association of Southern Women for the Prevention of Lynching, its leaders, their backgrounds, and their distinguished efforts to bring about change.

3   *p   ABLES, L. ROBERT. "Second Battle for the Alamo." *Southwestern Historical Quarterly* 70 (January 1967): 372-413. Notes, illus.: Clara Driscoll, Corpus Christi leader and writer; Adina de Zavala, San Antonio leader and teacher; map and photo of the Alamo.

   Two branches of the Daughters of the Republic of Texas contended for custody of the Alamo, site of the 1836 battle in San Antonio. The branches were founded in 1891 in Galveston and Houston, under the leadership of Clara Driscoll of Corpus Christi and Adina de Zavala of San Antonio, to seek custody of the chapel at the fort between the years 1903 and 1912. Each group had a different plan to acquire more property at the historical site, but found it difficult to raise the necessary funds to carry out their plans.

4   *c   ACTON, HUL-CEE MARCUS. *The Pierian Club of Birmingham*. Birmingham, Ala.: Banner Press, 1962. xviii, 243 pp. Indexes, illus.: 18 photos, including Virginia Franklin Acton and other officers; a group photo.

   In 1897, fourteen women in East Lake, Alabama, organized a literary and social club to give papers, provide music and readings, and share discussion. In the first year, ancient history was the general topic of study. Acton provides a biography for each of the 171 members, giving their maiden names, family history, dates of club membership, church affiliation, name and occupation of husband, physical characteristics, educational background, nickname, address, membership in other clubs, committee work, children, and, if pertinent, job or career. In separate sections, the policies on attendance, absenteeism, funding, social activities, educational programs, scholarships, child welfare projects, and library assistance are stated. Seven chapters enumerate the history chronologically: origins, activities from 1906 through World War I, projects during that war, those during the years between the two world wars (a better-film campaign, stopping jazz, countering the menacing liquor traffic, tree planting, the creation of a Junior Pierian Club in 1924, refusal to join the General Federation of Women's Clubs for fear of being forced to integrate with black members), World War II projects (the Red Cross, prayer, conservation, a victory clothing drive), postwar activity, and "Odds and Ends," a miscellaneous collection of parties, anniversaries, and recollections of deceased members.

5   *p   ADAMS, FRANC L. "The Woman's Relief Corps as a Pioneer." *Michigan History Magazine* 4 (April-July 1920): 575-82.

Fifty-eight women formed the Woman's Relief Corps in Denver in 1883, as an auxiliary to the Grand Army of the Republic. This history first looks back to noble women of earlier ages who did good works, including Miriam, Ruth, Esther, Dorcas, Lydia, Cornelia, Joan of Arc, Florence Nightingale, Frances Willard, and, in the Civil War, Clara Barton, Mother Bickerdyke, and Marie Logan. The Woman's Relief Corps sought to care for the sick and afflicted veterans of the Civil War, to inculcate lessons of patriotism, and to perpetuate the commemoration of Memorial Day. Some 164,000 members (8,000 of them in Michigan's chapter, founded 1884) spent $5 million for relief of veterans of the Civil War and their dependents. During World War I, 75 percent of the Michigan members joined the Red Cross and made 36,000 garments in 95,000 hours. Working for the Commission for Relief in Belgium and the American Fund for French Wounded, buying Liberty Bonds, sending ammunition workers into factories, and contributing eight canteen workers constituted some of its other wartime labors.

6   *t ADDITION, LUCIA H. FAXTON. *Twenty Eventful Years of the Oregon Women's Christian Temperance Union, 1880-1900.* Portland, Oreg.: Gotshall Print Co., 1904. x, 112 pp. Bib., indexes, illus.: 30 portraits of state officers; Corvallis Women's Christian Temperance Union headquarters, the first built by a local chapter on the Pacific Coast.

This survey of WCTU history in Oregon begins in 1880, when Elizabeth A.P. White was appointed by national headquarters as the WCTU vice president for Oregon. Her mother, Rebecca Clawson, organized the first local group, in Portland in 1881. The second president, Mrs. H.K. Hines, traveled across the state to establish unions and was sufficiently successful that the Oregon State WCTU was organized in Portland in 1883. Speeches from the opening convention are excerpted. Organizational details are provided, the sixty women attending creating six districts and electing officers immediately. Sixteen departments of work were planned, and local unions, numbering thirty-two by 1884, undertook a wide variety of activities, holding socials in seamen's halls and meetings for sailors in YMCA rooms or homes of members, petitioning sellers of tobacco about their sales to minors, volunteering for prison work, and founding kindergartens. In 1891, Portland began to host Pacific Coast conferences of the WCTU. Resolutions from the meetings are listed here, including those regarding the establishment of a post of police matron in local jails. The women also sponsored a conference for Indians at the Umatilla Reservation. Several poems about temperance are collected here as are memorials to Frances Willard, who died in 1898. Twenty-five biographies of WCTU workers are provided, including details about their public and private life.

7 *r AGNEW, THEODORE L. "Reflections on the Woman's Foreign Missionary Movement in Late Nineteenth Century American Methodism." *Methodist History* 6 (January 1968): 3-16. Notes.

   The Methodist Woman's Foreign Missionary Society was founded in Boston in 1869 and quickly grew to include auxiliaries throughout the nation, a home missionary movement after 1884, and special auxiliaries for "young ladies" and for "colored sisters." The group also published the *Heathen Woman's Friend*. Rather than describing the work of the association or exploring its meaning for members and recipients of its service work, the author speculates about its success in the context of forces in American Methodism and in American history.

8 *y,c AHRENS, S. HELEN. "Young Women's Christian Association of Reading, Pennsylvania, 1897-1947." *Historical Review of Berkshire County* 13 (January 1948): 45-49. Illus.: 1947 YWCA Historical Pageant; old YWCA on N. Sixth Street; the present YWCA building.

   To celebrate the fiftieth birthday of the Young Women's Christian Association in Reading, Ahrens surveyed its history from its organization in 1897 through 1947. Fifty women founded the Y, rented headquarters, and set up committees to hire a general secretary, organize classes, and display exhibits. A board of trustees, composed of men only, was established; they are named here. By 1905, two hundred industrial girls, organized in factory clubs, were using the Y for recreation and religious activity. During its second decade, the organization erected a gymnasium, expanded its course offerings, and became allied with the Camp Fire Girls. During World War I, the Y engaged in relief work, knitting, and fund-raising, and sponsored first aid programs. It opened an international institute for foreign girls at this time. By 1919, twelve hundred young women belonged to the organization, participating in its summer camp, using its new pool, attending dances, and dining in the two cafeterias. A club of business girls was formed in 1921. During the early, lean years of the Great Depression, the Y managed to buy Blue Mountain Camp. The war years brought USO activities, a young matron's club, and welcoming programs for wives from overseas.

9   *m ALLEN, ELEANOR W. "Boston's Women's Educational and
      Industrial Union." *New England Galaxy* 6 (Spring 1965): 30-39.
      Illus.: Dr. Harriet Clisby; Mary Morton Kehew; Eva Whiting White.
          In 1877, the Women's Educational and Industrial Union was
      founded in Boston. Allen surveys its early activities, language classes,
      and moral and spiritual programs. She describes the accomplishments
      of the Domestic Science Bureau, the School of Housework, the New
      England Kitchen, the Woman's Exchange, the free medical clinic, and
      the research undertaken regarding working women's lives.

10   no entry

11   *f ALPHA PHI FRATERNITY. *The History of Alpha Phi
      Fraternity, 1872-1922.* New York: Century Co., 1923. xvii, 376 pp.
      Illus.: 84 photos of founders, officers, chapter houses; group photo of
      50th anniversary conference in Syracuse in 1922.
          On the occasion of the group's fiftieth anniversary, forty-two
      members cooperated to produce this history, under the supervision of
      assistant historian Olive Finley Singleton. The bulk of the text consists
      of the histories of twenty-six sorority chapters, providing their dates of
      founding, growth and development, budgets, projects, and officers. A
      "Who's Who" section provides thumbnail biographies of all members.
      Shorter sections deal with administration, organization, conferences,
      badges, publications, war work, alumnae chapters, and chapter houses.

12   *c ALSOP, ELLA G. *History of the Florida Federation of Garden
      Clubs, 1924-1943.* Jacksonville, Fla.: Cooper Press, 1943. 104 pp.
      Indexes, illus.: Ella G. Alsop; Mrs. W.H. Covington, president, 1941-
      43; gardens of members; garden projects supported by the club.
          In 1924, at the Second Annual Flower Show in Jacksonville,
      Florida, women participants decided there was a need for a state
      federation of garden clubs. The first president, Mrs. Joseph R. Ellicott,
      held the first convention in 1926 in Jacksonville. The Jacksonville
      Garden Club grew to be the largest garden club in the world, with 1,654
      members at the time this history was written. The Florida Federation
      was a charter member of the National Council of State Garden Club
      Federations. Alsop surveys each presidency and reports on the work
      accomplished at each convention. Among projects undertaken by the
      membership were tours of gardens, the formation of junior clubs and
      gardens for children, opposition to billboards defacing Florida
      highways, and the improvement of home and public gardens. A list of
      seventy-six clubs which joined the federation between 1925 and 1943 is
      provided.

13   *n AMES, JESSIE (DANIEL). *Association of Southern Women for the Prevention of Lynching.* Atlanta: Commission on Inter-racial Cooperation, 1942.

See Lewis T. Nordyke.

14   *w AMSTERDAM, SUSAN. "The National Women's Trade Union League." *Social Service Review* 56 (June 1982): 259-72. Notes.

Amsterdam portrays the Women's Trade Union League as a social reform organization of the Progressive Era, which assisted unorganized women workers to become unionized. Part 1 explores the historical background and origins of the league from 1903 to 1930. The membership consisted of two constituencies—educated, middle-class women who were professionals or volunteers, and working women. Both groups assisted working women in their relations with employers and with the male-dominated American Federation of Labor which undervalued women workers. Prominent leaders described are Leonora O'Reilly, Margaret Dreier, Mary Anderson, and Agnes Nestor. No working-class woman presided over the organization until 1921. Rose Schneiderman assumed the presidency in 1928, however, and held the post for twenty years. Part 2 examines the 1930s and finds the New Deal unable to overcome discrimination against working women. Part 3 traces the organization's progress during the 1940s and 1950s, at which time the WTUL voted to disband. The author observes that women's place in unions and the workplace continues to be fraught with inequities.

15   *t ANDERSON, ELIZABETH PRESTON. "Organization and Accomplishments of the WCTU in North Dakota." *Annals of the American Academy of Political and Social Science* 32 (November 1908): 522-25.

This brief account catalogs the work of North Dakota temperance advocates. With a treasury of sixty thousand dollars, the group published the *White Ribbon Bulletin* for eleven years and maintained a home for the needy. The political initiatives supported by the membership are enumerated.

16   *p ANDERSON, MRS. JOHN HUSKE (LUCY LONDON). *North Carolina Women of the Confederacy.* Fayetteville, N.C.: the author, 1926. 141 pp. Illus.: Confederate monument erected in North Carolina in 1868.

Mrs. William Parley founded the North Carolina Division of the United Daughters of the Confederacy in 1895, a year after initiating the Cape Fear chapter. Determined "to honor the memory of those who served and those who fell in the service of the Confederate States," the members decorated the graves of soldiers and erected monuments to them, and sought to perpetuate the memory of women who served in the war effort. This study traces the accomplishments of women who made flags, knitted, nursed the wounded, ran blockades, spied, managed households while sons and husbands were at war, and formed soldiers' aid societies. This history includes one-page anecdotes about individual women who served the war effort, making reference to the organizations with which they worked. It is likely that these accounts were written by the women's descendants in the North Carolina UDC.

17   *c *Annals of the American Academy of Political and Social Science*. Woman's Work and Organizations [special issue] 28 (September 1906): 1-118.

President Mrs. Percy Pennybacker summarizes the resolutions passed by the General Federation of Women's Clubs membership at its eighth biennial convention in St. Paul in 1906 (pp. 277-82). Care of delinquents, libraries, forest preservation, child labor, and pure food laws received attention, alongside social events, organizational business, and the association's cultural and educational components. Following her essay is a positive account of the improvement women's clubs brought to home and society by ten prominent men in philanthropy and the reform movement. Among them are Ben Lindsey, judge of the Denver Juvenile Court, H.M. Wiley, chief of the Bureau of Chemistry at the U.S. Department of Agriculture, and James B. Angell, president of the University of Michigan ("Men's Views of Women's Clubs: A Symposium," pp. 283-92).

See also Sarah Platt Decker, Mrs. A.O. Granger, Dorothea Moore, Mrs. John Dickinson, May Alden Ward.

18   *t *Annals of the American Academy of Political and Social Science*. Women's Christian Temperance Union [special issue]   32 (November 1908).

See Elizabeth Preston Anderson, Frances Ensign, Sara Hoge, Lillian Stevens, Katharine Lent Stevenson.

19   *t ANSLEY, LULA BARNES (MRS. J.J.). *The History of the Georgia Christian Temperance Union, 1883-1907*. Columbus, Ga.: Gilbert Printing, 1914. 262 pp. Appendixes, illus.: 22, of the author; officers of the Georgia WCTU; Frances Willard letter; 1906 Georgia prohibition map; male legislators who passed the 1907 prohibition laws.

Ansley surveys the origins of the Georgia temperance movement, beginning with a 1757 law outlawing the sale of over three gallons of alcohol to anyone at one time. The Georgia WCTU was founded in 1881, and the author documents the development of the state organization, the work of departments, the resolutions passed at each annual convention, and the efforts to pass temperance legislation. In 1890, the national organization held its convention in Atlanta. Soon after, the Georgia women refused to endorse women's suffrage, which had been supported by national president Frances Willard. Written in a chatty and detailed style, the book includes the names of hymns played at meetings and children's stories about alcoholic parents. Appendixes include 1890 and 1906 charters of the WCTU, tributes to five WCTU leaders, and a 1906 resolution favoring closing of saloons during an Atlantic race riot.

20 *s ANTELL, JOAN B. "The Suffrage Movement." *Current History* 70 (May 1976): 203-5, 231-32.

A brief outline of basic facts in women's suffrage history. The story begins in 1848 at the Seneca Falls, New York, conference which first called for women's enfranchisement. Twenty-sixty women and forty men attended. Elizabeth Cady Stanton called the meeting and listed social, legal, and economic grievances of women. Suffragists divided over the question of Negro enfranchisement in 1868, and in 1869, two suffrage groups were formed—the National Woman Suffrage Association and the American Woman Suffrage Association. Antell traces the progress of western states in giving women the vote.

21 *s ANTHONY, KATHARINE. *Susan B. Anthony: Her Personal History and Her Era* . Garden City, N.Y.: Doubleday, 1954. viii, 521 pp. Bib., indexes, illus.: 4 of Susan B. Anthony.

Although the author claims to have written not a history of the women's suffrage movement but the biography of a woman's life, the story of suffrage leader Anthony of necessity includes a great deal of material on women's organizational progress. The Daughters of Temperance in Rochester, New York, absorbed Anthony's attention early on and introduced her to associational activity. The third National Women's Rights Conference in 1850 in Syracuse, New York, was her first such meeting. She was involved in abolition organizations as well. She helped form the Women's National Loyal League in May 1863 to seek equal rights for women and blacks. The author uses correspondence with suffragists and reformers with whom Anthony worked. Her part in the Kansas campaign for women's suffrage, her role in the *Revolution*—a suffrage newspaper—and her pain when suffragists split into the National and American Women Suffrage associations are described. The reconciliation between the two groups twenty years later is documented. The last national convention Anthony participated in took place in 1905, in Portland, Oregon.

21a   *s ANTHONY, SUSAN B., and IDA HUSTED HARPER. *History of Woman Suffrage*. Vol. 4, 1883–1900. Rochester, N.Y.: Susan B. Anthony, 1902. Reprint. New York: Arno, 1969. xxxiv, 1144 pp. Notes (informational), index. Illus.: 35, of leaders of the woman suffrage movement.

Here is an encyclopedia of documents illuminating the national conventions of the National Woman Suffrage Association, from 1884 through 1889, and the national conventions of the National American Woman Suffrage Association, from its merger of the National Woman Suffrage Association and the American Woman Suffrage Association in 1890 through 1900. Clearly written by the advocates for the National Woman Suffrage Association, the work provides only a scant chapter on the story of the American Woman Suffrage Association prior to 1890. The volume also includes congressional hearings and reports on the question of woman suffrage from 1884 and 1887. It describes the founding of the International Council of Women in 1888 and its devotion to the suffrage cause. A chapter for each state outlines laws affecting women of the late nineteenth century. Nations of the world, especially Great Britain, are similarly surveyed. Chapter 75 provides useful information about fifty-six women's voluntary organizations, including origins, goals, projects, and size. The are: International Council of Women, National Council of Women, Women's Christian Temperance Union, American National Red Cross Society, Association of Collegiate Alumnae, Association for the Advancement of Women, General Federation of Women's Clubs, National Association of Colored Women, National Congress of Mothers, National Woman's Relief Society, International Sunshine Society, National Council of Jewish Women, Women's National Indian Association, National League of Women Voters, National Christian League for the Promotion of Social Purity, Young Ladies' National Mutual Improvement Association, National Kindergarten Union, Woman's Prison Association, National Household Economics Association, National Woman's Keeley Rescue League, National Federation of Music Clubs, Needlework Guild of America, Women's Foreign Missionary Society of the Methodist Episcopal Church, Woman's Home Missionary Society of the Methodist Episcopal Church, Woman's Baptist Foreign Missionary Society, Woman's Baptist Foreign Missionary Society of the West, Woman's Baptist Home Mission

Society, Woman's American Baptist Home Middion Society, Free
Baptist Woman's Missionary Society, Woman's Presbyterian Board of
Foreign Missions of the South West, Woman's Board of Home
Missions of the Presbyterian Church, Christian Woman's Board of
Missions, Woman's State Home Missionary Organization of the
Congregational Church, Woman's Centenary Association of the
Universalist Church, National Alliance of Unitarian and Other Liberal
Christian Women, Woman's Missionary Association of the United
Brethren in Christ, Woman's Foreign Union of Friends, Woman's
Home and Foreign Missionary Society of the General Synod of the
Evangelical Lutheran Church in the United States of America,
Woman's Missionary Society of the General Synod of the Reformed
Church, International Board of Women's and Young Women's
Christian Association, Woman's National Sabbath Alliance, Woman's
Relief Corps, Ladies of the Grand Army of the Republic, National
Alliance of the Daughters of Veterans of the United States of America,
Mt. Vernon Ladies Association of the Union, National Society of the
Daughters of the American Revolution, Society of the Daughters of the
American Revolution, Colonial Dames of America, National Society of
the United States Daughters of 1812, United Daughters of the
Confederacy, Supreme Hive Ladies of the Maccabees of the World,
Supreme Temple Rathbone Sisters of the World, Order of the Eastern
Star, Daughters of Rebekah, Grand International Auxiliary to the
Brotherhood of Locomotive Engineers, and Ladies' Auxiliary to the
Order of Railroad Conductors of America. An appendix includes a list
of eminent advocates of women suffrage (including senators,
congressmen, governors, university presidents, clergymen, American
men, American women, and international supporters), testimony from
states with woman suffrage (Colorado, Idaho, Utah, Wyoming, and also
New York and Washington), National American Woman Suffrage
Association officers, committees, life members, and convention
delegates.

See also Elizabeth Stanton et al. for volumes 1-3, and Ida
Husted Harper for volumes 5-6 of this account.

22   *b   APOSTOL, JANE.   "They Said It with Flowers: The Los
Angeles Flower Festival Society." *Southern California Quarterly* 62
(Spring 1980): 67-76.   Notes, illus.: broadside with rules and
regulations of Boarding Home of Flower Festival Society; 1890
boardinghouse interior with female tenants; President Mary Barnes
Widney; Hazard's Pavilion in 1887.

When the work committee of the Woman's Club of Los
Angeles investigated the low wages of working women, they decided to

establish a residence with reasonable rents.   In April of 1885, the members held a flower festival which raised $2,400 in five days through the sale of twenty-five-cent admission tickets to private rose gardens in the city.   A second festival, held the following year, raised $4,000.   In 1887, a new boardinghouse was opened, providing the kinds of services (dormitory space, meals, evening workshops) the YWCA would make available when it opened in 1893.   One of the rooms was a woman's industrial exchange, where housebound women could sell articles they made at home.   In the third year, the store make $6,500 on 3,600 articles and the Flower Festival Society kept 10 percent of sales for its charitable work.   The building also contained a free reading room for working women, a place for classes, and a job bureau.   The last festival held as a fund-raiser took place in 1891—an author's carnival, where the clubwomen dressed like favorite literary characters, such as Shakespeare, Mother Goose, and Harriet Beecher Stowe, while they supervised booths of festivities.

23   *n,s APTHEKER, BETTINA. *Woman's Legacy: Essays on Race, Sex, and Class in America.* Amherst: University of Massachusetts Press, 1982. xii, 177 pp. Notes, indexes.

   Two chapters deal with black women's efforts to participate in white women's organizations.   Chapter 2 analyzes the founding of the Female Anti-Slavery societies in the 1830s.   Especially in Boston and Philadelphia, black women made up a significant part of the leadership.   Among the individuals Aptheker discusses are Sara Parker Remond, Charlotte Forten, Sarah Mappa Douglass, Letetia Still, and the Forten sisters, Margaretta, Harriet, and Sarah. Chapter 3 attacks the racism of white women of the suffrage movement, especially Kate Gordon's efforts to unify southern white women around statewide enfranchisement over a federal amendment, to ensure exclusion of black women's vote.   The author identifies the work of Delta Sigma Theta; Equal Suffrage League in New York, founded by Sarah Garnet; the Woman's Era Club of Josephine St. Pierre Ruffin; and Ida B. Wells's Alpha Suffrage Club and its exclusion from planning for the 1893 Chicago World's Fair.

24   *c ASSOCIATION FOR THE ADVANCEMENT OF WOMEN. *Historical Account of the Association for the Advancement of Women, 1873-1893.* Dedham, Mass.: Transcript Steam Job Print, 1893. 78 pp.

   Women reformers active in suffrage and literary club movements banded together in 1873.   For twenty-five years, they held annual meetings of the Association for the Advancement of Women in different American cities, delivering three days of speeches on topics of interest to women. They hoped to encourage local women to form clubs that would address questions regarding women's capabilities. This history, available in the Gerritson Collection of Microfilms (no. A100), is the only full review of the content of twenty years of convention proceedings.

25 *c,s AULT, NELSON A. "The Earnest Ladies: The Walla Walla Woman's Club and the Equal Suffrage League of 1886-1889." *Pacific Northwest Quarterly* 42 (April 1951): 123-37. Notes.

Although the Woman's Club of Olympia, founded in 1883, has the distinction of being the oldest woman's club in Washington State, the next club formed was the Walla Walla Woman's Club, in 1886. The club was formed for the purpose of self-improvement through literary study and discussions on religion, but the group changed its focus in 1887, when women of Washington Territory lost their four-year-old right to vote. For two years, the group became an Equal Suffrage League, agitating for women's right to vote in the new state of Washington. Ault examines the speeches and arguments of Oregon suffrage activist Abigail Scott Duniway, who campaigned for her neighboring sisters. Washington women, however, were unsuccessful in their attempt to win the vote, and they disbanded their society in 1889.

26 *w AYARS, CHRISTINE M. "The Alaska Tour, 1922." *Alaska Journal* 7 (Autumn 1977): 227-39. Illus.: 5, including author and other club members en route to Alaska; author in Eskimo costume; members in miners' jackets.

The Inkowa Outdoor Club in New York City planned outdoor activities for city-dwelling business women. In 1922, the group headed for Alaska, taking the train to Seattle and the inside passage on the S.S. *Alameda* to Ketchikan. This is a firsthand tale of the journey told by a member who participated. She describes the glaciers, the taverns and roadhouses, the mines and railroads she and her colleagues encountered.

27 *r BACON, MRS. A.M. *Twenty Years' History of the Woman's Baptist Foreign Mission Society of the West*. N.p.: the organization, 1891.

28 *t BADER, ROBERT SMITH. *Prohibition in Kansas: A History*. Lawrence; University Press of Kansas, 1986. xiii, 322 pp. Notes, bib., indexes, figs., tables, illus.; 29 photos including WCTU of LeRoy (Coffey County) celebrating Temperance Day in early 20th

century; Dr. Usilla Wilson; Lillian May Early Mitchner; Minnie Johnson Grinstead; Laura Mitchell Johns.

The work of the WCTU is woven throughout Bader's chronological account of Kansas prohibition. Among the activities he recounts for the 1880s and 1890s are these: lobbying legislators, pressuring for a law to prohibit the sale of tobacco to children under sixteen, raising the age of consent from ten to eighteen for girls, and revising the textbooks to include temperance education in the schools. Bader also mentions the formation in 1929 of the Woman's Organization for National Prohibition Reform, initiated by New York's "smart set."

29   *r BAKER, FRANCES J. *The Story of the Woman's Foreign Missionary Society of the Methodist Episcopal Church, 1869-1895.* Cincinnati: Curts and Jennings; New York: Eaton and Mains, 1898. 438 pp. Illus.: 53, of missionaries; author; founders; officers; facilities abroad.

A detailed account of the origins and development of the Woman's Foreign Missionary Society of the Methodist Episcopal church. It was founded in Boston in 1869 and grew quickly, establishing auxiliaries in churches throughout the country. A publication, the *Heathen Woman's Friend*, publicized its missionary activity early on. Branch histories are provided here for groups in Boston, Chicago, Cincinnati, Baltimore, St. Louis, Des Moines, Topeka, Minneapolis, Atlanta, and Seattle. Baker describes the young people's branches; the camp meetings at Martha's Vineyard, Albion, Michigan and Ocean Grove, Long Island; and the results of society funding of schools and medical facilities in India, China, Japan, Korea, Bulgaria, Italy, Mexico, and Africa. In 1872, a St. Paul, Minnesota, group founded the German auxiliary of the society. The final chapter lists bequests and donations made by members to the association. A list of real estate owned by the society—sixty-three homes, schools, hospitals, orphanages, and sanitariums, valued at $474,000—is provided.

30   *p BAKER, HELEN DOW, ed. *Texas State History of the D.A.R.* Abilene, Tex.: Abilene Printing and Stationery Co., 1929. 269 pp. Illus.: dozens of portraits of officers.

This work quickly surveys the national society's history and moves to the biographies of the five Texas vice-presidents general since 1906, the national chairpersons, and state regents. Baker has written a historical sketch of the state society and compiled a roster of officers from 1894 to 1931. She details the cities where annual conferences were held from 1900 to 1928, the chapters in the Texas DAR, and the source of funds for war work from 1917 to 1921. Her primary purpose, however, is to provide histories of each of the fifty-nine chapters, including the names of founders, dates of origin, projects initiated, monies raised, and officers' biographies (with family genealogy, church affiliation, and club work).

31   *m   BAKER, PAULA. "Domestication of Politics: Women and American Political Society, 1780-1920." *American Historical Review* 89 (June 1984): 620-47. Notes.

Through this ambitious overview of women's organizations, rather than a historical study of a specific group or category of groups, Baker demonstrates that suffragists and antisuffragists alike argued that woman's place was in the home in the nineteenth century. It was on the ground of women's moral superiority to men, which they were supposed to have developed in the domestic sphere, that activists urged women to enter public life and spread their special talents widely. Opponents insisted that a public voice for women was inappropriate, even dangerous. Baker locates the roots of an ideology supporting women's public activity in the colonial period: women during the American Revolution engaged in political action in their homes. But the nineteenth century saw the rise of mass political parties, which separated males and females in politics. Women now used assumptions about womanhood and separate spheres to launch their own organizations to correct injustice. For example, they founded benevolent and moral reform societies, the Woman's Parliament of 1869, suffrage leagues, the Civil War's Sanitary Commission, and temperance societies, which enabled them to fuse domesticity and politics at a sophisticated level. By the turn-of-the-century Progressive Era, politics became domesticated, and suffrage could no longer be perceived as a radical demand or a challenge to the notion of separate spheres of men and women. Now home and politics were inextricable. Suffrage, activists argued, would not destroy the home but enhance family life. The suffrage victory in 1920 assisted women to move away gradually from a separate political culture to one that mixed men's and women's efforts.

32   *n   BARBER, HENRY E. "Association of Southern Women for the Prevention of Lynching, 1930-1942." *Phylon* 34 (December 1973): 378-89. Notes.

This essay explores the work of Jessie Daniel Ames, director of women's work in the Commission on Interracial Cooperation. In 1930 in Atlanta, she founded the Association of Southern Women for the Prevention of Lynching. Southern white women, who were supposed to be protected by lynching, began to speak out against it. Members came from the League of Women Voters, the Young Women's Christian Association, federated women's clubs, Parent-Teachers Associations, and women's groups in the Southern Baptist church, the Methodist Episcopal church, South, and the Southern Presbyterian church. Most southern states rapidly pledged support, although Florida did so only later. The association held no conventions or local meetings and collected no dues; rather, it trained speakers to persuade women to pressure sheriffs and newspaper editors to oppose lynching and published pamphlets, posters, and plays for schools. Some members even confronted angry mobs in person to calm them. In 1942, having turned public opinion against white lynching of black men, the organization disbanded.

33 *c BARRY, HARRIET H. "The Sixth Biennial." *Out West* 16 (May 1902): 557-65. Illus.: women's clubhouse of Los Angeles; 15 women prominent in the development of the organization; Caroline Severance; Mrs. Robert Burdette; Ione Cowles.

Because the General Federation of Women's Clubs would hold its sixth biennial convention in Los Angeles in 1902, Barry was prompted to reflect on the growth of the organization since its formation in 1890. Women's clubs began in 1868, with Sorosis in New York City and the New England Woman's Club in Boston; the federation now was composed of 683 clubs with 200,000 women members. Almost forty states had federations of their own, Maine being the first to have formed. California was enjoying fast growth in membership and in the building of many fine clubhouses. Caroline Severance, who had founded the Boston club in 1868, had moved to Los Angeles and initiated the Friday Morning Club. The California Federation was founded in 1900, with 50 clubs and 7,000 women. By 1902, it had grown to 100 clubs with 8,000 women. The upcoming meeting would vote on the question of black women's membership in the General Federation of Women's Clubs.

34 *b BARTON, CLARA. *The Red Cross: A History of This Remarkable International Movement in the Interest of Humanity.* Washington, D.C.: American National Red Cross, 1898. 684 pp. Illus.: 107, including drawings; maps; photos of projects, officers, headquarters.

The most famous nurse in America collected an enormous amount of historical material on women's efforts to meet catastrophes around the world. Embellishing her remarks are bulletins, speeches, and particular documents referring to the Johnstown flood, Russian famine, Sea Island hurricane, Armenian war, and Spanish-American war in Puerto Rico and Cuba. She surveys women's accomplishments in mitigating the sufferings of war, pestilence, famine, and other calamities. While providing reports on the relief efforts of Red Cross branches in every state and major cities of the Union, Barton does not overlook more modest contributions, such as the work of sewing circles during the Sea Island hurricane.

35   *c BASSETT, MRS. PHEBE D. "Jacksonville Sorosis Organized." *Illinois State Historical Society Journal* 18 (April 1925): 209-12.

In 1868, Illinois women heard about the efforts of New York City reformers to found a literary and scientific study club, Sorosis. Quickly, they acted to do the same. Five women met to elect an experienced clubwoman, Mrs. Harvey Milligan, their first president. In 1869, the group studied such topics as the abolition of capital punishment, women's suffrage, and Chinese immigration. In 1871, the club invited Bronson Alcott to speak at a meeting. For all its brevity, the article indicates the nationwide enthusiasm for study clubs that emerged after the Civil War.

36   *i BAUMAN, MARY KAY. "Madison Organization for International Peace and Freedom." *Wisconsin Then and Now* 12 (August 1965): 1-3. Illus.: Mrs. Eugena Zegarowicz and puppets; group photos at 50th anniversary banquet.

In 1915, the Women's Peace party (later the Women's International League for Peace and Freedom) was founded "to unite women in all countries who are opposed to every kind of war, exploitation and oppression to work for universal disarmament and for the solution of conflicts by the recognition of human solidarity, conciliation and arbitration, by world cooperation, and by the establishment of social, political and economic justice for all." In 1922, women in Madison, Wisconsin, formed a branch. One member, Mrs. Charles D. Rosa, was particularly active in the years 1928-34, and favored disarmament and American participation in the League of Nations and World Court. She inspired her colleagues to lobby for legislation for peace throughout their state. Two members attended the 1932 Geneva Disarmament Conference. Others performed songs and plays for children and adults, calling for neighborliness. They fought conscription in the late 1930s. Although the records have disappeared for the years 1941-47, it appears that the club disbanded and then revived in 1955. At that time, members urged the banning of nuclear weapons and opposed American involvement in the war in Vietnam.

37   *c   BEADLE, MURIEL, and THE CENTENNIAL HISTORY
      COMMITTEE. *The Fortnightly of Chicago: The City and Its
      Women, 1873-1973.* Chicago: Henry Regnery, 1973. vii, 360 pp.
      Index, illus.: Kate Newell Doggett; clubhouse at 120 E. Bellevue
      Place, both exterior and interior; Fine Arts Building interior at 410
      S. Michigan Avenue, a meeting place between 1893 and 1920; four
      club presidents; amateur theatricals in 1928 and 1972.
            The members of the Fortnightly Club of Chicago lovingly
      assembled a potpourri of materials about the progress of their club,
      from its founding by Kate Newell Doggett in 1873 through its
      centennial celebrations. Writing in a chatty and breezy style, the
      authors have collected lively quotations from a century of minutes,
      speeches, correspondence, committee reports, presidential addresses,
      toasts at club receptions, and even memoirs of leading members.
      Although the story is told chronologically, it meanders from desciptions
      of parties to summaries of papers delivered by members and guests to
      biographies of noteworthy members like pianist, composer, and music
      patron Elizabeth Sprague Coolidge. The tone much of the time is
      positive, but there are glimpses of conflict, such as a debate over
      honoring Jane Addams for her philanthrophic efforts while she
      advocated peace during World War I. Great exuberance is revealed
      over a feature story that *Town and Country* magazine published in 1929
      on the redecoration of their clubhouse, a McKim, Mead, and White
      Georgian mansion built in 1891 and occupied by club members after
      1922.

38   *m   BEARD, MARY RITTER. *Woman's Work in Municipalities.*
      New York: D. Appleton, 1916. Reprint. New York: Arno, 1938. xi,
      344 pp. Index.
            In this compendium of women's club accomplishments at the
      turn of the century, Mary Ritter Beard enumerates ten areas of
      Progressive Era reform (education, public health, social evil, recreation,
      assimilation of races, housing, social service, corrections, public safety,
      and civic improvement) and details local changes brought about by
      hundreds of women's organizations. The work of individual groups in
      large cities and small towns in every part of the nation is documented
      with quotations from primary resources such as newspaper clippings,
      speeches, legislation, and surveys. The result is a dazzling overview of
      women's wide interests and successful strategies for reforming their
      communities.

39   *z   BECKER, SUSAN. "International Feminism between the Wars:
      The National Woman's Party vs. the League of Women Voters." In

The Woman's Movement, 1920-1940 edited by Lois Scharf and Joan Jensen, 223-42. Westport, Conn.: Greenwood Press, 1983. Notes.

    This historian articulates the schism between the National Woman's party and the League of Women Voters, two influential women's political organizations of the 1920s. Whereas the League's social feminists supported wholeheartedly the establishment of protective legislation for women workers, the NWP opposed it. They favored the equal rights amendment and equal protection of workers under the law. Both applied their philosophies to the international organizations in which they had influence.

40   *z -----. *The Origins of the ERA: American Feminism between the Wars*. Westport, Conn.: Greenwood Press, 1981. 293 pp. Notes, bib.

    In a scholarly fashion, historian Becker has documented the history of the National Woman's party in the 1920s and 1930s. Standing nearly alone in its advocacy of the equal rights amendment as the best method for eliminating the remaining legal discrimination against women, the organization took on the social feminists in the League of Women Voters, the U.S. Woman's Bureau, the Women's Trade Union League, and the Consumers' League, who instead supported special protective legislation for women. Becker views the American Association of University Women and the National Federation of Business and Professional Women as neutral on the question of the ERA. The National Council of Jewish Women, the General Federation of Women's Clubs and the YWCA she defines as "not actively struggling against" the ERA. The history does not confine itself to the controversial issue of the ERA, however. Becker also examines the reorganization of the National Woman's party after the passage of the women's suffrage amendment, dissecting the goals of the leaders and exposing the inconsistencies among the members' views on men, motherhood, and women's special characteristics. Some stressed similarities rather than differences with men. She also unveils internal debates about strategies for change and documents earnest efforts to address feminist issues on an international scale.

40a   *s BEETON, BEVERLY. *Women Vote in the West: The Woman Suffrage Movement, 1869-1896*. New York: Garland, 1986. xii, 164.

    Notes, bibliographic notes, illus.: 32, including leaders of the national suffrage movement (Susan B. Anthony, Elizabeth Cady Stanton, Victoria Woodhull, Anna E. Dickenson, Belva Lockwood, Lucy Stone, Abigail Scott Duniway, Carrie Chapman Catt) and suffrage leaders of Wyoming (Amelia B. Post, Theresa Jenkins), Utah (Emily S. Richards, Sarah Kimball, Charlotte Iver Cobb Godbe Kirby, Emmeline

B. Wells), Colorado (Ellis Meredith Stansbury), and Idaho (Mrs. Milton Kelly, Senator William E. Borah).

Here is a study of woman suffrage in four western states, Wyoming (1869), Utah (1870), Colorado (1893), and Idaho (1896), the first to grant women enfranchisement. While the efforts of organized suffragists in these four states played a small role in the success of enfranchisement, Beeton does discuss the strategies of the Colorado Equal Suffrage Association and the Utah Territory Woman Suffrage Association. In addition, there is close attention to the reaction of the National Woman Suffrage Association, American Woman Suffrage Association, and National American Woman Suffrage Association leaders to the fortunes of suffrage for women in the west.

41   *s BENNION, SHERILYN COX. "The Pioneer: The First Voice for Woman's Suffrage in the West." *Pacific History* 25 (1981): 15-21. Brief bib., illus.: masthead; Emily Pitts-Stevens; Elizabeth Cady Stanton and Susan B. Anthony; Lucy Stone; the *San Francisco Chronicle*'s antisuffrage headlines.

Four years after teacher Emily A. Pitts moved from New York to San Francisco in 1865, she bought a half-interest in the *California Weekly Mercury*. As coeditor, only twenty-five years of age, she moved the focus of the newspaper from American literature to women's rights. For four years, until 1873, her periodical, renamed *Pioneer*, advocated women's suffrage in editorials and news stories. She featured the arguments of eastern suffragists Susan B. Anthony and Elizabeth Cady Stanton and their National Woman Suffrage Association. When she married, the editor hyphenated her last name to Pitts-Stevens. In 1872, she organized the Woman Suffrage Party of the Pacific Coast and served as president. In addition, she wrote for Women's Christian Temperance Union publications and joined the Equal Rights League.

42   *b   BENSON, SUSAN PORTER.   "Business Heads and Sympathizing Hearts: The Women of the Providence Employment Society." *Journal of Social History* 12 (1978): 302-12.

This study of the Providence (Rhode Island) Employment Society between its founding in 1837 and 1858 examines the lives of the fifty-two women who served on its board as managers. Having created the society to aid self-supporting seamstresses by providing employment, relief, and vocational education, the managers adopted the forms of male activity in the public sphere and then deliberately transformed them to their own purposes. They built on the skills and experience they had developed as household managers in their own homes. They participated in the organization with a network of friends and relatives. Their work complemented the public activity of the husbands and other men in their lives, but was distinctly separate and sometimes conflicting with them in execution.

43   *b BERG, BARBARA J. *The Remembered Gate: Origins of American Feminism: The Woman and the City, 1800-1860.* New York: Oxford University Press, 1978. xvii, 334 pp. Notes, indexes, bib., illus.: 5 paintings portraying stereotypical ideals of women of the era.

Although the first part of this study examines antebellum ideals of women as arbiters of morality, the second part contains five chapters of special interest to researchers on the history of women's involvement in female benevolent societies. Berg argues that women's formation of voluntary associations created a vibrant feminist ideology, which in turn sparked the demand for women's rights. She points to numerous female members, managers, and officers of female societies for the needy, including the Female Bethel (formed in 1832) to aid the destitute and suffering families of seamen, the Association for Relief of Respectable, Aged and Indigent Females, the New York Asylum for Lying-in Women, and the Boston Seamen's Aid Society. As women volunteers got to know the poorer women they served, they were "ultimately able to articulate kinship with all women as victims of society's oppression." Three New York City societies for deviant women are explored for the programs volunteers created to meet urban problems: the Female Benevolent Society, the Female Moral Reform Society, and the Women's Prison Association. The volunteers came to attack the subordination of all women in their society and attempted to transform their social milieus to liberate Manhattan prostitutes, Roman Catholic orphans, and poor black urban women from poverty, ignorance, and tradition.

44   *n BERNSTEIN, ALISON. "A Mixed Record: The Political Enfranchisement of American Indian Women during the Indian New Deal." *Journal of the West* 23 (July 1984): 13-20. Illus.: 2 of Ruth Muskrat Bronson.

This article features four native American women who worked during the New Deal of the 1930s to improve government relations with the Indian community. Ella Deloria, Ruth Bronson, Helen Peterson, and especially Gertrude Bonnin used women's organizations, notably the General Federation of Women's Clubs and the Young Women's Christian Association, to expose corruption at the Commission of Indian Affairs.

45   *c   BLACKMAN, LUCY WORTHINGTON. *The Florida Federation of Women's Clubs.* Jacksonville: Southern History Publishing Associates, 1939.

45a   *m -----. *The Women of Florida.* Vol. 1, *The Narrative,* xiv, 209 pp., illus.: 28, including Jacksonville Woman's Clubhouse, Miami Woman's Clubhouse, Palmetto Clubhouse, officers in clubs, groups assembled at conventions; vol. 2, *The Biographies,* 192 pp., illus.: 150 individual portraits of clubwomen. N.p.: Southern Historical Publishing Co., 1940.

    Although volume one begins with a discussion of Indian Women of the sixteenth century and women pioneers of Florida, the bulk of the text is devoted to summarizing the histories of organizations of women in Florida, the names of founders and officers, budgets, size of membership, and projects undertaken. The national organizations with Florida branches are Mount Vernon Ladies Association, Colonial Dames of America, Daughters of the American Revolution, Daughters of Founders and Patriots of America, Colonial Dames of the Seventeenth Century, Society of the Daughters of the United States of 1812, United Daughters of the Confederacy, American Legion Auxiliary, Gold Star Mothers, Florida Federation of Women's Clubs, League of Women Voters, Congress of Parents and Teachers, Florida Federation of Music Clubs, Florida Federation of Business and Professional Women's Clubs, Florida Federation of Garden Clubs, Junior League of Florida, Daughters of the British Empire, American Association of University Women, Zonta Club of America, and Order of the Eastern Star. The Florida women's organizations surveyed are the Women's Club of Jacksonville, Woman's Club of Miami, Woman's Club of Miami Beach, Palmetto Club of Daytona Beach, Colonial Dames Club of Tampa and Florida Stephen Foster Memorial (sponsored by the Florida Federation of Music Clubs).

    Volume two collects the biographies of 164 women prominent in Florida organizational life. The biography the author wrote about herself is typical of the selections. It includes birthdate; birthplace; genaeology; education; religious affiliation; husband's name, career, and a genaeology; date of marriage; number of children, grandchildren, and great grand-children; and clubs and institutions in which the subject was active.

46   *s   BLACKWELL, ALICE STONE. *Lucy Stone: Pioneer of Woman's Rights.* Boston: Little, Brown and Co., 1930. viii, 313 pp. Indexes, appendixes, illus.: 4 of Lucy Stone; 2 of husband; Henry

Blackwell; Julia Ward Howe; Mary Livermore; 1 of her sister-in-law, the Reverend Antoinette Brown Blackwell.

Alice Stone Blackwell has used accessible material, perhaps pitched to a young adult audience, to illuminate the life of her mother, Lucy Stone. Stressing Stone's early activism and skimping on her later life, Blackwell catalogs her participation in the burgeoning women's suffrage and women's rights movements via antebellum lectures and conventions for women and for the abolition cause. She recounts Stone's importance in drawing Susan B. Anthony and Julia Ward Howe into the cause of women's equality, her founding of the American Woman Suffrage Association and the New England and Massachusetts Woman Suffrage associations, her journalistic work for the *Woman's Journal* of Boston (a women's rights newspaper), and her enthusiasm for temperance and the dress reform and health movements. This political work ties Stone closely to the influential activity of women's organizations in the mid-nineteenth century.

47   *c   BLAIR, KAREN J. *The Clubwoman as Feminist: True Womanhood Redefined, 1868-1914.* New York: Holmes and Meier, 1980. xv, 199 pp. Notes, bib., indexes, illus.: group photo of Friday Morning Club in Los Angeles in 1903 with Caroline Severance and Charlotte Wills.

Blair traces the development of the women's literary club movement in the second half of the nineteenth century and explains its transformation into a civic reform movement after 1890. Although women's clubs flourished before the Civil War, it was the founding of Sorosis in New York City and the New England Woman's Club in Boston, in 1868, that ushered in a wave of nationwide enthusiasm for women's study clubs. The New York and Boston founders persuaded other women to initiate societies devoted to self-improvement by creating the Woman's Parliament in 1869 and the Association for the Advancement of Women (1873-97). Members would travel to distant cities to present papers on topics of interest to women. Literary clubs in Providence, Rhode Island, are examined, as are the Women's Educational and Industrial Unions of Boston and Buffalo. By 1890, the General Federation of Women's Clubs had been formed, uniting many of the United States and foreign clubs and pushing them to read less and engage more in "municipal housekeeping"—to establish public libraries and other social services in their communities. Women's reform energies were fueled by domestic feminism, the notion that their differences from men sensitized them to the special needs of their cities, so that they were suited to build a more humane environment for all the citizenry.

48   *c -----. "Education and Reform in Buffalo Women's Clubs, 1876-
     1914." *Urban Education* 18 (Winter 1984): 452-62. Notes.
          The cultural study and civic reform activity of nine Buffalo
     women's organizations are surveyed, demonstrating that the
     "universities for middle-aged women" not only developed the minds of
     their members but benefited the city of Buffalo. The clubs examined
     are the Literary Club of the Church of the Messiah, Women Teachers
     Association, Women's Educational and Industrial Union, Twentieth
     Century Club, the Scribblers, Monday Class, Women's Investigating
     Club, The Friends, and Graduates' Association of the Buffalo
     Seminary.

49   *c -----. "The Limits of Sisterhood: The Women's Building in
     Seattle, 1907-1921." *Frontiers* 8 (Spring 1985): 45-52. Reprinted in
     Women in Pacific Northwest History: An Anthology, edited by Karen
     J. Blair. Seattle: University of Washington Press, 1988. Notes.
          In anticipation of the 1909 Alaska-Yukon-Pacific Exposition in
     Seattle, the Washington State Federation of Women's Clubs lobbied
     legislators to fund a woman's building on the fair site at the new
     University of Washington campus. They agreed, with the stipulation
     that the women raise money for the furnishings. Campus and
     community organizations of women cooperated to establish an inviting
     center where women might rest during their sight-seeing at the
     exposition, entrust their children to a day care-center, dine on YWCA
     recipes, view exhibits of the art, literature, music, and needlework of
     Washington women, and attend lectures and receptions. Conventions
     of suffragists, temperance advocates, the National Council of Women,
     and other associations of women held meetings in the building. At the
     end of the fair, the building was refurbished for campus women's use.
     While the university women occupied the structure, from 1910 to 1916,
     it was a center for nurturing women students' strengths and their skills
     for use in later life in women's organizations devoted to civic
     improvements. When administrators claimed the Woman's Building
     for other uses, the campus women located no comparable space to
     develop their capabilities as "municipal housekeepers."

50   *c -----. "The Seattle Ladies Musical Club, 1890-1930." In
     Experiences in a Promised Land: Essays in Pacific Northwest History,
     edited by G. Thomas Edwards and Carlos A. Schwantes, 124-38.
     Seattle: University of Washington Press, 1986. Notes.

The Seattle Ladies Musical Club formed in 1891, with a membership of women with advanced training and substantial accomplishments in music, who were now housewives devoted to running households. This article surveys their activities from the founding year through 1930, cataloging the types of papers delivered by the members, the kinds of music they performed for one another, and the annual series of four recitals they sponsored from 1901 on. In addition, the members supported music for the community, paying for musical training for immigrants at the settlement house, donating money for the MacDowall Colony in Peterborough, New Hampshire, and pressuring their school system for increased musical training for young people. The club's activities did much to shape the musical taste in their city.

51   *r BLAKE, CARRIE RICHARDSON. *The Boston Pioneers of the Woman's Missionary Society; November 16, 1860-November 16, 1910; A Memorial.* Boston: Conant and Newhall, 1911. 26 pp.
        This item can be located as microfilm no. 6342 in the 1976 edition of the Women's History Series (New Haven: Research Publications). It was written as a tribute to the fiftieth anniversary of the formation of the Woman's Union Missionary Society of Boston, the first organization independent of denominational control to send single women to non-Christian lands. The only other group to do so was the Ladies' China Missionary Society of Baltimore. The women who organized the Woman's Union Missionary Society had earlier participated in other missionary endeavors. One founder served as secretary in 1832 to the Female Primary Foreign Missionary Society of the Second Baptist Church and Congregation of Boston. The immediate inspiration for the creation of WUMS was the encouragement by the wife of Rev. Dr. Francis Masion, Burma missionary, when she visited the home of Mrs. John D. Richardson. Mrs. Richardson's daughter, Mrs. Francis E. Blake, and Mrs. Harriet Gould became captivated by the idea of creating an organization hospitable to woman missionaries. Eventually, branches were formed in New York, Brooklyn, Philadelphia, and elsewhere, called the Society for the Promotion of Female Education in the East. Biographical tributes are written for the nine original founders and for Miss Sarah Hall Marson, the first woman missionary they sent abroad, in 1862.

52   *c BLANC, MARIE THERESE DE SOLMES. *The Condition of Woman in the United States*. Boston: Roberts, 1895.
    See under De Solmes, Madame Therese Blanc.

53   *s BLAND, SIDNEY R. "Fighting the Odds: Militant Suffragists in South Carolina." *South Carolina Historical Magazine* 82 (1981): 32-43. Notes.

    In South Carolina, where there were more black women than white, racist suffragists were unwilling to support the Congressional Union (later the National Woman's party) for a federal women's suffrage amendment to the U.S. Constitution. Seeking an "expedient" argument to persuade white women to join their movement, the CU/NWP insisted that the black women of South Carolina, if permitted by law to vote, would still be unable to pass the state-imposed literacy test or to pay the required tax on property valued over three hundred dollars. Thus, the argument went, their power needn't be feared by white women. In 1915, Susan Forst opened a South Carolina office supporting the work of the Congressional Union. She rose as an officer in the organization and, by April 1917, was able to point to a new South Carolina branch, formed during the controversial episode of suffragist picketing at the White House. Anita Pollitzer, another force at the NWP, enjoys attention in Bland's history. Although the South Carolina branch of the NWP never enrolled more than one hundred members, it made a strong impact by using innovative techniques to reach the public and educate them about the importance of a suffrage amendment.

54   *s -----. " 'Never Quite as Committed as We'd Like': The Suffrage Militancy of Lucy Burns." *Journal of Long Island History* 17 (Summer-Fall 1981): 4-23. Notes, illus.: 2 of Lucy Burns.

    This article surveys the activism of Lucy Burns in the Congressional Union (later the National Woman's party). She was, for years, a co-equal and co-partner with Alice Paul, the organization's much-heralded president, yet her contribution has been ignored. This biography explores her youth in Brooklyn, her Vassar education (1899), her arrests in the United States and England over women's suffrage issues, her two hunger strikes, her speeches at open air-meetings, her editorship at the *Suffragist* in 1915, her efforts to lobby, and her role as a chief organizer for the organization. She worked with Alice Paul to create the Congressional Union within the National American Woman Suffrage Association and then moved to separate it, inventing ways to publicize suffrage more ingeniously than NAWSA was content to do.

She traveled widely, campaigning against Democratic candidates in 1914 and 1916, organized pickets, and even flew over Seattle to drop suffrage leaflets in 1916. As Alice Paul continued to dominate policy-making at the NWP, tensions over the appropriate response to World War I led Burns in the summer of 1917 to withdraw from her role as steady activist.

55   *t BLICHFIELDT, E.H. "WCTU Field." *Chautauquan* 59 (June 1910): 127-34.
        See *Chautauquan*.

56   *t BLOCHOWIAK, MARY ANN. " 'Woman With A Hatchett': Carry Nation Comes to Oklahoma Territory." *Chronicles of Oklahoma* 59 (Summer 1981): 132-51. Notes, illus.: 3 of Carrie Nation; "All Nations Welcome But Carrie" banner on saloon.
        Carrie Nation is probably the most famous temperance advocate of the nineteenth century, but this article clarifies the Women's Christian Temperance Union's official opposition to her methods. Nation enjoyed considerable fame for her destruction of property in saloons and her speeches drew huge crowds and flamboyant headlines, but in 1904 the Oklahoma Territory WCTU criticized her behavior. Blochowiak documents Carrie Nation's attack on president Mrs. Abby Hillerman for failing to endorse her efforts on behalf of temperance.

57   *m BLUM, CAROL J. "The Cincinnati Women's Christian Association: A Study of Innovation and Change, 1868-1880." *Queen City Heritage* 41 (Winter 1983): 56-64. Notes, illus.: 1900 floor plan of vocational cottage; 3 of women working.
        As early as 1868, the Cincinnati Woman's Christian Association (later YWCA) began volunteer efforts for working girls. The city had seen efforts by the Female City Missionary Society to discourage the spread of the "social evil" in 1837, but now a new club supported a boardinghouse to serve sixty-three women who might otherwise have fallen victim to poverty and "sin." Gradually, the members moved to larger and larger quarters, building a structure of their own in 1929 on Ninth at Walnut Street, which held a library and a chapel. Funds were raised through the efforts of a Young Ladies Branch of the WCA. New programs were established regularly throughout the nineteenth century to meet the needs of working women—an industrial institute to teach sewing, an employment committee to teach the skills of domestic science, a laundry, a vacation cottage, an employment bureau, a program of mothers meetings to

teach poor mothers how to sew for themselves and their children, and the Sewing Society for Colored Women. In 1894, the group's official name was changed to the Young Women's Christian Association.

58   *r,c BLUMAUER, BLANCHE. "Council of Jewish Women in Portland, 1905." *Western States Jewish Historical Quarterly* 9 (October 1976): 19-20.

A reprint from the *Jewish Times and Observer* in San Francisco (17 February 1905), this article relates the history of the Council of Jewish Women in Portland, Oregon. The club was organized in 1895 for self-help among its members and assistance to others in the community. By 1905, it had 280 dues-paying members, both Reform and Orthodox Jewish women. Among their projects were the study of the Bible and the erecting of Neighborhood House, a settlement house for community social service work. The piece lists the names of all past presidents of the organization.

59   *w BOONE, GLADYS. *Women's Trade Union Leagues in Great Britain and the United States*. New York: Columbia University Press, 1942. 283 pp. Notes, appendixes, bib., indexes.

Here is a standard reference work on the history of the Women's Trade Union leagues. Boone devotes sections to the relationship between labor and feminism, to the history of the first chapter of the organization in Britain (1872-1921), and to the background of the origins of the National WTUL in the United States, with attention to the working conditions American women faced in the nineteenth century. She explores the early days of the organization, 1903-13, including the work at conventions and the many strikes it supported. For the period 1913-29, Boone narrates members' promotion of protective legislation, participation in international congresses, organizing of women into trade unions, and celebration of a twenty-fifth anniversary. After 1929, Boone asserts, progress was difficult, the Great Depression bringing a terrible scarcity of employment opportunities. She discusses the organization's relationship to New Deal legislation, to the American Federation of Labor, and to workers' education. She concludes with an affirmation of timely tactics and policies developed regularly by the organization to meet the ever-changing needs to women and determines that its major purpose, to assist working women to attain more decent conditions, has remained firm. Appendixes include three on workers and three on contributions in 1903, 1907, and 1936 of the National Women's Trade Union League of America.

60   *t BORDIN, RUTH. "'A Baptism of Power and Liberty': The Women's Crusade of 1873-1874." *Ohio History* 87 (Autumn 1978): 393-404. Reprinted in *Woman's Being, Woman's Place: Female Identity and Vocation in American History*, edited by Mary Kelley, 283-95. Boston: G.K. Hall, 1979. Notes, illus.: Drawing of Ohio saloonkeeper signing pledge to suspend sale of liquor and beer while women look on and crusaders pray outside Hillsboro saloon.

Bordin explains that the 1873 Woman's Crusade was the watershed for women's participation in the temperance movement. One year after women staged pray-ins at saloons all over Ohio and the Midwest, they formed the influential organization, the WCTU. The crusade legitimated women's expansion of their efforts from the home into the public world.

61   *t -----. *Frances Willard: A Biography*. Chapel Hill: University of North Carolina Press, 1986.

Frances Willard (1838-1897) was one of the most famous, respected, and influential women in nineteenth-century America, but no biography of her had been published in the last forty years. Having established herself as an able chronicler of the Women's Christian Temperance Union in *Woman and Temperance: The Quest for Power and Liberty, 1873-1900*, Ruth Bordin wrote this sound portrait of the temperance movement's primary exponent. Using diaries and scrapbooks that had been lost since the turn of the century, Bordin illuminates the private and public life of a skilled leader with a broad social vision. Willard appears not to have challenged society's accepted ideals about women's traditional virtues; rather, she pressed them into service, awakening hundreds of thousands of female temperance advocates in the Women's Christian Temperance Union to realize their own power by supporting a "Do Everything" policy for "Home Protection." Willard initiated impressive programs, from cooperative kitchens to free kindergartens, social purity, and women's suffrage, which her followers developed, ultimately making a great impact as reformers. Surprisingly, Bordin manages to avoid rehashing material she treated in her earlier book. Instead, she argues that Willard, the person, can be disentangled from WCTU history to demonstrate her strong commitment to a broad range of social and political causes, including christian socialism, transatlantic feminism, and the labor movement. Although Bordin praises Willard's eloquence as a public speaker, her astuteness as a politician, and her success in carrying out an ambitious social program, she does not ignore her shortcomings. Willard's hypocrisy on the issue of lynching, her selfishness in her personal relationships with Kate Jackson, Anna Gordon, and Lady

Henry Somerset, and her differences with the Methodist clergy, Elizabeth Cady Stanton, and the WCTU factions opposed to her support for woman suffrage and for the Prohibition party are all scrutinized. Bordin succeeds, too, at synthesizing, coherently but succinctly, the backgrounds of numerous mass movements Willard supported.

62   *t -----. *Woman and Temperance: The Quest for Power and Liberty, 1873-1900*. Philadelphia: Temple University Press, 1981. xviii, 221 pp. Notes, appendix, illus.: 6 of WCTU presidents.

Although there is a tremendous temptation to equate the history of the Women's Christian Temperance Union with the life of Frances Willard during the years of her presidency (1879-98), Bordin does not succumb to it. She gives Willard's views and strategies fair discussion, but she also examines the roles of other temperance leaders of the era. Caroline Buell, Lillian Stevens, J. Ellen Foster, Zerelda Wallace, and Annie Wittenmyer are studied for their contributions to the growth and development of the huge temperance organization. Bordin analyzes the growth, maturity, and decline of the WCTU from its founding in 1873 to the years right after Willard's death in 1898. The move from alcohol issues to prison reform, facilities for dependent and neglected children, and woman suffrage is treated to illuminate the WCTU's success at pushing members from churches to legislatures. Bordin argues persuasively that the organization had stunning importance in developing a feminist consciousness among the women of late nineteenth-century America. The appendix gives WCTU leadership patterns and tables on marital status of officers in 1874, 1884, and 1894.

63   *c BOURNE, MIRIAM ANNE. *The Ladies of Castine: From the Minutes of the Castine, Maine, Woman's Club*. New York: Arbor House, 1986. xi, 148 pp. Notes, illus.: by Louise Taber Bourne (author's daughter) of buildings in the town.

In 1913, twenty-five women in Castine, Maine, founded a club for "civic improvement and literary and social culture." The author's grandmother, Caroline Perkins Walker Caddie, was a founding member and served as secretary for many years. Drawing on the minutes of the meetings from the eve of World War I until the eve of World War II, Bourne illustrates the public work and private fun of the members. She also uses poetry and letters by members, town reports and newspaper articles, and colorful observations by old-time Castiners to narrate the relationship of the women's organization to the history of the town. Thus, recipes used for club refreshments sit side by side with accounts of members' efforts to oppose the common drinking cup in the town's school, to place rubbish receivers at street corners, to sponsor a concert by Indian Princess Watahwaso, and to endorse the State Reformatory of Women in 1915. The club belonged to both the Maine Federation of Women's Clubs and the General Federation of Women's Clubs.

64   *c BOWERS, ANN M. "White-Gloved Feminists: An Analysis of Northwest Ohio Women's Clubs." *Hayes Historical Journal* 4 (1984): 38-47. Notes, illus.: WCTU of Wood County, Ohio; Sixteen Club in Bowling Green, Ohio; Discoverers Club, Findlay, Ohio, programs from March 1899; New Century Club of Perrysburg, Ohio, bylaws; title page of Lilian Cole-Bethel's *Compendium and Question Book of Parliamentary Law* (1892); Mary Stewart's poem, "A Collect for Club Women."
        Bowers examines the public work of several northwestern Ohio women's clubs at the turn of the century, explaining that volunteer work in literary and civic organizations did not represent a retreat from the world but a link between home and community. She outlines the efforts to support parks, libraries, schools, and hospitals by the Port Clinton Literary and Social Club (1881), the Discoverers in Findlay, Ohio (1895), the New Century Club in Perrysburg, Ohio (1900), and the Sandusky Federation of Women's Clubs (1899).

65   *r BOYD, LOIS A., and R. DOUGLAS BRACKENRIDGE. *Presbyterian Women in America: Two Centuries of a Quest for Status*. A publication of the Presbyterian Historical Society, contribution to the Study of Religion, no. 9. Westport, Conn.: Greenwood, 1983. xiv, 310 pp. Notes, bib., indexes.
        This study is divided into two parts, the first of which is more useful to researchers of women's organizations. A great deal of research and an impressive bibliography support a thorough examination of women's Presbyterian organizations from 1789 to 1981. Boyd and Brackenridge describe "Pious Females" determined to build societies of pious women. Declaring 1870-80 to be the "Church Woman's Decade," the authors explain the creation of women's boards to carry out missionary work abroad and at home. From 1878 to 1923, the Woman's Boards flourished, but by 1923, they had suffered a reorganization that diminished their power and influence. Symbolically, their absorption into male-dominated church boards spelled inclusion, but the women lost the autonomy they once enjoyed. For the most part, material is drawn from three churches: United Presbyterian Church in North America, Cumberland Presbyterian

Church, and Presbyterian Church in the United States (Southern). The modern achievements, from 1933 to 1958, are cataloged. The second section of the book dwells on the story of women's ordination in the church and the work of lay participants in the clerical profession, but there is a chapter (pp. 207-24) devoted to the mission work organized not through large regional networks but at the local levels.

66 *b BOYLAN, ANNE M. "Timid Girls, Venerable Widows and Dignified Matrons: Life Cycle Patterns among Organized Women in New York and Boston, 1797-1840." *American Quarterly* 38 (Winter 1986): 779-97. Notes, tables, appendixes.

   Historian Boylan identifies three women's organizational traditions in the early nineteenth century: benevolent work, reform efforts, and feminism. Dismissing the latter, she has chosen here to examine the charitable and missionary efforts of the New York and Boston Female Missionary societies, reform societies that attempted to correct urban problems by establishing such institutions as orphan asylums, and antislavery societies. She analyzes seven hundred women in twenty-eight organizations in New York and Boston during the first four decades of the nineteenth century and gives tables on the marital status of officers and managers of benevolent organizations, distribution of ages at which women first joined benevolent organizations, the marital status of officers and managers of reform organizations, and the distribution of ages at which women first joined reform organizations. Appendixes list fourteen New York organizations and fourteen Boston organizations discussed.

67 *b -----. "Women in Groups: An Analysis of Women's Benevolent Organizations in New York and Boston, 1797-1840." *Journal of American History* 71 (1984): 497-523. Notes, appendixes.

   Boylan seeks to evaluate the ways in which early benevolent organizations affected individual women and to measure clubs' impact on women's status. Her examination of the records of eleven New York clubs and eleven Boston clubs and their members (including the Moral Reform Societies, Societies for the Relief of Poor Widows, Seamen's Aid, Female Bible Societies, and the Fragment Society) yielded the following generalizations. Women's club work was ambitious from its beginnings in 1797. Women were unaware of similar organizations in other towns and therefore repeated actions and mistakes made elsewhere. There is no evidence that the organizational activity itself led individuals from benevolent work to reform. Members were actively involved in creating the image of woman as mother. By the 1830s, members were willing to discuss prostitution openly and to associate with the prostitutes they sought to reform. Members took on political roles, lobbying and petitioning for change. Women retained a separateness from men's societies, which were devoted to similar issues, because women were suspicious that men would erode their autonomy. Societies enabled women from a variety of economic classes and religious backgrounds to work together.

67a   *n BRADY, MARILYN DELL. "Kansas Federation of Colored Women's Clubs, 1900-1930." *Kansas History* 9 (1986): 19-30. Notes, illus.: Mary Church-Terrell, Meta Vaux Warrick, Mrs. Arthur S. Gray, Mrs. Carrie Clifford Williams, Mrs. W.W. Buckner, Elizabeth Washington, Mrs. Martha H. Townsend, Nick Chiles, Kansas Association of Colored Women's Clubs, groups in 1940, 1965, 1966, Sarah Malone.

In June 1900, ten black women's clubs were represented by delegates to Topeka, where the State Federation of Women's Art Clubs was formed under the leadership of Elizabeth Washington, of the Topeka Oak Leaf Club. Its purpose was "to elevate our women to a higher standard in the art and musical world, and it is also a lesson that we must educate the hand as well as the brain." In the late nineteenth century, black women had formed associations and those in Kansas were no exception. It is probable that the oldest black women's club in Kansas was the Ladies' Refugee Aid Society, formed in Lawrence in 1864. Other clubs included Coterie (founded in 1889) in Topeka for the purpose of the study of Shakespeare, and the Women's League in Kansas City, which held sewing and literary classes for former slave women. Also, clubs were founded for temperance, antilynching, literary study, and needlework. The Kansas alliance formed in 1900 continued to grow, as the Kansas Federation of Colored Women's Clubs. In 1904, twenty-one clubs joined. By 1913, fifty-one.

Exhibits of needlework, designed to demonstrate the ability of black women, drew and delighted hundreds of white men and women. When Josephine St. Pierre, a black member of the New Era Club in Boston, was not admitted to the white women's General Federation of Women's Clubs, Kansas women did not attempt to challenge the all-white Kansas Federation of Social Science Clubs (the forerunner of the Kansas Federation of Women's Clubs). For this, black women of Kansas were praised by the white clubwomen of Kansas. Under the leadership of Beatrice Child, Kansas clubs of black women grew and thrived in the 1920s, joining the National Association of Colored Women, supporting antilynching legislation, holding art contests and displays, holding music competitions, and funding the Florence Crittenton Home for Colored Girls in Topeka, the only black

33

Crittenton Home in America. In 1924, it pioneered within the National Association of Colored Women in creating junior clubs for young women. The clubs provided important leadership roles and fought stereotypes of race and gender, meanwhile glorifying women's work as nurturers and homemakers.

68 *n,c,y -----. "Organizing Afro-American Girls' Clubs in Kansas in the 1920s." *Frontiers* 9, no. 2 (1987): 69-73. Notes.

The Kansas Federation of Colored Women's Clubs, at the invitation of the Topeka Oak Leaf Club, was formed in 1900 and grew to include sixty-five study clubs, needlework societies, and charity, social, and civic associations. The earliest of these were founded in the late 1880s to meet the racism of the era by defining and proclaiming the virtues of black womanhood and serving the needs of the community. In 1922, the federation joined the National Association of Colored Women and its members took a distinguished role in national administration. In 1924, the Kansas Federation led the nation in establishing junior clubs. In one year, they founded thirty clubs with 523 girls, studying music, child labor issues, community responsibility, the girls' industrial problems, and the necessity for better interracial relationships. Kansas junior clubs supporter Beatrice Childs wrote a regular column in *National Notes* on the work of the clubs. Brady says the clubs for girls were crucial in passing on racial pride and solidarity and concern for other women and for the race. The relationship between the Kansas Federation and its junior clubs provided a bridge between generations and a set of models for growing girls.

69 *b,t BRANDENSTERN, SHERILYN. "The Colorado Cottage Home." *Colorado Magazine* 53 (Summer 1976): 229-42. Notes, illus.: the home; Adrianna Hungerford, Colorado WCTU president, 1898-1942.

In 1866, an alliance between Charles Crittenton and the Woman's Christian Temperance Union in Colorado resulted in the founding of the Colorado Cottage Home for unwed mothers. This article surveys the development of the institution, which operated in Denver. At first, it served only nine young women, but gradually, with increased funding from the WCTU, the establishment housed more and more women in larger and better facilities. A matron supervised the home, male and female physicians provided medical care, and the Colorado Cottage Home enjoyed a reputation for its high rate of successful births. For the duration of World War I, the institution broadened its constituency and offered aid to soldiers' wives.

70 *p BRATTON, VIRGINIA MASON. *History of the South Carolina Daughters of the American Revolution, 1892-1936.* York, S.C.: the Organization, 1937. 162 pp. Illus.: Mrs. Frances Pickens Bacon, organizer and first State Regent, and the South Carolina Cottage, the first building at Tamasee Daughters of the American Revolution School.

      This study surveys forty-four years of the history of the South Carolina Daughters of the American Revolution. The bulk of the text consists of histories of the state chapters. In all, sixty-one clubs are briefly documented, with the date of organization, the officers, projects undertaken, size of budget, the origin of the name of the branch, and the topics studied by the membership. Thirteen biographies of the state regents are included, relating the achievements of each administration rather than providing an account of her private life. The work includes a list of five chapters formerly on the roster but now disbanded, a list of state officers since the founding of the association, and a list of conference cities between 1892 and 1936. Much attention is given to Tamassee, a mountain school founded and supported by the organization, which opened in 1919 after five years of planning and fund-raising. At first it was open to girls and in 1932 began to accept boys, providing both with well-rounded educations.

71 *w BRAY, FRANK CHAPIN. "National Consumer's League." *Chautauquan* 59 (June 1910): 106-15.
      See *Chautauquan*.

72 *m BRECKINRIDGE, SOPHONSIBA PRESTON. *Women in the Twentieth Century: A Study of Their Political, Social, and Economic Activities.* New York: McGraw-Hill Book Co., 1933. Reprint. New York: Arno Press, 1972. xi, 364 pp. Notes, appendixes, indexes.

      Written in 1933, this was the most comprehensive history of the development of women's organizations undertaken in America. Part 1 surveys the history of the General Federation of Women's Clubs growing out of Sorosis and other local women's cultural societies. Antedating the culture club movement was the evangelical and missionary movement, the Young Women's Christian Association, P.E.O. (1869), Daughters of Rebekah (1851), Degree of Honor (1873), auxiliary to the Ancient Order of United Workmen, Ladies of the Macabees (1886), the Ancient Order of Eastern Star (1876), Masons, and the Woman's Relief Corps of the Grand Army of the Republic (1883). Breckinridge catalogs the groups that were founded in the 1890s: the Daughters of the American Revolution, Colonial Dames (1891), United Daughters of the Confederacy (1894), National Council of Jewish Women (1893), National Association of Colored Women (1896), National Congress of Mothers (1897), and National Consumers' League (1899). Chapter 3 isolates the groups founded between 1900 and 1910: an auxiliary to the National Baptist Convention (a society of black women), the National Women's Trade Union League (1903), American Home Economics Association (1908), Young Women's Christian Association from a merger of the Women's and Young Women's Christian Association (1906), and Congress of Women for Home Missions (1908). Between 1910 and World War I were founded the Junior League in New York, women's professional organizations, and the Woman's Peace party (1914). Postwar groups (1918-32) included War Mothers of America (1917), Service Star Legion, an auxiliary to the American Legion, the National Council of Catholic Women (1920), the Parent-Teachers Association growing out of the Congress of Mothers (1924), the American Association of University Women growing out of the Association of Collegiate Alumnae, temperance groups, Jewish groups, Girls Friendly Society, League of Women Voters, National Woman's party, National Association of Colored Women, Grange, and National Council of Women. During this era, a great many clubhouses were built. The clubs' growth and projects, changing over time, are detailed. Other parts of this study examine the lives of working women and the story of women in government. The latter mentions such women's associations as the League of Women Voters, the Woman's Joint Congressional Committee, the General Federation of Women's Clubs, and Women's Christian Temperance Union for their efforts to shape law.

73 *p BREEN, WILLIAM J. "Southern Women in the War: The North Carolina Woman's Committee, 1917-1919." *North Carolina Historical Review* 55 (Summer 1978): 251-83. Appendixes, illus.: Mrs. Gertrude Sise Tufts; Mrs. Lucy Owen Robertson; ad in October 1917 *Charlotte Observer* for cooking school and week of classes; Julia A. Thorns; Mrs. Fannie Yarborough Beckett; Alice Dunbar-Nelson.

   In North Carolina, the Woman's Committee served as a clearinghouse for women's war relief efforts during World War I. In June 1917, sixty-eight women representing groups throughout the state met to organize. Laura Holmes Reilley of Charlotte, a clubwoman and suffragist, headed the new committee and found her male counterparts difficult to work with. Their condescension and inefficiency disappointed her. The women on their own, then, defined their role in the state's war mobilization effort. They stimulated the formation of Red Cross groups in every town and encouraged the work of the

Woman's Liberty Loan Committee. They registered women for volunteer service and supported increased food production by touting the benefits of victory gardens. In order to improve the conservation of food, members taught through home demonstration. They initiated recreation programs for soldiers and began a campaign for child welfare. The latter consisted of three plans—weighing and measuring babies, pressing for recreational activities, and urging children be sent back to school by parents. Public health nurses were hired as well. Mrs. Alice Dunbar-Nelson was invited in 1918 to organize the black women of the state, and integrated projects were envisioned, although not sufficiently well planned to have far-reaching effects on the separate work. Breen argues convincingly that the agenda of the Woman's Committee pushed the state to a new social consciousness, enabling North Carolina's progressive program by 1920 to enjoy the label "Wisconsin of the South."

74   *b   BRINKER, LEA J.   "The Charitable Impulse of Sarah Worthington King Peter." *Queen City Heritage* 42 (Winter 1982): 27-40.   Notes, illus.: Sarah Worthington King Peter; records of organization.

Sarah Worthington King Peter, an Ohio-born woman, married Edward King at the age of sixteen. She had five children with him and grew active in the reform activities of Cincinnati in the early nineteenth century. In 1836, King died and she moved to Philadelphia, marrying William Peter in 1840. When he died in 1853, she took up reform activities in Philadelphia. Having participated in the founding of the School of Design in Philadelphia, she moved to Cincinnati in 1854 and helped found the Cincinnati Academy of Fine Arts "to aid in the cultivation of public taste" by establishing galleries with copies of art and sculpture revered in that era. The piece describes the work of the eighteen women on the Board of Managers, prominent individuals who paid five dollars a year for membership, but who raised additional funds with speakers, concerts, and strawberry parties to buy paintings and open exhibits. Although the author found little material on the period 1855-64, it appears that the women resolved to abandon their efforts and hand over their assets to McMechen University's School of Drawing and Design.

75   *p   BROCKETT, L.P. *Woman's Work in the Civil War: A Record of Heroism, Patriotism, and Patience.* Philadelphia: Zeigler, McCurdy and Co., 1868.   799 pp.   Indexes, illus.: 16 engravings of individual women.

This giant encyclopedia of women's contribution to the Civil War includes a sizable chapter (pp. 523-716). "Ladies Who Organized Aid Societies." This section explores the Women's Central Association of Relief, Soldiers' Aid Society of Northern Ohio, New England Women's Auxiliary Association, New England Soldiers' Relief Association, Northwestern Sanitary Commission, General Aid Society for the Army in Buffalo, Michigan Soldiers' Aid Society, Woman's Pennsylvania Branch of the United States Sanitary Commission, Wisconsin Soldiers' Aid Society, Pittsburgh Branch of the United States Sanitary Commission, Department of the South, St. Louis' Ladies Union Aid Society, Ladies' Aid Society of Philadelphia, the Women's Relief Association of Brooklyn and Long Island, and the special efforts of Mrs. Elizabeth M. Streeter, Mrs. Curtis T. Fean, Mrs. A.H. Hoge, Mrs. Mary A. Livermore, and Mrs. Elizabeth S. Mendenhall.

76 *n BROWN, IRA V. " 'Am I Not a Woman and a Sister?': The Anti-Slavery Convention of American Women, 1837-1839." *Pennsylvania History* 50 (1983): 1-19. Notes.

Citing generously from the *Proceedings* of the three antislavery conventions of 1837, 1838, and 1839, Brown explores the history of the Anti-Slavery Convention of American Women. In 1832, black women in Salem, Massachusetts, had formed an antislavery society which had, by 1837, one thousand auxiliaries, seventy-five of which were exclusively female in membership. It was Lucretia Mott who led in founding the racially integrated Philadelphia Female Anti-Slavery Society. The Boston Female Anti-Slavery Society was also integrated. Such groups as these convened in New York City in 1837 and in Philadelphia the following two years to pass resolutions, provide a forum for antislavery speakers, and plan speaking tours.

77 *s -----. "Woman's Rights Movement in Pennsylvania." *Pennsylvania History* 32 (April 1965): 153-65. Notes.

A Philadelphia Quaker, Lucretia Mott, assisted Elizabeth Cady Stanton in holding the 1848 Seneca Falls New York Woman's Rights Conference. Brown argues that Pennsylvania women continued to play a critical part in the American women's rights struggle. He cites the work of the Philadelphia Female Anti-Slavery Society, the Pennsylvania Women's Rights Convention in West Chester (June 1852), the fifth national women's rights convention in Philadelphia (October 1854), and the publication of Jane Grey Swisshelm's *Pittsburgh Saturday Visitor*. He reminds readers of the existence of educational institutions for women, the Equal Rights Association forming in Philadelphia in 1866, and the Pennsylvania Woman Suffrage Association, organized in 1869 and presided over by Mary Grew until 1892. Finally, he describes the 1872-73 Pennsylvania debates on suffrage at the Constitutional Convention.

78 *s BROWN, OLYMPIA. *Acquaintances, Old and New, among Reformers*. Milwaukee: the author, 1911. 115 pp. Illus.: Olympia Brown; Elizabeth Cady Stanton; Susan B. Anthony; Lucy Stone.

With brevity, charm, and attention to the personalities of the people she encountered, Brown tells the story of her life, including her growing-up years, college experience at Antioch in Ohio, and her petition as organizer of the Boston convention at which the New England Woman Suffrage Association was founded. Other chapters are devoted to organizational work, such as her participation in the 1866 New York City conference of the American Equal Rights Association, the Kansas suffrage campaign of 1867, the organization of Mother Cobb's first Woman's Physiological Society in the United States, and the ideals and contributions of such noteworthy clubwomen as Julia Ward Howe, Caroline Severance, Abby Kelly Foster, Mary Livermore, Clara B. Colby, who edited the *Woman's Tribune* for twenty-five years, and Emma Smith DeVoe.

79 *s -----. *Democratic Ideals: A Memorial Sketch of Clara B. Colby*. Washington, D.C.: Federal Suffrage Association, 1917. 116 pp. Illus.: Clara B. Colby.

Although Clara Bewick Colby (1846-1916) is not now revered among the pantheon of nineteenth-century American women suffragists, she was appreciated in her own time for her activism, particularly as a journalist for women's rights. Brown's biography summarizes Colby's management of the 1882 suffrage campaign in Nebraska and her sixteen-year tenure as president of the Nebraska Suffrage Association. From 1883 to 1888, she edited the *Woman's Tribune* in Nebraska, providing suffragists with a forum for their opinions. In 1888, she moved the paper to Washington, D.C., and published it there until 1904. Moving to Portland, Oregon, she continued to edit the *Woman's Tribune* until 1909. Brown is careful to recount Colby's support, during the years 1902 until her death in 1916, for the organization Brown founded, the Federal Suffrage Association. In addition, Brown quotes poetry by Colby, memorial tributes to her, and a 1915 address she gave at the San Francisco Panama-Pacific International Exposition. The work also contains documents pertinent to the work of the Federal Suffrage Association.

80 *f,n BROWN, SUE M. (MRS. S. JOE). *The History of the Order of the Eastern Star among Colored People.* Des Moines, Iowa: the organization, 1925. 88 pp. Illus.: Mrs. Sue M. Wilson; Prince Hall, founder of the Negro Masonry; 5 of past grand matrons; 8 of Masonic Temples, Widows' and Orphans Home in Nashville, Tenn.

The author was a worthy matron of the International Conference of the Grand Order of the Eastern Star in the year she wrote this history. Organized in 1907 in Boston by Mrs. Letitia L. Foy, it was formed to cooperate in the labors of Masonry and grew to include thirty-five grand jurisdictions with 3,500 chapters, 100,000 members, and a collective treasury of a half million dollars. It met biennially at the same time and place as the International Conference of Knights Temples. Summaries of the early conventions indicate a concern with establishing rituals for the members and creating a "force to stimulate members to a more intelligent participation with civic, national and international affairs." Printed here is a 1924 address Mrs. S. Joe Brown delivered before the ninth biennial conference in Pittsburgh in 1924. In addition, she includes her reminiscences of her travels to western cities to meet Eastern Star members in Alaska, the Pacific Northwest, California, and Texas. Brown alludes to antagonism with rival chapters in Washington State, Missouri, Louisiana, and West Virginia, where two groups each claimed to be the authentic society. A chapter on buildings utilized by members, including temples and social service institutions, provides a sense of their strength and civic commitments. The author includes lists of the chapters and membership per state; the dates of chapter organization, officers in 1924-26, biennial meeting places between 1907 and 1926, and a copy of the constitution and bylaws.

81 *w BROWNE, GRACE GREENWOOD. "Michigan Woman's Press Association." *Michigan History Magazine* 24 (Summer 1940): 309-12.

The Michigan Woman's Press Association was organized in 1890 in Traverse City's Hotel Park Place. It was the idea of Mrs. M.E.C. Bates of the *Grand Traverse Herald.* She was confident that an association of newspaper women would facilitate "betterment and extension of good journalism among women journalists," especially for rural women readers "whose only touch with the outside world was largely confined to the newspaper and her small community." Twenty-seven women from fifteen cities gathered to organize. Their names, cities, and newspaper affiliations are listed here. Much attention is given to the structure of the organization, its officers, and membership, and there is also revealing material about the women's relief work during World War I, a patriotic effort.

82   *m BRUCE, H. ADDINGTON. *Women in the Making of America*. Boston: Little, Brown and Co., 1928. Notes, indexes, illus.: 10 of celebrated women such as Julia Ward Howe, Jane Addams, Mother Bickerdyke, and Martha Washington; Smith College Ivy Day procession.

  Here is a chatty survey of American women's history from the colonial era to the passage of the federal suffrage amendment, describing individual leaders and general trends in domestic economy. In chapter 7 "Consolidating for Progress," researchers will find a history of women's organizations, from Anne Hutchinson's scandalous discussion meetings in seventeenth-century Massachusetts to the formation of the General Federation of Women's Clubs. Along the way, Bruce mentions the Kalamazoo Ladies Library Society, the Minerva Club in New Harmony, Indiana, the Friends in Council in Quincy, Illinois, the New England Woman's Club, Sorosis, and the state federations of women's clubs devoted to progressive reforms in industry and conservation. Chapter 8 surveys women's volunteer work during World War I, via the National Defense Council's Woman's Committee. Chapter 9 describes the suffrage movement after the National American Woman Suffrage Association shared the limelight with Alice Paul's Congressional Union/National Woman's party.

83   *r BRUMMITT, STELLA WYATT. *Looking Backward, Thinking Forward: The Jubilee History of the Woman's Home Missionary Society of the Methodist Episcopal Church*. Cincinnati: the organization, 1930. 278 pp. Indexes, illus.: 31 of officers, missionaries, and projects, including nurses in Rapid City Hospital; children in Japan; leaders in Spokane; girls in Susannah Wesley Home, Honolulu; tea party at Italian kindergarten in New Orleans; springtime at Buffalo settlement; handicraft classes in Epworth School for Girls; class in typewriting at Olive Hill, Kentucky; also 17 buildings, including Harwood Industrial Home and School, Albuquerque, New Mexico; Esther Hall for Young Women, Cincinnati; June Lee Home, Seward, Alabama; Browning Home, Camden, South Carolina; Highland Boys Community Home, Brighton Canyon, Utah; Ethel Harpst Home, Cedertown, Georgia; Navajo Indian Mission, Farmington, New Mexico; Erie School, Olive Hill, Kentucky; Helen Kelly Manley Center, Portland, Oregon; Baby Fold, Mothers' Jewels Home, York, Nebraska; Brewster Hospital, Jacksonville, Florida; Medical Mission Dispensary, Boston; Blodgett

Memorial Community House, Hazelton, Pennsylvania; Marcy Center, Chicago; Epworth School for Girls, Webster Groves, Missouri; Oram Community Hall, Ponca Indian Mission, Ponca City, Oklahoma; Peek Orphanage, Polo, Illinois.

This history of the Woman's Home Missionary Society of the Methodist Episcopal church begins in 1880, with a description of women's roles in society and the problems of the post-Civil War era in which they lived. The organization credits the early work of the 1832 Lynchburg Auxiliary to the Methodist Episcopal church, but surpassed it mightily by raising $50 million in fifty years for its projects. Buildings supported by them were valued at $1.5 million at the time of publication. Brummitt is thorough, detailing the early conventions, officers, publications, training schools, rest homes, hospitals, young people's programs at home, and missionaries abroad. A separate chapter is devoted to the work with immigrant women in China, Japan, and Korea and in American cities of New York, Philadelphia, East Boston, San Francisco, Los Angeles, and Seattle. Histories of individual institutions for blacks, Native Americans, and whites in America, plus portraits of children's homes, orphanages, clinics, leper colonies, and industrial schools in Alaska, Puerto Rico, the Dominican Republic, and the Spanish Southwest are provided. Final chapters catalog clubwomen's activities with temperance, evangelism, mite boxes, prayer mission study, and fund-raising, and describe the twenty-fifth, fortieth, and fiftieth anniversary celebrations of missionary work at home and around the world.

84 *r BRUNGER, RONALD A. "The Ladies Aid Societies in Michigan Methodism." *Methodist History* 5 (January 1967): 31-48. Notes.

The author explains that before the Woman's Society of Christian Service was organized in 1940, virtually every Methodist church had a Ladies Aid Society. For three quarters of a century, an important role in the Methodist church was played by the members, but it has been ignored by historians. Determined to rectify the neglect, Brunder outlines the founding of the Woman's Foreign Missionary Society in 1869, the Woman's Home Mission Society in 1880, and the local Ladies Aid societies formed as early as 1850 in Michigan. During the Civil War, the women united to form the Soldiers' Aid Society. Brunger makes extensive and ingenious use of newspaper accounts of the meetings to tell of oyster suppers, strawberry festivals, ice-cream socials, quilting bees, and other festivities to raise money for church and relief projects. He details the progress of the Michigan Ladies Aid

Society, which raised $584,000 in 1928, $227,000 in 1933, and $372,000 in 1940, the last year of its existence before reorganization.

85   *y BUCKLER, HELEN, MARY F. FIEDLER, and MARTHA F. ALLEN, researchers, comps., and eds. *Wo-He-Lo: The Story of Camp Fire Girls, 1910-1960*. New York: Holt, Rinehart and Winston, 1961. 308 pp. Bib., notes, illus.: 12 engravings from manuals; 38 pictures of Luther Halsy Gulick, Charlotte Vetter Gulick, and girls enjoying Camp Fire activities.

This history stresses the organizational and structured story of Camp Fire Girls, at the expense of addressing the activities of the girls in local camps and clubs. In 1910, Dr. Luther Halsy Gulick and his wife, Charlotte Vetter Gulick, conducted a camp for girls on Lake Sebago near South Casco, Maine. Unifying recreation for girls around work, health, and love, they founded Camp Fire Girls. They created costumes, three ranks, a manual, and a publication. By the end of 1913, there were one thousand independent clubs plus others in churches, YWCAs, schools, settlement houses, playgrounds, camps, libraries, and miscellaneous institutions. The study examines the effort of the leadership to reach out beyond middle-class girls to include a broad membership. Projects changed, depending on the needs of each generation of girls. Social welfare became an important objective, necessitating cooperation with other agencies. The final section of the volume provides excerpts from documents, letters from Girls' Count Books, leader's reports, and poems written by members.

86   *z,s BUHLE, MARI JO. *Women and American Socialism, 1870-1920*. Urbana: University of Illinois Press, 1981. xix, 345 pp. Notes, indexes, illus.: 24 of women leaders in American socialism.

The role of women's organizations plays a large part in the information and analysis of this work. Buhle asserts that "the Gilded Age woman's movement did not provide a massive constituency for the later Socialist movement, but it did set standards for those native-born women who would participate." She examines several organizations that worked for social change, including Sorosis, New England Woman's Club, Women's Educational and Industrial Union, and Women's Christian Temperance Union. Buhle then describes the grass-roots origins of women's Socialist clubs during the years 1900-8, defining their ideals and noting their resemblance to other women's organizations of the day. Close attention is paid to the work of the Women's National Committee from 1908 to 1913, whose founding "marked a major turning point in the Socialist women's movement." Despite the insistence of a few clubs, like Chicago's Socialist Woman's

League and the statewide Women's Socialist Union of California, on retaining their autonomy, the National Committee succeeded in coordinating many aspects of the socialist woman's movement. The work of Anna A. Maley and Caroline Lowe is featured. The priorities of the National Committee included carrying its literature to women everywhere, publishing the *Progressive Woman*, providing rigorous training in a materialist conception of history as related to women's status, and disseminating a standard lesson plan to study groups. Buhle devotes a chapter to the woman suffrage question, baring the tensions and points of cooperation between socialist women and members of the National American Woman Suffrage Association.

87   *w BULARZIK, MARY J. "The Bonds of Belonging: Leonora O'Reilly and Social Reform." *Labor History* 24 (Winter 1983): 60-83.

Bularzik examines Leonora O'Reilly's identity as a single Irish woman worker, who went to work at the age of eleven and remained in the labor force. She developed a class consciousness, which deepened her outlook as a political activist. Her insights were gained from her ethnic community, feminist ideology, and trade union work. These provided both a sense of support and conflict for her, and the author defines the extent and limits of these forces in supporting her public reform efforts. Details are provided on O'Reilly's participation in the Working Women's Society, Social Reform Club, United Garment Workers, settlement house movement, Pratt Institute, Manhattan Trade School for Girls, New York branch of the Women's Trade Union League, National Association for the Advancement of Colored People, Socialist party, and New York Woman Suffrage party.

88   no entry

89   *i BUSSEY, GERTRUDE, and MARGARET TIMS. *Pioneers for Peace: Women's International League for Peace and Freedom, 1915-1965.* London: the organization, 1965, 1980. 255 pp. Indexes.

Here is a survey of the work of the Women's International League for Peace and Freedom from its origins in 1915 through its fiftieth anniversary. Originating during World War I in 1915, it was called the Woman's Peace party. After the war, however, members changed its name. Bussey and Tims discuss the international peace conferences in which the organization participated in the 1920s, its nuclear disarmament proposals, and its responses to international tensions throughout its history. The authors are generous with quotations from Woman's Peace party/WILPF documents, its conference proceedings, and resolutions its members passed at regular conventions.

90   *r BUTLER, MRS. F.A. *History of the Woman's Foreign Missionary Society, Methodist Episcopal Church, South*. Nashville: Publishing House of the Methodist Episcopal Church, South, 1904. 181 pp. (Microfilm 5299 of New Haven: Research Publications, 1976 [History of Women], from Collection of the Schlesinger Library, Radcliffe College, Harvard University, Cambridge, Massachusetts.)

Originally, Butler's history was serialized in the *Woman's Missionary Advocate* as "The Story of Our Work," in 1898-99. The Woman's Foreign Missionary Society of the Methodist Episcopal Church, South, was organized in 1878 in Atlanta, Georgia. Women had been active earlier, as wives of missionaries to China and as members of clubs in New York and Boston. Chapters of church women throughout the South were established to raise money for women teachers in China, Mexico, Brazil, and the Seminole Academy in Oklahoma Territory. In 1882, members raised $41,000 for five women missionaries. The account stresses the prosperity for missionary projects that arose from the devotion of organization members.

91   *r CALHOUN, MRS. R.W. "History of the Woman's Auxiliary Synod of Oklahoma." *Chronicles of Oklahoma* 25 (Winter 1947-48): 358-81.

Here is a survey of the work of the Presbyterian woman's society for home and foreign missions, the Oklahoma Synodical Auxiliary, founded in 1915. Using quotations from annual reports through 1945, the author traces the work of the group. Projects include fund-raising for missions, establishing vacation Bible schools, supporting the young people's encampment, hosting missionaries from abroad, holding conferences for black women, and providing money for Indian boys to attend a seminary. In 1940, there were fifty auxiliaries with 1,151 members, which had declined by 1943 to thirty-seven auxiliaries with 1,057 members.

92   *c CAMPBELL, BARBARA KUHN. *The "Liberated" Woman of 1914: Prominent Women in the Progressive Era*. Studies in American History and Culture, no. 6. Ann Arbor: UMI Research Press, 1979. xviii, 220 pp. Notes, bib., indexes.

This historian surveyed the biographies of nine thousand American women of 1914, using John William Leonard's *Woman's Who's Who*. Although the reference source ignored black women and Roman Catholic nuns, Campbell was able to compile many statistics on the patterns in women's family environment, education, careers, religion, political activities and interests, and club work. Chapter 6 (pp. 147-76) discusses and provides tables illuminating club membership patterns among many distinguished women of the era. Campbell provides an overview of club history, beginning with the founding of culture clubs in the 1860s and culminating with the establishment of the General Federation of Women's Clubs in 1890. She features the work of the Chicago Woman's Club. Campbell's women belonged to literary, alumnae, professional, patriotic and genealogical clubs. Of the women she studied, 77 percent had joined women's clubs and 49 percent had held or were currently holding office. Among the noncareer women, the figures were higher: 85 percent joined clubs and 54 percent were leaders. Among professional women, 79 percent belonged to clubs and 57 percent were leaders. As for women in education, 71 percent joined clubs and 42 percent were leaders. In the arts, 70 percent became club members and 39 percent were leaders. Regionally, differences appeared. Southerners dominated club life: 83 percent belonged to clubs, 55 percent as leaders; among midwesterners, 82 percent joined and 52 percent were leaders; among easterners, 75 percent joined and 45 percent were leaders; westerners ranked lowest with 70 percent membership and 49 percent leaders.

93   *p CAMPBELL, D'ANN. *Women at War with America: Private Lives in a Patriotic Era*. Cambridge, Mass.: Harvard University Press, 1984. xiv, 304 pp. Notes, indexes.

Campbell outlines two types of voluntary organizations in which women participated during World War II. Approximately a quarter of a million women civilians pitched in, especially housewives in their thirties and forties, and women who were established residents in communities. Least likely to volunteer were mothers of young children, older women, newcomers in town, and workers. Also active were college-educated women and working-class women if their political and civic community groups gave out assignments. The USO—recreational centers serving bases, large cities, and transportation points—was staffed by women volunteers. The centers were informal meeting places for servicemen and service wives. Volunteers were screened and expected to meet dress codes while they served as hostesses and dance partners at the centers. Black hostesses were instructed to refuse to dance with white servicemen. The Red Cross was a second arena for women volunteers. Half a billion volunteer-hours were spent, perhaps not on really useful war projects, but of benefit to participant morale in wartime. Its mandate included providing home thrift classes, nutrition and accident prevention lectures, and canteen services for soldiers.

Four to five million women knit garments and rolled billions of surgical dressings for the soldiers.

94   *t CANUP, CHARLES E. "The Temperance Movement and Legislation in Indiana." *Indiana Magazine of History* 16 (March 1920): 3-37; 16 (June 1920): 112-52.

This survey of temperance reform activity includes material on the Daughters of Temperance, which formed in Indiana in 1849. It sponsored the "Hatchet Crusade" in 1854, when fifty Winchester women destroyed several saloons. In 1874, the Women's Christian Temperance Union formed in Fort Wayne, with 250 women from twenty-two counties. Half of them picketed saloons in Greencastle and others held prayer vigils outside the Shelbyville "tippling houses." The article gives figures on the growth of membership, and mentions publications, additional projects, and societies for youth sponsored by the WCTU.

95   *z CARLSON, AVIS. *The League of Women Voters in St. Louis: The First Forty Years, 1919-1959.* St. Louis: the organization, 1959. vi, 115 pp. Indexes, appendixes, illus.: 34 of officers.

This history of the League of Women Voters in St. Louis outlines the origins of the National League of Women Voters organization in the National Woman Suffrage Association, which had won the federal suffrage amendment in 1920 and sought to continue its work among women on political questions. Carlson describes the "Years of Experiment (1920-25)" in which the members groped toward a new agenda and decided not to affiliate with a political party or to launch a party of its own. Instead, it enforced nonpartisanship and stressed adult education in citizenship to create a more informed voting population. For the years 1926-30, Carlson elaborates on the St. Louis organization's structure, finances, and service programs for voters. During the 1930s, the organization emphasized interracial commitment and adult education programs. During the years of World War II, the St. Louis league formed war service units and engaged in patriotic efforts. After the war, St. Louis members worked on civil rights issues, conservation, public schools, and foreign policy. Appendixes list legislative achievements, and officers of the St. Louis league from 1919 to 1959.

96   *z CARLSON, MRS. HARRY. "The First Decade of the St. Louis League of Women Voters." *Bulletin of the Missouri Historical Society* 26 (1969): 32-52. Notes, illus.; members of the Equal

Suffrage League of St. Louis (1916), League of Women headquarters in St. Louis in the early 1920s.

The League of Women Voters was born in St. Louis when the local suffrage organization modified its goals upon winning enfranchisement. Carlson surveys the early work of the Equal Suffrage League of St. Louis. Members staged a "Golden Lane" of seven thousand women carrying yellow parasols and wearing white dresses to silently line the streets as Democratic delegates headed for their national convention. They also provided a tableau, with the Goddess of Liberty and twelve nymphs, to persuade president-makers to include women's rights on their platform. Women in St. Louis also established citizenship schools in the summer of 1919 to educate women in how to use their new enfranchisement thoughtfully. Suffragists pressured for ratification with parades, costumes, and flamboyant spectacles. In November 1919, with ratification assured, the St. Louis Equal Suffrage League transformed itself into a new organization, the League of Women Voters, several months before the national transformation in February 1920. Carlson outlines the cooperative efforts of the members with other organizations including those of black women. She documents their difficulty in raising money, in attracting membership, and in remaining nonpartisan. She surveys the issues the organization supported in the 1920s, such as women serving as factory inspectors, the age of consent rising from fifteen to sixteen, the establishment of Workmen's Compensation, passage of the Sheppard-Towner Act, and encouragement to vote in elections.

97 *t CARPENTER, CHARLES K. *The Origin of the Woman's Crusade and the WCTU*. N.p.: Mines Press, 1949. 29 pp.

Not a weighty source, this is a reminiscence of a man who witnessed the Woman's Crusade in Washington Courthouse, Ohio, at the age of eight, seventy-six years before writing this pamphlet. His mother marched to the saloon and kneeled in the snow, praying until eleven o'clock at night to persuade the owner to close. Although the author assisted his mother to write her own memoirs of the occasion, he quotes from those infrequently. He does draw on reminiscences of other participants and on Frances Willard's accounts of the origins of the Women's Christian Temperance Union in 1874 from the momentum of women's success with the crusade.

98 *p CARR, ANNIE CALL, ed. *East of Antelope Island*. N.p.: Daughters of Utah Pioneers, 1948.

See Daughters of Utah Pioneers [Davis County Company].

99   *c CARRAWAY, GERTRUDE SPRAGUE. *Carolina Crusaders: The History of the North Carolina Federation of Women's Clubs*. Vol. 2. New Bern: Owen G. Dunn Co., 1941. 142 pp. Illus.: 41, of officers in the North Carolina Federation of Women's Clubs; Raleigh Woman's Club house.

The author, who was also a leader in the Daughters of the American Revolution, provides a highly general survey of North Carolina Federation of Women's Clubs activity from 1901 to 1941. She lists all officers in the organization for these years and gives the presidential address of Mrs. Lindsay Patterson at the 1941 convention. Details are sparse, however, on the projects undertaken by the organization.

See Sallie Southall Cotten for volume 1 of this account.

100   *t CARTER, PAUL A. "Prohibition and Democracy: The Noble Experiment Reassessed." *Wisconsin Magazine of History* 56 (April 1973): 189-201. Notes, illus.: Mrs. Charles H. Sabin, women's organizer for the National Prohibition Reform; Mrs. Ella Boole, national president of the Women's Christian Temperance Union.

This scholar documents the battle in 1930 between two groups of temperance women. The members of the Women's Christian Temperance Union, led by national president Mrs. Ella Boole, supported Prohibition, the law of the land. The Woman's Organization for National Prohibition Reform, led by Mrs. Charles H. Sabin, along with Mrs. Pierre Du Pont and Mrs. August Belmont, sought to repeal Prohibition and make alcohol production and consumption legal once again. Carter articulates their opposing stances and describes their efforts, like side-by-side booths at state and country fairs, to persuade the public of the wisdom of their perspective.

101   *s CATT, CARRIE CHAPMAN, and NETTIE ROGERS SHULER. *Woman Suffrage and Politics: The Inner Story of the Suffrage Movement*. New York: Charles Scribner's Sons, 1923. Reprint. Seattle: University of Washington Press, 1970. xxiii, 504 pp. Indexes.

Carrie Chapman Catt (1859-1947) joined the Iowa Woman Suffrage Association in 1887 and remained an active leader in the suffrage struggle until its achievement in 1920. Rather than focusing on her own biography and her presidency of the National American Woman Suffrage Association from 1900 to 1904 and from 1915 to 1920, she and Shuler trace the broad story of woman suffrage from the Seneca Falls Convention in 1848 through the passage of the Nineteenth Amendment. She discusses the reorganization of woman suffrage forces after the passage of the constitutional amendment granting black men the vote after the Civil War. The history gives special attention to suffrage campaigns in the states of Illinois, Ohio and Iowa, but concentrates most closely on the decade just prior to success, 1910-20. Instead of dwelling on the split from NAWSA by the National Woman's party, the study documents state- and federal-level efforts to win the support of legislators to the suffrage cause. It is harsh in its criticism of antagonistic politicians and the liquor industry's opposition to a woman suffrage amendment.

102   *c   *Chautauquan* [special issue on women's clubs] 59 (June 1910). Clubs.   Illus.: Mrs. Philip N. Moore, president of the General Federation of Women's Clubs; Sarah Platt Decker; Dimies T.S. Denison; Women's Club House in Cincinnati; club house of Good Citizenship League in Flushing, New York; 4 views of home and school gardens under management of the Cincinnati Women's Club; the exterior and the interior court of the Ebell Club House in Los Angeles; library at Cody, Wyoming, built by the Women's Club, 1907-08; dump converted to a park by the West Side Forestry Club of Topeka, Kansas; interior of the Mothers and Daughters Club House in Plainfield, New Hampshire; Dr. Anna H. Shaw, president of the National American Woman Suffrage Association; Laura Drake Gill, president of the Association of Collegiate Alumnae; H.E. Countess of Aberdeen, president of the International Council of Women; Emilie McVeas, dean of the University of Cincinnati; Woman Suffrage Association postcard; anti-woman suffrage postcard; Mrs. William H. Taft, National Civic Federation; Lillian M.N. Stevens, WCTU president; Cynthia Westover Alden, president of the International Sunshine Society; Daughters of the American Revolution Continental Memorial Hall in Washington, D.C.

The entire issue of this periodical is devoted to the history of women's organizations in America.   Mary I. Wood, "Woman's Club Movement," (pp. 13-64) asserts that clubs' watchword is "service," and she acknowledges a debt to Jane Cunningham Croly in founding Sorosis in New York City in 1868 and the General Federation of Women's Clubs in 1890.   Wood lists the first club in each state and describes early conventions, leaders, the Bureau of Information which she directed, the state federation system, the education and library extension work, and civics programs. Essentially, this is a condensation of her book on the history of the General Federation of Women's Clubs which she published two years after this article.   She also examines the International and National Councils of Women (pp. 65-68) and the split and merger of the suffrage camps, the National

Woman Suffrage and American Woman Suffrage associations (pp. 69-83) in the National American Woman Suffrage Association. Mrs. Barclay Hazard's "New York State Association Opposed to Woman Suffrage" (pp. 84-89) reports on the founding of the organization in 1895, its counterpetition to the 1905 New York State Constitutional Convention which considered woman suffrage, its decision not to hold public conventions, its dissemination of literature, and its officers. Mabell S.C. Smith, "Association of Collegiate Alumnae" (pp. 90-95), clarifies resolutions of the club based on a 1909 study of self-supporting women and of college women. "Southern Association of College Women" (pp. 96-98) is an essay describing the founding of the organization at the University of Tennessee in 1903. Its objects were to unite colleges in the South for the promotion of higher education for women, to raise the standard of education for women, and to develop preparatory schools for young women. Philip Davis, in "Shirtwaist Maker's Strike," (pp. 99-105), discusses conditions of labor that caused the strike of thirty thousand. Frank Chapin Bray, "National Consumers' League" (pp. 106-15) makes a case for the importance of efforts to obtain better working conditions for women by patronizing establishments and buying products from factories with fair standards. He quotes Florence Kelley's survey article of 26 March and the Supreme Court decision on Oregon's ten-hour law. Jane A. Stewart, "National Woman's Trade Union League" (pp. 116-20), outlines six objects of the organization founded in 1903 to promote unionization for working women. "Woman Leaders of Washington Uplift" (pp. 121-22) reprints a New York World article (14 February 1910) about three women in the Welfare Committee of the National Civic Federation, trying to improve working conditions of government employees in the District of Columbia. E.H. Blichfeldt, "WCTU Field" (pp. 127-34), moves from a story of the Woman's Crusade of 1873 to the development of the WCTU's "Do Everything" policy. James Ravenel Smith, "YWCA" (pp. 135-41), narrates the origins of the first Y in Boston, in 1866, and the first student association, in 1872. Lunch rooms, travelers' aid, education, inexpensive membership, and headquarters at Chautauqua are among the topics he reviews. Jane A. Stewart, "National Patriotic Societies" (pp. 142-46), deals briefly with the work of the Daughters of the American Revolution, National Society of Colonial Dames of America, Woman's Relief Corps, Ladies of the Grand Army of the Republic, and Daughters of the Cincinnati. "International Sunshine Society" (pp. 146-47), tells of Cynthia W. Alden founding the organization fifteen years before; it grew to have three thousand branches and 300,000 members, all working to cheer up shut-ins.

103 *p CHIDESTER, IDA SARGENT, and ELEANOR BRUHN. *Golden Nuggets of Pioneer Days*. Panguitch, Utah: Daughters of Utah Pioneers, 1949.

    See Daughters of Utah Pioneers [Garfield County Chapter].

104 *n CHITTENDEN, ELIZABETH F. "As We Climb: Mary Church Terrell." *Negro History Bulletin* 38 (February-March 1979): 351-54. Bib., illus.: 3 of Mary Church Terrell.

    This biography of Mary Church Terrell includes material on her work with women's organizations. In 1890, she spoke before the National American Woman Suffrage Association. In 1892, she founded the Colored Woman's League of Washington, which became the National Association of Colored Women. She also organized the Women's Republican League of Washington. In 1920 and 1932, the Republican National Committee asked her to direct a campaign among "Negro women" in the eastern part of the United States. In 1940, she applied for membership in the District of Columbia branch of the American Association of University Women. She was rejected because she was black, but she fought the decision for three years and won black women the right to join the AAUW.

105 *c CHRISTIAN, STELLA L. *The History of the Texas Federation of Women's Clubs*. Houston: Dealy-Adey-Elgin Co., 1919, viii, 398 pp.

    Christian collected details on the officers, conventions, resolutions, projects, and committee work of ten administrations of the Texas Federation of Women's Clubs, from its founding in 1897 through 1917.

106 *c CHRISTIE, MRS. W.J. "The Women's Clubs of Montana." *Rocky Mountain Magazine* 2 (March 1901): 579-91. Illus.: 10 of clubwomen; the following issue (April 1901) also contains 15 photos of individual portraits of clubwomen.

    Here is a broad but detailed survey of the work and goals of women's clubs in Montana history, from the founding of the first club in Deer Lodge in 1889. Among the societies discussed are in Deer Lodge: the Chaminade Music Club; in Helena: Alvalea Girls Club, Fortnightly (1890), Current Topics Club (1892), Woman's Club of Helena (1896), and Students' Musical Club (1897); in Butte: the Home Club, Atlas, Woman's Club of Butte, West Side Shakespeare Club, Ethical Culture Club, Charity Organization Society, Daughters of the American Revolution, and Needle Work Guild of America (Butte also formed a city federation of women's clubs to unite efforts and avoid duplication of projects) in Kalispell: the Century Club (1893) and

Nineteenth Century Club (1897); in Dillon: the Shakespeare Club; in Bozeman: State Housekeepers' Society (1894) and Woman's Social, Domestic, and Literary Society (1898); in Billings: Woman's Club (1899); and in Great Falls: Shakespeare Club and Tuesday Morning Musical Club.

107   *c,f CLAPP, STELLA. *Out of the Heart: A Century of P.E.O., 1869-1969.* Des Moines: the organization, 1968. ix, 365 pp. Index, bib., illus.: 136 of officers.

P.E.O. is a secret society (even its initials represent a secret name) that was founded in 1869 at Iowa Wesleyan College for philanthropic and educational purposes. The early constitution stated its object: "general improvement, which shall comprehend more especially the following points--first individual growth in charity toward each P.E.O. and toward all with whom we associate, and in the qualities of Faith, Love, Purity, Justice and Truth; second improvement in our manners at home and in society; third to seek growth in knowledge, and mental culture, to obtain stores of wisdom from nature, art, books, study and society, and to radiate all the light possible by conversation, by writing and by the right exercise of any talent we possess; fourth to aim at moral culture, self-control, equipoise and symmetry of character and at temperance in opinions, speech and habits." On its hundredth anniversary, the sorority produced this history for its 165,000 members in 4,500 chapters throughout the United States and Canada. Three educational philanthropies took precedence for the membership: a revolving loan for college women was established in 1907, Cottey Junior College for Women in Nevada, Missouri, was supported, and an International Peace Scholarship to assist foreign students to attend graduate school in North America was established in 1949. This history surveys the organizations, development and expansion in the early years, lists the projects undertaken, and provides biographies of founders and past presidents, and one-page histories of the state, district and provincial chapters and of homes and chapter houses.

108   *t CLARK, ROGER W. "Cincinnati Crusaders for Temperance: 1874." *Cincinnati Historical Society Bulletin* 32 (Winter 1976): 185-99. Notes, illus.: interior and exterior of Wesley Chapel where the Cincinnati Crusade was launched in 1874; exterior of Nineth Street Baptist Church where crusaders met for prayers before visits to bars; 2 sketches of women outside a saloon kneeling in prayer; Esplanade (Fountain Square) where women assembled for prayers.

Clark describes the efforts of Cincinnati women to halt the consumption of alcohol in their city in the winter of 1874. He attributes their mobilization to the remarks of Dr. Dio Lewis, a compelling lecturer of the day. Cincinnati women met, organized, and prayed in their churches for temperance and then embarked on a series of street demonstrations. Clark examines the backgrounds of the eight most active women, especially their religious affiliations, and lists the names of forty-three martyrs arrested for their participation in the public protests.

109   *p CLARKE, IDA CLYDE. *American Women and the World War.* New York: D. Appleton and Co., 1918. xix, 545 pp.

Through this veritable encyclopedia of material on women's voluntary efforts during the First World War, Clarke created a definitive study of wartime relief projects. After stating the goals of the Woman's Committee, as defined by the secretary of war, she articulates the general plan and early activities of women to organize for defense work. Women, often through existing women's voluntary organizations, registered for service. Clarke describes their work in food conservation, child welfare, health and recreation, patriotic education, and selling Liberty Loans. Although she discusses the contribution of two million women working in factories, the bulk of her study revolves around the achievements for the Red Cross, National League for Women's Service, General Federation of Women's Clubs, Daughters of the American Revolution, Colonial Dames, United Daughters of the Confederacy, Council of Jewish Women, Young Women's Christian Association, Navy League, and Congress of Mothers. She devotes separate chapters to the contributions of each of the state organizations of the Woman's Committee. Part 3 documents the efforts of Women's War Relief Organizations abroad, especially in Europe. Finally, Clarke provides a directory of leading women's organizations doing defense work. Here is a comprehensive examination of patriotic endeavors of volunteer women.

110   *f CLARKE-HELMICK, ELIZABETH ALLEN. *The History of Pi Beta Phi Fraternity.* N.p.: David D. Nickerson and Co. 1915. ix, 272 pp. Indexes, appendixes, illus.: 91 of officers, chapter houses, groups.

This sorority, known also as I.C. Sorosis, was founded in 1867 at Monmouth College, in Monmouth, Illinois, by eleven young women. They earnestly worked for a national organization, and additional chapters were quickly formed. Brief histories are collected here of the forty-eight active and twenty-five inactive chapters and of alumnae and their organizations. Included are reports of the national conventions held between 1868 and 1912, presented in great detail that extends to excruciating minutiae. Even the names of convention participants appear, the long lists no doubt invaluable to serious researchers of the group's history, but not of interest to the casual reader. Still, in the descriptions of scholarship winners, it is possible to discover that a charter member at the University of Washington, photographer Imogene Cunningham, won an award in 1910 that enabled her to do graduate work in Europe. Such a tidbit might be a treasure to a researcher of women and the arts.

111 *f CLAWSON, MARY ANN. "Nineteenth Century Women's Auxiliaries and Fraternal Orders." *Signs* 12 (Autumn 1986): 40-61. Notes.

This sociologist has examined fraternal orders of the late nineteenth and early twentieth centuries, such as the Masons, Odd Fellows, and Knights of Pythias, and determined the needs of the women who participated in the auxiliaries. Clawson asserts that the women sought to reconcile their conflicting desires for feminine autonomy and masculine approval. She identifies negotiation, accommodation, and challenge as key features of the Odd Fellows' Rebekah Degrees, the Masonic Eastern Star, and the Pythian Sisters, from the time of their origins in the mid-nineteenth century. In examining differences between the men's and the women's groups, especially the absence of rituals to define rites of passage for women, she locates close and respectful ties between male and female members, finding considerable mutuality between them, despite their separation.

112 *s,t,c CLIFFORD, DEBORAH P. *Mine Eyes Have Seen the Glory: A Biography of Julia Ward Howe.* Boston: Little, Brown and Co., 1978. 313 pp. Notes, bib., indexes, illus.: 8 of Julia Ward Howe and her family.

Clifford surveys the early life of Julia Ward Howe, including her ancestry, girlhood in New York, her marriage to Samuel Gridley Howe, her married life in South Boston, her published writing, and her raising of a large family. During the Civil War, her popular lyrics to the "Battle Hymn of the Republic" made her a celebrity. Her husband's death signaled the beginning of her public life and career as a respected reformer. In 1868, she attended her first woman suffrage meeting and quickly became a leader in the women's rights issues of her day. She was elected president of the New England Woman Suffrage Association and an officer in the New England Woman's Club. In 1869 she became a leader in the new American Equal Rights Association, and the American Woman Suffrage Association and, in 1873, the Association for the Advancement of Women. This biography contains much detail about Howe's earnest activity on behalf of the nineteenth-century woman's movement, most of it undertaken through her leadership within women's voluntary organizations.

113   *t -----. "The Women's War against Rum." *Vermont History* 52 (Summer 1984): 141-60.   Notes, illus.: Women's Christian Temperance Union Temple in Burlington, Vermont; Francis Willard; pledge card; membership card; chart with the characteristics of selected Vermont WCTU leaders.

    Starting her story in the spring of 1874, when Vermont women heard Dr. Dio Lewis's speech on temperance reform, Clifford describes the audience's march to the saloons and hotels of St. Albans, Montpelier, and Rutland to seek pledges from barmen to stop selling alcohol. A Women's Christian Temperance Union, rooted in the Chautauqua movement, soon spread across the state. The 1880s saw the highpoint of leadership and solidarity among temperance advocates in the state, President Anna C. Park of Bennington opposing the politicization of the organization, but suffragist Maria Hidden successfully pressing for National president Frances Willard's political program.

114   *c COATES, ALBERT. *By Her Own Bootstraps: A Saga of Women in North Carolina.* N.p.: the author, 1975. xiv, 231 pp. Illus.: 4 leading North Carolina women including clubwoman Sallie Southall Cotten.

    Chapter 5, "Woman's Fight for Community Betterment" (pp. 60-138), consists of a three-tier study of women's organizations—at the national level, in the state of North Carolina, and in the city of Raleigh. Coates excerpts generously from club reports and documents to summarize the work of the National American Woman Suffrage Association, General Federation of Women's Clubs, National Colored Parents and Teachers Organization, National Congress of Parent-Teacher Associations, American Association of Junior Leagues, and National League of Women Voters. He then explores the ways that the national policy was translated locally by the North Carolina Federation of Women's Clubs, North Carolina Congress of Parents and Teachers, North Carolina Congress of Colored Parents and Teachers Organization, North Carolina Junior Federation of Women's Clubs, North Carolina Association of Junior Leagues, Garden Club of North Carolina, and North Carolina League of Women Voters. Coates also surveys the size, issues, projects, and financial structure of these groups. For the city of Raleigh, he documents the histories of the Woman's Club of Raleigh, Junior Woman's Club of Raleigh, Junior League of Raleigh, Raleigh Garden Club, League of Women Voters of Raleigh/Wake County, and Raleigh Fine Arts Society. At the end of the volume is a two-page biography of clubwoman Sallie Southall Cotten.

115 *r COLE, LUCY (MRS. CHARLES F.) *History of Woman's Work in East Hanover Presbytery.* Richmond, Va.: Richmond Press, 1938. 151 pp. Notes, bib., illus.: 3 of Mrs. Sarah Milnor Price and Mrs. Calvin Stewart.

Using a highly formal writing style that obscures the personalities of leaders and the controversial issues of this woman's organization, Cole outlines the institutional development of the Presbyterian women in East Hanover County, Virginia. The Presbyterian church began there in 1755, and women's groups devoted to charitable work, Bible study, and foreign and home missions grew numerous. The author surveys several of the nineteenth-century antecedents to the Woman's Foreign Missionary Union, formed in 1888. Mrs. Sarah M. Price presided from 1888 to 1896 and encouraged all the Presbyterian women in the country to form societies to stimulate, systematize, and unite their efforts for Presbyterian missions abroad. They convened five times a year for devotions, addresses, and union business. By 1904, the women had won church approval to extend their efforts throughout the Synod of Virginia, and energetic young women reorganized the group's work to include funding for home missions. In 1914, the group underwent reorganization again and became the Women's Auxiliary of East Hanover Presbytery, which emphasized home mission work, including prayer services, and visits to homes, hospitals, and prisons, provided charity to the local needy, and distributed Christian literature. In 1920, the group built a Richmond home for the use of women missionaries and they continued to maintain it. In 1922, members began an annual Colored Woman's Conference, providing classes on the Bible, home nursing, and sewing. They continued to provide some assistance to foreign missions, sending, for example, medical supplies to Chinese hospitals.

116   *w   CONN, SANDRA.   "Three Talents: Robins, Nestor, and Anderson of the Chicago Women's Trade Union League." *Chicago History* 9 (Winter 1980-81): 234-47.   Bib., illus.: working women including Agnes Nestor, Mary Anderson, and Margaret Dreier Robins; the 1915 Women's Trade Union League delegation to D.C. women's peace resolution; the 1915 Women's Trade Union League convention in New York.

Here are three biographies of women of different backgrounds who pooled their talents and energy to improve the working conditions of American women, in the National Women's Trade Union League. Conn focuses on the interests of Agnes Nestor, Mary Anderson, and Margaret Dreier Robins and the ways the WTUL benefited and was shaped by their talents and visions.

117   *p   COOK, ANNA MARIA GREEN. *History of Baldwin County, Georgia.* Anderson, S.C.: Keys-Hearn, 1925.   482 pp. Illus.: Anna Maria Green Cook; Cook's home; important buildings in Colorado; bronze tablets placed by the Daughters of the American Revolution.

Although most of this volume addresses the history, institutions, and reminiscences about Baldwin County, Georgia, and collects biographies of early families, chapter 4, "Regents of the Nancy Hart Chapter, Daughters of the American Revolution and a History of Their Work," by Leola Selman Beeson (pp. 151-265) will interest researchers of women's organizations.   Etta Kincaid Chappell organized the chapter in 1900 with fifteen members. They purchased the site of the cabin of Nancy Hart, Revolutionary War heroine. They also offered an American history prize in the schools after 1903 and held regular teas at which members wore colonial costumes. The chapter surveys each administration of a project, through 1925, listing projects undertaken such as placing bronze tablets on historical sites and forts and planting a Liberty Tree on the grounds of the old capitol.

118   *i   COSTIN, LELA B.   "Feminism, Pacifism, Internationalism and the 1915 International Congress of Women." *Women's Studies International Forum* 5 (1982): 301-15. Notes.

Most suffragists in America supported American participation in World War I, many of them bent on demonstrating their competence and energy in patriotic endeavors in order to win acknowledgment of their ability as citizens and their capability to use enfranchisement wisely. A handful of women defied the norm however, and actively opposed the war. In January 1915, before the American entrance into the fighting, Carrie Chapman Catt and Jane Addams called a national conference which was attended by representatives of the National Women's Trade Union League, the Women's National Committee of the Socialist Party, and the General Federation of Women's Clubs. They formed the Women's Peace party, which would be known after the war as the Women's International League for Peace and Freedom. Costin also lists the forty-seven leading American women who attended the international conference at The Hague from 28 April to 1 May 1915. The women passed twenty resolutions in seven areas (including peace, international cooperation, women's protest against war, education of children) and defined the actions they would take to implement their plans. Several, for instance, visited heads of belligerent and neutral nations immediately after the conference. Jane Addams, who had enjoyed respect before the war, lost prestige in 1915 for her opposition to fighting. She was vindicated in 1931, when she won the Nobel Peace Prize.

119   *b COTT, NANCY F. *Bonds of Womanhood Woman's Sphere in New England, 1780-1835.* New Haven Yale University Press, 1977. xii, 225 pp. Notes, bib., indexes.

This monograph documents the formation of several New England women's societies formed under the auspices of the Protestant church in the antebellum era. With sophisticated and persuasive analysis, Cott argues that the associations provided women with a public voice, that they were an important extension to their domestic world. Women met in maternal and moral reform societies and missionary and charitable societies, raising money and seizing the decision-making power to define the social problems they wished to address and the means by which they sought to solve them. Among the societies described Female Religious and Cent Society of Jericho Center, Vermont (formed 1805), and Young Ladies' Society (1812) which merged to form the Female Cent Society of Jericho in 1816; Female Charitable Society of Greenfield, Massachusetts (1815), and Maternal Association (1816); Female Religious Biographical and Reading Society (1826); Boston Female Society for Missionary Purposes; Boston Female Reform Society; and maternal associations in Dorchester, Massachusetts, Portland, Maine, New London, Connecticut, and Hamilton, Massachusetts.

120   *z -----. "Feminist Politics in the 1920's The National Woman's Party." *Journal of American History* 71 (June 1984) 43-68. Notes.

After surveying quickly the work of the National Woman's party from its origins in 1913 through passage of the woman suffrage amendment in 1920 Cott concentrates on the period of the early 1920s, when the association reorganized its priorities to select a single issue to which it might devote itself. Rejecting disarmament, racial injustice, and other possible issues, the leaders decided to focus on the equal rights amendment. This emphasis displeased some supporters. "Besides those who did not join the reorganized NWP because their principal goal, suffrage, had been achieved, many women more strongly committed to black rights, pacifism, birth control, or social revolution departed." Cott airs the views of those who felt Alice Paul "welshed on the Negro question" and those who felt the leadership to be too elitist, narrow, and authoritarian to build a grass-roots constituency for issues of women's equality.

121 *c COTTEN, SALLIE SOUTHALL. *History of the North Carolina Federation of Women's Clubs, 1901-1925.* Raleigh, N.C.: Edwards and Broughton Printing Co., 1925. 214 pp. Illus. 1909 North Carolina Federation of Women's Clubs; 1925 North Carolina Federation of Women's Clubs Executive Board.

    The author, a leading clubwoman in North Carolina, presents a readable narrative, relying on quotations from North Carolina Federation of Women's Clubs convention proceedings. Beginning with the founding of the federation in 1901 with twenty-five clubwomen from seventeen federated clubs, she summarizes the work of twenty-three annual conventions through 1925. She names the officers elected, surveys the accomplishments of the committees (education, library extension, village improvement, state charities), and asserts the importance of club news conveyed through *Keystone* Magazine. Each convention is described in a separate chapter and includes the figures on the growing membership, the entertainments provided to the delegates by the host club, and the topics covered by local and nationally known speakers. Detail is rich on the 1916 American history pageant and the war relief work accomplished during World War I. As a leader also in the King's Daughters, the author coaxed her two networks to cooperate in supporting the North Carolina Industrial Training School for Boys, and details on their success are provided in this history.

    See Gertrude Sprague Carraway for volume 2 of this account.

122 *c COURTNEY, GRACE GATES, comp. *History of the Indiana Federation of Clubs.* Edited by Arcada Stark Balz. Authorized by the Board of the Indiana Federation of Clubs at Turkey Run Hotel, 8 July 1936. Fort Wayne, Ind.: Fort Wayne Printing Co. 1939. xii, 587 pp. Index, illus. 80, mostly of club officers; executive board; group photo at St. Paul convention; 11 clubhouses.

Indiana has a long and rich history of women's clubs, starting with the Minerva Club of 1859 at the home of Mrs. Robert Dale Owen in the experimental New Harmony Community. The story of the formation of the Indiana Federation of Clubs is a complicated one. It formed in 1911 from a merger of two rival federations. In 1890, the Indiana Union of Literary Clubs had been formed and held regular conferences from 1890 to 1906. It was unusual in that men were participants in the organization. In fact, Prof. John Benjamin Wisely, from the Men's Terre Haute Literary Club, presided over the federation in 1898. This text documents the group's development, giving charter clubs, officers, constitution, biographies of presidents, projects undertaken, convention summaries, and department work in fine arts, education, home economics, and business. In 1906 it consolidated with the Indiana State Federation of Women's Clubs, which had formed in 1900 and was more typical of women's federations of the era. We learn here of its early officers and programs, its magazine, annual art exhibition, student loans and honor society, and of eleven clubhouses built by member clubs. The merger, because it included men, was called the Indiana State Federation of Clubs, but it was reorganized in 1911 and conformed, as the Indiana Federation of Clubs, to national norms set by the General Federation of Women's Clubs.

123   *c CRANE, MAMIE D. "The Sorosis Club of Sweetwater, Texas, 1899-1950." In *West Texas Historical Association Yearbook, 1950*, Abilene: West Texas Historical Association Year Book, 1950, pp. 76-83.

The author, a pioneer member of the West Texas Sorosis Club in 1899, credits Mattie Trammell from South Texas with organizing her friends for cultural study and self-improvement. Their motto was "What others have done, we can do." Their first topic of study was Oliver Wendell Holme's book, *Autocrat of the Breakfast Table*. Rotation in office being their policy, members elected twenty-seven presidents in fifty years. The club was limited in size to twenty-one members. They awarded an annual prize to the highest honor graduate in Southwater High School. The group was active in the Texas Federation of Women's Clubs. Social activities were important to the members, although the group was not frivolous.

124   *w,y,p CREEDY, BROOKS SPIVEY. *Women behind the Lines The YWCA Program with War Production Workers, 1940-1947*. New York Woman's Press, 1949. 227 pp.

.

61

This volume studies the impact World War II had on civilian women, stressing the ways the Young Women's Christian Association used its resources for war-related service programs in which women participated. There is considerable attention to USO (United Service Organizations) programs, the American War Community Services, and the regular operations of the national board of the YWCA and its local branches. These "helped people in war production communities maintain emotional and moral stability, assisted in integration of newcomers, developed leisure time programs, and improved standards for living and working conditions." The officials and staff cooperated with labor and churches and interracial boards to fund, publicize, seek, and train women and girls to become volunteers. The Y provided crafts, food, day care, a bookmobile, work with tenant associations, swimming, movies, tennis, badminton, softball, dance classes, charm schools, and discussion groups. The USO provided supper clubs where girls could cook and eat together on an around-the-clock basis. Night Owls, Early Birds, and Dawn Patrols catered to women workers in the swing shift or graveyard shifts of wartime workplaces. For families, the Y sponsored covered-dish suppers, picnics, holiday celebrations, movies, square dances, and hobby nights. A case study demonstrating the services of an interracial program serving both military personnel and war production personnel illuminates the work in Bridgeton, New Jersey among the Japanese-American, white, and Jamaican communities. This history also describes the Niagara Falls, New York, recreation project through American War Community Services, an alliance of six agencies, to discourage juvenile delinquency. Although the title and introduction to the study promise to explore postwar efforts of the YWCA, the examination of the national and local associations in fact dwells on wartime endeavors.

125 *b CRITTENTON, CHARLES NELSON. *The Brother of Girls The Life Story of Charles Nelson Crittenton as Told by Himself.* Chicago World's Events Co., 1910. 247 pp. Illus. Charles N. Crittenton; Florence Crittenton, Charles's "Mother Mission" in New York City; Mrs. Kate Waller Barrett.

Although much of this volume is an autobiography of the millionaire evangelist who created shelters and training centers for unwed mothers in late nineteenth- and early twentieth-century American cities, two chapters discuss the assistance provided by the Women's Christian Temperance Union. In 1884, Crittenton made his headquarters in the WCTU Temple in Chicago while preparing his book, *The Traffic in Girls*, which was published by the WCTU. Local branches took financial responsibility for the maintenance of several of the homes. In addition, the Young Women's Christian Association took a hand in the Crittenton homes by establishing branches in the homes for the residents.

126   *c CROLY, JANE CUNNINGHAM [Jennie June, pseud.]. *The History of the Woman's Club Movement in America.* New York Henry G. Allen and Co., 1898. xi, 1184 pp. Indexes, illus.: hundreds of individual club leaders; exterior and interior of clubhouses and clubrooms.

This is the largest compilation available on the history of the women's culture club movement for self-improvement and civic reform. Croly articulates her philosophy of women's responsibility to public reform in her introduction, "The Moral Awakening of Women." She features some of the early clubs in the federation she started, including Sorosis of New York City, the New England Woman's Club in Boston, Friends in Council in Quincy, Illinois, Fortnightly in Chicago, Chicago Woman's Club, Civic Club of Philadelphia, and the network of Working Girls clubs. She outlines the inception of the General Federation of Women's Clubs, reprinting the "Call" that invited club representatives to form an alliance, the constitution, bylaws, and proceedings of the founding conference, and summarizing the biennials of 1892, 1894, and 1896. A small section is devoted to the work of clubs abroad, founded by American women in India, Australia, England, and Mexico. The bulk of the volume consists of reviews of the work of 926 American clubs, written by members, and detailing the goals, officers, projects, and accomplishments of each. For Arkansas, there are 25 entries; Alabama, 10; California, 13; Colorado, 34; Connecticut, 18; Delaware, 3; District of Columbia, 13; Florida, 1; Georgia, 9; Idaho, 6; Illinois, 30; Indiana, 28; Iowa, 13; Kansas, 12; Kentucky, 10; Louisiana, 12; Maine, 88; Maryland, 3; Massachusetts, 98; Michigan, 35; Minnesota, 42; Missouri, 19; Montana, 5; Nebraska, 17; New Hampshire, 53; New Jersey, 20; New Mexico, 2; New York, 95; North and South Dakota, 14; Ohio, 44; Oregon, 5; Pennsylvania, 23; Rhode Island, 13; South Carolina, 5; Tennessee, 7; Texas, 13; Utah, 16; Vermont, 23; Washington, 20; Wisconsin, 26; and Wyoming, 4.

127   *c CROSBY, MRS. ROBERT R. *Fifty Years of Service; 1929-1979: History of the National Council of State Garden Clubs, Inc.* St. Louis: the organization, 1979. 160 pp. Illus.: 43 of officers and projects including children's gardens, making Christmas trees, winning flower arrangements, and headquarters.

In six sections, Crosby addresses, thematically, the fifty year work of the National Council of State Garden Clubs and its branches.

The group was founded in 1929, with 23,800 women in 314 clubs. The founders, record of incorporation, seal, bylaws, membership and dues, national meetings, and publications like the *National Gardener*, issued 1948-79, are surveyed. Headquarters for twenty-nine years was in New York. In 1957, the officers moved to St. Louis at Missouri's Botanical Garden, and Crosby describes the facilities. Brief one-page summaries address the issues undertaken by the membership environmental concerns, land trust, birds, Blue Star Memorial Highway, memorial gardens, historical trails, Bicentennial, civic development, roadsides, billboards, legislation, garden therapy, and world gardens. In an effort "to transmit knowledge on gardening, landscape design and horticulture, the association has operated through study courses, garden centers, flower shows, awards, scholarships, and youth groups," which are described here. A section is devoted to biographies of the women who served as president before 1965, and the author provides a list of patrons, members, and friends of the organization throughout its history.

128 *f CROW, MARY B. "The Sorority Movement at Monmouth College." *Western Illinois Regional Studies* 4 (1981): 37-49. Notes, illus.: Holt House; Stewart House; Kappa founder Minnie Stewart; Kappa founder Lou Stevenson Miller.

    Two of the oldest and largest sororities for women were founded at Monmouth College in Illinois—Pi Beta Phi and Kappa Kappa Gamma. At the time of this publication, the organizations had 200,000 members in two hundred United States and Canadian chapters. In 1867, twelve young women in Jacob Holt House organized a secret society called I.C. Sorosis Society (later Pi Beta Phi). In 1870, six students organized Kappa Kappa Gamma fraternity in the home of a Judge Stewart. Although chapters quickly spread, the Presbyterian church in 1875 banned fraternities from its campuses. Campus administrators took two years to enforce the new regulation, however, so the sororities did not close until 1878. When the ban was lifted in the 1920s, the sororities again flourished. But even at the turn of the century, Zeta Epsilon Chi was formed by women students.

129 *b CUMBLER, JOHN T. "The Politics of Charity Gender and Class in Late Nineteenth Century Charity Policy." *Journal of Social History* 14 (Fall 1980) 99-111. Notes.

    Cumbler asserts that women moved into positions of control over the charity movement, notably in the Associated Charities of Lynn and Fall River, Massachusetts, and he determines that this affected both the policy and the orientation of the organization in the late nineteenth century. Before the women took charge, welfare programs were few and intense concern over welfare cheaters dominated the interest of officers. Once women led the organizations, the programs, especially those addressing woman-related issues such as child care and police matrons, increased and improved. The women surveyed the textile workers and indicted landlords for their treatment of workers. The upper-class women who joined the organizations interacted with the poor women who were recipients of the charitable programs, both as "Friendly Visitors" and as organizers and shapers of a more generous form of charity.

130   *c CUNNINGHAM, MARY S. *The Woman's Club of El Paso Its First Thirty Years*. El Paso: Texas Western Press, University of Texas at El Paso, 1978. xii, 270 pp. Notes, bib., indexes, illus.: 70 of officers and of El Paso.

   The author, president of the Woman's Club of El Paso from 1943-44, wrote this lovingly detailed account of the achievements of the club between the years of its founding in 1894 through 1924. Each of the twenty-two chapters is named for the president of that year and describes her administration, projects, meetings, and parties. Karen J. Blair contributed a brief introduction linking the El Paso efforts to the national movement of literary and civic reform clubs.

131   *f DALGLIESH, ELIZABETH RHODES. *Alpha Chi Omega: The First Fifty Years, 1885-1935*. 5th rev. ed. Menasha, Wis.: George Banta Publishing Co., 1936. x, 487 pp. Indexes, illus.: hundreds of photographs of members, founders, and chapter houses.

   The author is a former officer of this musical sorority, who has revised earlier editions (1911, 1916, 1921, 1928) of the history, to provide a full detailed account of its development. She provides biographies of the national presidents between 1891 and 1935 and an account of each campus chapter at colleges and universities all over the United States. The sixth national Greek-letter fraternity to be founded, Alpha Chi Omega was created at Indiana Asbury University (renamed DePaul University in 1884), a Methodist Episcopal school. Funding for the MacDowell Colony in Peterborough, New Hampshire, was a priority of the sorority. They supported the creative endeavors of musicians, painters, and writers at this summer haven, named for the American composer, by building a studio in 1911 for an artist to work in and maintaining repairs on it. Members also funded the endowment and gave a fellowship to the colony in 1931-33. Details on their sorority publication, *Lyre*, is provided as are lists of award winners of their musical competitions.

See also the following entry.

132   *f -----. *The History of Alpha Chi Omega 1885-1948*. Menasha, Wis.: George Banta Publishing Co., 1948. xi, 499 pp. Indexes, illus.: hundreds of photographs including officers, charter members, and chapter houses.

An updated edition of entry 131, this book provides new photographs and new detail, especially on relief work in wartime and size of membership in each chapter. The motto of this organization, "Ye daughters of Music come up higher," is honored in their zealous endeavors to further musical and social service programs, generously described in the reports of the national conventions and Panhellenic conferences.

133   *t DANNENBAUM, JED. *Drink and Disorder Temperance Reform in Cincinnati from the Washingtonian Revival to the WCTU*. Urbana: University of Illinois Press, 1984. xii, 245 pp. Notes, indexes, illus.: sketches of temperance and intemperance from the nineteenth century.

Chapter 7 (pp. 212-33) explores the ways in which the Woman's Crusade against saloons in 1873-74 developed into the Women's Christian Temperance Union. The emphasis is on the crusade itself, however, rather than on women's organizational history. Dannenbaum asserts that Frances Willard's election to the WCTU presidency in 1879, over incumbent Annie Wittenmyer, represented membership support for a newly political phase of its development. Dannenbaum has uncovered valuable material about women's antebellum temperance activism. In the late 1820s, their organizational role was circumscribed in temperance associations dominated by men. Women could not hold office, vote, or speak at meetings. Arguing on moral grounds, women found themselves useless in the 1850s arena of political fights for temperance legislation at the state level. Nevertheless, beginning in 1853 in Ohio, and forecasting the Woman's Crusade of 1873-74, dozens of women's state organizations were founded, forming bands to destroy liquor stocks of saloons.

134   *p DAUGHTERS OF THE AMERICAN REVOLUTION [California], (Mrs. Frank R. Mettlach, Chairman of the DAR State History Committee). *History of California State Society Daughters of the American Revolution; 1938-1968*. San Diego: Neyenesch, 1968. 599 pp. Indexes, illus.: the fifteen state regents between 1938 and 1968.

This encyclopedia of the history of the Daughters of the American Revolution in California provides a biography of each state president between 1938 and 1968, a history of each committee and its accomplishments, and the history of each of 163 chapters in the state, including its leaders, treasuries, and accomplishments.

135   *p   DAUGHTERS OF THE AMERICAN REVOLUTION [Idaho]. *History and Register, Idaho State Society, Daughters of the American Revolution.* Caldwell, Idaho: Caxton Printers, 1936. 124 pp. Indexes, illus.: group photo at 1930s conference; officers; 9 markers and monuments; pioneer cabin in Boise, Idaho.

The pioneer chapter of this organization formed in Boise in 1909. Twelve chapters followed, holding an annual convention to define new historical and patriotic projects. This survey includes one-page biographies of each of the state regents in the association's twenty-seven-year history, giving ancestry, education, husband's name and occupation, organizational involvement, and pet projects in the DAR. Histories of each chapter follow, including the descriptions of historical markers placed throughout the state. Lists are given of state officers elected, committee Chairpersons appointed, and all members of the organization.

136   *p   DAUGHTERS OF THE AMERICAN REVOLUTION [Massachusetts]. *History of the Massachusetts Daughters of the America Revolution.* N.p.: the organization, 1932. 425 pp. Illus.: 32, mostly of officers and chapter houses; 1925 statue dedicated to Pilgrim Mothers.

At the time of its writing, this history reported an organization of 8,630 members with state committees devoted to better films, conservation and thrift, Constitution Hall, finance, correct use of the flag, children of the American Revolution, student loans, Ellis Island, genealogy, girl homemakers, historical and literary club reciprocity, historical research and preservation of records, international relations (including essay contests in high schools and fund-raising appeals for famine-stricken populations in Europe), U.S. Congress legislation, *DAR* magazine, manual of information for immigrants, membership, national defense, national old trails, patriotic education, preservation of historic spots, publicity, revolutionary relics, state board of hospitality, radio, world war service, and Sons of the Republic. Priorities of the group included establishing the DAR State Forest in Massachusetts, maintaining their memorial fountain at Plymouth, and caring for graves of Revolutionary soldiers. The bulk of the text consists of histories of each Massachusetts chapter, with background on the origins of the chapter's name, biographies of the regents including their family genealogy, the projects undertaken; size of treasury and size of membership, and the charter members. Lists are provided of the state conferences, state officers, and official songs of the organization. Biographical sketches of the national officers from Massachusetts and of the Massachusetts state regents are collected here.

137 *p DAUGHTERS OF THE AMERICAN REVOLUTION [Washington State Society]. *History and Register, Washington State Society of the DAR*. Seattle: the organization, 1926. 211 pp. Indexes of honor roll names, illus.: 60 of officers and memorials.

This volume surveys the history of each of the thirty-eight chapters of the Daughters of the American Revolution in Washington State. In addition, there is a roster of all members. Biographies of the officers, a brief history of the national organization, and a survey of the founding and development of the organization in Washington State round out the information here.

138 *p DAUGHTERS OF THE FOUNDERS AND PATRIOTS OF AMERICA. *History of the National Society of Daughters of Founders and Patriots of America, for the Tenth Year, Ending May 13, 1908*. Washington, D.C. the organization, 1908.

139 *p DAUGHTERS OF UTAH PIONEERS [Beaver County Chapter]. *Monuments to Courage: A History of Beaver County*. Milford, Utah: Beaver Press, 1948. 367 pp. Illus.: Jane Mumford, founder and Beaver County president; officers and county presidents; clubhouse; historian.

The Daughters of Beaver County, formed in 1921, comprised women "whose ancestors came to the West before the advent of the railway in 1869," "for the purpose of perpetuating the names and achievements of the men and women who were the pioneers in founding the commonwealth of Utah." Preservation of historical records was a priority of the members. The final chapter explains that one of the four "companies" of Beaver County's Daughters of Utah Pioneers erected a home in 1934 at the site of the 1868 Stake Tabernacle (Mormon) with labor and logs coming from the federal WPA. The club raised eight hundred dollars for their center through entertainments. This volume preserves local history more than it touts DUP activities, for it surveys the history of the county, including Indian life, the founding of towns and ranches and forts by white settlers, social life, geography, schools, medicine, industries, communication, the Church of Jesus Christ of Latter-Day Saints, historical buildings, military and political history, mining, and railroads. Information on pioneer women, including their mutual improvement associations, is sprinkled throughout the text.

140   *p   DAUGHTERS OF UTAH PIONEERS [Davis County Company]. *East of Antelope Island.* Bountiful, Utah the organization, 1948. 519 pp. Illus.: 1946-48 officers; 2 group photos of women pioneers; Daughters of Utah Pioneers marker at 1852 grist mill; a cannon.

Most of this volume is a regional social history of a Utah county, including biographies of women pioneers by club members. Housekeeping, family life, suffrage, Sunday schools are studied alongside accounts of towns, churches, schools, politics, farms, industries, amusements, cemeteries, military, post offices, old buildings, Indian and Negro life. Of interest to researchers on women's organizations is the final chapter, which provides brief histories of the "camps" devoted to historical preservation in the association Aurelia Rogers Camp (founded 1917), Sessions Camp (1920), John Park Camp (1921), Phillips Camp (1922), Sunflower Camp (1924), Helen Mar Miller Camp (1924), Kimball (1925), Columbine (1927), Camp Eutaw (1928), Sagamore (1929), Hollyhock (1929), North Canyon (1934), Ann Roberts Dustin (1940), Oak Leaf Camp (1944), Rachel Layton Warren Camp (1947), and Sego Lily (1947).

141   *p   DAUGHTERS OF UTAH PIONEERS [Garfield County Chapter]. *Golden Nuggets of Pioneer Day: A History of Garfield County.* Panguitch, Utah: Garfield County News, 1949. 374 pp. Indexes, illus.: 22 of DUP members; men and women involved in settlement, development of war service, merchandising, amusements, newspaper, Indian school, Presbyterian Church, establishment of a National Forest in Colorado, World War I and World War II Honor Roll.

An assemblage of historical material about the growth of Garfield County is capped by a final chapter on the history of the Daughters of Utah Pioneers in Panguitch, Garfield County, Utah, who sponsored and wrote the volume. Organized in 1921, the women united residents over the age of eighteen whose ancestors had come to Utah before the railroad in May 1869. Women of any creed, church, or color were welcome to join. Lists of officers are provided, histories of the camps or branches are included, and details on the ceremonies and public parades, exhibits, open-air concerts, and pageants of the society are described. In 1940, the group erected a monument on the site of a fort built in 1864. In 1949, they dedicated a monument at the Old Tithing Office.

142 *p DAVIES, WALLACE E. *Patriotism on Parade: The Story of Veterans' and Hereditary Organizations in America, 1783-1900.* Cambridge, Mass.: Harvard University Press, 1955. xiv, 385 pp. Notes, bibliographic essay, index.

Davies argues that women's patriotic societies should be viewed in the context of the woman's civic reform movement. As teachers of history, donors of American flags, preservers of historical buildings, and shapers of immigration policy, he sees the membership as typical clubwomen of the late nineteenth and early twentieth century. Davies mentions the work of numerous women's patriotic societies, among them, the Daughters of the American Revolution, Dames of the Revolution, Daughters of the Revolution, Woman's Relief Corps, Ladies of the Grand Army of the Republic, Colonial Dames of America, National Society of the Colonial Dames of America, Mount Vernon Ladies' Association, Daughters of Liberty (an auxiliary to the Order of United American Mechanics), Daughters of Veterans, Union Veteran's Women's Relief Union, Ladies of the Naval Veteran Association, Dames of the Loyal Legion, Ladies Aid of the Sons of the Veterans, National Association of Nurses of the Civil War, Veteran Nurses of the Civil War, Daughters of the Cincinnati, Daughters of the Holland Dames, Society of New England Women, Daughters of the Founders and Patriots, Daughters of the Lone Star Republic, and Daughters of the Republic of Texas.

143 *p,n -----. "The Problem of Race Segregation in the Grand Army of the Republic." *Journal of Southern History* 13 (August 1947), 354-72. Notes.

In discussing color prejudice in the Grand Army of the Republic in the American South, Davies examines the racism in the women's counterpart, the Woman's Relief Corps, which was founded in 1883. By the turn of the century, 120,000 women in three thousand local corps took part in patriotic club work. Black corps were founded, called "Detached Corps," which met separately from all-white groups. Leaders feared the establishment of an all-black group in a southern town, for it tended to discourage the formation of any white groups. Mrs. Julia Layton of Washington, D.C., a former slave who became an official organizer for the Woman's Relief Corps among southern black women, pressed strongly for the organization of black corps. The organization did not endorse segregation, but black and white women sat separately at conventions and luncheons sponsored by the organization.

144　*w　DAVIS, ALLEN F.　"The Women's Trade Union League Origins and Organization." *Labor History* 5 (Winter 1964) 3-17. Notes.

　　　　Biographies of Mary and Margaret Drier, key leaders in the Women's Trade Union League, amplify Davis's account of the organization which wedded middle-class progressives like settlement workers with women wage workers in the cause of improved working conditions and unions for factory workers. Davis observes distrust between the two factions, but emphasizes the considerable activity of settlement workers, including strike support, organization of unions, and the defense of secondary boycotts, which won the cooperation of many labor leaders.

145　*n,c　DAVIS, ANGELA Y.　"Black Women and the Club Movement." In *Women, Race and Class*. 127-36, 260-62. New York: Random House, 1981. Notes.

　　　　Featuring the biographies of two outstanding black clubwomen, Mary Church Terrell and Ida B. Wells, Davis documents the determination of black women to unify for social activism in the late nineteenth century.　Citing the racism in 1900 of the General Federation of Women's Clubs' excluding Boston's black delegate Josephine St. Pierre Ruffin of the Woman's Era Club, the author illuminates the context in which black women federated. When black women of Boston held the First National Conference of Colored Women in 1895, they did so because of their conscious need to challenge the racism around them. Wells spoke there against lynching and against the exclusion of blacks from the planning of the Chicago Exposition of 1893.　Terrell founded and first presided over the National Association of Colored Women's Clubs. Speeches from the meetings, such as one by Fannie Barrier Williams, are quoted. In 1896, the two groups merged and created the National Association of Colored Women in Washington, D.C.

146　*n,c　DAVIS, ELIZABETH (LINDSAY). *Lifting as They Climb*. Washington, D.C.: National Association of Colored Women, 1933. 424 pp. Indexes of names, illus.: hundreds, including Elizabeth Davis; founders; officers; clubhouses; meeting places; groups.

　　　　Written by a prominent Illinois clubwoman, this large history of the National Association of Colored Women offers an impressive collection of documents and details concerning the growth and development of black women's clubs in America. The organization formed in 1896, with the merging of the National Federation of Afro-American Women and the National League of Colored Women. The author provides summaries of the early organizational meetings and of the biennial conventions from 1899 through 1930. She describes *National Notes*, the official publication of the organization from 1897, the assumption in 1916 of responsibility for the Frederick Douglass Memorial Building, the scholarship program, and the national headquarters facility at 1140 O Street NW, in Washington, D.C. Presented here are the presidential statement on the goals and administration of the organization and an account of the establishment of the National Association of Colored Girls, which offer a club life to girls aged five to twenty-five. Work of committees on home life ("Mother, Home, and Child") and working conditions ("Negro Women in Industry") is documented. Two invaluable sections summarize the projects of state branches (California, Colorado, Delaware, Florida, Georgia, Illinois, Indiana, Iowa, Kansas, Kentucky, Michigan, Minnesota, Mississippi, Missouri, Montana, New Jersey, Ohio, Oregon, Pennsylvania, Rhode Island, Texas, Washington, West Virginia, Wisconsin, and Washington, D.C.) and the lives of dozens of black leaders in the club movement. Their religious, educational, familial, business, political, and club backgrounds are surveyed, providing an encyclopedia of black women active in public life.

147   *n,c -----. *The Story of the Illinois Federation of Colored Women's Clubs, 1900-1922.* Chicago: Illinois Federation of Women's Clubs, 1922. 136 pp. Appendixes, illus.: 51 photos of officers in the federation and 10 of institutions created by club members.

The author—an educator, a charter member of the National Association of Colored Women's Clubs to which the Illinois Federation belongs, and a twenty-four-year president of the Phyllis Wheatley Club of Illinois—has created a treasure trove of detail about early twentieth-centruy black women's literary and civic clubs pledged "to the cause of education, the integrity of the home, and the interest and support of the best women of every community." She quickly describes the organizational meeting of the federation in 1899 and its early efforts to engage its member clubs in pressuring public schools to create kindergartens. The civic, philanthropic, educational, and social programs grew, as did the number of clubs and the size of their memberships. The meat of the text is the description of fifty-seven clubs and their work. Included among them is the Autumn Leaf Club, the "oldest Colored Woman's Club in Illinois" (1890); the Imperial Art Club, originally devoted to embroidery but expanding to address public issues; and the Sojourner Truth Club. A section entitled "Who's Who" provides seventy-one biographies of distinguished clubwomen, with family background, education, club work, church affiliation, and volunteer projects. The chapter on "Institutions" describes twelve social service institutions funded by the clubs, including the Phyllis Wheatley Home for Self-Supporting Girls, a nursery, hospital, community center, and Home for Aged and Infirm Colored People. A top priority for the federation, interracial cooperation, receives a chapter of its own. The work "to promote a just and amiable relationship between white and colored people and remove disabilities from which the latter suffer in their civic and political life" and the "encouragement of equal opportunities" are discussed here. For the future, the author forecasts issues of racial equality to be addressed by the federation. The appendixes provide lists of meetings held between 1900 and 1922, officers elected between 1900 and 1922, deceased members and 77 clubs and their dates of organization as well as the constitution and bylaws, chronology of important events between 1899 and 1922, clubwoman's prayer, and federation club song.

148 *w DAVIS, PHILIP. "Shirtwaist Maker's Strike." *Chautauquan* 59 (June 1910): 99-105.
See *Chautauquan*.

149 *s,c DAVIS, REDA. *California Women: A Guide to Their Politics, 1885-1911*. San Francisco: California Scene, 1967. v, 201 pp. Bib.
While Davis covers the kindergarten movement, charitable endeavors of women, and efforts of working girls to organize for better working conditions, she stresses the suffrage campaigns of 1896 and 1911 and the contributions of literary and civic clubs. She has reprinted a huge though incomplete 1892 list of women's organizations in California, compiled by the California Bureau of Labor. At the back of the book are eighty-nine biographies of California women who supported suffrage, including their club affiliations, and thirty-eight biographies of men who supported suffrage.

150 *c DE SOLMES, MADAME THERESE BLANC. *The Condition of Woman in the United States*. Boston: Roberts Brothers, 1895. 285 pp. Illus.: Madame Therese Blanc De Solmes.
This French visitor to the United States in 1893 surveyed the work of several women's clubs and reported on them in her study of American women. She visited two clubs in Chicago, the Fortnightly literary club and the Woman's Club of Chicago. At the Fortnightly she admired the members' critical sense in discussing Amelia Gere

Mason's paper, "Old and New Types of Women." She found that they spoke the truth, even if it was unpleasant. They drank tea and exuded a reasonable tone throughout their interactions. At the Woman's Club of Chicago, the author saw a broader range of activity. The five hundred-member club formed six committees (reform, philanthropy, education, housekeeping, art and literature, science and philosophy). President Sarah Stevenson, M.D., created a protective agency for women and children which had collected $1,249,000 in fraud, injustice, and divorce cases from 7,197 complaints. The clubwomen also awarded a prize at the Art Institute, supported an industrial school for homeless boys, lobbied for compulsory school attendance for children ages six to fourteen, collected clothing for the needy, and formed a Municipal Reform League to clean up the city of Chicago. Our narrator reported on other women's associations and women's club leaders she encountered: at the Woman's Building at the 1893 Fair in Chicago; at the Woman's Temple of the Women's Christian Temperance Union; at Hull House; with Julia Ward Howe, founder of the New England Woman's Club; with Anna Ticknor, founder of the Society for the Encouragement of Study at Home; and with Grace Dodge, founder of the association of Working Girls' Societies.

151   *c DECKER, SARAH S. PLATT. "The Meaning of the Women's Club Movement." *Annals of the American Academy of Political and Social Science* 28 (September 1906): 198-204.

This president of the General Federation of Women's Clubs credits the club Sorosis of New York City with founding the women's club movement and nurturing its development. She cites its own origins in 1868 and its call on its twenty-first birthday to other clubs around the nation to form the General Federation. The GFWC motto, Unity in Diversity, was carried through after 1890, with programs in art, education, pure food laws, forestry preservation, and home economics.

152   *p DEERING, MARGARET (PERKINS). *Forty Years of the National Society of Colonial Dames of America in California.* San Francisco: the organization 1935. 22 pp. Illus.: 7 officers; a donated sundial in Golden Gate Park.

In 1895, the national president of the Colonial Dames of America, Mrs. Howard Townsend in New York, appointed Mrs. Selden Stuart Wright of San Francisco to found a California chapter. She did so and presided over it for nineteen years. In 1906, when the organization had attracted over one hundred members, the Great Fire destroyed the early records. Charter members' recollections enabled Deering to reassemble many details, however. The group met in San

Francisco homes until 1926, when it grew too large and engaged a room in the Seven Arts Club. Members held breakfast meetings with a preacher's benediction and speeches by guests, including legislators and other public officials. The women raised $336 for Spanish-American War hospital supplies for the government ship *Solace* and set up a soldiers' library in Manila. They sent money to the Florida chapter for a commemorative tablet at Fort Augustine and funded the planting of two trees in Roger Williams Park, Rhode Island. They presented a sundial with the names of discoverers of California to Stanford University, the school having been founded by member Jane Lathrop Stanford. They sent $25 in 1910 to the Pocahontas Memorial Association and provided support for the preservation of trees in Yosemite Reservation. In 1915, Los Angeles organized its own chapter and grew to include 239 members in 1935. This chapter engaged in much Red Cross work during World War I and raised money for Liberty Bonds. Members knit hundreds of garments and collected and published a book of American war songs. They prepared a civic primer for immigrants and financed an English-language class at the YWCA. In 1923, they initiated an undergraduate scholarship for prize-winning essays on early american colonial history. Awards, given to men as well as women, spot-lighted studies of frontier women, Quakers, and Salem witchcraft. The Los Angeles group also established the Hewitt Cottage for Americanization work in a factory district of the city. Both groups donated colonial artifacts to San Francisco and Los Angeles museums and prepared Christmas boxes for Indian schools in California.

153   *i DEGEN, MARIE LOUISE. *The History of the Woman's Peace Party*. Baltimore: Johns Hopkins Press, 1939. Reprint. New York: B. Franklin Reprints, 1974. 266 pp. Notes, bib., indexes.

Degen's serious treatment of the Woman's Peace party from its founding in 1915 through its activities during World War I and immediately afterward is a solid scholarly endeavor. The organization was founded in January 1915, after World War I had begun in Europe but not yet in America. Several leading figures in the woman's movement, among them Jane Addams, Carrie Chapman Catt, and Fannie Fern Andrews, drew on the cooperative spirit of the International Council of Women of 1888. As early as 1896, the ICW delegates passed resolutions for peace and arbitration throughout the world. Degen labels the founding of the Woman's Peace party "an offspring of women's ideals," which flourished when three thousand women attended the 1915 conference to create a platform of eleven peace principles. Immediately, forty-seven members attended The Hague International Congress of Women with other American delegates from the Women's Trade Union League, the Oregon State Federation of Women's Clubs, and the Daughters of the American Revolution; they joined 1,136 representatives from twelve nations of the world. They created a Program for Constructive Peace Abroad in the effort to stop world conflict. Following the April meeting, many of the conferees visited statesmen of the world, delivering their message of peace. In America, the newspapers attacked Jane Addams for her activities. When Henry Ford sponsored a peace ship which traveled from the United States to Europe, the action reinforced many Woman's Peace party ideals and Addams spoke in support of his project. In this text are supporting speeches by pacifist Harriet Stanton Blatch, daughter of suffragist Elizabeth Cady Stanton, and by Lucia Ames Mead. Degen devotes a chapter to the growing martial spirit in America, the preparedness movement which developed, and the support for militarism which the Woman's Peace party opposed. Jane Addams's statements are quoted extensively, as are the news attacks against her. After the war, members objecting to the harsh terms of the armistice called an International Committee of Women for Permanent Peace in 1919 in Paris, sending twenty-five American women to the meetings. This impressive and thorough work lays the groundwork for understanding organized women's peace efforts throughout the 1920s and beyond.

154 *f DELTA GAMMA. *An Historical Sketch of the Delta Gamma Fraternity, 1874-1934.* Menasha, Wis.: George Banta Publishing Co., 1934. 66 pp. Illus.: trio of founders and Leulah Judson Hawley, first secretary of Delta Gamma.

In 1874, three girls at the Lewis School in Oxford, Mississippi, founded a secret society. The biographies of the three—Anna Boyd Ellington (1856-1907), Eva Webb Dodd (1855-1934), and Mary Comfort Leonard (1856-still living in 1934)—are included here. In 1877, the sorority extended its influence to Water Valley, Mississippi, and Fairmont College in Mont Eagle, Tennessee. By 1883, eight chapters had been formed, although only three remained active. Chapters soon formed throughout the country, however, and in 1913, a Toronto, Canada, chapter formed. A publication, *Anchora*, appeared in 1884. A student loan fund was established in 1909 and a list of winners and prizes was compiled for this edition. During World War I, relief work became a priority. The five thousand members acquired a house for destitute and ailing children at Ossendrecht, Holland. They bought $11,000 worth of Liberty Bonds. In 1899, the sorority authorized the formation of alumnae organizations. The first convention was held in 1881, but this history provides only skimpy details on the business conducted at conventions. The group was active in the National Panhellenic Congress. Lists of inactive chapters, active chapters, and officers from 1874 to 1934 are provided.

155 *c,n DICKSON, LYNDA F. "Toward a Broader Angle of Vision in Uncovering Women's History: Black Women's Clubs Revisited." *Frontiers* 9 no. 2 (1987): 62-68. Notes.

The author, who was writing a dissertation on the history of black women's clubs in Denver at the time of this article, examines the pitfalls she encountered and methods she devised to resolve the tangles. She embarked on a difficult topic, for black women's clubs have been unexamined by scholars of both black history and women's history. She focused on clubs formed between 1900 and 1925 that still existed in Denver. Earlier clubs had formed, however, including the Colored Ladies Legal Rights Association, the Colored Women's Republican Club, and the Woman's League. Dickson examined the Pond Lily Art and Literary Club (formed 1901), the Carnation Art Club (1903), Self-Improvement Club (1903), and the Taka Art Club (1904). She found herself disappointed in their emphasis on literary activities, art, needlework, and social interaction, and found them to be condescending in their charity work and rigid in their views about running a proper household. These women were not fighters for their race she concluded. Dickson decided to view her material in the light of the question "What were the forces exerting an impact on club formation and the activities during the period in question?" in order to understand the sources most fully. She also rejected the idea that white women's clubs were the norm for the era.

156 *r DONOVAN, MARY SUDMAN. "Zealous Evangelists: The Woman's Auxiliary to the Board of Missions." *Historical Magazine of the Protestant Episcopal Church* 51 (1982): 371-83. Notes, illus.: 1 of Julia Chester Emery, secretary of the organization 1876-1914 [*sic*, 1872-76].

The Woman's Auxiliary to the Board of Missions of the Protestant Episcopal church formed in 1872. Two sisters were especially instrumental in its success. Julia Chester Emery was secretary 1872-76 and her sister, Mary Abbot Emery, succeeded her for forty years. The association took on the financial and psychological support of foreign as well as home missions. It communicated with its branches through a woman's column in the church's national periodical. In 1899-1900 it raised $191,000 through missionary boxes for supplies for missionary families. The members provided life insurance for all missionaries to foreign countries. They established scholarships for children of missionaries. They created special benefits for missionary widows and schools for girls in the western part of the United States.

157   *z DONOVAN, RUTH GODFREY. "The Nebraska League of Women Voters." *Nebraska History* 52 (Fall 1971): 311-28. Notes, illus.: 1921 meeting of the League of Women Voters in Lincoln, Nebraska; car parade by the Lincoln Equal Franchise League, forerunner of Nebraska League of Women Voters; broadside for a National Citizenship School in 1920.

With sparse analysis, Donovan provides a detailed overview of the activities of the Nebraska League of Women Voters, which was organized in June 1920 at the dissolution of the Nebraska Woman Suffrage Association. Women's new enfranchisement geared members up to establish a nonpartisan association devoted to creating citizenship schools, informing voters about election issues, holding public meetings for candidates, conducting a "get out the vote" campaign, establishing branches at colleges, publishing a newsletter, supporting peace in 1921 with a "No More War" demonstration, and lobbying for the Sheppard-Towner maternity and infant care act, a child labor amendment, and a law permitting women on juries (Nebraska did not grant women the right to sit on juries until 1943). In the Great Depression, the organization turned to issues of relief, in the 1940s, to war and Red Cross service, and in modern times, to sanitation and water pollution issues.

158   *s,t DORR, RHETA CHILDE. *Susan B. Anthony: The Woman Who Changed the Mind of a Nation*. New York: Frederick A. Stokes and Co., 1928. xiii, 367 pp. Indexes, illus.: 13, including photos of Susan B. Anthony and suffrage leaders.

In this biography of a major suffrage agitator, Dorr praises the "quality of leadership that amounted to genius" which Anthony possessed. Part 1 documents Anthony's early life, including her opposition to inequality within the New York State Sons of Temperance and her role in the Woman's State Temperance Society. Part 2 recounts her leadership in the Woman's Loyal League, her disappointment in the legislators' failure to grant women the vote after the Civil War, and her importance in the formation of the National Woman Suffrage Association and its publication, The *Revolution*. Part 3 covers the merger of the National Woman Suffrage Association with the American Woman Suffrage Association in 1890, and the growing politicization of the Women's Christian Temperance Union and General Federation of Women's Clubs, albeit along lines of moral reform. Dorr makes much of Anthony's protest, at the convention of the New York State Federation of Women's Clubs, regarding the seating in Congress in 1899 of a Mormon representative, Brigham H. Roberts of Utah, who was a polygamist. She outlines Anthony's work on the *History of Woman Suffrage* and her presiding over the International Suffrage Alliance in Berlin.

159   *w   DREIER, MARY E. *Margaret Dreier Robins: Her Life, Letters and Work*. New York: Island Press Cooperative, 1950. xviii, 278 pp. Indexes, illus.: 23 including photos of Margaret Dreier Robins; her parents; 1907 convention of the National Trade Union League in Norfolk, Va; group photo of 8 women, officers of the Women's Trade Union League and strikers.

    Margaret Dreier Robins (1868-1945) is here eulogized by her sister, Mary. Although the story includes some detail about her private life, including parents, childhood, husband, marriage, and favorite books, the author concentrates on Robins's public life in women's organizations, particularly those for working women. In 1907, Robins was elected president of the National Women's Trade Union League and was also president of the Chicago League. Much attention is given to the strategies of the association to make improvements in women's working lives, including pressuring the Illinois State Legislature for better laws, holding conventions, and supporting strikes. Speeches, news clippings, convention resolutions, and private correspondence are quoted extensively. This biographer does not shortchange the contribution of her sister to other women's organizations, however. She documents Robins's wartime service in World War I, her participation in the first three International Congresses of Working Women in Washington, D.C., Rotterdam, and Vienna. Robins organized a YWCA in Hernando County, Florida, where she had a winter retreat. The author asserts that the toney Chicago Woman's City Club blackballed her sister for her "extreme labor views."

160   *c   DRURY, CLIFFORD M.   "The Columbia Maternal Association." *Oregon Historical Quarterly* 39 (June 1938): 99-122. Notes.

    The Columbia Maternal Association, claimed to be the first woman's club organized by American women west of the Rocky Mountains, was founded in 1838 near the site of present-day Walla Walla, Washington. At the Marcus and Narcissa Whitman mission at Waiilatpu, six women assembled to assist their spouses in establishing a Protestant outpost in the Pacific Northwest. They were Narcissa Whitman, Eliza Spalding, Mary Augusta Dix, Mrs. Elkanah Walker, Mrs. Cushing Eells, and Mrs. A.B. Smith. They met on the second and last Wednesdays of each month to read *Mother's Magazine*, published by the Utica, New York, Maternal Association, to meditate and pray and to discuss child-raising and current events. Additional women joined over the years and the club met regularly until 1847, when the Indian massacre closed the mission. Documents are included by the author the constitution, the first annual report, resolutions of members, subjects addressed, names of members and their children, deaths of members, and Narcissa Whitman's letter to Mother's Magazine, which was printed in volume 14, 1846.

161   *s DUBOIS, ELLEN CAROL. *Feminism and Suffrage: The Emergence of an Independent Women's Movement in America, 1848-1869*. Ithaca, N.Y.: Cornell University Press, 1978. 220 pp. Notes, bib., indexes.

Ground-breaking in its close analysis of the roots of the post-Civil War fight for women suffrage, this monograph moves from a survey of the antebellum struggles for women's rights to scrutinize the American Equal Rights Association. Historian DuBois exposes the tension between abolitionism and feminism among the members who defined goals and strategies to attain a Fourteenth Amendment to the U.S. Constitution. There is considerable attention also to the Working Women's Association of New York, the focus in 1868-69 of suffragist effort to organize women to demand their own enfranchisement and emancipation. A result of an alliance between women suffragists and labor reformers, it was a pioneering attempt to build a working women's feminism to address economic and political grievances. When the Fourteenth Amendment was passed to enfranchise black males only, an independent suffrage movement emerged with the formation of the American Woman Suffrage Association and National Woman Suffrage Association.

162   *s -----. "Radicalism of the Woman Suffrage Movement: Toward the Reconstruction of Nineteenth Century Feminism." *Feminist Studies* 3 (Fall 1975): 63-71. Notes.

This landmark article argues that the radicalism of the woman suffrage movement in the last century lay in its challenge to the familial role for women and its determination to give to women a voice in the public sphere. The Women's Christian Temperance Union is scrutinized here for its success in urging women to enter the public arena and to work eventually for suffrage to protect the primacy of the private, domestic sphere and woman's position within it.

163   *b   DULLES, FOSTER RHEA. *The American Red Cross: A History*. New York: Harper and Brothers, 1950. ix, 554 pp. Bib.

  The contribution of women to the Red Cross is ignored throughout most of this history, with the exception of chapter 22 "Volunteer Activity," (pp. 379-96). Here Dulles provides figures on women's activity as motor car drivers, canteen servers, hospital volunteers, and knitters.

164   *c   DUNN, JAMES TAYLOR. "St. Paul's Schubert Club: Musical Mentor of the Northwest." *Minnesota History* 39 (Summer 1964): 51-64. Notes, illus.: two concert halls; one program; Mrs. Warren S. Briggs; and Mme. Ernestine Schumann-Heink and her accompanist, Mrs. Frank L. Hoffman.

  In 1882, forty women met at the home of Mrs. Charles McIlrath and formed the Ladies Musicale. The club changed its name in 1888 to the Schubert Club and became renowned for bringing internationally famed recitalists to perform in St. Paul. The women performed for St. Paul's citizens in hospitals, prisons, and rest homes. In 1932, its music school provided two hundred music lessons each week at ten centers for the underprivileged in settlement houses, orphan asylums, and other social service facilities. The article enumerates the prizes and scholarships awarded by the members to musical students in their city. For a time, the members created an orchestra and chorus from its own ranks. Clearly, the club functioned successfully to provide members and the city of St. Paul with good music.

165   *w   DYE, NANCY SCHROM. *As Equals and as Sisters: Feminism, the Labor Movement, and the Women's Trade Union League of New York*. Columbia: University of Missouri Press, 1980. 200 pp. Notes, bib., indexes.

  This strong and serious history documents the work of the New York City Women's Trade Union League. The organization's origins lie in the poor working conditions of wage-earning women at the turn of the century. Women of privilege united with their working-class sisters to persuade the labor movement to integrate women into its ranks. The League was founded in 1904 and began to create branches. It met success in the garment trades between the years 1909 and 1913, which Dye thoroughly examines. The author also dissects sisterhood and class conflict among the membership, and the movement to emphasize woman suffrage after 1913 at the expense of trade union issues. The fight for protective legislation in the first quarter of the twentieth century led to WTUL opposition with the National Woman's party and its equal rights amendment. Although the WTUL existed until 1955, after World War I it was impoverished and limited its program to social welfare projects. In its heyday, in 1909, it assisted thirty thousand shirtwaist makers, 85 percent of them women, to go out on strike, creating the largest woman's strike in labor history. Dye insists, that 1913 was the group's turning point when it emphasized women's problems and women's suffrage over the labor issues of women in industry.

166   *w   -----.   "Creating a Feminist Alliance: Sisterhood and Class Conflict in the New York Women's Trade Union League, 1903-1914." *Feminist Studies* 2 (1975): 24-38. Notes.

Dye argues that upper-class women disenchanted with conventional philanthropic and social reform activities in the early twentieth century made efforts to cooperate with labor organizations, especially those of garment workers, to help the industrial sister "find her way through the chaos of industry." Dye suggests that the women enjoyed only limited success in achieving the goal of egalitarian cross-class alliances. Personal, cultural, and political strife dominated the interactions and resulted in a schism over woman's movement versus labor movement priorities. Dye sees as significant the loss of the presidency in the 1914 organizational election by immigrant Rose Schneiderman to American-born worker Melinda Scott, symbolizing the victory of woman's movement politics over workers' issues. In the 1910s and 1920s, woman suffrage and protective legislation efforts overshadowed attempts to organize trade unions.

167   *w   -----.   "Feminism or Unionism? New York Women's Trade Union League and the Labor Movement." *Feminist Studies* 3 (Fall 1975): 111-25. Notes.

This article explores the strategies devised by the New York City Women's Trade Union League, between the years 1903 and 1912, to integrate working women into the established trade unions. The difficulties were great, for the leadership in the American Federation of Labor was antagonistic to the unionization of women. Dye's analysis reveals the problems feminists faced in synthesizing their commitment to the woman's movement with a commitment to organized labor.

168 *m EAGLE, MARY KAVANAUGH OLDHAM, ed. *The Congress of Women Held in the Woman's Building, World's Columbia Exposition, Chicago, USA, 1893.* Cincinnati: E.R. Curtis and Co., 1894. 824 pp. Indexes, illus.: 298 portraits of speakers whose remarks are collected here and members of the Board of Lady Managers.

Eagle collected 180 speeches prepared by 198 authors for the Congress of Women held in the Woman's Building of the 1893 Chicago World's Columbia Exposition. Most of the presenters were women who had prepared this material for women's club meetings. Their remarks on inequities women have faced in politics, arts, careers, and religion all over the world and throughout history provide an impressive breadth of information and insight about the turn-of-the-century woman's movement. Many of the essays deal with the histories of women's organizations in the United States. Among them are "The Women's National Indian Association" by Mrs. Amelia S. Quinton, who founded the association in 1887 to appeal to the governor to improve the status of American Indians. Another is "What the Women of Kansas Are Doing Today" by Mrs. Eugene F. Ware, which discusses the developing women's club movement in her state.

169 *t EARHART, MARY. *Frances Willard: From Prayers to Politics.* Chicago: University of Chicago Press, 1944. vi, 418 pp. Notes, bib., indexes, illus.: 21, of Francis Willard; her mother; father; Lady Henry Somerset; documents pertaining to Willard's life.

Easily one of the most influential women of the nineteenth century, Frances Willard (1839-98) held the presidency of the Women's Christian Temperance Union from 1879 until her death. Not only did she develop it into the largest and most powerful women's organization of her day, but she tapped the respect and appeal she enjoyed from her constituency to coax members to support a variety of social programs beyond the abolition of alcohol. Woman suffrage, improved conditions for laborers, and social services for the needy were among the "Do Everything" policies she championed. Because so much of her life was devoted to public issues, the biography is heavily intertwined with the history of the Women's Christian Temperance Union, but the author also gives some attention to Willard's private life. Her Puritan ancestry, devotion to her mother and to other relatives, her friendship with Lady Henry Somerset of England, and their cooperation to build an international temperance association are recounted. Because Willard's devoted followers shaped her public image long after her death, Earhart's story is the only nonpartisan work that was published prior to recent years.

170   *c   EBERT, EVELYN O., comp. and ed. *The Thirty-Fifth Year: History of the National Council of State Garden Clubs, Inc..* St. Louis: the organization, 1965. x, 182 pp. Illus.: 13, of presidents; logos of state garden clubs.

This history surveys the eight administrations of the National Council of State Garden Clubs between 1949 and 1965. The author devotes one section to the work of the National Council, including the headquarters from which officers operated and the meetings at which policy was made. She outlines the projects of the National Council committees, including birds, Blue Star Memorial Highway, conservation, high schools, junior gardening, and litter bugs. She provides brief histories of the regions in the organization and the state federations and notes contributions of foreign affiliates and the Men's Garden Clubs of America.

171   *b,t   EDHOLM, CHARLTON. *Traffic in Girls and Florence Crittenton Missions.* Chicago: Women's Temperance Publishing Association, 1893. 307 pp. Illus.: 9 Florence Crittenton Missions in New York, Oakland, San Jose, Sacramento, Los Angeles, San Francisco, Atlanta, Denver, and Chicago; Women's Christian Temperance Union Temple; Charles N. Crittenton; Florence Crittenton; Charlton Edholm; Francis Willard; Lady Henry Somerset; Josephine Butler.

To memorialize the death of his daughter, Florence, Charles Crittenton sponsored the founding of numerous missions for troubled girls in America. In several cases, he cooperated with the local Women's Christian Temperance Union, which undertook to provide financial support and supervision of many of the individual centers. This volume concentrates on documenting the problems faced by prostitutes, but details are also provided on the WCTU missions in New Brunswick, New Jersey, Portland, Oregon, Denver, Fargo, and Chicago. Edholm includes names of officers and personnel, describes projects like the Sabbath school, and prints letters and clippings about the women assisted, enabling researchers to get a sense of the volunteerism that kept the missions running.

172   *w   ELLERBE, ROSE LUCILE. *History of the Southern California Woman's Press Club: 1894-1929.* Los Angeles: Foster Co., 1930. 68 pp. Illus.: Rose Lucile Ellerbe.

Ellerbe served as president of the Southern California Woman's Press Club in 1916, a group devoted to "promoting acquaintance, good fellowship, and co-operation among the women writers of this coast, and to advance their professional interests." The text is rich in original documents and information, including the 1894 constitution and bylaws, correspondence with the National Woman's Press Association, a *Los Angeles Herald* account of an 1894 reception, lists of officers and titles of their published writings, lectures presented by experts at meetings, and a report by member Rebecca Spring on her European visit to Thomas Carlyle in 1846 with her friend Margaret Fuller. Although my focus in this annotated bibliography is on volunteers rather than on working women networking for career advancement, the tone of Ellerbe's history so diminishes the workplace and careers and so thoroughly emphasizes excursions, banquets, fundraising with tableaux, failed plans to build a clubhouse, and war relief, that the study will well serve to document social interaction among club members. To be sure, the members met in sections devoted to reading, discussing, and criticizing the short story, music, verse, fiction, features, and drama, but in the Ellerbe interpretation, the study and career advancement aspects of club life recede.

173   *c ELLIOTT, MAUD HOWE, ed. *Art and Handicraft in the Woman's Building of the World's Columbian Exposition, Chicago, 1893.* Chicago: Rand, McNally and Co., 1894. 320 pp. Illus.: 228 photos of women's art on display in the building; 30 photos of the fair; 18 of prominent American and foreign women officials at the fair.

Elliott's collection of material on the decorative arts, fine arts, and crafts at the 1893 Chicago Exposition's Woman's Building contains three essays on women's voluntary organizations. Elizabeth W. Perry (pp. 101-6) described "The Work of Cincinnati Women in Decorated Pottery." In 1879, the Pottery Club of Cincinnati formed among a group of women who developed the distinctive Rookwood Pottery. Among the members who enjoyed greatest acclaim for their original glazes were Mrs. Bellamy Storer and Miss McLaughlin. In another essay, Julia Ward Howe (pp. 175-85) examines the "Associations of Women." Culminating in the formation of the General Federation of Women's Clubs in 1890, two clubs began twenty-five years before this fair, inspiring multitudes of similar clubs to form. Sorosis in New York City and the New England Woman's Club in Boston provided, in 1868, a central meeting place and regular social and intellectual meetings. The Boston club permitted a few men to participate, New York did not. Sorosis, in 1873, created the Association for the Advancement of

Women, whereby clubwomen traveled to a different American city each year to present speeches on women and encourage new women to form clubs. Howe provides a list of fifty-four organizations that were granted space in the Woman's Building, thereby demonstrating that the movement flourished in the late nineteenth century. A third essay was written by Bertha Honore Palmer (pp. 17-30) on "The Growth of the Woman's Building." This is a history of the Board of Lady Managers of the Chicago fair which organized the ambitious Woman's Building exhibitions and congresses.

174   *t   ENSIGN, FRANCES H. "Organization and Accomplishments of the WCTU in Ohio." *Annals of the American Academy of Political and Social Science* 32 (November 1908): 525-27.

Ensign explains that it was Ohio women who founded the first branch of the Women's Christian Temperance Union in 1874. She praises the educational efforts in the association's history, including members' success at raising the age of consent, putting scientific instruction into the schools on the effects of alcohol, pressuring for local option laws to prohibit saloons, and establishing 1,150 dry townships and 500 dry villages.

175   *t   EPSTEIN, BARBARA LESLIE. *The Politics of Domesticity: Women, Evangelism, and Temperance in Nineteenth Century America.* Middletown, Conn.: Wesleyan University Press, 1981. viii, 188 pp. Notes, bib., indexes.

This historian argues that women's religious activity of eighteenth- and nineteenth-century America gave rise to a "proto-feminism" that combined protest against female subordination with a commitment to Victorian morality which, while circumscribing women, also provided paradoxically the grounds for their self-assertion. Epstein focuses on the lives of white, Protestant, middle-class women of the Northeast and Midwest. Phases one and two on the first and second Great Awakenings of 1740-47 and 1797-1840 are not as pertinent to researchers on women's voluntary associations as the final two phases she discusses. The section on the Women's Crusade of 1873-75 describes the first "sit-in," consisting of women's marches to Ohio saloons where they prayed until intimidated saloonkeepers closed their establishments and pledged to refrain from selling alcohol. This activity spread widely and yielded the Women's Christian Temperance Union, whose "Home Protection" and "Do Everything" policies propelled thousands of women to support progressive causes like woman suffrage.

176   *n ERGOOD, BRUCE. "Female Protection and the Sun Light:
Two Contemporary Negro Mutual Aid Societies." *Florida Historical
Quarterly* 50 (July 1971): 25-38. Notes.

The Female Protective Society of Alachua County in North
Florida was founded in 1903 to care for the sick, bury the dead, and
relieve distressed members. For those who belonged to the association
for two years, it would provide a fifty-dollar burial, five dollars worth of
flowers, and one hundred dollars in cash to the bereaved. The founder
was Mrs. Mathilda Halle of Jonesville, a Methodist. Four lodges
meeting at an annual convention provided an important outlet for
female leadership. The organization was not affiliated with any church.
In 1868, it moved its monthly meeting time from Friday to Sunday to
permit working women to attend. The Sun Light Pall Bearers
Charitable Society was founded in 1898 in Thomasville, Georgia by
Mattie J. Shaw Cohens. By 1936, it had a membership of 450; by 1969,
5,000. This society was closely related to the Baptist Church and used
secret rituals in its meetings.

177   *b EVANS, RICHARD XAVIER. "The Ladies Union Benevolent
and Employment Society, 1850." *Columbia Historical Society Record*
39 (1938): 159-66.

This is a speech delivered at the District of Columbia
Historical Society in 1935. The Ladies Union Benevolent and
Employment Society was founded before 1850, but the presidency of
Mrs. Eliza Barnwell Mills is the only administration documented by her
personal papers. Evans relates the story of the organization's work,
using quotations from Mills's papers generously. Feeling a "religious
and moral duty to help the great family of mankind," the members
raised money to aid the poor, visited the needy, and found employment
for seventy widows and orphans. The account provides examples of the
poverty encountered by the membership, lists the "Committee of
Gentlemen" who assisted in fund-raising, enumerates nine regulations
of the society, and names the four women directors and fourteen
women managers who served as the group's administrators.

178   *r FALLS, HELEN EMERY. "Baptist Women in Mission Support
in the Nineteenth Century." *Baptist History and Heritage* 12 (1977):
26-36.

This article summarizes the history of women's mite societies
from Mary Webb's Boston Society of 1800 through the post-Civil War
missionary societies. The Woman's Missionary Union, founded in
1888, is described here.

179 no entry

180 *p,n FARLEY, ENA L. "Caring and Sharing Since World War I:
The League of Women for Community Service—A Black Volunteer
Organization in Boston." Umoja 1 (1977): 1-22. Notes.

 Middle-class black women in Boston, married to husbands
with professional careers, founded a Soldiers' Comfort Unit in 1918-19.
Determined to assist black soldiers stationed in Boston during World
War I, they offered hospitality in the form of dinners, dances, and visits,
and gave them knitted mufflers. To accomplish their goals, they
formed committees for publicity, hospitality, entertainment, music,
supplies, visiting, knitting, and Red Cross. After the war, they changed
their name to League of Women for Community Service, buying a
building for use by other groups serving the black community, such as
the Young Women's Christian Association and a day nursery. In 1919,
they added a Girl's Business Club to their list of projects. In 1921 they
formed a soup kitchen. Much credit belongs to Maria Louise Baldwin,
who steered the work of the club until 1922.

181 *s FARNAM, ANNE. "Isabella Beecher Hooker as a Woman
Suffragist: A Centennial Frame of Reference." Connecticut Review
5 (October 1971): 70-82.

 This biography of Isabella Beecher Hooker emphasizes her
participation in the Connecticut Woman Suffrage Association. She
founded the organization in 1869 and presided over it until her death in
1907. The author is generous with quotations from Hooker's speeches
as an advocate for women's enfranchisement throughout the late
nineteenth century.

182 *m FEINSTEIN, KAREN WOLK. "Kindergartens, Feminism and
the Profession of Motherhood." International Journal of Women's
Studies 3 (January-February 1980): 28-38. Notes.

 The author focuses on the growth of kindergartens between
the years 1860 and 1920 in the United States, explaining their popularity
as institutions that pioneered new roles for women and new approaches
to early childhood education. She mentions the support provided by
several all-women's or mostly womens' organizations, especially the
National Congress of Mothers, General Federation of Women's Clubs,
National Council of Women, National Education Association, National
Kindergarten Association, International Kindergarten Union, and
National Federation of Settlement Houses.

183   *w FELDBERG, ROSLYN L. "Union Fever: Organizing among Clerical Workers, 1900-1930." *Radical America* 14 (May-June 1980): 53-67. Notes, illus.: 8 of women as typists and clerks in early years; Women's Trade Union League demonstration.

     The origins of associations of stenographers, typists, and bookkeepers lie not with labor unions but with mutual benefit societies. In 1902, six hundred female stenographers in Toledo, Ohio, planned a restaurant to serve their members. Pittsburgh stenographers soon subscribed to a cooperative luncheon for themselves. In 1904, the Women's Trade Union League campaigned to organize clerical workers, becoming the first organizers sympathetic to working women before trade unions evidenced concern.

184   *m FENDELMAN, EARL. "An Empire of Women." *American Heritage* 35 (August-September 1984): 70-76. Illus.: Egyptian Building, 1906, headquarters of *Women's National Daily*; 2 of women.

     In June of 1910, the first American Woman's League Convention was held in a suburb of St. Louis. One thousand women attended, invited by Edward Gardner Lewis (1869-1950), editor of the *Woman's Magazine* and *Woman's Farm Journal*. Using women as his army of magazine subscription salespeople, he built thirty-eight chapter houses for his members. Three of these still stand, in Corning, California, Kissemmee, Florida, and Avon, Montana. In 1911, however, he declared bankruptcy. Fifty-two dollars or fifty-two subscriptions made a woman a lifetime member. Half of her contribution went to the League, the other half to Lewis. In return, she was allowed to join a free postal library with the latest books and phonograph records. A loan society, woman's exchange, and correspondence course in the arts were among other benefits membership bestowed.

185   *p FENHAGEN, MARY F. PRINGLE, comp. *A History of the Maryland Society of the Colonial Dames of America from April 1891 to April 1951*. N.p.: the organization, 1951. 48 pp.

     In 1891, at the suggestion of members of the Pennsylvania and Philadelphia chapters of the Colonial Dames of America, several Maryland women met to form a Maryland society of the organization. Dividing her history by presidential administrations, Fenhagen details the projects of the membership. These include a loan exhibition of historical relics, a colonial costume party, speeches on colonial government, society on genealogy, sponsorship of several courses of lectures at Johns Hopkins University, and care for neglected graves of early colonists and of Baltimore author Edgar Allan Poe. Included is an early speech by a member on colonial women of Maryland, which was published in a 1900 issue of the Maryland Historical Society magazine. In 1898, members sent delicacies to the Spanish-American war hospital ship *Solace*. In 1902, they helped erect a monument to soldiers and sailors killed in the 1898 war. To Florida they sent financial support for a tablet at the city gates of St. Augustine, and to Jamestown, money for a statue of Pocahontas. Between 1906 and 1920, Mrs. William Reed provided classes in church silver of the colonies. Full citations for this and other scholarly articles by members published in Maryland's historical publications are provided. During World War I, the group helped with veterans' and Americanization programs. In 1917, the association moved its headquarters into Mount Clare, a 1784 house in Baltimore. Sixty years of historical activity are documented in this volume.

186   *s FENNER, MILDRED SANDISON. "One Hundred Years Ago History Was Made at Seneca Falls." *NEA Journal* 37 (November 1948): 534-35. Illus.: three-cent U.S. postage stamp with Elizabeth Cady Stanton, Carrie Chapman Catt, and Lucretia Mott.

One hundred years after the Woman's Rights Conference was held in Seneca Falls, New York, a three-cent U.S. postage stamp commemorated the efforts of three suffragists, Elizabeth Cady Stanton, Carrie Chapman Catt, and Lucretia Mott. This brief chatty account of suffrage history contains excerpts from the Declaration of Rights of Women signed in 1848 and the 1923 version of the equal rights amendment.

187   *m FERGUSON, CHARLES W. *Fifty Million Brothers: A Panorama of American Lodges and Clubs*. New York: Farrar and Rinehart, 1937 viii, 389 pp. Bib., index.

As his title suggests, Ferguson is most concerned with the history of men's organizational life, but his study includes material on women's clubs and secret societies as well. His chapter on temperance provides a glimpse of the Frances Willard years at the Women's Christian Temperance Union (pp. 61-66), and he provides an entire chapter on the history of the General Federation of Women's Clubs (pp. 82-93). Another chapter explores the Daughters of the American Revolution (pp. 203-16), focusing in a critical way on the conservatism of the organization: "By every device at their command they have made patriotism as real as indigestion" (p. 213). He considers the work of the National Society of Colonial Dames and the United Daughters of the Confederacy in a chapter on clubs formed around the concept of ancestry. And finally, he surveys the Woman's Patriotic Association for

Diminishing the Use of Imported Luxuries, founded in New York City in 1863, when twenty-five hundred women pledged "to refrain from imported articles of luxury for which those of home manufacture or production can be substituted" for the duration of the Civil War. Ferguson's writing is readable but general and provides only a once-over-lightly survey of club activity.

188   *m FLAK, FLORENCE. "District History, BPW." *Palimpsest* 52 (1971): 143-45.
      See *Palimpsest*.

189   *s FLEXNER, ELEANOR. *Century of Struggle: The Woman's Rights Movement in the United States*. New York: Atheneum, 1959, 1971. xviii, 385 pp. Notes, bib., indexes, illus.: 25 of leaders of the woman's movement in America.
      Flexner divides American women's history into three sections: part 1 deals with the period 1800 to the eve of the Civil War, part 2, the Civil War to the turn of the century, and part 3 the twentieth century. One of the earliest surveys of women's history, this is impressively thorough. The first section treats early organizational efforts among women, including anti-slavery societies, sewing circles, and benevolent and suffrage associations for black and white women. The middle part develops the suffrage struggle, the early trade union movement, and the intellectual gains of women. Chapter 13 examines the growth of women's organizations and includes material on the Women's Christian Temperance Union, the Colored Women's League, the National Association of Colored Women, and the General Federation of Women's Clubs. The final section scrutinizes the suffrage struggle from 1906 until passage of the federal amendment in 1920.

190   *c FORDERHASE, NANCY. " 'Limited Only by Earth and Sky': The Louisville Woman's Club and Progressive Reform, 1900-1910." *Filson Club History Quarterly* 59 (July 1985): 327-43. Notes, illus.: Patty Hill; 30 prominent women.
      In 1890, deciding to "form an association for mutual sympathy and counsel and united effort to further reform and improve the community in which we live," suffragist Susan Look Avery inspired the founding of the Louisville Woman's Club. In the first decade, the organization's members stressed moral purity in their projects, urging that a prison matron be hired at the city jail and that the age of consent be raised in the state. In addition, they engaged in literary study. During the second decade, they created concrete reform proposals for the improvement of the urban environment. They supported

settlement houses, charitable institutions like the children's home, the playground movement, the Consumers' League, educational reform, kindergartens, social welfare programs, and the abolition of child labor.

191   *m FOSTER, MARY DILLON, ed. and comp. *Who's Who among Minnesota Women: A History of Women's Work in Minnesota from Pioneer Days to Date, Told in Biographies, Memorials, and Records of Organizations*. N.p.: the author, 1924. 380 pp. Indexes, illus.: 1 with each of the 700 biographies.

Mary Dillon Foster compiled seven hundred biographies of white women and two of black women engaged in Minnesota reform. For each woman, she provides a photograph, and details about her birth place, parents, education, marriage, and activity in women's voluntary associations.   For writers like Alice Ames Winter, she includes titles of their published novels. Among the Minnesota groups given attention are Alternates of Minneapolis; Austin Ladies' Floral Club; Bethesda Sick Benefit Society of Deaconess Hospital; Brainerd Musical Club; Buchanana Bible Study Club; Business and Professional Women's Clubs; Camp Fire girls; Child Interest Club of Little Falls; Civic Improvement League of Minneapolis and that of Dover; Class Room Teachers' Association; Cobb Hospital Auxiliary; Colony of New England Women; Concordia Society of Swedish Hospital; Coterie Club; Council of Jewish Women in Duluth, Minneapolis, and St. Paul; Daughters of the American Revolution; Dames of the Round Table; Detroit Literary Club; Dome Club of Minnesota; Duluth Council of Catholic Women; Ebenezer Old Folks' Home Woman's Auxiliary; Ever Ready Sunshine Club; Every Woman Progressive Council of St. Paul; Federated Fraternal Women of Minnesota; Fergus Falls Woman's Club; Schumann Club; General Council of Mothers' Clubs and Parent-Teachers Associations; Girl Scouts; Guild of Catholic Women in St. Paul; Hennipin Republican Club of Colored Women; Home Garden Club; Home for the Friendless, Junior League; Lester Park Literary Club in Duluth; Little Falls Civic Improvement League; Lutheran Women's Inner Mission League of Minneapolis; Matinee Musicale in Duluth; Masonic Women of St. Paul; Merriam Park Woman's Club; Minneapolis College Women's Club; Minneapolis League of Catholic Women; Minnesota Federation of Colored Women's Clubs; Minnesota Federation of Women's Clubs; League of Women Voters; Parent-Teachers Association, Monday Club; Mozart Club; Musical Art Club; National Woman's party; Needlework Guild; New Century Club; Philolectian Club; Ramsey County Suffrage Club; Ramsey County Republican Woman's Club; Council of Rural Mothers' Clubs; St. Paul Housewives League; Sisterhood of Mount Zion Temple; Stillwater

Woman's Club; Students' Wives' Association of Luther Seminary in St. Paul; Minneapolis League of Catholic Women, Thursday Club; Twentieth Century Club; Utopian Study Club; Visiting Nurse Association; Wanderlust Hiking Club; Woman's Christian Association; Women's Christian Temperance Association; Women's Club of Litchfield and that of Moorhead; Minneapolis Woman's Cooperative Alliance; Woman's Council; Woman's Welfare League; Woman's Relief Corps; Women's Civic League; Women's City Club of St. Paul; Women's International League of Peace and Freedom; Women's Guild of Little Falls; Women's Literary Club in Springfield; Women's Mission Society; Women's Nonpartisan Clubs of Minnesota; Women's Overseas League; Women's Welfare League; Women's Lincoln Club; and Young Women's Christian Association.

192   *s FOWLER, ROBERT BOOTH. *Carrie Catt: Feminist Politician.* Boston: Northeastern University Press, 1986. xx, 226 pp. Notes, bib., index, illus.: 9 of Carrie Chapman Catt.

In nine succinct chapters, Fowler handily surveys the life and suffrage career of National American Woman Suffrage Association leader Carrie Chapman Catt. His introductory chapter on her early years, beginning with her 1859 birth in Wisconsin and her growing-up years in Iowa, quickly moves to her two marriages and her preoocupation with politics. His chapter on her private life is strong, emphasizing her female friendships with Clara Hyde, Maud Wood Park, Rosika Schwimmer, Alda Wilson, Mary Peck, and Mary Garrett Hay with whom she elected to be buried. Chapters 4 through 6 generalize about Catt's theories of politics and chapters 7 through 9 specify her roles and contributions at the National American Woman Suffrage Association at the turn of the century and on the eve of victory. Fowler is critical of some aspects of his subject's political vision for women. He cites her distance from the equal rights amendment in the 1920s, her practice of "practical" politics, her caution in style and strategy, her limited program for women's self-mastery, and her avoidance of women's sexual and reproductive issues.

193   *s FOX, KAROLENA M. "History of the Equal Suffrage Movement in Michigan." *Michigan History Magazine* 2 (January 1918): 90-109. Notes.

Fox examines the history of the fight for woman suffrage in the state of Michigan, from Ernestine L. Rose's 1846 speech in the legislature through the constitutional convention rejections of the amendment in 1908, 1911, 1912, and 1913. In the years between, the Michigan Suffrage Association formed in 1870 and faced overwhelming defeat in an 1874 referendum. In 1881, school suffrage was granted to parents and guardians of children of school age and an era of more efficient suffrage lobbying began. Public interest in the issue recurred periodically, as did organized opposition, but women participated in greater public service. When the Michigan Equal Suffrage Association formed in 1884, its members worked for municipal suffrage, raising the age of consent from fourteen to sixteen, police matrons, women on the state boards of the insane, factory inspections, a ten-hour day, and increased cooperation among all types of women's organizations for common programs.

194 *m FRANK, DANA. "Housewives, Socialists, and the Politics of Food: The 1917 New York Cost-of-Living Protests." *Feminist Studies* 11 (Summer 1985): 255-85. Notes, illus.: 4 of women demonstrating.

In the late autumn of 1916, the Mothers' Anti-High Price League formed in New York City, when Rachel Panken harnessed the efforts of immigrant Jewish working-class housewives from the Socialist Housewives League in Brooklyn and the Socialist Consumers' League of the Bronx. They organized a series of demonstrations and mass meetings on food issues. For two weeks, they boycotted chickens, fish, and vegetables, and delivered five thousand demonstrators to a Madison Square mass meeting. Frank quotes the speeches of the activists, which called for direct distribution of free food. By the second week of March, prices dropped and the women ended their work.

195 *c FRANK, HENRIETTE GREENEBAUM, and AMALIE JEROME HOFER, comps. *Annals of the Chicago Woman's Club for the First Forty Years of Its Organization: 1876-1916*. Chicago: Chicago Woman's Club, 1916. Indexes, illus.: 1 of Caroline M. Brown.

Dividing the fifty-year history of the Chicago Woman's Club by administrations, the authors narrate the progress of the clubs arts and civics committees, its cooperation with other organizations involved with civic issues in the city, and its speakers, philanthropies, parties, and guests. The summary is taken from minutes and speeches and argues persuasively that the "solidarity" of the members and their seriousness in tapping their talents and resources resulted in impressive programs, including industrial arts education for working girls, scholarships, jobs for destitute women, juvenile courts, schoolchildren's aid, vacation schools, beautification of parks, schools in jails, support of a teacher for "feeble-minded children," and investigations of child labor and public sanitation facilities.

196   *t FRANKLIN, JIMMIE L. "That Noble Experiment: A Note on Prohibition in Oklahoma." *Chronicles of Oklahoma* 43 (Spring 1965): 19-34. Notes.

        This article gives only scant attention to the contribution of the Women's Christian Temperance Union, led by Miss Abbie Hillerman, in the November 1906 elections for delegates to the Oklahoma Constitutional Convention where temperance was addressed as a state issue.

197   *t -----. "The Fight for Prohibition in Oklahoma Territory." *Social Science Quarterly* 49 (March 1969): 876-85. Notes.

        Oklahoma was admitted to statehood in 1907 as a dry state. It remained so until 1959. The Women's Christian Temperance Union and Anti-Saloon League were successful in mobilizing sentiment against the whiskey traffic. Franklin traces the history of the WCTU to 1888 in Oklahoma, but this is a brief piece and provides only sparse accounts of the groups contribution. Mention is made of Carrie Nation's Prohibition Federation, which cooperated with the two more established reform groups to win prohibition in Oklahoma.

198   *m FREEDMAN, ESTELLE. "Separatism as Strategy: Female Institution Building and American Feminism, 1870-1930." *Feminist Studies* 5 (Fall 1979): 512-29. Notes.

        This important article credits the strong woman's culture of nineteenth-century America, with its personal networks, rituals, and relationships among women, as the basis of the strong public female sphere which launched women's public voice and influence between 1870 and 1930. The separate sphere helped mobilize women to gain political leverage in the larger society and therefore served as a political strategy. Groups like Sorosis, the General Federation of Women's Clubs, Women's Christian Temperance Union, Women's Trade Union League, Consumers' League, National American Woman Suffrage Association, National Woman's party, and League of Women Voters attracted women who believed, to varying degrees, that they possessed a unique identity that obligated them to solve public problems. Freedman suggests that the weakness of women in politics of the 1920s reflected the devaluation of woman's culture in general and of the previously vital separate female institutions in particular.

199   *p FRENCH, ELLA M., comp. *History of Department of California and Nevada, Woman's Relief Corps, 1883-1934.* Modesto, Calif.: Cavell, 1934. 154 pp. Illus.; Woman's Relief Corps Home at Evergreen, opened in 1889 and destroyed by fire in 1920; ex-Senator

A.E. Osborne donating new home and 18 acres near San Jose in 1921; memorial window of Woman's Relief Corps in post chapel at Presidio, San Francisco; chapel in 1934.

In 1884, California and Nevada formed a Woman's Relief Corps with nine corps which convened in San Francisco the following February. These women served as an auxiliary to the Grand Army of the Republic, a patriotic association of Civil War veterans. A list of the officers elected, the names of the corps in the region, and a list of 158 members are provided along with one-page summaries of each annual convention. The city, place, date, officers, new corps joining, and projects for veterans and their dependents are enumerated. Among the work accomplished: the dedication in 1934 of a chapel, presentation of flags to churches and schools, financial support during the 1930s to the Soldiers Home, Memorial Day events, Andersonville Prison, Near East Relief, child welfare, flowers for shut-ins, scholarships for boys and girls, Boy Scouts, and the National Council of Women. In World War II, members provided thirty-two thousand hours of Red Cross assistance and collected thousands of pounds of rubber and grease. They also placed historical markers on the highways.

200   *s FRY, AMELIA. "Along the Suffrage Trail: From West to East for Freedom Now." *American West* 6 (1969): 16-25. Bib., illus.: 6 of Sara Bard Field campaigning for suffrage; Congressional Union Freedom booth at Panama Pan-International Exposition in 1915; 4 of December 1915 suffrage parade in Washington, D.C.

Four women—Sara Bard Field, Mabel Vernon, Miss Kindstedt, and Miss Kindborg of the Congressional Union—made an auto campaign for suffrage in 1915, beginning at San Francisco's Panama-Pacific International Exposition and winding up at the December 1915 suffrage parade in Washington, D.C. Along the way, the women collected signatures for a petition to be presented to President Woodrow Wilson, gave speeches, held receptions, and staged parades and rallies. The article traces their flamboyant expedition, charting their itinerary through Sacramento, Reno, Salt Lake City, Denver, Colorado Springs, Kansas City, Topeka, Lincoln, Des Moines, Cedar Rapids, Chicago, Indianapolis, Columbus, Detroit, Cleveland, Buffalo, Syracuse, Albany, Providence, New York, Newark, Philadelphia, Wilmington, and Baltimore.

201   *s,z FULLER, PAUL E. *Laura Clay and the Woman's Rights Movement*. Lexington: University Press of Kentucky, 1975. x, 217 pp. Notes, indeses, bib., illus.: Laura Clay alone and in 2 group photos with suffragists in 1910 and 1916.

Fuller links Laura Clay's career as a woman suffragist to Kentucky and national woman's rights politics. He devotes a chapter to Clay's first fifteen years, from 1849 to 1866, but dwells on her growth as a suffragist from 1866 to 1888, her work with the Kentucky Equal Rights Association from 1888 to 1895, her leadership among southern suffragists from 1892 to 1896, her prominence in her state and the nation at the turn of the century, her fight against eastern dominance in the National American Woman Suffrage Association in 1909, her legacy to Madeline McDowell Breckinridge who replaced her as president of Kentucky's suffrage forces in 1912, her antipathy to the federal amendment when a state suffrage plan would successfully exclude black women voters, her ambivalence about the Women's Christian Temperance Union, her role in the Kentucky Federation of Women's Clubs, and her cooperation with the Democratic party and with Al Smith's candidacy in 1928.

202 *s FULLER, STEVEN J., and ALSATIA MELLECKER. "Behind the Yellow Banner: Anna B. Lawther and the Winning of Suffrage for Iowa Women." *Palimpsest* 65 (May-June 1984): 106-16. Illus.: 1908 parade for Anna Howard Shaw; Anna Bell Lawther.

Iowa became the tenth state to ratify the federal amendment granting women the vote, but not without five decades of agitation by earnest suffragists. This essay highlights the efforts of Anna B. Lawther, who served as president of Iowa's Equal Suffrage Association after 1916. She led her supporters in lobbying efforts at the legislature and, as Iowa director of the Women's Committee of the Council of National Defense, in relief work during World War I. In 1921, Lawther was appointed the first woman to head the state's Board of Education, a post she held until she retired in 1941. A dormitory at the University of Northern Iowa is named for her.

203 *z FURLOW, JOHN W., Jr. "Cornelia Bryce Pinchot: Feminism in the Post-Suffrage Era." *Pennsylvania History* 43 (October 1976): 329-46. Notes, illus.: Cornelia Bryce Pinchot.

Although biography is the focus of this portrait of the wife of a Pennsylvania governor, Cornelia Bryce Pinchot (1881-1960), the author discusses her involvement in social feminism with the Pennsylvania Woman's Suffrage Association, Pennsylvania Republican Women's Committee, and the League of Women Voters.

204 *z,w GAMMAGE, JUDIE K. "Pressure Group Techniques: The Texas Equal Legal Rights Amendment." *Great Plains Journal* 16 (Fall 1976): 45-65.

In 1919, the National Federation of Business and Professional Women's Clubs established a branch in Texas. In 1937 the members officially came out in support of the National Woman's party and its efforts to win congressional support for an equal rights amendment. They also approved of jury service for women. By 1957, the organization had 185 clubs in Texas, representing 8,400 members. They hired attorney Hermine Tobolowsky to lobby in the state Senate in Austin for ERA. In 1966, the National Organization for Women also assisted in pressuring Texas lawmakers for a state ERA. In 1971, the women were successful. Although young people thought passage represented a victory of the contemporary women's movement, older Texans understood it was the culmination of a long and difficult women's rights struggle.

205 *c *Garden Club of America: History, 1913-1938.* New York: the organization, 1938, 177 pp. Illus.: Elizabeth Price Martin, founder and first president.

Here is a summary of twenty-five years of Garden Club history. For each annual convention, the volume summarizes the resolutions passed, projects initiated, and the accomplishments of conservation programs. In addition, lavish entertainments at luxurious garden settings at each convention site are described.

206 *p GARDNER, VIRGINIA ATKINSON. *A History of the Massachusetts Society of the Colonial Dames of America, 1893-1937.* Boston: Thomas Todd Co., 1937. 26 pp. Illus.: the Quincy House which the Massachusetts Society of the Colonial Dames restored.

In 1893, the Massachusetts Society of the Colonial Dames of America was founded to collect and preserve manuscripts, traditions, relics, and mementos of bygone days; preserve and restore early buildings; diffuse information on the past; stimulate patriotism; and impress on the young their sacred obligation of honoring heroic ancestors. This volume recognizes the charter members, officers elected, and efforts to join with the national society, organized in Philadelphia in 1891. Gardner provides rich detail on the programs members supported, prizes for essays on colonial history for women college students (including Radcliffe's "Bacon's Rebellion" and Mount Holyoke's "Fifty Years of Liquor Legislation in Massachusetts Bay"), and financial assistance for the 1901 dedication of a bronze tablet to the memory of Wannalanset, last sachem of the Merrimac River Indians, a Pilgrim memorial in Southampton, England (1912), Americanization programs, a hundred-dollar prize for a competition in paintings on a colonial subject, and history and civics classes in Italian and Russian communities in Boston. The women purchased 164 volumes in American history for Girls' Normal School, established scholarships, provided relief for fire victims, held an exhibit of pewter, published a book of American samplers, collected early military uniforms for the national museum in Washington, D.C., and celebrated the 1920 Tercentenary of the Landing of the Pilgrims at Plymouth Rock. In 1901, they leased the Quincy Homestead in Massachusetts to restore the home and open it to the public.

207   *r,y GATES, SUSA YOUNG. *History of the Young Ladies' Mutual Improvement Association of Jesus Christ of Latter-day Saints: From November 1869 to June 1910.* Salt Lake City: Deseret News, 1911. viii, 488 pp. Notes, illus.

      Here is a study useful to researchers on the contributions of organized Mormon women. After providing fifty-eight biographical sketches of leaders in the Young Ladies' Mutual Improvement Association, Gates provides sixty-four portraits of branches (stakes) that developed after 1869. Local societies were organized all over Utah and its environs, and by 1889, a periodical, the *Young Woman's Journal*, was regularly published. At the turn of the century, while engaged in restructuring the religious association for young women, the group allied with the National Council of Women.

208   *z GEIDEL, PETER. "The National Woman's Party and the Origins of the Equal Rights Amendment." *Historian* 42 (August 1980): 557-82. Notes.

      Battles between two factions in the women's movement of the 1920s are described here. After the passage of the suffrage amendment to the U.S. Constitution in 1920, "social feminists," or traditional reformers, such as women in the League of Women Voters and National Consumers League, continued to advance the cause of protective legislation for women, while "feminists" in the National Woman's party advocated an equal rights amendment that was likely to undermine protective legislation.

209   *p GIBBS, MARGARET. *The DAR.* New York: Holt, Rinehart and Winston, 1969. i, 244 pp. Bib., indexes.

Here is an extremely detailed and critical study of the conservatism of the Daughters of the American Revolution organization. The organization began in 1890, when women were excluded from the Sons of the Revolution, and the founders squabbled from the start about the direction the group should take. Much minutiae is provided on patriotic service during World War I, support for the League of Nations in 1919, Americanization programs in the 1920s, and participation in the Red Scare of that decade, with special emphasis on the "Blue Menace," whereby members, using the *Woman Patriot*, accused suffragist Carrie Chapman Catt, Jane Addams, Women's Trade Union League member Rose Schneiderman, and other progressive public leaders of subverting the United States with Bolshevik sympathies. Another chapter attacks the organization for its refusal to permit black singer Marion Anderson to sing in their auditorium, Constitution Hall, in 1930. After describing the group's earnest support of World War II, Gibb's examines its interest in censorship of textbooks.

210   *c GIBSON, MARY S. *A Record of Twenty-five Years of the California Federation of Women's Clubs, 1900-1925.* N.p.: the organization, 1927. 368 pp.

This leading clubwoman of California's federated civic and self-improvement associations summarized the administration of each presidency in the California federation, from its founding in 1900 through 1925. She includes the official presidential message delivered at each annual convention and reprints speeches, resolutions, reports on committee accomplishments, and figures on the membership's growth over time. This compendium can serve as a primary source, as it includes financial and treasurer reports, and lists of officers and committee members through 1915.

210a *f GIDDINGS, PAULA. *In Search of Sisterhood: Delta Sigma Theta and the Challenge of the Black Sorority Movement.* New York: William Morrow, 1988. 336pp.

211   *b GILMAN, AMY. "From Widowhood to Wickedness: The Politics of Class and Gender in New York City Private Charity, 1799-1860." *History of Education Quarterly* 24 (1984): 59-74. Notes.

Gilman makes the case that charitable organizations changed in character from the beginning of the nineteenth century to the mid-century. In 1799, Isabella Graham and her daughter, Joanna Bethune, established the Society for the Relief of Poor Widows with Small Children. It was the first private charity organization directed and managed entirely by women. It became typical of a type, whereby elite women managed and controlled private benevolence in New York City. The women managers viewed the recipients of the charity as women much like themselves, deserving women who had simply come on hard times. By the 1850s, however, the system had been transformed into one in which men replaced women as directors and managers of private charities. Instead of providing sewing for genteel women, they established Children's Aid Societies with a network of industrial schools stressing industrial skills, aggressive work programs, and stringent discipline.

212   *r GINGERICH, MELVIN. "Mennonite Woman's Missionary Society, I and II." *Mennonite Quarterly Review* 37 (April 1963): 113-25; 37 (July 1963): 214-33.

Part 1 of this study locates the origins of the Mennonite Woman's Missionary Society in late nineteenth-century sewing circles within the Mennonite churches in Lancaster, Pennsylvania. By 1911, eastern Pennsylvania had a network of Pioneer Regional circles, devoted to earning money for home missions and orphans. The author is generous with the names of women leaders of individual groups in Mennonite communities. Part 2 features the leadership of Clara Eby Steiner, who led women to do more ambitious work for missionary efforts. Their success met opposition in 1915. The men of the church, fearing competition and independent action from the women, curbed the women's spending by channeling their expenditures through the district mission board. By 1922, however, the new Mennonite Woman's Missionary Society had 131 societies with seventeen hundred members and a treasury of twenty thousand dollars; they had provided seventeen thousand garments for charity. Their relief work for the Soviet Union and Turkey was impressive, but the 1920s saw the undermining of the women's strength through administrative restructuring. Scholars will appreciate the extensive quotations from organizational records.

213   *b GINZBERG, LORI D. " 'Moral Suasion Is Moral Balderdash': Women, Politics, and Social Activism in the 1850s." *Journal of American History* 73 (December 1986): 601-22. Notes.

This article exposes the growing conservatism in women's benevolent organizations of the 1850s. Earlier, the ideology of women's unique moral calling seemed to hold potential for radical activism and social change in antislavery societies and Moral Reform societies. Now, however, reformers began to move away from faith in the possibilities of a moral transformation of American society. They focused instead on formalizing institutional benevolence, permitting men to serve on boards, and concentrating on elections and institutional administration.

214 *f GIST, NOEL P. Secret Societies: A Cultural Study of Fraternalism in the United States. *University of Missouri Studies* 15 (October 1940): 1-184. Notes, bib., indexes.

Although women's secret societies receive a scant amount of attention here in comparison with that offered about men's fraternal organizations, the study is noteworthy for its details about ranks in the women's lodges, names of female auxiliaries paired with men's groups, symbolic titles, and group mottoes. Gist provides definitions and classifications for secret societies and discusses the rise and development of fraternalism in the United States, the process and structure in secret societies, theories and legends of origin, ritualism, symbolism, selection and control of members, dogma and doctrine, and economic and social functions. The women's groups that are discussed include Ladies of the Royal League, Job's Daughters, Ancient Order of Hibernians' Ladies Auxiliary, Ladies of the Maccabees, Daughters of Mokanna, Shepherd's Consistory, Order of the Eastern Star, Daughters of the Nile, Mysterious Witches of Salem, White Shrine of Jerusalem, Heroines of Jericho, Order of the Amaranth, True Kindred, Order of Beauceant, Order of the Rainbow, Women of the Mooseheart Legion, Home Chapter of the Moose, Nomads of Anrudaka, Daughters of Norway, Patriotic Order of Daughters of America, Daughters of St. George, Ladies of the Royal Arcanum, Dames of Malta, Woodmen Circle, Daughters of Ruth, Degree of Honor Protective Association, Women of the Ku Klux Klan, Daughters of Hermann, Daughters of Isabella, Companions of the Forest, Lady Knights, Household of Ruth, Pythian Sisters, Pythian Sunshine Girls, Ladies of Omega of the World (Negro), Daughters of the Sphinx, Daughters of Jerusalem, Daughters of Tabor, Ladies of Honor, Ladies of Security, Ladies of the Cross, Ladies of the Knights, and Hospitalers of St. John of Jerusalem.

215 *m GITTELL, MARILYN, and TERESA SHTOB. "Changing Women's Roles in Political Voluntarism and Reform of the City." *Signs* (Supp.) 5 (1980): 567-78. Notes, illus.: class of immigrant mothers learning English in 1910.

Although women in national and municipal electoral political organizations have been marginal in influence, they used voluntary associations to channel their interests and energies effectively. The authors survey the organizational vehicles for women's activity, beginning with the New York City Female Moral Reform Society of 1834 and moving to the Charity Organization Society, National Council of Jewish Women, General Federation of Women's Clubs, Women's Christian Temperance Union, settlement movement, Women's Trade Union League, League of Women Voters, and National Consumers' League. Finally they examine 1960s and 1970s activism through neighborhood organizations linked to the Congress of Neighborhood Women and the National Welfare Rights Organization.

216 *s GLAZER, PENINA MIGDAL. "Organizing for Freedom." *Massachusetts Review* 13 (Winter-Spring 1972): 29-44. Notes, bib.

Glazer exposes differences among suffragists at the turn of the century. Left-wing radicals, as different as anarchist Emma Goldman and millionaire Alva Vanderbilt Belmont, could agree that women's rights should be expanded, but they diverged on most other questions. The leadership in the National American Woman Suffrage Association was limited in its vision, and one must look to settlement house workers and the Women's Trade Union League to locate reformers alert to the needs of working-class women.

217 *w GOLDSTEIN, MARK L. "Blue-Collar Women and American Labor Unions." *Industrial and Labor Relations Forum* 7 (October 1971): 1-35. Notes.

Examining women's long efforts to organize in the workplace, Mark L. Goldstein cites the 1835 founding of a citywide federation of women's unions called the Female Improvement Society for the City and County of Philadelphia. It represented five hundred women who pressured for better wages. In the 1840s, the more widely known Lowell Female Reform Association formed. Goldstein surveys the support offered by the American Woman Suffrage Association, the Working Women's Protective Union established by the National Woman Suffrage Association, and the National Women's Trade Union League and its aid to the 1910 "Uprising of the 20,000," its training school for labor organizers, and its assistance to the International Ladies Garment Workers Union. In Part 2 of his essay, he discusses the women's organizations during World War I, notably the National Consumers' League and the National Woman's Trade Union League. Part 3 moves to contemporary questions raised by women in the workplace.

218 *r GOLOMB, DEBORAH GRAND. "The 1893 Congress of Jewish Women: Evolution or Revolution in American Jewish Women's History." *American Jewish History* 70 (September 1980): 52-67. Notes.

In 1893, the Jewish Women's Congress was held in Chicago in conjunction with the World's Columbia Exposition. The conferees upheld traditional standards of femininity and propriety, but devised new routes for female thought and action independent of men. The roots of the new voluntarism lay in local charitable and study societies. In 1819, for example, Rebecca Gratz founded the Female Hebrew Benevolent Aid Society of Philadelphia, the first Jewish woman's organization in the United States. Philadelphia women organized a Sunday school in 1838, and Baltimore women founded a Ladies Sewing Society. In 1846, New York City women established lodges in connection with the Independent Order of True Sisters. Excluded from Christian organizations and unwelcome in suffrage associations, the Jewish women gravitated to clubs of their own, where they addressed many of the public issues that other women's organizations spotlighted. If the nineteenth-century groups were not feminist in content or implication, they were nevertheless pivotal in enabling a Jewish women's collectivity to take shape.

219   *m   GOOD, BARBARA J.   "Significance of Woman's Organizations in the Advancement of Women in the United States." *Indian Journal of American Studies* 13 (July 1983): 97-100.

The author, a worker for the U.S. National Commission for UNESCO, has collected information on the status of women and the history of their voluntarism in the United States. In her survey, she includes the work of the abolitionists, early suffragists, American Association of University Women, Young Women's Christian Association, General Federation of Women's Clubs, National Woman's party, League of Women Voters, National Federation of Business and Professional Women, religious organizations, labor unions, National Organization of Women, Girl Scouts, and new groups of blacks, Chicanas, students, farmwomen, and radical feminists. In these groups, Good views women as taking initiative, mobilizing their communities, breaking with traditional roles for women, helping other women, and acquiring leadership skills.

220   *m,c   GOODFRIEND, JOYCE D., and DONA K. FLORY. "Women in Colorado before the First World War." *Colorado Magazine* 53 (Summer 1976): 201-28. Notes, illus.: 7 of women at school, work, and with families.

Goodfriend examines women's lives in four arenas--in their personal lives, in education, in the work force, and in voluntary organizations. She lists clubs, archives, and sources available to scholars of Colorado women's groups, and discusses the achievements of the Northside Woman's Club in Denver. One of its leaders, Martha A.B. Conine, moved on to become a state legislator.

221 *f,b GOODHUE, LAURA S. *History of the International Order of the King's Daughters and Sons. Vol. 2, 1931-1946.* Plainfield, N.J.: the organization, 1946. v, 323 pp.

A sequel to the Gugle study on 1886-1930 (see Sara F. Gugle), this work only summarizes briefly the early history of the organization. In 1886, ten women in New York formed a circle "to develop their own spiritual life and to help them be a blessing to the world." In 1888, the group incorporated as "The Order of the King's Daughters." In 1891, however, men and boys desired membership and Canada and foreign missions had established branches, so the name was changed to the International Order of the King's Daughters and Sons and the object articulated as the "development of spiritual life and the stimulation of Christian activities." The author is highly sympathetic to the organization. She served as an officer in her home state of Ohio and became the executive secretary of the order at headquarters in New York for eight years. Part 1 is organized chronologically, providing a report of events of 1931 through events of 1946. These chapters summarize the annual meeting of the Central Council, including the entire roll call of participants, the annual meeting of the general convention, and the week of sponsored activities at Chautauqua, New York. Officers, speakers, projects for good works, and efforts to expand membership are covered. Part 2 provides a history of departments and branches, each written by a different woman member. Departments surveyed include around the world, Indian (Native American), young people's, and young women's. Also examined are thirty-four states, northern California, southern California, unorganized states, Canada and six of its provinces, and Shanghai. All are treated for the numbers of circles, the types of relief work accomplished, especially during World War II, the dates and places of regional conventions, and the contributions of significant officers. Attention is paid to the building of headquarters at 144 E. 37th Street, New York City (in 1933) and the reception room at the Century of Progress Exposition in Chicago in 1933. The religious motivation for the organization is woven throughout this richly detailed account.

222 *t GORDON, ELIZABETH PUTNAM. *Women Torch-Bearers: The Story of the WCTU.* Evanston, Ill.: the organization, 1924. xiii, 320 pp. Illus.: 31 of officers' facilities created by Francis Willard; fountain in Chicago, float in a Waterbury, Connecticut, parade; headquarters.

Written in 1924, this book celebrates both the fiftieth anniversary of the Women's Christian Temperance Union and the passage of the Eighteenth Amendment to the U.S. Constitution. In ten chapters, it surveys anecdotally the history and beliefs of the organization. Although it contains some detail about donors, officers, and international conferences, this is a persuasive and readable tract, not a compendium of facts and statistics. Beginning with the roots of the organization in the 1873-74 Woman's Crusade, it moves to discuss mobilization and organization, "Fight for a Clear Brain" (expert analysis of the dreaded results of alcoholism and WCTU campaigns to publicize the horrors of drink), the world organization, legislative achievements, patriotism and war, Prohibition, the story of the passage of the Eighteenth Amendment, the story of the passage of the Nineteenth Amendment for woman suffrage, and a survey of accomplishments at the fifty-year mark.

223 *s GORDON, FELICE D. *After Winning: The Legacy of New Jersey Suffragists, 1920-1947.* New Brunswick, N.J.: Rutgers University Press, 1986. x, 262 pp. Notes, bib., appendix, indexes, illus.: representatives of Consumers' League of New Jersey and other women's organizations looking on as Governor George Silzer signs night work bill into law on 21 March 1923.

After surveying the long fight by New Jersey women to win the vote from 1857 to 1920, Gordon examines the direction taken by political women. Some joined the League of Women Voters, "a non-partisan organization created to inform citizens and work to pass specific legislation that would improve the welfare of home and the larger community." "Moral Plodders" of the 1920s worked through the New Jersey State Federation of Women's Clubs, the Consumers' League, peace organizations, and the New Jersey Woman's Committee for Law Enforcement. The author examines the "Equal Righters," who attempted to make an impact in the Republican and Democratic Parties. She describes the work of the New Jersey branch of the Woman's party to secure passage of an equal rights amendment. She features the work of six women: Helena Simmons, Lena Anthony Robbins, Caroline Wittpenn, Miriam Lippincott, Mary Philbrook, and Lillian Feickert. For the Great Depression of the 1930s, Gordon traces the development of the women's organizations already mentioned. For the 1940s, she explores their efforts to revise the state constitution and their failure to agree to support the ERA. Gordon's conclusion pinpoints the split among women over the magnitude of their differences from men. The appendix gives social characteristics of ninety-three suffragists of 1910-20.

224 *s -----. "After Winning: The New Jersey Suffragists in the Political Parties, 1920-1930." *New Jersey History* 101 (Fall-Winter 1983): 12-35. Notes, illus.: Lillian Ford Feickert; all-woman jury in 1920.

Some suffragists joined mainstream political parties in New Jersey in the 1920s, where they failed to win true political equality. Gordon blames the men as well as the women. Lillian Ford Feickert, who had been president of New Jersey's Woman Suffrage Association, was placed in charge of the Republican women. Florence Randolph organized the State Federation of Colored Women's Clubs for the Republican party. The two women successfully delivered a broad base of supporters to the party, sixty thousand members in 1922. The women were isolated from policy-making, however, and had little impact on the Republican party. By 1925, a faction of disgruntled "Official Women" replaced the old "Independents," abandoning aspirations to win official support for women's issues. Divided, the Women's Committee collapsed and disbanded in 1930. The group was superseded by the Women's State Republican Club of New Jersey. Gordon emphasizes, then, the isolation of women's issues in the early 1920s in the New Jersey Republican party and says the issues were ignored in the late 1920s. In both eras, women's politics made no inroads.

225 *b GORDON, JANET, and REISCHE, DIANA. *The Volunteer Powerhouse: The Junior League.* New York: Rutledge Press, 1982. 252 pp. Notes, indexes, illus.: 78 of clubhouses, officers, projects.

Cognizant of the relationship of the Junior League of America to the rest of the women's rights movement, Gordon surveys its history. She explains its origins in the turn of the century in the context of the burgeoning movement for woman suffrage, colleges, settlement work, and voluntary organizations. She explores the new socially responsible roles that debutantes like Mary Averell Harriman took on in creating a service organization for her peers. She documents the Junior League's growth and development, war service work during World War I, and the group's reorganization after the war at the hands of Dorothy Whitney Straight. In the 1920s, programs in children's theater and other arts were supported by League branches throughout the United States. In the depression, the members devoted themselves to relief programs. World War II brought renewed attention to war service. The postwar period brought "re-tooling for new realities" and participation in the civil rights movement, the women's rights movement, training for organizational activity, "projects for the people, 1960-82," and programs for the arts, history, and urban renewal. A recent move has been to tap the services of the increasing numbers of working women among their membership. The Junior League, no longer the exclusive domain of debutantes from the upper crust of society, recruits for a wider membership to enable stronger programs to be developed and carried out.

226   *y,f GORDON, LYNN D.   "Co-education on Two Campuses: Berkeley and Chicago, 1890-1912." In *Women's Being, Women's Place*, edited by Mary Kelley 171-93. Boston: G.K. Hall and Co., 1979. Notes.

Gordon compares women's campus clubs at two universities— University of California at Berkeley and University of Chicago—at the turn of the century. Among the groups she examines are the Associated Women Students of the University of California (founded in 1884), the XYZ Club for math, and Chemistry Friends.

227   *m GRADWOHL, REBECCA J. "Jewess in San Francisco, 1896." *Western States Jewish Historical Quarterly* 6 (July 1974): 273-76. (First published in *The American Jewess*, New York, October 1896.)

Jewish women were active in several turn-of-the-century San Francisco women's organizations. Among them were the Fruit and Flower Mission, Occidental Kindergarten, and Woman's Exchange. Mrs. I. Lowenberg presided over the Philomath Club, the only Jewish literary club of the city. She also headed the Laurel Hill Association Literary Circle, with a nonsectarian policy on membership.

228   *y,w GRAHAM, ABBIE. *Grace H. Dodge: Merchant of Dreams*. New York: Woman's Press, 1926. 329 pp. Illus.: Grace H. Dodge.

In a fourteen-chapter biography of Grace Dodge (1856-1914), two chapters are devoted to her work in women's organizations. Chapter 5, "The Best Known Working Women's Club Woman in America," discusses her efforts to found a network of clubs for working women. To the first national convention, held in 1890, seventy-five clubs representing 2,151 girls sent delegates. The author uses quotations from Dodge's speeches and from newspaper clippings about the organization. There is no documentation from the working women themselves, and the book neglects the dates of particular events discussed. Chapter 12 surveys Dodge's presidency of the National Board of the Young Women's Christian Association from 1906 and uses correspondence extensively to outline the accomplishments of her administration.

229 *t GRAHAM, FRANCES W. "Organization and Accomplishments
of the WCTU in New York." *Annals of the American Academy of
Political and Social Science* 32 (November 1908): 518-21.

The New York State Women's Christian Temperance Union
was founded in 1874 as a result of Dr. Dio Lewis's inspirational words
in a Fredonia public address. Graham explores the changes made over
time in the official pledge, describes the projects and issues supported
in the "Do Everything" policy, and surveys the work of state
conventions held in thirty-four years of activity.

230 *c GRANGER, MRS. A.O. "Effect of Club Work in the South."
Annals of the American Academy of Political and Social Science 28
(September 1906): 248-56.

Twelve southern states, including Oklahoma and the Indian
Territory, had active women's club federations. Granger surveys their
projects, including those devoted to arts and crafts, libraries,
kindergartens, manual training, music, civic improvement, civil service
reform, and child labor.

231 *s GRANT, MARILYN. "The 1912 Suffrage Referendum: An
Exercise in Political Action." *Wisconsin Magazine of History* 64
(Winter 1980-81): 107-18. Bib., illus.: 3 of Ada James with
colleagues in strategy session in 1912; Olympia Brown, Theodora
Winton Youmans, newspaper woman and president of the
Wisconsin Suffrage Association, 1913-20; Mrs. Katherine
McCullough speaking at Sister Bay, Dover County, 1912; a suffrage
gathering; State Senator David James with suffragists at 1919
ratification; 1912 broadside by antisuffragists; 1920 suffragists voting
in Racine polling place.

In 1885, Wisconsin women won support for a bill to authorize
women's participation in school elections, but worked longer to achieve
a referendum, in 1912, for woman suffrage in the state. The Reverend
Olympia Brown was a leader of the suffrage movement, presiding over
the Wisconsin Woman Suffrage Association for twenty-five years. By
1900, her leadership was stale, and only seventy members belonged to
the organization. Since Mrs. Brown refused to relinquish control of her
organization, Senator David James's daughter, Ada James, presided
over a new Political Equality League. Her administration brought in
assertive political action, a speakers bureau, outdoor meetings, labor
gatherings, film showings of *Votes for Women*, foreign-language
speakers, and author junkets. In 1913, the two suffrage organizations
merged for the final push to win state suffrage in Wisconsin.

232 *p GREEN, FLETCHER M. "Women of the Confederacy in War Times." *Southern Magazine* 2 (1935): 16-20, 47-48.

Declaring southern women in the War between the States to have been as brave as Joan of Arc and humanitarian as Florence Nightingale, Green reviews their organizational success in assisting the war effort. Described is the work of the Sewing Circles (or Thimble Brigades), Soldiers Friends Associations, societies for relief, Refreshment Saloons, and Ladies Defense Associations which raised funds for supplies via fairs and bazaars. In 1862, Georgia women founded a Ladies Gunboat Association to raise money for gunboats. Richmond women followed, building the *Richmond*.

233 *n,c GRIDLEY, MARION E. *American Indian Women*. New York: Hawthorn Books, 1974. vi, 178 pp. Indexes, illus.: 16.

Included in this series of biographies of American Indian women is the life of clubwoman Roberta Campbell Lawson (1878-1940), "Leader of Three Million Women." She served as president of the General Federation of Women's Clubs from 1935 to 1938. Born in Alluwe, Indian Territory, her mother was Emeline Journeycake of Delaware and her father was Scottish. She attended Hardin College and majored in music. She translated old Delaware Indian melodies, collected chants, wrote songs, wrote a book on Indian music, and gathered a collection of Indian musical instruments. At the age of twenty-three, she married Eugene B. Lawson and organized the first woman's club in Nowata. She went on to serve with the Young Women's Christian Association and preside over the Oklahoma Federation of Women's Clubs. She also directed Tulsa's Oklahoma Historical Society, served as the only woman trustee at the University of Tulsa, and raised one son.

234 *r GRIPE, ELIZABETH HOWELL. "Women, Restructuring and Unrest in the 1920s." *Journal of Presbyterian History* 52 (Summer 1974): 188-89. Notes.

"Having spent a century building a million-dollar enterprise, culminating in the incorporation of the Woman's Board of Home Missions in 1915, Presbyterian women had seen that enterprise—and their one power base in the church—restructured out of existence in the Reorganization and Consolidation of the board and agencies in 1923" (p. 188). Gripe documents the explosion of Presbyterian women's mission work in the 1880s, only a short time after founding a network to sponsor women's home missions in 1878. The church fathers resisted women's authority over their spending and undermined their organizational strength by restructuring their board in the early 1920s.

235 *z GRUBERG, MARTIN. *Women in Politics: An Assessment and Sourcebook*. Oshkosh, Wis.: Academia Press, 1968. viii, 336 pp. Notes, bib., indexes.

    General and brief portraits of several women's organizations are included in this sourcebook. Among them are the Women's Divisions of the Republican and Democratic parties, League of Women Voters, National Congress of Parents and Teachers Associations, auxiliaries to male veterans' organizations, patriotic organizations of descendants of early Americans, Women's International League for Peace and Freedom, the National Woman's party, National Council of Women, American Association of University Women, National Organization for Women, National Federation of Business and Professional Women's Clubs, National Consumers' League, Young Women's Christian Association, Women's Christian Temperance Union, and General Federation of Women's Clubs.

236 *z GRUENEBAUM, JANE. "Women in Politics." *Proceedings of the Academy of Political Science* 34 (April 1981): 104-20. Notes.

    Three stages of women's organizational life are analyzed. For the period 1840-70, the author discusses the split of suffragists into the American Woman Suffrage Association and the National Woman Suffrage Association over the Civil War amendments granting political rights to the black males. For the era 1890-1920, Gruenebaum examines the alliance between temperance and suffrage forces and the organization of groups for specific reform issues. Among the social feminists she names are those forming the Women's Trade Union League, General Federation of Women's Clubs, National Consumers' League, League of Women Voters, and National Woman's party. For the post-1960s era, the author examines the efforts of the National Organization for Women.

237 *s,z GUETHLEIN, CAROL. "Women in Louisville: Moving toward Equal Rights." *Filson Club Historical Quarterly* 55 (April 1981): 151-78. Notes.

    In her survey of women's rights activism in Kentucky history, Guethlein provides biographies of national women's rights figures who visited Louisville in the middle of the nineteenth century, including Elizabeth Cady Stanton and Lucy Stone. She also reviews the careers of local opponents like Presbyterian minister Stuart Robinson and Henry Wattermon, editor of the *Courier Journal*. In 1881, the National Woman Suffrage Association held its eleventh convention in Louisville and organized the Kentucky Woman Suffrage Association. Although Kentucky activist Laura Clay participated in the national organization, the local one did not flourish. However, Susan Howes Look Avery, founder of the Woman's Club of Louisville in 1890, ushered in a wave of interest in issues pertaining to the legal status of women, women's vote in school elections, women matrons in the jails, and an improvement of women's working conditions. An 1894 act to permit women to vote in school elections in the second-class cities of Kentucky was appealed in 1902, since "ignorant and degraded and especially Negro women voted in such large numbers as to outweigh the influence of educated and public-spirited women." This unveiled a racist tone in the suffrage movement of Kentucky. The author documents a rejuvenated movement after 1910. The Louisville Woman Suffrage Association opened headquarters in 1914 and launched a public effort to assist in wartime relief. After women won the federal amendment for suffrage in 1920, Louisville suffragists rallied to the League of Women Voters, only a small number joining the National Woman's party.

238 *f GUGLE, SARA F. *History of the International Order of the King's Daughters and Sons: Vol. 1, 1886-1930.* Columbus, Ohio: the organization, 1931. 437 pp. Illus.: 201 of officers.

Forty-five years before the writing of this study, ten women formed the International Order of the King's Daughters and Sons to develop spiritual life and stimulate Christian activity. In 1930, it had grown to include sixty-five thousand members and spend two million dollars annually on service for the needy. Much of the text consists of histories of the thirty-two state branches and six Canadian branches. For each, we learn of the number of circles, the size of membership, the name of the first president, services provided, cooperation with churches, educational institutions, hospitals, homes for the aged or for epileptics, restrooms for factory women on their lunch hours, and Travelers' Aid societies. Many state histories include lists of conventions. In the chapters on Maryland and Mississippi are references to "colored circles," which seem to have been dropped at some point in history. The ten founders each enjoy a biography and reports from the general conventions provide details about the work of the president, secretary, and treasurer, plus projects undertaken, deaths of members, awards given, activity in Chautauqua, and resignations among the officers.

See Laura S. Goodhue for the second volume of this history.

239 *t GUSFIELD, JOSEPH R. *Symbolic Crusade: Status, Politics and the American Temperance Movement.* Urbana: University of Illinois Press, 1963, 1972. 198 pp. Notes, indexes.

A sociologist, Gusfield examines moral reform as a political and social issue in U.S. history. He focuses on temperance because of the issue's persistence and power in the American past. He weaves the work of the Women's Christian Temperance Union throughout his portrait of the late nineteenth-century temperance movement and gives the organization credit for securing laws in every state for public school instruction on temperance. Gusfield asserts that the WCTU, in criticizing the existing social order, attracted members and supporters from conservative as well as progressive corners of America. Its endorsement of women's rights, including woman suffrage, the Populist party, and Christian socialism demonstrate President Frances Willard's success in rallying progressives to affirm issues of social control. The material in this study also appeared in Gusfield's doctoral dissertation and in his "Social Structure and Moral Reform: A Study of the WCTU," *American Journal of Sociology* 61 (November 1955): 221-32.

240 *c GWYNN, DOROTHY. "Friends of American Writers: Encouraging Writing and Thoughtful Reading." *Chicago History* 10 (1981): 38-43. Bib., illus.: Oak Park Library where Friends of American Writers organized in 1922; Anne Morgan's studio in Fine Arts Building; a meeting place founder, Nettah Bohr; 1933 group with Carl Sandburg; speakers Dorothy Thompson and Phyllis Bottome; 1980 awards luncheon; 1981 group photo.

In 1922, a leader of the Illinois Federation of Women's Clubs, Mrs. John Bohr of Oak Park, Illinois, founded Friends of American Writers. The object of this organization was to "study American literature, encourage high standards and promote literary ideals among American writers." The members, determined "to counteract jazz in literature and sensationalism in journalism," invited writers to read or lecture on literary topics to the group. Membership peaked at four hundred in the 1940s, and dipped to two hundred in 1981. Members also met to review books at literary teas. Between the years 1924 and 1928, the club established neighborhood reading groups all over the city. The club also sought donations and held fund-raising events to fund awards in literature.

241 *m HALL, CLARENCE W. "America's Amazing Women." *Reader's Digest* 67 (July 1955): 17-22.

Hall surveys the growth of women's organizations in the post-World War II era, asserting that American women even made an impact abroad, insofar as German and Japanese women observed U.S. soldiers' wives effecting change through voluntary associations and might have been inclined to emulate them. The author estimates that 20 million women belonged to 115 women's associations with 110,000 local chapters. At least half of the membership gave at least three hours per week to local community welfare activity, providing services worth $2.25 billion a year if one calculated their worth at merely minimum wage. Special attention is given to the work of the Junior League and Red Cross, although women, from girls to senior citizens, were eager participants in the movement.

242   *n HALL, JACQUELYN DOWND. *Revolt against Chivalry: Jessie Daniel Ames and the Woman's Campaign against Lynching.* New York: Columbia University Press, 1979, xiv, 373 pp. Notes, bib., indexes, illus.: 1 photograph of Jessie Daniel Ames.

Hall is a serious historian who carefully surveyed primary material in thirty-four collections of papers and conducted twenty-seven interviews with women who participated in the Association of Southern Women for the Prevention of Lynching founded in 1929 by Jessie Daniel Ames. This work is a biography of the founder, whose early participation in public life included activity in the Texas Woman Suffrage Movement. In 1919, when suffrage was won, Jessie Daniel Ames became the first president of the Texas League of Women Voters. She also became a representative from Texas to the Atlanta-based Committee on Interracial Cooperation. Ames moved to Atlanta and formed the ASWPL, which was successful in mobilizing a membership devoted to discouraging lynching in the 1930s. Hall does a thorough job, documenting Ames's success at cooperating with church women's groups to build her organization.

243 *n -----. "A Truly Subversive Affair: Women against Lynching in the Twentieth Century South." In *Women of America: A History*, edited by Carol Ruth Berkin and Mary Beth Norton, 360-80. Boston: Houghton Mifflin Co., 1979.

Hall provides a biography of Jessie Daniel Ames, founder of the Association of Southern Women for the Prevention of Lynching. She was born in East Texas in 1883, married, and had three children. Widowed in 1914, she moved to Atlanta and became active in voluntary associations. She founded the interracial organization for which she is known in 1930. Hall provides a sophisticated analysis of the issues its membership addressed.

244 *n -----. "Women and Lynching." *Southern Exposure* 4 (Winter 1977): 53-54. Notes, illus.: Jessie Daniel Ames in 1919; Alabama leaders meeting in 1938.

"Unlike most suffrage leaders, Jessie Daniel Ames brought the skills and political consciousness acquired in the women's movement to bear on the struggle for racial justice." To strengthen the Association of Southern Women for the Prevention of Lynching which she founded in 1930, she drew on evangelical women's missionary societies, the League of Women Voters, and Joint Legislative Council. She was able to collect forty-four thousand signatures on antilynching pledges. In the fourteen years of its existence, her group made impressive strides against the problem of lynching.

245 *c HARCUM, MRS. HARRY, et al., comps. and eds. *History of the Maryland Federation of Women's Clubs, 1899-1941*. Vol. 1. Federalsburg, Md.: J.W. Stowell Printing Co., 1941. 455 pp. Illus.: 100 of individual officers of the Maryland Federation of Women's Clubs; group photo of club members; sheet music of song (and pledge); furnished interiors of club houses.

Harcum surveys the early club movement in Maryland, discussing such antebellum societies as the Quaker settlement's Mutual Improvement Association in Sandy Spring. She goes on to survey the first thirty years of the Maryland Federation of Women's Clubs, or eight presidential administrations (1900-1930), including that of Mrs. John F. Sippel, became president of the entire General Federation of Women's Clubs. The peak of activity occurred between 1922 and 1926, when the Maryland Federation grew from 79 clubs to 120. The author features the work during the Great Depression, the junior clubs, the publication—*Maryland Clubwoman*—and the achievements of the six districts. Her portraits of each of the latter document the size, programs, conferences, and speakers of each district. Finally, she analyzes the relationship of the Maryland Federation to the General Federation and lists all resolutions made by the Maryland women between 1927 and 1940.

246   *r HARGROVE, BARBARA, JEAN MILLER SCHMIDT, and SHEILA GREEVE DAVANEY. "Religion and the Changing Role of Women." *Annals of the American Academy of Political and Social Science* 480 (July 1985): 117-31. Notes.

Between the 1860s and 1890s, women's foreign missionary societies were founded in thirty-three denominations of Protestantism and home missionary societies in seventeen. The authors observe that the decade of the 1920s saw the consolidation of women's missionary boards, usually accomplished by male clergy without consulting the women. Special attention is given to the work of Jewish women, who formed in 1893 the National Council of Jewish Women, to unite Reform Jews engaged in religious, educational, and philanthropic work. Conservative and Reform Jewish women united in Hadassah in 1912, the Woman's Division of the Zionist Organization of America. The survey also discusses the impact of the feminist movement on the church in the 1970s.

247   *m HARLEY, SHARON. "Beyond the Classroom: Organizational Lives of Black Female Educators in the District of Columbia, 1890-1930." *Journal of Negro Education* 51 (Summer 1982): 254-65.

Black female educators in Washington, D.C., played a role in the black urban community through voluntary associations during the years 1890-1930. Single women put great zeal into their organizations, which were secular rather than religious in purpose. The author explores the work of the National Association for the Relief of Destitute Colored Women and Children (founded in 1863), the Colored Woman's League (1892) which founded a day nursery, kindergarten, and a night school and held cooking and sewing classes for young women, the Colored Social Settlement (1902), Colored Young Women's Christian Association (1904), Women's Christian

Temperance Union, Harriet Beecher Stowe Mothers Club, Ladies' Auxiliary Committee, Sojourner Truth Home for Working Women and Girls, the National Training School for Women and Girls, Home for Friendless Girls, Woman's Republican League (1920), National Association of College Women (1924), National Association for the Advancement of Colored People, and the National Urban League.

248 *m HARPER, IDA HUSTED. *Associated Work of the Women of Indiana*. Indianapolis, Ind.: W.B. Burford, 1893. 52 pp. Indexes.

 "The watchword for today is organization," wrote Ida Husted Harper, an activist clubwoman herself. Here she surveyed the club accomplishments of her Indiana peers, first explaining that "literary clubs are not literary. No two are exactly alike. They are a body of women organized for mental improvement and social intercourse. The club provides a stimulation that domestic life alone does not." Harper lists eighty women's clubs in Indiana thriving in 1893. She then examines the histories of the Shakespeare Club, Fortnightly, Jewish Culture Club, Coterie, Tourist Club, Monday Club, History Class, Reform School for Girls and Women's Prison sponsored by women, orphan homes run by Propylaeum, which also built a Romanesque clubhouse in Indianapolis, Free Kindergarten and Children's Aid Society of Indianapolis, Women's Christian Temperance Union, suffrage associations, industrial clubs, Daughters of Rebekah, Eastern Star, Pythian Sisters, Ladies Auxiliary to the Brotherhood of Railroad Trainmen and Locomotive Firemen, Association of Collegiate Alumnae, Art Association, and Missionary Society. For each, she provides the date of origin, the goals asserted at national headquarters, the size in Indiana today, the projects, budgets, and branches developed. Unlike many such encyclopedias by local clubwomen, Harper does not provide portraits of individual club leaders.

249 *s,t -----. *The Life and Work of Susan B. Anthony*. 3 vols., Vol. 1, Indianapolis: Bowen-Merrill Co., 1898, xxiv, 1-513, illus.: 24, of Susan B. Anthony and her friends, activists in the women's rights movement. Vol. 2, Indianapolis: Bowen-Merrill Co., 1898, xi, 515-1110, indexes, appendixes, illus.: 24, of Susan B. Anthony and her suffragist friends. Vol. 3, Indianapolis: Hollenbeck Press, 1908, xvii, 1111-1633, indexes, appendixes, illus.: 23, of Anthony and suffragists.

 Susan B. Anthony spent her life in women's organizations devoted to women's rights issues, especially woman suffrage. Volume 1 of Harper's massive account, surveys her early participation in temperance, suffrage, and the antislavery movements. After the Civil War, she helped found the Women's Loyal League and campaigned for woman suffrage in New York State and Kansas. At the end of the 1860s, she founded the National Woman Suffrage Association and traveled the nation, speaking on behalf of the issue. Volume 2, which studies Anthony's suffrage activity between 1880 and 1897, includes her cooperation with women's clubs, the Women's Christian Temperance Union, the Woman's Building at the 1893 Chicago Exposition, the International Council of Women, and her speaking tours to organize for women suffrage. The third volume, published separately from the first two, examines her later life from 1898 to 1907, including her last efforts to achieve woman suffrage in the United States and abroad through the International Council of Women. Appendixes to volumes 2 and 3 contain supporting primary documents.

250 *s -----. "Woman Suffrage in Six States." *Independent* 71 (2 November 1911): 967-70.
On the heels of the passage of woman suffrage in Washington State and the eve of victory in Oregon, Harper surveys the earliest states to grant women the vote: Wyoming, Colorado, Utah, and Idaho.

251 *s HARPER, IDA HUSTED, ed. *The History of Woman Suffrage.* New York: National American Woman Suffrage Association, 1922. Vol. 5, *1900-1920,* xxiv, 817 pp., appendixes, indexes, illus.: 10 of Dr. Anna Howard Shaw, Elizabeth Cady Stanton, Susan B. Anthony, Lucy Stone, Lucretia Mott, Millicent Garrett Fawcett; Warren, Ohio, Court House (headquarters of NAWSA, from 1903-10); Susan B. Anthony House, headquarters until 1895; group photo in Washington, D.C., at suffrage headquarters on balcony. Vol. 6, *1900-1920,* viii, 899 pp., notes, appendixes, indexes, illus,: Carrie Chapman Catt; Susan B. Anthony Memorial Building at the University of Rochester.
Volume 5 covers the history of the woman suffrage movement from 1900 to 1920. After discussing the founding of the National American Woman Suffrage Association, Harper surveys each annual convention with generous quotations from addresses and local newspaper accounts of the meetings. She reports on the work accomplished at conventions in Washington, D.C., in 1902; New Orleans in 1903; District of Columbia, 1904; Portland, 1905; Baltimore, 1906; Chicago, 1907; Buffalo, 1908; Seattle, 1909; District of Columbia, 1910; Louisville, Kentucky, 1911; Philadelphia, 1912; District of Columbia, 1913; Nashville, 1914; District of Columbia, 1915; Atlantic City, 1916; District of Columbia, 1917; no wartime meeting in 1918; St. Louis in 1919, where President Carrie Chapman Catt led the celebration of the passage of the woman suffrage amendment and

called for a new organization, the League of Women Voters; and Chicago, 1920. Harper then provides a history of the federal suffrage amendment, beginning with the failure of women to win suffrage as part of the Civil War amendment to the Constitution. She surveys the work of various women suffrage associations, League of Women Voters, women suffrage in presidential conventions, and war service by suffragists.

The first forty-nine chapters of volume 6 consist of surveys of the history of woman suffrage in each state. Harper cites authors who were activists in a particular state, documenting the groups, leaders, campaigns, referenda, votes by legislators, names of supportive influential men, and strategies used in the twenty years previous to the passage of the suffage amendment. The quality and size of each chapter varies. Six pages on New Mexico appear, while New York enjoys ninety. Chapter 50 analyzes woman suffrage campaigns in the territories of Alaska, Hawaii, and the Philippines. Other chapters examine the struggle for woman suffrage abroad: in Great Britain, British colonies, and Europe. Finally, Harper provides a history of the International Woman Suffrage Alliance, which developed out of the International Council of Women. She quotes widely from addresses to these congresses: Berlin in 1904; Copenhagen, 1906; Amsterdam, 1908; London 1909; Stockholm, 1911; Budapest, 1913; Geneva, 1920.

See also Elizabeth Cady Stanton, et al. for volumes 1-3 of this account, and Susan B. Anthony and Ida Husted Harper for vol. 4.

252   No entry

253   *t HARRIS, KATHERINE. "Feminism and Temperance Reform in the Boulder WCTU." *Frontiers* 4 (Summer 1979): 19-24. Notes.

The Boulder Women's Christian Temperance Union in Colorado was organized in 1881 for social reform activity, especially the prohibition of alcohol. Its underlying objectives included an extension of women's autonomy and a rise in the status of women. Justifying its programs by invoking the wisdom of the "Christian Mother," the group established a reading room for young men, worked for a series of legislative reforms, supported education, and established in 1886 a Cottage Home for Unwed Christian Mothers. In 1893, it participated in the successful campaign to win women the vote. In 1914, the group saw Colorado pass prohibition.

254   *m HARTMANN, SUSAN M. "Women's Organizations during World War II: The Interaction of Class, Race, and Feminism." In

Mary Kelley, editor, *Woman's Being, Woman's Place*, edited by Mary Kelley, 313-28. Boston: G.K. Hall and Co., 1979. Notes.

Although feminism was alive in autonomous women's groups like the American Association of University Women, National Federation of Business and Professional Women, and Women's Trade Union League, middle-class clubwomen often ignored issues of primary concern to black women. Alpha Kappa Alpha and the National Council of Negro Women, for example, opposed discrimination, lynching, and the poll tax, and supported a permanent Fair Employment Practices Commission. Hartmann exposes the divisiveness arising from two different points of view.

255 *s HAUSER, ELIZABETH J. "The Woman Suffrage Movement in Ohio." *Ohio Magazine* 4 (February 1908): 83-92. Informational notes, illus.: exterior of headquarters of the National Woman Suffrage Association in Warren, Ohio, county courthouse; interior of headquarters; Harriet Upton Taylor; Caroline Severance; Enra Taylor (prosuffrage congressman); Rev. Antoinette Brown Blackwell; Rosa L. Segur; Caroline McCullough Everhard.

Ohio was hospitable to women and organizations devoted to women's rights. Early in the nineteenth century, it was the home of education and abolitionist leaders who would have a national impact on politics. In 1850, a woman's rights convention was held in Salem, and another the following year in Akron. In 1852, the Ohio Woman's Rights Association was founded in Massillon, the first state society of its kind. In Cleveland in 1869, the American Woman Suffrage Association formed under the leadership of Hannah Tracy Cutler.

256 *r HAYES, FLORENCE (SOOY). *Daughters of Dorcas: The Story of the Work for Home Missions Since 1802*. New York: Board of National Missions, Presbyterian Church in the United States, 1952. 158 pp. Appendix.

Presbyterian women formed Dorcas societies to support home missions through their churches as early as 1802. Members sewed together to collect money "for ailing missions among the heathen." A network of women's auxiliaries to the Board of National Missions was created in 1834. In 1878, the women formed their own Women's Executive Committee of Home Missions. By quoting correspondence and regulations, and relating stories sprinkled with observations by members on individuals, programs, and finances of the organization, Hayes leaves the reader with an understanding of the work with Indians, blacks, immigrants at Castle Green, New York, industrial workers in Chicago, and Hispanics. The women's meetings are described from the opening Bible reading and group prayer to adjournment. An appendix lists all female societies organized between 1803 and 1853, and includes a partial list of women on the board and staff.

257 *t HAYS, AGNES D. (MRS. GLENN G.) *The White Ribbon in the Sunflower State: A Biography of Courageous Conviction, 1878-1953.* Topeka: Women's Christian Temperance Union, 1953. 125 pp. Notes, illus.: Kansas delegation to the national WCTU convention in Denver, 1950; author, an Ohio and national officer; Elizabeth P. Hutchinson, Ohio and national officer; WCTU Building in Chautauqua Park, Winfield, Kansas; Willard Hall in Forrest Park, Ottawa, Kansas; 8 early presidents, 1879-99; 3 recent presidents, 1944-51; narcotic education exhibit; 1905 photo of twelve members with fifty-four children; Fort Scott White Ribbon recuits with their children, 1953.

    Hays surveys the organization of the Kansas WCTU in 1878 by Amanda Way of Lawrence; the WCTU campaign in 1880 for prohibition; humanitarian and charitable activities like the founding of an industrial school; the summer assemblies and the building of Frances Willard Memorial Hall, a headquarters, in Forrest Park in 1903; charitable projects like the Protective Home for Colored Aged and Orphans; Waifs Aid Society; work among soldiers and sailors; "Cookie Jar" campaign for soldiers; Carrie A. Nation Home for wives and children of drunkards; prohibition in Kansas since 1881; 21 biographies of women leaders in Kansas temperance including the notorious Carrie Nation; temperance education in the schools and colleges; work with young women; support for suffrage; *Our Messenger*, their publication; and prohibition repeal in 1948.

258 *s HAZARD, MRS. BARCLAY. "New York State Association Opposed to Woman Suffrage." *Chautauquan* 59 (June 1910): 84-89.
    See *Chautauquan.*

259 *n HEDGEMAN, ANNA (ARNOLD). *The Trumpet Sounds: A Memoir of Negro Leadership.* New York: Holt, Rinehart and Winston, 1964. 202 pp.
    This black woman's autobiography deals with her career as a staff woman in black branches of the Young Women's Christian Association from 1924 through the 1930s in Springfield, Ohio, Hersey City, New Jersey, Harlem, New York City, Philadelphia's Catherine Street Branch, and Brooklyn, New York, until the New York City mayor appointed her to serve in government. The author earned her

B.A. in 1922 in Hamline University in St. Paul, a Methodist school, and became a teacher at Rust College in Holly Springs, Mississippi. She describes her first encounters with Jim Crow trains and cabs en route to her work in the South. Much of her story deals with the separate black facilities established by the YWCA. Black branches had inferior facilities and steered her to become an activist for civil rights.

260　*m　HEFNER, LORETTA L. "The National Women's Relief Society and the U.S. Sheppard-Towner Act." *Utah Historical Quarterly* 50 (Summer 1982): 255-67. Notes, illus.: Amy Brown Lyman; Cottonwood Stake Maternity Hospital in 1924; Sen. William H. King, foe of the act.

　　　　A Mormon woman's organization, the National Women's Relief Society of the Church of Jesus Christ of Latter-day Saints, was in the forefront of important social legislation in the 1920s. This study examines the efforts of the membership between 1921 and 1928 to secure federal support for maternal and infant health care. The issue was painted by opponents as part of a Bolshevik plot to centralize social services in the United States, but the organization fought for its passage and renewal to ensure health centers, maternity homes, layettes for babies, and a reeducation in maternal and infant mortality. While the program was in existence, Utah was one of the five safest states in the nation for new mothers and babies. When the federal government withdrew its support for the act in 1928, Utah provided a state program until 1935.

261　*y　HENDEE, ELIZABETH RUSSELL. *The Growth and Development of the Young Women's Christian Association: An Interpretation*. New York: Woman's Press, 1930. ix, 83 pp. Notes.

　　　　A general study, with few facts to support its generalizations, this flowery essay illuminates the growth and development of the Young Women's Christian Association. It identifies the religious revivals of the 1850s as the impetus for women's prayer circles in New York, which became the foundation for the YWCA in 1858. Bible classes, an employment bureau for working women, and suitable boarding places were the hallmark of the new organization. In the following year, Boston women attempted to create a similar association, but ministers there opposed the program. Nevertheless, branches were founded in many American cities. In 1873, the first student YWCA was formed, in the Midwest, and it became common in midwestern coeducational schools of higher learning. New branches of the organization devised new programs, needlework exchanges for housebound widows with talents as seamstresses, travelers' aid bureaus to protect new girls in town from "white slavery," and day nurseries for working women. In 1887, a junior department was created for adolescent girls, stressing religion, education, recreation, employment, and housing. Thus, women of all ages, races, and classes enjoyed the services of the early YWCA.

262 *w HERRON, BELVA MARY. "The Progress of Labor Organization among women, Together with Some Considerations concerning Their 'Place in Industry.' " *University Studies* (University of Illinois) 1, no. 10 (May 1905): 1-70. Notes, indexes.

This study provides a history of the Women's Union Label League (1899) to encourage women to purchase union-made goods, to abolish child labor, and to gain a universal eight-hour workday. It also provides a chapter, however vague, on the Women's Trade Union League in America, inspired by an organization of the same name in Great Britain. The bulk of the essay, however, deals with women's trade unions, including those for boot and shoe workers, ladies garment workers, typographers, bookbinders, glove makers, cigar makers, potters, telegraphers, shirtwaist/laundry workers, bakery and confectionery workers, building tradeworkers, meat cutters, and teachers.

263 *n,s HERSH, BLANCHE GLASSMAN. *Slavery of Sex: Feminist Abolitionists in America.* Urbana: University of Illinois Press, 1978. xi, 280 pp. Notes, bib., indexes.

In a study of fifty-one women, Hersh relates the origins of feminism to the antebellum abolitionist movement. Although she is more concerned with biographies of individuals, her work is rich in references to women's voluntary organizations, including the Philadelphia Female Anti-Slavery Society, Massachusetts Female Emancipation Society, Anti-Slavery Society of Boston, Daughters of Temperance, and the Women's Temperance Society of New York State.

264 *m HEWITT, NANCY A. *Women's Activism and Social Change, Rochester, New York, 1822-1872.* Ithaca, N.Y.: Cornell University Press, 1984. 281 pp. Notes, indexes, tables.

A thoughtful and meticulous study, Hewitt confronts a web of women's voluntary associations in early Rochester, New York, and orders them to illuminate the extensiveness, permanence, and position of women's public labors. She identifies clubwomen in sync with the ideals of their spouses and class interests. In fact, she emphasizes that women's efforts and methods were determined by their families and social circles, reflecting the experiences and expectations they shared with men. To show this, the author dissects the techniques, goals, and leadership in Rochester's Female Charitable Society, Orphan Asylum Association, Home for Friendless and Virtuous Females, Industrial School, Female Moral Reform Society, Ladies' Anti-Slavery Society, and New York State Women's Temperance Society. Hewitt begins her monograph with the founding of the first secular philanthropic society in 1822 and ends on the date of Susan B. Anthony's famous attempt to vote in the election of 1872. Hewitt identifies the woman activists who reached beyond the domestic sphere as mostly white, Protestant, and middleclass. She divides them into three categories. First, she labels as "benevolents" the women from pioneer elite families, who established the earliest major social welfare institutions. They were the most cautious, apparently encountering little opposition to their public charitable efforts to aid the victims of circumstance. Second were "perfectionists," or bourgeois evangelicals, the wives of the merchants and trades prospering from the commercialization and urbanization of the Erie Canal city. These women were fueled by aspirations ignited by the Great Awakening and evangelist Charles Finney. At first they sought to eradicate the problems of a newly burgeoning city. In the face of criticism regarding the propriety of ladies' acquaintance with debauchery, they retreated, settling for the salvation of potential prey to vice. Hewitt paints these two groups as closely allied, differing only in emphasis. The final category, "ultrasists," consists of agrarian Quaker radicals, the most marginal of the women, who had fewer resources to lighten their domestic responsibilities and leave time for work. These, however, organized around issues of alcoholism, slavery, capital punishment, communitarianism, spiritualism, health reform, dress reform, and women's rights. The author neatly explores the three groups' changes and interactions over time. Twenty-two tables spell out details on the profiles of club members analyzed in the text, including composition of households, occupations of husbands, religious affiliation, marital status, number of children, and birthplace.

265   *p HILL, FRANK ERNEST. *The American Legion Auxiliary, A History: 1924-1934.* Indianapolis, Ind.: American Legion Auxiliary, 1935. viii, 286 pp. Indexes, illus.: presidents' and officers' portraits.

After World War I, veterans founded the American Legion. Soon afterward, they created a women's auxiliary to support their aims. The membership drew on the forty thousand American women who saw active service in the war in addition to near relatives of Legionnaires. The history surveys women's contributions to the war effort and documents the 1920s programs for Americanism, rehabilitation, child welfare, and national defense, and the drive for legislation to compensate disabled veterans and dependents of certain deceased soldiers. Hill summarizes the accomplishments of regular conventions of the auxiliary and details the building of American Legion headquarters in Indianapolis with a suite for women. He devotes specific chapters to women's work in the hospitals, care for war children, participation in the Poppy Crusade, support for the Paris Conference in 1928, and the formation of a World Auxiliary. By 1930, with a membership of 406,000 women members, the auxiliary launched a broad campaign to serve the veteran in the Great Depression.

266　*r　HILL, PATRICIA R. "Heathen Women's Friends: The Role of the Methodist Episcopal Women in the Women's Foreign Mission Movement, 1869-1915." *Methodist History* 19 (April 1981): 146-54. Notes.

In 1869, eight Boston women met to finance the work of women missionaries who sought to educate the secluded women of India and China. Their efforts spread to eleven American branches of the Methodist Episcopal Women's Foreign Mission Movement. By 1896, a half million women participated in fund-raising work for foreign missionary work by women, and by 1915, there were 3 million members. Hill asserts that foreign mission work provided an ideal arena for relatively conservative, middle-class women who wanted to engage in social service and reforms but felt threatened by radical feminism. The organization was successful, between the years 1869 and 1915, in sending 687 female missionaries to stations abroad.

267　*r　-----. *The World Their Household: The American Woman's Foreign Mission Movement and Cultural Transformation, 1870-1920.* Ann Arbor: University of Michigan Press, 1985. 231 pp. Bib., indexes.

This scholarly book traces the growth and development of four white Protestant American women's organizations devoted to foreign missions, from 1869 through their decline just before World War I. The author ingeniously uses fiction, largely from association periodicals, to illustrate early fervor among the huge membership for fund-raising fairs and personalized adoptions of foreign children in mission schools. Less attention was devoted to Bible study and poetry. Hill also documents the professionalization and secularization of the association at the turn of the century, when businesslike managers, efficient financial campaigns, and systematic courses of study attracted younger members but alienated the founders. Despite its care to remain distant from the feminist movement of the era, the foreign mission organizations declined after 1915, owing to the appeal of new sources of activities for American women. Here is a serious examination of a heretofore neglected field in which "proper ladies" acquired skills and social benefits of all kinds and came to wield considerable influence abroad and within their own churches.

268 *t HILLERMAN, ABBIE B., comp. *The History of the Women's Christian Temperance Union of Indian Territory, Oklahoma Territory, State of Oklahoma*. Sapulpa, Okla.: Jennings Printing and Stationery Co., 1925. 111 pp. Illus: 21, of officers including founders L. Jane Stapler, Mrs. GB Hester and the author, Abbie B. Hillerman.

The Women's Christian Temperance Union had two organizations in Oklahoma until a merger took place in 1908. Hillerman first documents the history of the WCTU in the Indian Territory, founded in 1888 under the leadership of Jane Hicks Stapler, daughter of Chief Elijah Hicks, who commanded the first thousand Cherokee during their removal from Georgia to the Indian Territory in 1836-37. While no early records of the organization were available to Hillerman, her account examines each convention before 1908, listing the place of the meeting, the names of officers, guest speakers and committees, budgets, size of membership, projects undertaken, resolutions passed, music performed, and devotionals that took place. The second section of her book surveys the history of the WCTU, which was founded immediately after the Oklahoma Territory was opened to homestead settlement in 1889. For 1890 through 1908, she summarizes the work of each WCTU convention and elaborates on the victorious struggle to attach prohibition to statehood in 1907. The author of this volume was instrumental in this campaign. Part three of the work examines the merger of the two groups in 1908 and its projects through 1925, including wartime relief work, support for woman suffage, and a huge celebration for the federal suffrage amendment to the constitution.

269 *p HINTON, MARY HILLARD. "Practical Work of the Daughters of the Revolution in North Carolina." *Magazine of History* 12 (November 1910): 253-60.

In 1896, on the anniversary of the surrender of Cornwallis, Mrs. Spier Whitaker, who was a lineal descendant of William Hooper, founded the Daughters of the Revolution in North Carolina. Devoted to history, literature, and patriotism, the sixty-six members embarked on a program of delivering papers, publishing eleven volumes of articles in the *North Carolina Booklet*, and placing a memorial tablet in Raleigh at the Capitol Rotunda to commemorate the Edenton Tea Party of

1774, when fifty-one North Carolina women pledged to boycott British tea. The author surveys the work of each chapter in the state, praises the work of the genealogy department of the organization, and enumerates the exhibits members have placed in the Hall of History in Raleigh and the contributions they have made to the establishment of historical monuments.

270   *p HOAR, JAY S. "Susan Haines Clayton, American Lady, 1851-1948." *Oregon Historical Quarterly* 84 (Summer 1983): 206-10. Notes, illus.: Tom and Susan Clayton; Mrs. Clayton in her nineties.

This biography of Susan Haines Clayton, a Union nurse in the Civil War, documents her founding in 1875 of the first Women's Relief Corps in Kansas. She went on to found a branch of the same organization in Columbia Falls, Montana. She moved to Oregon in 1905 and spent the rest of her life there, joining the Daughters of Union Veterans.

271   *m HODER-SALMON, MARILYN. "Myrtle Archer McDougal: Leader of Oklahoma's 'Timid Sisters.' " *Chronicles of Oklahoma* 60 (Fall 1982): 332-43. Notes, illus.: Myrtle Archer McDougal.

Myrtle McDougal was a leading figure in the woman's club movement, suffrage fight, Democratic party politics, and health reform and world peace efforts. This biography surveys her work in Sapulpa, Oklahoma, where she founded the Current Events Club, Red Cross, and Daughters of the Confederacy's Thomas Wells Chapter. In 1905, she served as president of her city's federation of women's clubs. She was also active as a temperance lecturer. Between the years 1906 and 1913, she presided over the Indiana Territory Federation of Women's Clubs.

272   *z HOFF-WILSON, JOAN, ed. *Rights of Passage: The Past and Future of the ERA.* Bloomington: Indiana University Press, 1986. xx, 140 pp. Bib., indexes, illus.: 8 of political cartoons.

A collection of eleven essays, this work illuminates the history of several women's organizations. "Alice Paul and the ERA," by Amelia R. Fry (pp. 8-24), relates the National Woman's party support for an equal rights amendment, an issue disdained by social reformers in the National Consumers' League, National Women's Trade Union League, Women's Christian Temperance Union, National Mothers and Parent-Teachers Associations, American Association of University Women, National Council of Jewish Women, and the federal government's Woman's Bureau. By 1938, however, some groups had moved to support the ERA. These included the National Federation of

Business and Professional Women, National Federation of Colored Women, Women's International League for Peace and Freedom, and national professional associations of women workers. Kathryn Sklar has contributed "Why Were Most Politically Active Women Opposed to the ERA in the 1920's?" to this collection. She concludes, "By far the chief origin of resistance to the early ERA was the fear generated among opponents that the amendment would invalidate a wide range of labor and health legislation that women reformers during the past thirty years had struggled to obtain for American working and poor women" (p. 26). In focusing her remarks on the career of Florence Kelley, Sklar discusses the work of the National Consumers' League, in which Kelley was a key participant. In "The ERA: Postmortem of a Failure in Political Communication" (pp. 76-89), Edith Mayo and Jerry K. Frye also document the split ERA engendered between the National Woman's Party and other women's voluntary associations in the 1920s.

273 *s HOFFECKER, CAROL E. "Delaware's Woman Suffrage Campaign." *Delaware History* 20 (Spring-Summer 1983): 149-67. Notes, illus.: Mabel Vernon; Delaware headquarters of Congressional Union, W. Florence Bayard Hilles, Alice Steinlein, and Mary Conkle; F.B. Hilles; Mary Wilson Thompson, antisuffragist; crowd scene at a suffrage rally on Dover Green in 1920; cartoon depicting Delaware as country bumpkin blocking passage of suffrage.

Delaware's first woman suffrage organization was born as the Franchise Department in the Women's Christian Temperance Union (1888). By 1896, however, Delaware's Equal Suffrage Association was formed and it affiliated with the National American Woman Suffrage Association. Only ninety members belonged to it by 1911, however, and it took Alice Paul to revive the suffrage issue. She recruited Mabel Vernon of Wilmington, a fearless stump speaker, to open a Delaware office. In May 1914, four hundred marchers participated in the Wilmington suffrage parade. Vernon went to Washington, D.C., to heckle President Woodrow Wilson, and she was arrested and jailed for her White House demonstrations. The author also details the arguments of the antisuffragists in Delaware and documents the racism lingering in the former slave state. The House of Representatives in Delaware voted against bringing the suffrage amendment before it for ratification, indicating the strong forces opposed to woman suffrage in the state.

274 *t HOGE, SARA H. "Organization and Accomplishments of the WCTU in Virginia." *Annals of the American Academy of Political and Social Science* 32 (November 1908): 527-30.

The Women's Christian Temperance Union formed a Virginia branch in Richmond in 1883. A long list of legislation supported by the membership is included in this history. The organization established a newspaper of its own, the *Virginia Call*, used here by Hoge to illustrate the group's activism on a wide range of social issues.

275 *t HOHNER, ROBERT A. "Prohibition Comes to Virginia: The Referendum of 1914." *Virginia Magazine of History and Biography* 75 (October 1967): 473-88. Notes.

The Virginian Women's Christian Temperance Union had a membership of six thousand in 1914, and the organization was tremendously active and effective in winning prohibition. Hohner details the efforts of the women in distributing leaflets, putting seven posters in Virginia stores, holding parades, and calling public meetings in the summer before Election Day, 1914. Virginia prohibition took effect on 1 November 1916.

276 *b HOLMES, ANNE MIDDLETON. *Southern Relief Association of New York City, 1866-1867*. New York: Mary Mildred Sullivan Chapter, United Daughters of the Confederacy, 1926. 115 pp.

Between February 1867 and June 1867, the Southern Relief Association of New York City raised and donated $10,800 to the Confederacy. Holmes's study includes fifty letters from southern white women asking for aid during wartime. Printed in full is the 1868 report of the association, listing all contributors and clergymen to whom funds, from $25 to $1,200, were distributed. The women officers and managers of the organization are named.

277 *y HOOK, ALICE P. "The YWCA in Cincinnati: A Century of Service, 1868-1968." *Cincinnati Historical Society Bulletin* 26 (April 1968): 119-36. Notes, illus.: Mrs. John Davis, first president, 1868-81; headquarters from 1905 to 1929 at 1820 E. 8th Street; exterior of the Norwood branch that opened in 1921; 1920 Blue Triangle at 704 W. 8th Street for Negro girls; World War I class in auto mechanics.

In 1868, Cincinnati women incorporated to form a Christian institution to serve self-supporting women. Founders raised money for a home, opened a library, and embarked on city missionary work with women in the workhouse, county jail, hospital, city prison, and House of Refuge. Hook details their fund-raising efforts and the services they provided with their profits. Women held an apron festival in 1870, and raised $763 with an 1872 program of tableaux vivants. The Young Women's Christian Association provided sewing classes, initiated an Industrial Institute which sponsored a laundry, offered business courses in bookkeeping and stenography, held picnics and summer camping trips, and expanded its facilities by creating branch homes all over the city.

278 *m HOOPER, PAUL F. "Feminism in the Pacific: The Pan-Pacific Southeast Asia Women's Association." *Pacific Historian* 20 (Winter 1976): 367-78. Notes, illus.: Jane Addams in Honolulu at 1928 conference; group photo of 1930 delegates; 1975 group photo.

    The Pan-Pacific Women's Association (now known as the Pan-Pacific and South East Asian Women's Association) was founded in 1930 by women from Hawaii, who were internationalists with transcultural goals. The idea for the group grew out of two conferences held on the status of women in the Pacific, in 1928 and 1930. The meetings were attended primarily by middle-class clubwomen, social feminists who belonged to the League of Women Voters and American Association of University Women. Attending the 1928 meeting were 274 women, emphasizing research and discussions more than activism. Peace and friendship dominated their concerns, and they supported the United Nations in 1949. The theme of their 1952 meeting was "Pacific in Today's World," in 1958, "The Role of Women in Community Development in the Pacific and in South East Asian Countries."

279 *b HOPKINS, DANIELLE L. *Fruit and Flowers: The History of Oregon's First Day Care Center*. Portland, Ore.: Fruit and Flower Child Care Center, 1979. xiii, 103 pp. Bib., appendixes, indexes, illus.: 31 of staff, children served, founders, and structures utilized.

    In 1885, eight schoolgirls, aged ten to fourteen, founded the Children's Flower Mission in Portland to deliver flowers to hospital patients and shut-ins. Disbanding in 1888, they reorganized in 1893 as the Portland Flower Mission, and in 1911 as the Portland Fruit and Flower Mission and Portland Fruit and Flower Day Nursery. Thus for nearly a century, their members visited the sick, brought baskets of food to the poor, and sewed for babies in foundling homes. Biographies are provided for the families of the girls who founded the organization. The day nursery opened in 1906, with a second branch attempted between the years 1912 and 1915. One section is devoted to fund-raising efforts and administration. Appendixes give a chronology of events from 1885 to 1978, a map of Portland with the residences of five founders and eight locations of nurseries used between 1906 and 1979, and a list of forth-seven board presidents between 1893 and 1979.

280 *b HORNBEIN, MARJORIE. "Frances Jacobs: Denver's Mother of Charities." *Western States Jewish Historical Quarterly* 15 (January 1983): 131-45. Notes, illus.: stained-glass portrait from Colorado State Capitol; Francis Jacobs Hospital of Denver, 1892.

      This biography of Frances Jacobs details the volunteer efforts of a Jewish woman in Denver. In 1887, she served as first vice president of the Denver Ladies' Relief Society. With the Reverend Myron Reed and Father William O'Ryan, she formed the Charity Organization Society. Among the volunteer programs she supported were a free kindergarten and a tubercular hospital. When she died at the age of forty-nine in 1892, the hospital for which she worked was named the Frances Jacobs Hospital of Denver.

281 *p HORNE, FLORA B. "History of the Society of the Daughters of Utah Pioneers." *Utah Genealogical and Historical Magazine* 3 (April 1912): 96-104.

      In 1897, when the state of Utah celebrated its fiftieth anniversary of the pioneers' entrance into the Great Salt Lake Valley, the Society of Utah Pioneers decided to form to honor those pioneers. Horne lists the names of the women who attended the 1901 conference, many of them daughters of the original 1847 pioneers. They decided to invite any female descendants, over the age of eighteen, of ancestors who had come to Utah before 1853, collected family genealogies, and held an annual encampment to elect officers. Branches in many counties were formed to expand the work of the organization.

282 *m HORVITZ, ELEANOR F. "The Jewish Woman Liberated: A History of the Ladies Hebrew Free Loan Association." *Rhode Island Jewish History Notes* 7 (November 1978): 501-12. Notes, illus.: Mrs. Harvey Shatkin; group of members; loan application; 2 officers.

      The Ladies Hebrew Free Loan Association was founded in 1931 in Rhode Island, offering twenty-five dollars to women who applied without the endorsement of their husbands. Since 1903, a Hebrew Free Loan Association had provided services to men, but now the women decided to provide for their own. A list of the charter members is provided here, along with an account of their first decade of accomplishments. In 1936, for example, sixty-seven women borrowed from the association, drawing on the dues and donations. The members celebrated their tenth anniversary with a luncheon and bridge party. In 1953, they supplied five thousand dollars to the building fund of the Jewish Home for the Aged in Rhode Island. In

1965, the group disbanded, feeling that the need for their service no longer existed.

283　*r -----. "The Years of the Jewish Woman." *Rhode Island Jewish History Notes* 7 (November 1975): 152-70. Notes, illus.: group photos in 1950, 1952, and 1953; festival picnics in 1961 and 1963.

This article discusses the various benevolent organizations Jewish women established in Rhode Island between the years 1877 and 1975. Included among them are: Montefiore Lodge Ladies Hebrew Benevolent Association (1877); Ladies Hebrew Union Aid Association (1887), which founded the Jewish Home for the Aged; and the Ladd School at Exeter, Rhode Island. The author quotes and documents the organizations and lists the names of officers. She describes charitable projects undertaken and fund-raising methods that met with success.

284　*c HOWE, JULIA WARD. "A Chronicle of Boston Clubs." *New England Magazine* 34 (July 1906): 610-15. Illus.: Julia Ward Howe.

Consummate Boston clubwoman Julia Ward Howe here describes the history of several local clubs. She examines the work of the Daughters of Liberty; Boston Sewing Circle; music clubs; Ladies' Social Club, or "The Brain Club"; Metaphysical Club, an offshoot of the Concord Summer School of Philosophy; the Society to Encourage Studies at Home (1873), the brainchild of Anna Eliot Ticknor; the New England Woman's Club; and the Saturday Morning Club. Of the last two, Howe speaks from personal experience.

285　*c,s -----. Reminiscences: 1819-1899. Boston: Houghton Mifflin and Co., 1899.

Although most of the twenty chapters in this autobiography catalog family and friends of the author, she devotes chapter 17 to the woman suffrage movement (pp. 372-400). Among the women's organizations she links to her own campaign for women's rights: the New England Woman's Club, Sorosis, and Association for the Advancement of Women.

286　*r HOWELL, MABEL KATHARINE. *Women and the Kingdom: Fifty Years of Kingdom Building by the Women of the Methodist Episcopal Church, South, 1878-1928.* Nashville: Cokesbury Press, 1928. 283 pp. Notes, bib., illus.: Miss Lochie Rankin, pioneer missionary in China for 50 years to whom volume is dedicated.

Ten chapters divide this history of the women's missionary work in the Methodist Episcopal Church, South, between the years 1878 and 1928. When the organization was founded, the slogan adopted was "Woman's Work for Women," but Howell makes the point that the motto was outgrown, as members demonstrated "Woman's Work *with* Women." Calling the effort a "missionary sisterhood, or cooperative movement for the Christianization of womanhood around the world," the author begins with church authorization for women to organize to "take the gospel of Christ to womanhood in other lands." Wives of male missionaries first alerted members to the needs of foreign women, and churchwomen began to raise money for projects to solve women's problems abroad. Howell lists the fifteen pioneer societies formed in 1878-79, describing their growth, publications, prayer and Bible study activity, as well as missionary projects. Going on to stress the accomplishments of the women rather than their interaction at home, she details their support of colleges, high schools, elementary education abroad, evangelistic work, and medical and social services.

287　*c　HUBBARD, ALICE. "Flat Women Are Sharp Minded." *Alaska Life Magazine* 8 (April 1942): 9-10, 18. Illus.: 4 including a group photo of 6 of the charter members of the Thursday Club in Flat, Alaska.

An isolated mining town in Alaska, the town of Flat was the site of a woman's club founded in 1937 by ten women who desired to socialize and study together. Meeting the last Thursday of each month, they called themselves the Thursday Club. Each meeting included a paper delivered by a member, a discussion of current events, and a table with three types of refreshments. The members acquired a library for the town by donating books; the doors opened with a collection of twenty-four volumes. The women also sponsored the town's Fourth of July celebration and cleaned the cemetery. In 1938, they invited every woman in town to join and the group grew to twenty-four members. The club name was also changed to the Woman's Club of Flat. World War II relief work was uppermost on the club's agenda in the 1940s.

288　*c　HUBBELL, THELMA LEE. "The Friday Morning Club: A Los Angeles Legacy." *Southern California Quarterly* 50 (March 1968): 59-90. Illus.: exterior of Friday Morning Club in 1924.

Caroline Severance founded the Friday Morning Club in Los Angeles in 1891. The biography provided here explains that she was already an experienced clubwoman, having founded one of the first woman's clubs in America, in Boston in 1868—the New England Woman's Club. When she moved to California in 1875, she attempted to create a counterpart, but it fell apart when she left town for a New England visit. In the 1880s, however, organized women of Los Angeles formed the Ruskin Art Club and the Flower Festival Home Society. This author is generous with detail about the early women officers of the Friday Morning Club including Eliza Donner and Charlotte Wells, and lists all presidents from 1894 to 1963.

289   *n HULL, GLORIA R., ed. *Give Us Each Day: The Diary of Alice Dunbar-Nelson*. New York: W.W. Norton and Co., 1984. 480 pp. Indexes, illus.: 42, including Alice Dunbar-Nelson; delegates to Delta Sigma Theta sorority convention; Dunbar-Nelson and 3 clubwomen in New York City in the late 1920s.

Alice Dunbar-Nelson's diaries, as well as the biography by editor Gloria T. Hull in the introduction, contain considerable detail about the club activity of this black teacher, suffragist, wife of poet Paul Laurence Dunbar, writer and speaker (1875-1935).   Among the woman's clubs in which she was active: National Federation of Colored Women's Clubs, National Association of Colored Women, Delta Sigma Theta sorority, Woman's Committee of the Council of National Defense, International Council of Women of the Darker Races, Inter-racial Council of the Federal Council of Church Women, League of Colored Republican Women, New Jersey State Federation of Colored Women's Clubs, Philadelphia Professional Woman's Club, Research Club, Temple of the Daughters of Elks, and Fireside Club. She was the first black woman to serve on the State Republican Committee of Delaware (1920).

290   *n HUNDLEY, MARY S. "The National Association of College Women." *Opportunity: Journal of Negro Life* 3 (June 1925): 185.

This is a survey of the first two years of accomplishment of the National Association of College Women. It was founded in 1923 in Washington, D.C., "to unite all colored college women to improve education." Branches formed in eleven cities, devoted not to social or political activity but to surveys of living conditions among colored girls in northern colleges, creation of a research bureau to publish the findings, and improvement of interracial relations. Hundley provides a complete list of officers of the organization.

291   *b HUNT, MARION. "Women and Child-Saving: St. Louis Children's Hospital, 1879-1979." *Missouri Historical Society Bulletin* 36 (January 1980): 65-79. Notes, illus.: Mrs. Frank Blair and 3 succeeding presidents of the board; first home, St. Louis Children's Hospital, 1879-84; children's and mothers' waiting room of the dispensary.

In 1879, the St. Louis Children's Hospital opened its doors with fifteen beds. Each woman on the board pledged to raise at least two hundred dollars each year by selling five dollar subscriptions. The article stresses institutional growth rather than details about the prominent women who followed Mrs. Appoline Blair who founded the institution.

292   *p HURN, ETHEL ALICE. *Wisconsin Women in the War between the States*. Madison: Wisconsin History Commission, 1911. xix, 190 pp. Indexes, illus.: Mrs. Cordelia A.P. Harvey; orphan home; soldiers home; office of soldiers; aid society.

Considerable detail is provided here regarding the work of Wisconsin women volunteers during the Civil War. The history begins with an account of the services women provided for the departing regiments, including the presentations of flags and the banquets for soldiers. Women formed Soldiers' Aid Societies as branches of the Sanitary Commission, and members knit articles and packed boxes of supplies for Wisconsin soldiers. Hurn lists the amounts contributed to the cause by each branch of volunteers. She features the work of the Milwaukee Soldiers' Aid Society, under the leadership of Henrietta Colt. The author explores the sacrifices made by wartime women, who coped with inflation, ran family farms and businesses, suffered destitution at home, and/or engaged in philanthropic efforts. She quotes women's letters to the front and celebrates their work in the hospitals. Hurn lauds the work of Cordelia A.P. Harvey, details the efforts of the Christian Commission which assisted the army chaplains by sending money and reading matter to the soldiers, and describes the embroideries and fancywork sent to the Northwest Sanitary Fair of 1863. Finally, she documents the history of women's fund-raising efforts to support the Milwaukee Soldiers' Home in 1894.

293   *m HURWITZ, EDITH F. "International Sisterhood." In *Becoming Visible: Women in European History*, edited by Renate Bridenthal and Claudia Koonz, 325-45. Boston, Houghton Mifflin Co., 1977. Notes, illus.: Carrie Chapman Catt.

This article surveys late nineteenth- century and early twentieth-century alliances between American and European women's rights advocates. In 1888, May Wright Sewall founded the International Conference of Women at a Washington, D.C., conference. Eleven women's societies affiliated with it numbered 6 million in membership. Until 1904, American leadership dominated the organization, which worked for political feminism (the vote) as well as social feminism (to correct women's disabilities through legal reform, temperance, higher education, career opportunities, and charitable work). In 1902, the International Woman Suffrage Alliance was founded by Carrie Chapman Catt, who was more single-mindedly devoted to the fight for woman suffrage around the world. In the 1920s, with suffrage granted in many nations of the world, women retained international ties, cooperating until World War II for peace and the League of Nations. In 1926, Catt's group changed its name to the International Alliance of Women for Suffrage and Equal Citizenship, signifying a broadening of the issues it considered. In 1925, a Joint Committee of Representative Women's Organizations coordinated efforts of the Women's International League for Peace and Freedom, the World's Women's Christian Temperance Union, the World's Young Women's Christian Association, the International Council of Nurses, World Union of Women for International Concord, and the International Federation of University Women.

294   *s HUTCHESON, AUSTIN E., ed. and intro. "The Story of the Nevada Equal Suffrage Campaign: Memoirs of Anne Martin." *University of Nevada Bulletin* 42 (August 1948): 1-19. Notes, illus.: Anne Martin, president of the Nevada Equal Franchise Society, 1912-14.

Austin E. Hutcheson, history professor at the University of Nevada, has provided biographical material on the life of Anne Martin and edited her remembrances of her leadership in the 1912-14 campaign to enfranchise Nevada women. The narrative is told in the third person and begins with her apprenticeship to British suffragist Emmeline Pankhurst in England from 1909 to 1911. In 1912, however, Martin returned to her home state of Nevada and led the Nevada Equal Franchise Society to pressure Nevada's legislators and voters to pass and ratify woman suffrage. Although Martin is generous in naming the other officers and pioneer organizers for suffrage throughout her state, it is clear that her three-thousand-mile auto tour around the state with Mabel Vernon made her the most visible suffragist in Nevada. Her travels, speeches, pamphlets, and organizational efforts won the support of labor. She chastises the Nevada Federation of Women's Clubs for endorsing suffrage only in the late stages of the campaign. Martin recounts the help from the College Equal Suffrage League, and suffragists who came from outside the state, and financial help from both the National American Woman Suffrage Association and the National Woman's party. When the vote was won, the Nevada Equal Franchise Society became the Nevada Woman's Civic League.

295 *m INGHAM, MRS. W.A., *Women of Cleveland and Their Work,
Philanthropic, Educational, Literary, Medical and Artistic, a History.*
Cleveland: W.A. Ingham, 1893. xiv, 362 pp. Indexes.

In thirty chapters, devoted to one thousand women and the
organizations in which they developed programs for medicine,
temperance, education, literary study, and the Woman's Exchange,
Ingham provides lists of leading Cleveland clubwomen and histories of
their clubs. Anecdotes as well as factual details are provided in this
dense reference work.

296 *w "Iowa Business and Professional Women, 1919-1970."
Palimpsest 52 (1971): 129-42.

See *Palimpsest*.

297 *t IRONMONGER, ELIZABETH HOGG, and PAULINE
LANDRUM PHILLIPS. *History of the Women's Christian
Temperance Union of Virginia and a Glimpse of Seventy-Five Years,
1883-1958.* Richmond, Va.: Cavalier Press, 1958. 325 pp. Bib.,
indexes, illus.: Frances E. Willard statue in Statuary Hall, Capitol
Building, Washington, D.C.; 8 national presidents; Broad Street
Methodist Church in Richmond, Virginia, where Willard spoke in
1881; Seventh Street Christian Church in Richmond, site of the first
state convention of the WCTU of Virginia in 1893; 8 Virginia state
presidents; 2 groups of children; group of women planning First
Youth Temperance Education Week in 1945; Hastings, England, site
of 1950 World's WCTU convention; White Rock Pavilion in
Hastings, England; state and general secretaries; proceedings of the
Youth Temperance Education Week; group and individual photos of
state and county officers; Emily O.L. Price, president of the Virginia
Sojourner Truth WCTU in 1955 (black group organized 1945); 1952
health exhibit by Norfolk WCTU for doctor's health exhibition; ad
and drawing of their Norfolk retreat for the sick in 1891.

To celebrate the diamond jubilee of the Virginia Women's
Christian Temperance Union, Ironmonger surveys the work of the
organization from its founding in 1883 through 1958. After providing a
brief history of the founding of the national organization in 1874 and
two-paragraph biographies of the eight national presidents, 1874-1953,
the author explores the history of these early Virginia WCTUs: Lincoln,
Alexandria, Charlottesville, Staunton, Harrisonburg, Church Hill, and
Dayton. She devotes a section to the organization of the Virginia
WCTU, quoting minutes from the first meeting, constitution, bylaws,
and proceedings of the first convention. She summarizes the
accomplishments of each presidential administration, describing the

various departments of work as they were initiated. Among those that enjoy rich description are the departments for armed services, child welfare, Christian citizenship, flower mission and relief, health, historical files, interrelations for peace, legislative, natural fruit beverages, publicity, radio-TV, scientific temperance instruction, speech contests, spiritual life, temperance education in church schools, and visual education. Conference resolutions are cataloged, budgets are given and the author includes poems by members, names of delegates to world conferences, and speeches given at conferences. Programs establishing a day camp for children, sending fruit juice to Korean soldiers, calling for a chemical test for drunken drivers, cooperating with Norfolk's Florence Crittenton Home, and founding the Youth Temperance Council for young ladies are described. Finally, the author provides biographies of the editors of the *Virginia Call*, the organization's publication, for 1897-1958. By county, she also includes histories of the organization and development, projects, and officers of local unions. This is a thorough compendium of Virginia temperance history.

298   *m IRWIN, INEZ HAYNES. *Angels and Amazons: A Hundred Years of American Women.* Garden City, N.Y.: Doubleday, Doran and Co., 1933. x, 531 pp. Appendix.

This study is divided into three "Books," each containing a chapter of interest to researchers on the history of women's voluntary associations. In the first Book, chapter 5, "They Begin to Organize," discusses antebellum benevolent and philanthropic organizations, temperance societies, women's rights associations, and abolitionist leagues. In the second Book, chapter 3 discusses late nineteenth-century trade unions, temperance societies, women's literary clubs, and suffrage associations. In the third Book, covering the post-1930s era, Irwin discusses temperance, and the postsuffrage endeavors of the members of the National American Woman Suffrage Association and the National Woman's party. The especially useful appendix lists eighty-five women's organizations, containing much rare information. She includes the location of headquarters, the object of the group, its size, and names of officers. Many of these groups have never commissioned a history or have been the object of scholarly inquiry.

299   *s -----. *The Story of Alice Paul and the National Woman's Party.* Fairfax, Va.: Denlinger's Publishing, 1964, 1977. viii, 501 pp. Indexes, illus.: 20 including 1 of Alice Paul; Lucy Burns; Inez Milholland; demonstrators in Washington, D.C.; 3 cartoons on suffrage by Nina Allender.

This is not a biography of Alice Paul, but rather the story of her leadership in the Congressional Union and National Woman's party in its fight for a woman suffrage amendment, between the years 1913 and 1920. The story is divided into four parts. The first, concerning 1913-14, provides some background on Alice Paul and on Lucy Burns and then launches into their efforts to create a congressional committee within the National American Woman Suffrage Association. Their split with NAWSA to form the Congressional Union is explained sympathetically. A second section describes the transformation of the CU into the National Woman's party. A third section deals with the group's wartime activity in 1917, its picketing of the White House to embarrass president Wilson for his failure to support woman suffrage at home while leading a nation to fight for democracy abroad. There is considerable detail on the arrests of the women and their hunger strikes. The final section deals with the victory of the suffrage forces and their great efforts to win ratification in the states. This volume can serve as a compilation of documents relating to the suffrage struggle, for Irwin uses many long quotations, headlines, newspaper accounts, *Suffragist* reports, speeches, and even lyrics of suffrage songs to recount her story.

300 *s -----. *The Story of the Woman's Party*. New York: Harcourt Brace and Co., 1921. Reprint. New York: Kraus Reprint Co., 1971. 486 pp. Indexes, illus.: Alice Paul; Lucy Burns; 3 suffrage cartoons by Nina Allender; Inez Milholland; Joy Young; pickets at the White House; police arresting pickets; Watchfire of Freedom.

See previous entry.

301 *c JACKSON, PAULINE P. "Life and Society in Sapulpa." *Chronicles of Oklahoma* 43 (Autumn 1965): 297-318. Notes, illus.: group photo of 1898 Social-Literary Society.

This survey of organizations and institutions in Sapulpa, Oklahoma, includes brief histories with names of key officers of the following women's societies: Social and Literary Society (founded 1897); Reading Club (1905), which helped organize the Sapulpa Federation of Women's Clubs in (1906); Ladies' Library Club (1901), which supported the town library until 1917; P.E.O., a secret lodge for women (1907); Daughters of the American Revolution (1912); and Tuesday Club (1903), devoted to euchre, whist, and bridge playing. In 1901, Mrs. Charles Whitaker became the first president of the Ladies' Library Club, which raised money to build a library building for Sapulpa and provide one hundred volumes for it. The women's club supported the library until 1917, when it became a Carnegie library.

The author outlines the accomplishments of other women's organizations in the town, such as the Reading Club, P.E.O, Daughters of the American Revolution, Tuesday Club, Morning Bridge Club (1903), and the Business and Professional Women's Club. Founders, officers, and goals are articulated. Jackson also documents the contributions of men's organizations in Sapulpa.

302 *w JACOBY, ROBIN MILLER. "Feminism and Class Consciousness in the British and American Women's Trade Union League, 1890-1925." In *Liberating Women's History* edited by Bernice A. Carroll, 137-60. Chicago and Urbana: University of Illinois Press, 1976. Notes.

Jacoby compares the health of feminism and class consciousness in the British and American Women's Trade Union leagues at the turn of the century and discusses their relationship to woman suffrage. She discusses the WTUL's efforts to educate the broader public about the needs of working women and to support progressive legislation.

303 *w -----. "Women's Trade Union League and American Feminism." *Feminist Studies* 3 (Fall 1975): 126-40. Notes.

Founded in 1903, the Women's Trade Union League was an alliance of middle-class suffragists and working-class factory workers. Its goals were to improve the situation of female workers by facilitating the growth of trade unions and lobbying for legislation to improve working conditions and to secure woman suffrage for women of all classes. Until the organization faltered in the mid-1920s, the middle-class women's alliance with the woman's movement took precedence over workers' causes, so the members achieved less for women in the labor movement than for leisured women seeking the vote.

304 *p JAMES, BESSIE ROWLAND. *For God, for Country, for Home: The National League for Women's Service, A Story of the First National Organization of American Women Mobilized for War Service.* New York: G.P. Putnam's Sons, 1920. xv, 260 pp. Illus.: chairman, Miss Maude Wetmore; 1st vice-chairman, Mrs. Coffin Van Rensselaer; 2nd vice-chairman, Mrs. John A. Logan, Jr; treasurer, Miss Anne Morgan; commandante and secretary, Miss Grace Parker; receiving ship canteen in Brooklyn, New York; motor corps: Denver, Colorado, Kings County, Herkemer County, Portland, Oregon, Dayton, Ohio, Milwaukee, Wisconsin, canteen units: Germantown, Pennsylvania, New York City, Brooklyn, New York, Seattle, Washington; community cannery: Asheville, North

Carolina; fruit conservation in Everett, Washington, Chelan County, Washington; canning kitchen in Rensselaer County, New York, and Portland, Oregon; Navy canteen in Pelham Bay, New York; Soldiers and Sailors Club in Pueblo, Colorado, and Seattle, Washington; Sailors Club in Philadelphia, Pennsylvania; War Hospitals Library Committee in Hamilton, Ohio; Win-the-War Kitchen, Florence, South Carolina; Win-the-War Kitchen for Colored Women, Florence, South Carolina; Junior Service Corps; flag presentation ceremony; ambulance service at Camp Mills and Colonie, New Jersey; shopping bureau, New York City, New York; Camouflage Corps printing USS *Recruit*, New York City; signal practices at Fort Tolten; volunteer bringing flowers to convalescing veteran; reading room in San Francisco National Defenders' Club (for soldiers and sailors); official roadhouse in Montgomery, Alabama; typical workroom of the National League for Women's Services; first wireless class in New York City, March 1917 at Hunter College.

During World War I, the women of the United States coordinated their efforts toward three patriotic goals: to establish a clearinghouse of information on women's voluntary organizations, to coordinate women's organizations and resources, and to register women to form a federated woman's bureau to deal with women's work and welfare in wartime. Eleven divisions of effort were constructed: social and welfare work (including providing soldiers with coffee and sandwiches at canteens), home economics, agriculture, industry, medicine and nursing, motor driving, general service, health, civics, signaling, and camping. The author lists names of officers, staff, and trained organizers who participated in this effort in New York State. She is generous with examples of the ways that women donated their talents to war-related activities, from avoiding extravagance, planting vegetables instead of flowers in their gardens, giving patriotic lectures in Greek, Lithuanian, and Syrian languages, and knitting for refugees. Two hundred thousand motor corps drivers, aged twenty-one to forty-five, earned state chauffeurs' licenses and transported people, equipment, fertilizer for school gardens, and jars for canneries. Women farmed as well "for [the] woman with the hoe must defend the man with musket. If you cannot be a fighting soldier be a farming soldieress. Potatoes are as necessary as bullets. Send them to the front." The author devotes chapters to food conservation by women, volunatrism in service clubs, knitting, and relief efforts after the war. This volume proivdes an impressive amount of detail about wartime voluntarism among women.

305 *s JAMES, LOUISE BOYD. "Woman Suffrage Issue in the Oklahoma Constitutional Convention." *Chronicles of Oklahoma* 56 (Winter 1978-79): 379-92. Notes, illus.: Mrs. M. Carter, supporter; Robert L. Owen, supporter.

This article narrates the defeat in 1906 of prosuffrage forces at Oklahoma's Constitutional Convention in Guthrie. Lobbying for women's enfranchisement was the Oklahoma Woman Suffrage Association under the leadership of President Kate H. Biggers and bolstered by representatives of the leadership of the National American Woman Suffrage Association. The author lists the names of Oklahoma officers who worked for the vote and also quotes the legislators who opposed or supported the measure.

306 *s JENNINGS, MARY KAY. "Lake County Woman Suffrage Campaign in 1890." *South Dakota History* 5 (Fall 1975): 390-409. Notes, illus.: 2 of women; 3 of men including Reb Hager and Hearst.

Here is the history of one South Dakota county's unsuccessful fight for the vote in November 1889. Under territorial law, South Dakota women could vote at school meetings after 1879. Six years later, the Dakota Territorial Council and House of Representatives both passed a woman suffrage bill. It was the governor, Gilbert A. Pierce, who vetoed it. Susan B. Anthony came to win support. Both Rebecca Hager, an activist in the Women's Christian Temperance Union, and her husband, a Methodist minister, took leadership roles in the Lake County Equal Suffrage Association. The publisher of the *Sentinel* endorsed women's enfranchisement and so did the Farmer's Alliance. Antisuffragists, however, wrote to the newspapers voicing the fierce opposition within the county. Jennings makes extensive use of the local newspapers to explore the sources of antagonism and support for the issue of women's enfranchisement.

307 *s JENSEN, BILLIE BARNES. "Colorado Woman Suffrage Campaigns of the 1870's." *Journal of the West* 12 (April 1973): 254-71. Notes.

A careful, serious, and solid study, Jensen's article argues that the 1893 victory of Colorado women in achieving suffrage was rooted in the campaigns of the 1870s. Quoting newspapers, legislators, Margaret Campbell (president of the woman suffrage organization in Colorado), and speeches of national lecturers Lucy Stone, Susan B. Anthony, and Henry Blackwell, Jensen explores the issues debated in the 1870s and the strategies women attempted to attain victory. That is, suffragists tried to secure passage of suffrage through the territorial legislature, they tried again through the 1876 state constitution, and the following year, they sought victory via a referendum. The women's serious tone and organized machinery provided the foundation for woman suffrage in 1893.

308 *s -----. "Let the Women Vote." *Colorado Magazine* 41 (Winter 1964): 13-25. Notes, illus.: 1 of woman at polling place; 3 political cartoons about suffrage.

In this survey of the Colorado woman suffrage campaign, Jensen focuses on the three strategies suffragists used to win over public opinion between 1868 and 1893, to see passage of woman suffrage. Leaflets, newspapers, and lectures are dissected for their arguments in favor of women's enfranchisement.

309 *n,c JENSEN, JOAN M. "After Slavery: Caroline Severance in Los Angeles." *Southern California Quarterly* 48 (June 1966): 175-86. Notes, illus.: Caroline Severance.

This biography of clubwoman Caroline Severance features not the early years of the Boston clubwoman but her public career after 1875, when she moved to Los Angeles at the age of fifty-five. She founded women's literary societies such as the Friday Morning Club, participated in the suffrage struggle, advocated Christian socialism, and played an important role in the 1902 biennial of the General Federation of Women's Clubs. At that convention, the question of race was to be addressed. At issue was the controversy over whether to admit integrated women's clubs into the organization. Allowing white southern racists to dominate, Severance advocated that each club should be permitted to decide its own policy. Rather than advocating that the national organization determine that integration must be the rule, Severance participated in the perpetuation of all-white clubs representing the American South.

310 *z -----. "All Pink Sisters: The War Department and the Feminist Movement in the 1920s," In *Decades of Discontent: The Woman's Movement, 1920-1940*, edited by Lois Scharf and Joan Jensen, 199-222. Westport, Conn.: Greenwood Press, 1983. Notes.

In the early 1920s, immediately after the passage of the woman suffrage amendment to the Constitution, the large network of women's organizations felt strong. By the end of the decade, however, they emerged battered and divided about the best ways to change women's status in society. Jensen examines the external and internal pressures faced by the Women's International League for Peace and Freedom. She articulates the moderate route taken by Carrie Chapman Catt in shaping the National American Suffrage Association into the League of

Women Voters. She documents the alliance Alice Paul built between her National Woman's party and WILPF. In 1922, when WILPF singled out militarism as the chief cause of war, the secretary of war staged a public campaign to increase the visibility of the army and attack "silly pacifists who are seeking universal peace through undermining with insidious propaganda the ability of the United States to protect itself." WILPF campaigned against candidates who urged increased appropriations, but the group was denounced with rancor. Finally, the War Department's Chemical Warfare Service built a "Spider Web Chart," interlocking eleven women's organizations that were said to threaten the American government. Although the Woman's Joint Congressional Committee forced the secretary of war to back down with his allegations and destroy the Spider Web Charts, the Red Scare harmed the vigor of many women's groups that had been targeted and those that feared wider attacks.

311   *s -----. "'Disfranchisement Is a Disgrace': Women and Politics in New Mexico, 1900-1940." *New Mexico Historical Review* 56 (January 1981): 5-35. Notes, illus.: 1 of 4 women in an automobile.

Jensen divides women's political history of New Mexico into four periods. In the pre-1890s there was no organized women's movement. From 1900 to 1920, political pressure groups formed and suffrage was attained. From 1920 to 1940, women began voting, participating in political parties, and holding office. After 1940, women took active roles in political participation at all levels of state and local government except the highest elective offices. Focusing on the two middle periods, Jensen asks why New Mexico women had to wait for suffrage through the federal amendment and what they did do with the vote once they achieved it. In part, the slowness to win enfranchisement occurred because the women's clubs did not federate until 1909. In fact, few had formed before the turn of the century. Senatorial leadership in the state opposed suffrage as well. Although the Women's Christian Temperance Union and Congressional Union would eventually provide support for the suffrage, New Mexico did not see the a network of women's organizations preparing the way for suffrage until late in its history. After 1920, women's voter turnout was low. Hispanic women during the New Deal, however, helped swing elections for the Democrats. During this era, both Anglo and Hispanic women moved into officeholding.

312   *z JOHNSON, DOROTHY E. "Organized Women as Lobbyists in the 1920's." *Capitol Studies* 1 (Spring 1972): 41-58. Notes.

Here is a good survey of 1920s women's nonpartisan organizations that attempted to influence federal legislation. Johnson determines that these six organizations were the most active: General Federation of Women's Clubs, National Consumers' League, National Women's Trade Union League, National Federation of Business and Professional Women's Clubs, League of Women Voters, and American Association of University Women. These six lobbied individually and were charter members of the original ten forming the Women's Joint Congressional Committee, founded in 1920 to lobby for issues collectively appreciated. The committee grew to include twenty-one women's groups by 1925 and launched support for a child labor amendment, federal Department of Education, vocational training in home economics, World Court, Women's Bureau and Children's Bureau within the Department of Labor, reclassification of civil service, and protective legislation rather than an equal rights amendment. Most of these groups also allied for world peace, participating in Carrie Chapman Catt's Committee on the Cause and Cure of War, headquartered in Washington, D.C., and holding international conferences calling for cooperation and disarmament. Women's first major victory was passage in 1921 of the Sheppard-Towner Act, offering federal aid for maternal and infant health. This was opposed by the Daughters of the American Revolution and the Woman Patriot Publishing Company, a remnant of the National Association Opposed to Woman Suffrage. They charged that this legislation amounted to a Communist conspiracy. Johnson details other battles as well, stressing women's actions to pressure Congress for their causes.

313   *s JOHNSON, KENNETH R. "Florida Women Get the Vote."
Florida Historical Quarterly 48 (January 1970): 299-312.

Florida legislators were the last to ratify the Nineteenth Amendment to the U.S. Constitution granting women enfranchisement. Not until 1969, fifty years after the rest of the nation moved to extend suffrage to women, did Florida support it. Nevertheless, Florida women organized to support suffrage in the decade before 1920. In 1912, Jacksonville women organized the Florida Equal Franchise League. The next year, in Orlando, the Florida Equal Suffrage Association united twenty-eight leagues, five of which were men's prosuffrage associations. Suffrage support came from urban rather than rural areas of the state, and legislative campaigns of 1913, 1915, 1917, and 1919 met resistance. The author quotes the legislative opponents, including racists who opposed black women's enfranchisement. More success was met at the local level, twenty three cities awarding municipal suffrage to women, largely in southern Florida cities.

314   *s -----. "Kate Gordon and the Woman-Suffrage Movement in the South." *Journal of Southern History* 38 (August 1972): 365-92. Notes.

The southern suffrage campaigns began in the 1880s. Two methods for success were available to suffragists, a call for a federal amendment or one for state suffrage. Miss Kate Gordon of New Orleans was a powerful adherent of state suffrage, which could prevent black women from voting. She established the Southern States Woman Suffrage Conference in 1913, competing with the National American Woman Suffrage Association which labored for the federal amendment. Gordon saw success in 1918, when the Louisiana legislature passed a woman suffrage amendment for its state constitution. The amendment was defeated for ratification, however. Gordon and her cohorts remained determined to see state suffrage amendments, however, and worked in both Louisiana and Mississippi to prevent ratification of the federal suffrage amendment.

315   *n JONES, BEVERLY W. "Mary Church Terrell and the National Association of Colored Women, 1896-1901." *Journal of Negro History* 67 (Spring 1982): 20-33. Notes.

In 1896, the National Association of Colored Women was founded by the merger of the National Federation of Afro-American Women and the Colored Women's League. One hundred delegates from twenty clubs in ten states participated in shaping a black women's club network which had more ambitious goals than its white counterpart, the General Federation of Women's Clubs. Forming in an era of deep discrimination, the "nadir of the Negro," when Jim Crow legislation disenfranchised blacks and prohibited integration in public facilities, the group worked to provide social services for black people and to challenge racism. Mary Church Terrell, the first president of the organization, steered the membership to provide kindergartens, day nurseries, domestic science programs, and social service centers for girls, along the lines of the Young Women's Christian Association. In Louisiana and Tennessee, members petitioned the state legislatures to repeal the Jim Crow laws. They also condemned the barbarity of the convict lease system for female prisoners.

316   *f JONES, IMOGENE MULLINS. *The Golden Years of Delta Theta Tau*. N.p.: the organization, 1954. 112 pp. Illus.: 66 of founders and officers.

Written by a member and documented with sources held by the organization, this history begins with the story of the founding of the sorority in 1903 by five high school girls in Muncie, Indiana. Hard-to-come-by material on the pranks played on pledges is provided here. In 1906, the sorority convened with other sororities in neighboring cities and began to work to establish chapters widely. Materials on songs, parties, civic and benevolent projects, and the publication of *Grit*—which emphasized the philanthropic efforts of local chapters— are divided by decade. One section is devoted to the 1920s, another to the 1930s, another to the wartime years of 1941-45 which were dominated by emergency relief work, and the last to postwar peacetime projects. Occupational therapy projects in hospitals and modernization of the Kentucky mountain school facility are featured. A description of the 1952 golden anniversary celebration is full and joyous.

317   *c JONES, IRMA T. "History of the Michigan State Federation of Women's Clubs." *Michigan Historical Magazine* 10 (January 1926): 60-75; 10 (April 1926): 221-32; 10 (October 1926): 534-49; 11 (January 1927): 41-48; 11 (April 1927): 265-70; (October 1927): 621-29; 12 (January 1928): 70-76; 12 (April 1928): 302-8; 12 (July 1928): 499-504; 12 (October 1928): 695-704; 13 (January 1929): 113-20; 13 (April 1929): 245-51; 13 (October 1929): 544-54; 14 (April 1930): 299-310; 14 (July 1930): 455-62; 14 (October 1930): 680-88. Illus.: Portraits of officers of the organization.

Although it is serialized, this massive history, in toto, constitutes a major history of the Michigan State Federation of Women's Clubs. Jones begins with the history of the woman's club movement nationally, the founding of the General Federation of Women's Clubs in 1890, and the earliest Michigan women's club, the Kalamazoo Ladies Library Association. In August of 1894, however, representatives of twenty-two Michigan women's clubs came together to form the Michigan State Federation of Women's Clubs. By March of the following year, sixty-four clubs sent 110 delegates to the Lansing meeting, electing President Clara A. Avery as presiding officer. With great love, care, and respect, Jones documents the work of the annual conventions, quoting the addresses, listing officers, recording budgets, and detailing the formation of standing committees. Each administration is documented, with its resolutions, projects, scholarships, entertainments, growth, relationship with national leadership at the General Federation of Women's Clubs, and civic programs undertaken.

318 *r JUDD, BERTHA GRINNELL. *Fifty Golden Years: The First Half-Century of the Woman's American Baptist Home Missionary Society, 1877-1927.* New York: the organization, 1927. 281 pp. Bib., illus.: 60 photos, including Alice B. Coleman; devotional exercises at the Japanese Women's Home, Seattle; 2 Lithuanian women talking to their Christian Americanization Friend; Puerto Rican Sunday school class; 4 girls at an orphanage; churches around the world; Boston Baptist women in 1877.

In 1877, the Woman's American Baptist Home Mission Society formed for the "evangelization of women among the freed people, the Indians, the heathen immigrants and the new settlements of the West." The members raised money to support missions among blacks, Indians in Kodiak, Chinese in San Francisco, and Scandinavians in the midwest. Women were uniting for suffrage, temperance, and foreign missions, so Michigan women initiated an alliance for the cause of home missions. In 1877, headquarters was established first in Chicago, and then in Boston, where New England women had already been active in this work. Judd's chapter on education enumerates support for multitudes of institutions. For blacks, they contributed to the Mather Industrial School, Spelman College, Hartshorn Memorial College, Storer College, Florida Normal and Industrial Institute, and Americus Institute; for Indians, Indian University at Tahlequah, Bacone College, and Seminole Academy. The organization also established missions for the Chinese in Ogden, Utah, and in Fresno, Sacramento, and San Francisco, California; for Latin Americans, in Mexico, Puerto Rico, Nicaragua, and El Salvador. Christian social settlements were established as well, providing church services, Bible lessons, vacation Bible schools, athletic programs, health clinics, bathrooms with hot water, and English and citizenship classes. In Seattle, the Japanese Women's Home, run by Mrs. Okazaki, wife of a Japanese pastor, provided a "suitable Christian hotel for Japanese women." Members visited non-English-speaking mothers at home to teach them English. This detailed reference work on missionary work also contains valuable lists of important events in the organization from 1877 to 1926, officers from 1877 to 1909, and fifteen golden anniversary projects undertaken by the general membership.

319 *m KAMINER, WENDY. *Women Volunteering: The Pleasure, Gain and Politics of Unpaid Work from 1830 to the present.* Garden City, N.Y.: Doubleday and Co., 1984. xix, 237 pp. Notes, bib., indexes.

Although much of this book consists of interviews with contemporary clubwomen, chapter 3 is entitled "Volunteering in

Recent History: A Summary of Volunteering and the Status and Image of Women in America, from the 1830's through the 1920's." Here, Kaminer surveys cursorily the efforts of women's groups devoted to charity, religion, abolition, suffrage, temperance, consumerism, and trade unions.

320   *b KATZ, VIRGINIA. "The Ladies' Hebrew Benevolent Society of Los Angeles in 1892." *Western States Jewish Historical Quarterly* 10 (January 1978): 157-58.
        Under the leadership of Mrs. Rosa Newmark of Los Angeles, Jewish women formed the Ladies' Hebrew Benevolent Society in 1870. These southern California women administered relief to the poor, sick, and needy and prepared the dead for interment.   They took responsibility for seeing that the dead received every honor and rite the Hebrew religion accorded. By 1892, the organization had spent twenty thousand for charitable purposes. Katz provides a list of the founding officers and those leading the group in 1892.

321   *s KATZENSTEN, CAROLINE. *Lifting the Curtain: The State and National Woman Suffrage Campaigns in Pennsylvania As I Saw Them*. Philadelphia: Dorrance, 1955. xi 376 pp. Appendixes.
        The author of this memoir was executive secretary of the Pennsylvania Woman Suffrage Association. Involved with the suffrage campaign between 1910 and 1920, she was one of twenty-three American leaders on the Suffrage Special, a tour of twelve western states to generate support for women's enfranchisement. Part 1 of her study consists of sixteen chapters on the history of the Pennsylvania suffrage movement after 1910. Part 2 devotes thirteen chapters to her view of the national movement, especially the divisiveness between the National American Woman Suffrage Association and the Congressional Union. She excerpts internal documents, testimony at hearings, correspondence received at Pennsylvania headquarters, and speeches given to persuade a reluctant Pennsylvania legislature to endorse the woman suffrage amendment. Her four appendixes reprint the 1848 Seneca Falls Declaration of Sentiments, the Nineteenth Amendment, the equal rights amendment, and her essay on women and life insurance.

322   *r KELLER, ROSEMARY SKINNER. "Creating a Sphere for Women in the Church: How Consequential an Accommodation?" *Methodist History* 18 (January 1980): 83-94.
        Expressing ideas rather than uncovering facts, Keller surveys the collective accomplishments of the Methodist women in the

Women's Foreign Missionary Society and Women's Home Missionary Society. In 1880, Methodist women channeled their public concerns through an all-women's organization, for they were excluded from decision making and ordination within their church. Supporting missionary work at home and abroad and sponsoring Sunday schools, they developed their own talents, visions, publications, representatives to send abroad, and institutions. Although their organizational efforts were a result of their exclusion from the male sphere, they built leadership skills and sisterhood through their networks.

323   *c,t,y KELLEY, MARY, ed. *Woman's Being, Woman's Place: Female Identity and Vocation in American History.* Boston: G.K. Hall and Co., 1979. xiii, 372 pp. Notes.
     See Ruth Bordin, Lynn D. Gordon, Susan M. Hartmann, Charles E. Strickland, Joan G. Zimmerman.

324   no entry

325   *r,s KENNEALLY, JAMES J. "Catholicism and Woman Suffrage in Massachusetts." *Catholic Historical Review* 53 (April 1967): 43-57.
     Kenneally asserts that the period 1885-1920 saw a shift in the Roman Catholic position on woman suffrage. In 1885, Catholic clergy desired to prevent "a moral deterioration" which they insisted suffrage would bring, and they feared "the development of a political structure and social climate deleterious to Catholicism." In 1888, native-born American women voting on local issues did seek to limit Catholic influence in schools. When the National Birth Control League was organized by women involved with the National American Woman Suffrage Association and Massachusetts Woman Suffrage Association in 1915, Catholics who felt women's role was to perpetuate the race discovered additional reasons to oppose woman suffrage. A sinister link between suffrage and birth control was assumed by members of the Massachusetts Association Opposed to the Further Extension of Suffrage to Women. Kenneally also provides a history of Catholics who supported suffrage. When the Massachusetts Suffrage Association formed in 1895, there were some prominent Catholic supporters, both laymen and clergy. Among them was John F. Fitzgerald, grandfather to President John F. Kennedy. By 1911, Catholic union members saw suffrage as a means to improve working conditions. Catholic women formed a Massachusetts State Suffrage Association in the decade before enfranchisement, and the Catholic Order of Foresters came out in support of the woman suffrage amendment.

326 *w -----. "Women and Trade Unions 1870-1920: The Quandary of the Reformer." *Labor History* 14 (Winter 1973): 42-55.

This article examines the tensions with the American Federation of Labor and the Women's Trade Union League. The AFL was reluctant to cooperate with their Department of Women's Work, established in 1886. Able organizers, among them Leonora Barry and Mary E. Kenney (O'Sullivan), established the WTUL, during an AFL convention, to meet the needs of working women. The reluctance among AFL leadership to permit women to play participatory roles continued throughout the period 1870-1920.

327 *w,r KESSLER-HARRIS, ALICE. "Organizing the Unorganizable: Three Jewish Women and Their Union." *Labor History* 17 (Winter 1976): 5-23. Notes.

Here are biographies of Pauline Newman, Fannie Cohn, and Rose Pesotta, three Jewish organizers for the International Ladies Garment Workers Union. Realizing that the unions did not care about women workers and suffragists did not care about workers, the three women supported the establishment of the Women's Trade Union League. WTUL was supposed to address the needs of suffragists and women workers, but the middle-class women's dominance in the leadership positions undermined the success of the organization in dealing with working women's needs.

328 *w -----. *Out to Work: A History of Wage-Earning Women in the United States*. New York: Oxford University Press, 1982. 400 pp. Notes, bib., indexes.

Voluntary organizations devoted to the needs of working women are surveyed (pp. 203-14). They include the Women's Trade Union League, National Consumers' League, National Woman's Party, and the National Federation of Business and Professional Women's Clubs.

329 *b KIHLSTROM, MARY F. "The Morristown Female Charitable Society." *Journal of Presbyterian History* 58 (Fall 1980): 255-72.

Seventeen Presbyterian women in Morris County, New Jersey, formed the Morristown Female Charitable Society in 1813 "to devise some means of caring for the poor and distressed persons in the village." For its first sixty years of existence, no men were permitted to join. The women united, in part, to protest against the harshness of public poor relief laws in their community. Indigents, even children, were consigned to almshouses or indenture. By contributing dues and soliciting donations from citizens and businesses, the women assisted the poor they located.

330   *r   KLINGELSMITH, SHARON.   "Women in the Mennonite Church, 1900-1930." *Mennonite Quarterly Review* 54 (July 1980): 163-207.

While the leadership of the Mennonite church was dominated by men, late nineteenth- and early twentieth-century churchwomen began to develop opportunities for their participation too. The major area in which this took place was in the Mennonite Woman's Missionary Society, in which women, under the leadership of Clara Eby Steiner and Mary Burkhard, began to raise money for missionaries and for World War I relief. As early as the 1860s, Sunday school projects enlisted the work of women. By 1890, almost every church had a Sunday school where women taught children, and an 1892 conference attended by the instructors brought great numbers of women together. At Bible meetings of the 1890s, women also participated publicly. Writers for major church periodicals were women. In the mission field, 66.6 percent of the twenty-two workers in 1905 were single or married women. Sewing circles of women supported new mission efforts and these united in 1911 into the Associated Sewing Circles of the Lancaster Mennonite Conference. Certainly the church opposed woman suffrage, believing that women's kingdom was in the home, but the church women made decisions about girls' schools they sponsored in India, and they assumed greater independence and control of their volunteer work. The church board attempted to limit the women's autonomy by changing the thrust of their work in the 1920s, placing emphasis on sewing efforts of the auxiliary and changing the name to the General Sewing Circle Committee of the Mennonite Board of Missions. This diminution of women's leadership roles resulted in women's decreasing support for missionary work of the church.

331   *t   KNIGHT, VIRGINIA C.   "Women and the Temperance Movement." *Current History* 70 (May 1976): 201-3.

Here is a succinct survey of women's contribution to the history of temperance activity throughout the nineteenth century. Because women felt themselves to be guardians of morality and because liquor brought misery to their own lives, women began to exert control over their problems by participating in the Woman's Crusade in Ohio in 1893 and in the Women's Christian Temperance Union. WCTU president Frances Willard supported woman suffrage, and this drew temperance advocates, especially rural women, into the mainstream of American political debate.

332   *c KNOX, JULIE LECLERC. "The Julia C. Dumont Club of Vevay, Indiana." *Indiana Magazine of History* 46 (June 1950): 165-78.

The author, a member of the Julia L. Dumont Club in Vevay, Indiana, recalls its founding in 1886 by Mrs. Estelle Dufour Barker. The name of the club honors the pioneer educator and its members who devoted themselves to literary study. Longfellow, Shakespeare, the history of Germany and Holland, and the question of whether the United States should assume possession of Caribbean and Pacific islands were all topics the members discussed. They gave plays and operettas and made an effort to secure regulations requiring that pigs and cows in Vevay be "put up." Members held art exhibits, sponsored lectures, made donations to the hospital and other charities, gave a prize to the high school senior with the best record in English, conducted ceremonies on Arbor Day, and supported food conservation in World War I. Using the printed yearbooks of 1886-1950, the author lists all the general subjects studied in the history of the club.

333   *m KOHLSTEDT, SALLY GREGORY. "In from the Periphery: American Women in Science, 1830-1880." *Signs* 4 (Autumn 1978): 81-96. Notes.

Although the bulk of the essay considers the women scientists of the mid-nineteenth century, the author briefly addresses the role of three amateur study clubs for science, the Dana Society of Natural History of the Albany Female Academy, the Chautauqua Literary and Scientific Study circles, and the Society for the Encouragement of Study at Home.

334   *m -----. "Maria Mitchell: The Advancement of Women in Science." *New England Quarterly* 51 (March 1978): 39-63. Notes.

Kohlstedt provides a biography of scientist Maria Mitchell and examines her role in support of the Association for the Advancement of Women, which was founded in 1873 and held annual conferences on women's issues around the nation until 1897. Mitchell spoke on the higher education of women at the 1874 meeting and served as the organization's second president in 1875. She was reelected in 1876 and used her role to press for the entrance of more women in science. Through questionnaires, she collected information on women's achievements and problems, their education and skills. She sought to analyze data and provide greater visibility for women's successes. She withdrew from the work of the organization in the 1880s, when it moved away from its earlier emphasis on women's participation in the professions and stressed their role in philanthropy.

335 *s,n KOLMER, ELIZABETH. "Nineteenth Century Woman's Rights Movement: Black and White." *Negro History Bulletin* 35 (December 1972): 178-80. Notes, illus.: Mary Church Terrell; Josephine St. Pierre Ruffin; Lucy Stone; Elizabeth Cady Stanton with Susan B. Anthony.

Examining the racial attitudes of suffragists, Kolmer observes the antebellum support for abolition which was common. After the Civil War, however, Susan B. Anthony and Elizabeth Cady Stanton opposed the amendments that gave the franchise only to black men. The National American Woman Suffrage Association took no stand on race, but the 1903 New Orleans meeting of the association affirmed the policy of states' rights, which permitted white southern suffragists to exclude black members from their ranks. In the 1890s, black women organized to serve their own race. The Colored Woman's League formed in Washington, D.C., in June 1892 under the presidency of Helen Cook. The organization sponsored night classes in literature and language, sewing, gardening, home care, and day nursery care and provided a model kindergarten with a training school for young women interested in employment at day-care centers. Josephine St. Pierre Ruffin, president of the Woman's Era Club in Boston, founded the National Federation of Afro-American Women, with Mrs. Booker T. Washington assuming the presidency. The two groups merged in 1896 to create the National Association of Colored Women, whose first president was Mary Church Terrell.

336 *c,n KORNBLUH, ANDREA TUTTLE. "Woman's City Club: A Pioneer in Race Relations." *Queen City Heritage* 44 (Summer 1986): 21-38. Notes, illus.: 4 homes of the Woman's City Club; exterior of the Shoemaker Health and Welfare Center they supported; 3 group photos of Shoemaker Center activities; group photo of Colored Girls' Council; clinic for black community; Elsie Austin, only black woman lawyer in Cincinnati; 2 news clippings, one about the 1949 election of 2 Negro women to the Woman's City Club and the other, a 1953 article on race relations.

Here is a survey of the Woman's City Club of Cincinnati and its efforts to deal with black people of the city. Since 1915, the white women's organization had debated whether to admit black women to membership. Members formed a Race Relations Committee in 1927. They sponsored a home for "delinquent and pre-delinquent colored girls," underwrote music lessons for West End teenagers, and sponsored a Christmas concert. The club worked for federal antilynching legislation, the Wagner-Costigan Anti-Lynching Bill of 1934. By 1945, members still did not advocate racial integration, but two black women joined the club in 1949. The Junior Department, founded as a subcommittee at the club in 1926, refused to change its racial policy when the larger club did and finally disbanded in 1960 over the struggle within the organization.

337 *s KRADITOR, AILEEN S. *Ideas of the Woman Suffrage Movement, 1890-1920.* Garden City, N.Y.: Doubleday and Co., 1965. xi, 262 pp. Notes, bib., indexes.

The major contribution of this scholarly work is articulated in chapter 3. Turn-of-the-century feminists increasingly argued for their right to vote on the basis not of the justice of suffrage but of its expediency. That is, early feminists, who had insisted that equality was a natural right and the absence of a woman's franchise an impediment to equality with men, found themselves sharing center stage with another view. Some now emphasized the differences between men and women and forecast that women's special sensibilities, harnessed to a vote, would ameliorate the complex social conditions aggravated by the influx of immigrants. The latter ideology smacked of racism and nativism, but frustrated leaders used any argument that commanded attention. Most sources are taken from the views expressed by women reelected to national office in the National American Woman Suffrage Association and the National Woman's party at least twice between the years 1890 and 1918. Kraditor also examines suffrage leaders' views on home, state, religion, and marriage, and antisuffragists. Inter- and intraorganizational disputes about principles, strategy, and tactics are aired.

338 *f KRIEG, SHIRLEY KREASAN. *The History of Zeta Tau Alpha, 1898-1928.* Vol. 1. N.p.: the organization, 1928, 1939. xxvi, 510 pp. Notes, bib., table, maps, illus.: 211 of officers; conventioneers; documents pertinent to history of the organization; and chapter houses.

This sorority was founded at the State Teachers' College in Farmville, Virginia, in 1898. Generous quotations by the young women who founded it fill the early chapters. Chapters cover the official family, with biographies of officers, of editors of *Themis*, the sorority's publication, and of the historians of the organization. Krieg includes histories of the founders, reports on the ten national conventions of 1903-26, summaries of the work of the grand chapter meetings, and details on organization, government, expansion and development, insignia and heraldry, mythology of the Greek goddess Themis, publications of the organization, and budgets of loan funds, endowments, and philanthropies. One section is devoted to the homes of Zeta Tau Alpha: eighteen chapters own their own houses, fourteen chapters live in rented houses, and fifteen chapters maintain chapter rooms. Tables give members of each state in 1927, territorial expansion of Zeta Tau Alpha from 1898 to 1928, and a directory of grand officers.

339   *f -----. *The History of Zeta Tau Alpha: 1898-1928*, Vol. 2. N.p.: the organization, 1929, 1932, 1935, 1940. xvii, 647 pp. Notes, illus.: 124 of chapters; charter members; officers; conventions; installations; chapter houses.

This volume contains material on the alumnae chapters of the sorority, the first one established in 1905 in Newport News, Virginia, and called Hampton Roads Alumnae Chapter. A brief history of each alumnae chapter follows. The bulk of the text, however, consists of histories of the campus chapters. Both active and inactive chapters are recorded, naming charter members and enumerating projects undertaken. Many of the chapters are in southern colleges, but there are also many others in the Midwest and West. No chapters existed in New England. A big section on customs, traditions, and politics is provided. The eleventh national convention of 1928 is documented in detail. A chapter roll consists of a list of all sixty-two chapters, their size, dates of founding, and college affiliation.

340   *s,n KUGLER, ISRAEL. *From Ladies to Women: The Organized Struggle for Woman's Rights in the Reconstruction Era*. Westport, Conn.: Greenwood Press, 1987. xiv, 221 pp. Notes, bib., indexes, illus.: 11 portraits of feminist leaders Elizabeth Cady Stanton, Susan B. Anthony, Lucretia Mott, Lucy Stone, Francis Harper; Wyoming women at the polls in 1870; Victoria Woodhull testifying in Congress in 1871; women shoebinders turn out in Lynn, Mass., in 1860; an 1888 sweatshop; the *Call* to attend the funeral of the Triangle Fire victims in 1911.

Tracing the history of the American Equal Rights Association from 1866 until 1869, Kugler examines the leadership roles of four founders—Elizabeth Cady Stanton, Susan B. Anthony, Lucy Stone, and Lucretia Mott. He documents their debate over and support for inclusion of woman suffrage in the Fifteenth Amendment to the U.S. Constitution, using records of the post-Civil War annual New York City conventions. When they were disappointed in 1869, the "Negro's Hour" enfranchising black men but not women, the suffrage leaders and their supporters split into two factions. For twenty years, the American Woman Suffrage Association and the National Woman Suffrage Association worked for suffrage through separate channels, with different officers, publications, conferences, and branches. Not until 1890 did the antagonists of the 1860s bury the hatchet and cooperate to achieve woman suffrage.

341   no entry

342   *t KYRIG, DAVID E. "Women against Prohibition." *American Quarterly* 28 (Fall 1976): 465-82.
      In 1933, the Eighteenth Amendment to the Constitution, the prohibition Aaendment, was repealed. This was due in no small part to the efforts of female antiprohibitionists who founded the Women's Organization for National Prohibition Reform in 1929. Wealthy members, of high social position, assumed leadership in this organization. Earlier, women's auxiliaries to the Association against the Prohibition Amendment, the Molly Pitcher Clubs, lobbied for repeal in New York State in 1923. Small, with little influence, these disappeared in 1928. Pauline Morton Sabin of New York, who founded the Women's National Republican Club and served as its first president in 1921, complained of the hypocrisy of the law, the lack of enforcement of Prohibition, the growing prestige of bootleggers, and children growing up with a lack of respect for the law. By 1933, she had built an organization with 305,000 women, mostly in the northeastern part of the United States and weakest in the states of the Old Confederacy. It informed women's clubs, Parent-Teacher Associations, political candidates, newspapers, and radio stations about Repeal Week and other efforts to abandon the prohibition amendment. After a victory celebration at the end of 1933, the group disbanded.

343   *p LADIES AUXILIARY TO THE VETERANS OF FOREIGN WARS OF THE UNITED STATES. *Record of the First Twenty-Five Years, Silver Jubilee, Ladies Auxiliary to the Veterans of Foreign Wars of the United States, 1914-1939.* N.p.: the organization, 1939. 191 pp. Illus.: national president; 14 women in first auxiliary in Columbus, Ohio; men and women delegates leaving Milwaukee for 1922 Senate encampment; 55 women at Pittsburgh founding; 1938 past national president; president cutting 25th anniversary cake at 1938 Columbus encampment; national headquarters at Kansas City, Missouri, with its 5 rooms presenting flags; Michigan orphanage; history of Veterans of Foreign Wars; 1925 Children's Village for children of deceased or disabled veterans in the National Home in Eaton Rapids, Michigan.
      The Silver Jubilee of the Ladies Auxiliary to the Veterans of Foreign Wars of the United States was observed by the compilation of a history of the organization's accomplishments. Forming in 1914

before American entrance into World War I, it functioned to assist the fifteen-year-old American Veterans of Foreign Service. After twenty-five years of work, it had attracted a membership of 60,752 women in 1,757 auxiliaries. The group's projects are cataloged: recreation center, Americanism programs, high school essay contests on "What the Statue of Liberty Means to the American People," floral tribute for the Tomb of the Unknown Soldier, visits to hospitals, observation of patriotic holidays with parades and drill teams, regular pages in *Foreign Service Magazine*, Children's Village for children of deceased or disabled veterans in Eaton Rapids, Michigan, pressure to make "The Star-Spangled Banner" the national anthem in 1931, and a prize-winning pair of binoculars to the Annapolis and West Point midshipman who improved most in his fourth year of school. This history reprints the minutes of early conventions, lyrics to the "Song of Jubilation," and essays by prize-winning students.

344 *p LAMAR, CLARINDA HUNTINGTON (PENDLETON). *A History of the National Society of the Colonial Dames of America from 1891 to 1933*. Atlanta: Walter W. Brown, 1934. iii, 272 pp. indexes, appendix, illus.: 35 of historical sites sponsored; headquarters at Dumbarton House.

The original constitution of this patriotic organization stated that its object was "to commemorate the success of the American Revolution, perpetuate the memory of those who, in any important service by act or council, contributed to the achievement of American independence." Its members are women descended from ancestors who came to reside in an American colony prior to 1776 and as a statesman or officer contributed to the achievement of American independence. This history surveys the members' war work in the Spanish-American war of 1898 and during World War I; its steady relief efforts; its establishment of monuments at Arlington National Cemetery and Plymouth, Massachusetts; and its restoration of a Jamestown, Virginia, church, of Sulgrave Manor in England, home of George Washington's ancestral family, of Dumbarton House, a colonial estate the organization acquired for its headquarters in 1927, and of Gunston Hall, a colonial mansion in Virginia. The group also published historical works such as *Old Silver in American Churches* (1913), *Letters of Richard Henry Lee* (1911-14), and *American War Songs* (1925). There is a chapter on the founding of the national society from the 1890 New York branch and 1891 Pennsylvania branch, its councils, and the composition of its national board. A list of officers is provided and a chronology of important events in the organization's history between 1891 and 1933. An appendix lists gifts and loans to Dumbarton House and the corporate societies.

345 *s LARSON, TAFT A. "Idaho's Role in America's Woman Suffrage Crusade." *Idaho Yesterdays* 18 (Spring 1974): 2-15. Notes, illus.: Margaret Roberts; Permeal French, elected superintendent of public institute in 1898; Governor Brady, Senator Borah, and David Davis; 3 women elected to the legislature in 1898.

Idaho was one of the first states to grant women the vote. The suffrage was achieved in 1896, with the aid of the Idaho Equal Suffrage Association, the *Idaho Statesman* (Boise) under the editorship of William Balderston, and eastern members of the National American Woman Suffrage Association. Instead of stopping at the time of victory, Larson goes on to list the women who won seats in the Idaho House of Representatives between 1898 and 1918, document the support Governor Brady gave to suffragists outside the state, and recount the creation of the National Council of Women Voters, which was a forerunner to the League of Women Voters. The organization, formed in Idaho from 1911 to 1920, included suffrage supporters from Idaho, Washington State, Colorado, Utah, and Wyoming. Under the presidency of Emma Smith DeVoe, who presided over the Washington Equal Suffrage Association when Washington women won the vote in 1910, it pressured Idaho senator Borah to support women suffrage, and it assisted member states without suffrage to attain it.

346 *s -----. "Montana Women and the Battle for the Ballot." *Montana, the Magazine of Western History* 23 (January 1973): 24-41. Illus.: Butte, 1914, auto with women and banners; Susan B. Anthony; Francis Willard; Civilian Conservation Corps; Emma Smith DeVoe; Hiram Knowles and Henry B. Blackwell; Harriet P. Sanders; Sarepta Sanders; Ella Knowles Haskell; Jeannette Rankin; Mary Long Alderson; Anna Howard Shaw.

Montana women won the vote in November of 1914. Larson traces the history of the effort, noting that no early pressure developed in territorial days, as it had in Wyoming and Utah. By 1887, however, women were permitted to vote for school trustees if they were taxable residents. Two years later, the state rejected full suffrage for women. In 1890, then, Helena women organized Montana's first suffrage club, which collapsed quickly. In 1895, as a result of Emma Smith DeVoe's lecture tour throughout the state, a Montana conference of thirty-three interested delegates formed the Montana Woman's Suffrage Association. The size of the state made it difficult to organize, but Harriet P. Sanders, the wife of the U.S. senator, served as president and presumably won support for the cause in her state. Still, enthusiasm built slowly. DeVoe revived defunct clubs and started new ones, but the membership dues did not even pay her expenses. At the second conference in 1896, the organization elected a lawyer as their president, Ella Knowles Haskell, who represented the Helena Business Women's Suffrage Club. Her administration secured twenty-five hundred signatures for the 1897 legislators. Success was elusive, despite this burst of activity, and at the turn of the century, all but one suffrage club, in Helena, had disbanded. National officers visited to revive the fight, and Jeannette Rankin of Missoula in 1910, marshaled support from the Women's Christian Temperance Union and Missoula Teachers' Suffrage Committee, overrode the objections of prominent antisuffragists, and held a parade at the 1914 state fair. Boy Scouts waved banners declaring, "I want my mother to vote." Opposition from the powerful Amalgamated Copper Company did not abate, even in 1914, but was not strong enough to prevent the passage of woman suffrage in Montana.

347 *s -----. "Woman Suffrage in Western America." *Utah Historical Quarterly* 38 (1970): 7-19. Notes, illus.: Susan B. Anthony, two U.S. maps of states granting suffrage, in 1896 and 1914.

Larson surveys the efforts to bring suffrage to the western states of Utah, Wyoming, Idaho, Colorado, California, and Washington, emphasizing the work of governors, legislators, and newspaper editors, and minimizing the contribution of women and women's suffrage organizations. When he discusses the public reform activity of Abigail Scott Duniway of Oregon, he mentions that she belongs to suffrage organizations, but does not specify her affiliations. He does remark that the merger of the National Woman Suffrage Association with the American Woman Suffrage Association in 1890 assisted in reviving the woman suffrage struggle.

348 *s -----. "Woman Suffrage Movement in Washington." *Pacific Northwest Quarterly* 67 (April 1976): 49-62. Notes, illus.: Abigail Scott Duniway; members of the Washington Equal Suffrage Association putting up posters; Emma Smith DeVoe; May Arkwright Hutton.

The father of Seattle, Arthur A. Denny, introduced the first woman suffrage bill to Washington Territory's legislature in 1854. It lost, eight to nine. In 1871, lecturing with Oregon suffragist Abigail Scott Duniway, Susan B. Anthony traveled west to win public support and sway the legislature, but they met with hostility. Women voted briefly in the territory during the 1870s, however, through an oversight in constitutional language until their suffrage was successfully challenged in the courts. Duniway, the sixteen-year editor of the feminist newspaper *New Northwest*, did not support temperance and thereby incurred dissension, even with suffrage supporters. In 1889, upon the granting of statehood, Washington women hoped the Constitutional Convention would grant them the vote, but they were defeated by nineteen thousand votes. The defeat disintegrated the Washington Equal Suffrage Association. In 1906, however, Emma Smith DeVoe moved to Tacoma. Born in Illinois, she had been a key organizer of suffragists in other states. Now she led a ladylike assault on antisuffrage forces. Her methods ran contrary to those of flamboyant activist May Arkwright Hutton of Spokane, however, and their rivalry led to an admonition to both sides by national leaders at the 1909 National American Woman Suffrage Association conference in Seattle. Despite the internal divisiveness, Washington women won the vote in 1910.

349 *s -----. "The Women's Rights Movement in Idaho." *Idaho Yesterdays* 16 (Spring 1972): 2-15, 18-19. Notes, illus.: Abigail Scott Duniway; Mrs Kate Green; Rebecca Mitchell of the WCTU.

As early as 1870, Dr. Joseph Williams Morgan urged the Idaho legislature to pass a woman suffrage amendment, but he met an opponent in W.H. Van Slyke. Larson examines the men in government who supported suffrage. He also documents the women who urged suffrage, including Mrs. Carrie F. Young and Abigail Scott Duniway. Since Duniway, an antiprohibitionist, antagonized many potential supporters, President Carrie Chapman Catt of the National American Woman Suffrage Association got Emma Smith DeVoe of Illinois to tour and organize in 1895. The suffrage campaign of 1896 was successful. The author lists the votes for and against suffrage in each county, discusses the budget of the campaigners, and tells of the public's fear that Mormon polygamists would wield unusual clout at the polling places in Idaho.

350 *s,z -----. "Wyoming's Contribution to the Regional and National Women's Rights Movement." *Annals of Wyoming* 52 (Spring 1980): 2-15. Illus.: Mary G. Bellamy; Therese A. Jenkins; Dr. Grace Raymond Hebard.

The first government in the world to give women full rights to vote and hold office was that of the Wyoming Territory, in December 1869. Republican governor John A. Campbell signed the bill which was passed by an all-Democratic legislature governing a population of eight thousand male citizens and one thousand women. The territory had no woman suffrage organization. By 1870, three women had been appointed justices of the peace, Esther Morris had become the first woman judge, and six women had served on a Laramie jury. The following year, opponents tried to repeal woman suffrage and met Governor Campbell's opposition. Nationally prominent suffragists Elizabeth Cady Stanton and Susan B. Anthony lectured in Cheyenne and Laramie, in an effort to combat criticism that women didn't know enough about politics to vote intelligently. They argued that women refined the process. Larson embellishes here the history of the Council of Women Voters, founded by Emma Smith DeVoe, from 1911 to 1920, which he articulated in his article on the history of Idaho suffrage. Wyoming, Washington, Idaho, Colorado, Oregon, and Idaho delegates cooperated there. Here, however, he finds fault with Wyoming suffragists, in their failing to assume responsibility for supporting suffrage struggles in neighboring states. Wyoming delegate Mary G. Bellamy did not even attend the original meeting in Tacoma in 1911. Cheyenne, however, did host the 1916 conference during Frontier Days.

351   *b LASSER, CAROL S. " 'A Pleasingly Oppressive Burden': The Transformation of Domestic Service and Female Charity in Salem, 1800-1840." *Essex Institute of Historical Collections* 116 (July 1980): 156-75. Notes.

The Salem Female Charitable Society was established in 1801 when 146 women, inspired by religious impulses, directed their benevolent work toward the relief of the less fortunate members of their sex. In particular, they served eighty-two girls between the ages of three and ten who were orphaned or whose parents were unable to support them. Until 1837, the society provided a governess who supervised and taught the girls in an "asylum house" and indentured them, at the age of ten or eleven, as domestic servants. In 1837, the society dismantled its project and shifted its emphasis to assisting respectable but indigent widows. Lasser suggests that the change occurred because of the breakdown of deference by servants to mistresses and the introduction of wages. The old-fashioned roles between donor and recipient had disappeared.

352   *c LAWS, ANNIE, comp. and ed. *History of the Ohio Federation of Women's Clubs for the First Thirty Years: 1894-1924.* Cincinnati: Ebbert and Richardson Co., 1924. 350 pp. Illus.: 17 of presidents from 1894 to 1924.

Author Annie Laws served as president of the Ohio Federation of Women's Clubs from 1907 to 1909. She surveys the work of fourteen administrations, from 1894 to 1924, summarizing the accomplishments of twenty-eight annual conventions, collecting memorials to three founders, and listing early clubs, and officers and delegates to conferences. Laws scrutinizes the projects, committees, and resolutions initiated by the Ohio Federation, dividing the study into three eras—1900-1910, 1910-17, 1917-24.

See Ohio Federation of Women's Clubs for volume 2.

353 *f LAWTON, RUTH JENNINGS, et al. *The History of the United Daughters of the Confederacy.* Vol 1, 1894-1929. Raleigh, N.C.: Edwards and Broughton Co., 1929. 226 pp. Illus.: 28 of officers.

The United Daughters of the Confederacy was founded in 1895 when a few patriotic organizations of women joined together in Nashville, eliminating duplication of efforts for relief of Confederate soldiers, their wives and children, and veterans' widows. This history traces their growth and early work. Establishment of monuments and memorials was a priority, and the group placed Jefferson Davis monuments in Richmond and Arlington, Virginia, Fairview, Kentucky, and Shiloh; a memorial window to Mrs. Jefferson Davis; a bust of Gen. Robert E. Lee at the Royal Military College in Sandhurst, England; and a Lee Memorial Chapel in Washington and Lee University; they also had the Jefferson Davis National Highway named for the Confederate leader. The book includes a lengthy list of recipients of scholarships awarded by the group between the years 1907-29. They also funded dorms in normal schools and built mountain schools. Their Mrs. Simon Baruch University Prize gave one hundred dollars annually for an essay on a Confederate subject by a student at Teachers College, Columbia University. Lawton examines the historical work of the association, its relief work in peacetime and during World War I, the *Confederate Veteran*, its official publication, and the Mary Custis Lee Children of the Confederacy organization, founded in 1896 "to unite children and youth of the South in some work to aid and honor ex-Confederates and their descendants and, in so doing, link the name of Mrs. Mary Custis Lee with her husband's, General Robert E. Lee."

See Mrs. Albert Lee Thompson for volume 2 of this work.

354 *p LEACH, MRS. FRANK SAYRE. *Missouri State History of the Daughters of the American Revolution.* Sedalia, Mo.: the author, 1929. 882 pp. Indexes, illus.: Mrs. Frank Sayre Leach; national and state officers; Washington, D.C., headquarters; sundial marking Santa Fe Trail at Boonville and memorial drinking fountain.

This huge history begins with an account of the national organization of the Daughters of the American Revolution, a network of 2,336 chapters formed between 1890 and 1928. It includes noteworthy lyrics submitted to competition for the state song, addresses by officers, and portraits of Missouri citizens like poet Sara Teasdale and novelist Winston Churchill. In addition, there is a history of the Missouri DAR and reminiscences by early officers. Leach includes information on the proper way to display the American flag and tells the story of the 1922 restoration of the Old Tavern of 1830 at Arrow Rock, Missouri. The bulk of the text consists of detailed histories of each Missouri chapter, written by its members. A photograph of each regent or leader, with material on the accomplishments of her administration, accompanies her biography, the latter often rich with detail about her other organizational affiliations.

355   *c LEACH, LOTTIE A., comp. and ed. *The First Twenty Years: History of the National Council of State Garden Clubs, Inc., 1929-1949.* New York: the organization, 1949. 172 pp. Illus.: 16 photos, including officers; Tulsa Memorial Gardens; redwood grove; floral logo for each state or region.

This history is divided into three parts. The first section reviews the histories of the first ten administrations of the organization, which was founded in 1929. Lists of officers elected, issues sponsored, projects initiated, and committees appointed are generous. Part 2 discusses the work of twenty-six National Council Committees, including that to support the Blue Star Memorial Highway as a tribute to World War II veterans, and programs relating to birds, book service, conservation, headquarters, historians, junior gardening, radio, redwood grove, peace, dcholarships, and visiting gardens. Here is a list of life members and biographies of the organization's historians. Part 3 provides brief histories of the seven regions in the nation in which the National Council of State Garden Clubs is divided. The founding date, number of clubs, number of members, names of officers, goals, and projects are all succinctly narrated.

The final section of the study provides several primary documents, including bylaws, cities where national council meetings have been held in its twenty-year history, publications sponsored, and founding date and size of each state branch.

356   *s LEACH, ROBERTA J. "Jennie Bradley Roessing and the Fight for Woman Suffrage in Pennsylvania." *Western Pennsylvania Historical Magazine* 67 (July 1984): 189-211. Notes, illus.: 5 of political cartoons on suffrage.

Here is a biography of the political career of Jennie Bradley Roessing of Pennsylvania. She joined the suffrage movement in 1904, helping organize the Allegheny County Equal Rights Association, lobbying, fund-raising, touring for four months with the Liberty Bell of Suffrage, a huge bronze replica of the original Liberty Bell. In July of 1915, at the Pittsburgh Americanization Day ceremonies, she created a spectacle in Schenley Park, a parade with two thousand children and twelve groups of women waving banners supporting woman suffrage. In November of 1915, however, the referendum in Pennsylvania for woman suffrage failed. Opposing forces, such as the liquor interests, National Association Opposed to Woman Suffrage, and the Roman Catholic church, were sufficiently strong to defeat the suffragist efforts.

357 *m LEBSOCK, SUZANNE. *The Free Women of Petersburg: Status and Culture in a Southern Town, 1784-1860.* New York: W.W. Norton and Co., 1984. xx, 326 pp. Notes, bib., indexes.

Lebsock addresses the question of whether organized benevolence inhibited feminism by perpetuating the image of nurturer for women, creating the semblance but not the substance of power. Or did charity organizations yield a feminist consciousness in members? She wrestles with the subject, in chapter 7, by examining the Petersburg, Virginia, female benevolent societies, for both black and white women, during the years 1784-1860. Until 1858, voluntary organizations for charity were the exclusive province of women, especially through the churches. White women, for example, worked through the Dorcas Society of the First Baptist Church. Black women used the Gillfield Baptist Church, its Good Samaritan Sisters and Female Building Society. She determines that voluntary associations gave upper- and middle-class women a focus for sisterhood and ambition, and thus they heightened women's sense of their own significance.

358 *b LELOUDIS, JAMES L., II. "School Reform in the New South: The Women's Association for the Betterment of Public School Houses in North Carolina, 1902-1919." *Journal of American History* 69 (March 1983): 886-909.

In 1902, two hundred young women, white students at the Industrial College for Women at Greensboro in North Carolina, decided to form the Woman's Association for the Betterment of Public School Houses. Its goal was to upgrade the state's public schools for white children. The movement enlisted thousands of members and spread to Alabama, Arkansas, Georgia, Kentucky, South Carolina, Tennessee, Texas, and Virginia. The North Carolina association merged in 1919 with the Congress of Parents and Teachers, closing its state headquarters. Other state branches continued independently into the 1920s. The organization did not address racial, class, and regional inequalities, but it made an effort to modernize state educational life in an era when women were asserting their right to make changes in public life. At the first conference, held in 1902, ninety-six counties had representatives. Only the churches had organized women more completely. The author stresses the importance of self-discovery, competence, and resourcefulness exhibited by the membership but denies that they could be considered feminists.

359 *z LEMONS, J. STANLEY. "Sheppard-Towner Act: Progressivism in the 1920's." *Journal of American History* 55 (March 1969): 776-86. Notes.

The first venture by the federal government into the realm of social security legislation was through the Sheppard-Towner Maternity and Infancy Protection Act of 1921. It was the first major result of women's enfranchisement in 1920. Lemons argues that women's organizations helped force its enactment and later fought to preserve it from repeal. The National League of Women Voters, Children's Bureau, and Women's Joint Congressional Committee are among the women's alliances Lemons features. Opponents included the National Association Opposed to Woman Suffrage, Woman Patriots, and Daughters of the American Revolution. The act was an example of the persistence of progressive reformers and a link between the Progressive Era and Franklin Roosevelt's New Deal.

360 *z -----. "Social Feminism in the 1920's: Progressive Women and Industrial Legislation." *Labor History* 14 (Winter 1973): 83-91.

The author features the contribution of the National League of Women Voters in the 1920s to support for a variety of reform issues, including labor concerns of working women, protective legislation, and child labor.

361 *z -----. *The Woman Citizen: Social Feminism in the 1920's.* Urbana: University of Illinois Press, 1973, 1975. xiii, 266 pp. Notes, bib., indexes.

Lemons argues that social feminism as practiced by women in voluntary organizations during the Progressive Era did not disappear in the 1920s; it simply slowed down. This strong study of women's groups and their issues of the 1920s begins with a survey of members' efforts during World War I to support the emergency. He also deals with the pacifist women who refused to cooperate. The bulk of the text, however, elaborates on the new associations developed after the war, which defined new issues for members to address. The National Federation of Business and Professional Women, National Association of Bank Women, League of Women Voters, and National Joint Congressional Committee are among the groups Lemons uses. The issues the women's organizations lobbied for included the Cable Act and jury duty for women, participation in the Republican and/or Democratic party instead of the nonpartisan League of Women Voters, progressive reforms like city manager movement, consumer interests, civil service, the primary, the Sheppard-Towner Act for maternity and infancy protection, and National Woman's party's ERA versus protective legislation. Lemons determines that the insinuation of Bolshevism in women's groups and among the leadership undermined their vigor and resulted, in 1925-33, in an "ebb tide," or decline of social feminism.

362 *s LERNER, ELINOR. "Jewish Involvement in the New York City Women Suffrage Movement." *American Jewish History* 70 (June 1981): 442-61. Notes.

Arguing the importance of the Jewish population to the woman suffrage struggle, Lerner articulates the contributions of individuals and groups that participated in the movement for enfranchisement. The Equality League, Wage Earners' League, Women's Trade Union League, and suffrage organizations like the Political Equality League and the suffrage committee of the Socialist party are scrutinized for their suffrage support. Maud Nathan of the Consumers' League, Rose Schneiderman, an organizer at the International Ladies Garment Workers Union, and Lillian Wald at the Henry Street Settlement are also credited with significant activity within the suffrage struggle.

363 *b,n LERNER, GERDA. "Early Community Work of Black Club Women." *Journal of Negro History* 59 (April 1974): 158-67.

Lerner discusses the blossoming of the black women's club movement in the 1890s. In 1896, the National Association of Colored Women formed when three separate federations, with over one hundred black women's clubs, united. The author asserts that the importance of the work of the clubs has been underestimated, for they met a wide range of needs with ingenious solutions. The clubs created kindergartens, nursery schools, day-care facilities, orphanages, old folks' homes, and educational institutions. Using the Tuskegee Women's Club as a prototype, she outlines their efforts to create for its members social and recreational programs, literary discussions, forums for guest lecturers, and study circles. Membership denoted social standing, and like its white counterparts, displayed snobbishness, restrictiveness, strong class prejudices, patronizing attitudes, and a missionary attitude with the poor. In the 1890s, however, Ida B. Wells exposed the problem of lynching in her writing, and her speech inspired the formation of two black women's clubs. They were the Women's Loyal Union, with branches in New York and Brooklyn, and the Woman's Era Club, in Boston, under the leadership of Mrs. Josephine St. Pierre Ruffin. Lerner discusses the formation and early work of other black women's clubs, including the Ida B. Wells Club in Chicago (1893), Phillis Wheatley Club (1896), National Conference of Colored Women (1895), National Federation of Afro-American Women (1895), National League of Colored Women, Working Girls' Home Association in Cleveland (1911), Colored Women's League of Washington, D.C. (1892), and Atlanta Neighborhood Union (1908).

364　*b　LEVERING, PATRICIA W., and RALPH B. LEVERING. "Women in Relief: The Carroll County Children's Aid Society in the Great Depression." *Maryland Historical Magazine* 72 (Winter 1977): 534-46. Notes.

　　　In 1911, the state of Maryland formed a County Children's Aid Society for needy children in rural areas. By the 1930s, it had grown to include twelve district offices. In December 1928, the Carroll County branch was organized by Mrs. Frank T. Myers. She and her colleagues solicited donations from individuals, groups, and businesses to secure food and milk for needy children. The Rotary Club contributed thirty-eight for braces. Churches gave canned foods. The organization was overloaded in the Great Depression of the 1930s and needed assistance from government to meet the many emergencies, but the group continued to operate, under the labors of volunteer women, to expand its original mandate, to find jobs for the unemployed, sponsor gardens, and meet the broad variety of needs engendered by the depression.

365　*r　LINDSEY, DAVID. "Ministering Angels in Alien Lands." *American History Illustrated* 9 (1975): 19-27. Illus.: Emma Willard; missions in Hawaii; Mount Holyoke Female Seminary.

　　　In the United States, the rise of the crusade for foreign missions coincided with the rise of women's activity on behalf of their own emancipation. Lindsey surveys the women who served as missionaries or missionary wives, but also details the growth of voluntary associations at home which supported Protestant missions abroad. Briefly, he details the work of the Boston Female Society for Missionary Purposes (organized in 1800 by Mary Webb), Female Cent societies, Female Mite societies, Female Praying societies, Female Sewing societies, and the Boston Female Society for Promoting the Diffusion of Christian Knowledge (1801). By mid-century, over seven hundred groups existed. Among the most effective was the Women's Union Missionary Society of New York, founded in 1861 by Mrs. Thomas Doremus. Lindsey also features the Congregationalists' Women's Board of Missions, under the leadership of Mrs. Albert Bowker.

366   *p LIVERMORE, MARY A. *My Story of the War*. Hartford, Conn.: A.D. Worthington and Co., 1889.   760 pp.   Illus.: 13 engravings of war; and 48 state battle flags.

Although the great body of material in this large volume consists of Livermore's observations about the Civil War, its leadership, soldiers, and battles, she devotes chapters 3, 4, 5, 20, 21, and 22 to the history of the Sanitary Commission, especially in Chicago, where she organized the first great fair to raise money for the Union effort. She details the work of women volunteers to carry out all the relief programs and fund-raising efforts of the commission during wartime.

367   *p -----. *The Story of My Life*. Hartford, Conn.: A.D. Worthington and Co., 1897. 734 pp. Illus.: 122.

Thirty-five chapters and six lectures delivered by the author on the Lyceum circuit flesh out the story of Mary Livermore's public and private life. Much of her public career was devoted to the achievement of women's rights through membership and leadership in several women's organizations. Thus, her account is useful for its detail on the Civil War Sanitary Commission and other Civil War relief societies, the woman suffrage movement, and the temperance movement.

368   *s LOEWY, JEAN. "Katharine Philips Edson and the California Suffragette Movement, 1919-1920." *California Historical Society Quarterly* 47 (December 1968): 343-50. Notes.

Loewy catalogs the extensive and lifelong participation of Edson in California women's organizations. At the age of thirty, in 1900-1901, she launched a successful pure milk campaign, as chair of the Public Affairs Committee at the Friday Morning Club of Los Angeles. An ardent advocate of woman suffrage, she became cochair of the Los Angeles Political Equality League. When women achieved the vote in 1920, she assisted in the effort to transform the National American Woman Suffrage Association into the League of Women Voters. Her commitment to public affairs led to her investigating working conditions of women and to write California's minimum wage law of 1913. She was an early woman leader in the republican party and a delegate to the 1921 Washington, D.C., Conference on Limitations of Armaments. She built an impressive career as a progressive activist through the network of California women's voluntary associations.

369 *w LOGAN, MARY S. CUNNINGHAM (MRS. E.O. LORD).
History of the New England Woman's Press Association, 1885-1931.
Newton, Mass.: Graphic Press, 1932. 393 pp. Indexes, illus.: 6 of
founders; 40-year members; past presidents; poets; playwrights;
journalists; pioneers in domestic science; musical critic.

    Six women in the *Boston Herald* office founded the New
England Woman's Press Association in 1885. Lord provides generous
detail about each charter member and other outstanding journalists in
the club, including their educational and family background, volunteer
work, and newspapers for which they worked. The club was devised for
social interaction, the delivery of papers and speeches, and receptions
for guests like Jane Cunningham Croly, as well as career networking.
The author lists the members and their newspaper affiliations, the
rhymed toasts they gave, poems members wrote, a one-paragraph
summary of each meeting, and a description of the annual guest night,
its music, decorations, and guest list. In addition, Lord provides an
overview of the topics discussed at the meetings, from poetry to world
affairs, suggesting a membership with a broad range of career and
personal interests.

370 *m -----. *The Part Taken by Women in American History.*
Wilmington, Del.: Perry-Nalle, 1912. Reprint. New York: New
York Times Arno Press, 1972. xiii, 927 pp. Indexes, illus.: 13
photos.

    This reference work illuminates the size, goals, charter, and
officers of the Woman's Relief Corps, auxiliary to the Grand Army of
the Republic (1883), the National Society of the Daughters of the
American Revolution, United Daughters of the Confederacy, Woman
Suffrage Association, and Women's Christian Temperance Union. One
chapter, "Club Section" (pp. 386-421), surveys several types of clubs,
representing 850,000 women, and provides twenty-five biographies of
leaders. In chapters designed to document Jewish women, Catholic
women, philanthropic women, painters and writers, the author uses
biographies of prominent clubwomen to tell her story.

371 *c LORING, KATHARINE PEABODY. Forword to *The
Mayflower Club, 1893-1931.* Cambridge, Mass.: Riverside Press,
1933. ix, 59 pp. Illus.: 7 of early officers.

    This history of the Mayflower Club in Boston surveys the years
1893-1931 for the literary and social activity in which its members

engaged. Loring quotes reports of the organization and provides brief sketches of the charter members. She compiles several lists in this brief work of the officers, charter members, members of the club when it disbanded in 1931, and the five domestic workers hired at the club.

372 *s LOUIS, JAMES P. "Sue Shelton White and the Woman Suffrage Movement in Tennessee, 1913-1920." *Tennessee Historical Quarterly* 22 (June 1963): 170-90. Notes.

This biography explains that Sue Shelton White was the first woman to become a court reporter in Tennessee, in 1907. She also worked as state chairman of the Women's Committee of the Council for National Defense during World War I, a position awarded to clubwomen of great power. Not content to work with the tamer National American Woman Suffrage Association, she moved to the National Woman's party in 1917. It was asserted that White's silent pickets of 1916 at the Farmers' Institute Convention inspired NWP leader Alice Paul to use the technique for the NWP. When most white southern suffragists supported the Southern States Woman Suffrage Alliance which pressed for state suffrage, she worked for a federal amendment, unconcerned that it would enfranchise black women as well as white. Sue Shelton White picketed the White House in wartime, was jailed, and conducted a flamboyant one-month whistle-stop suffrage campaign attired in prison garb, speaking out for suffrage.

373 *b LUCKINGHAM, BRADFORD. "Benevolence in Emergent San Francisco: A Note on Immigrant Life in the Urban Far West." *Southern California Quarterly* 55 (Winter 1973): 431-43. Notes.

In a survey of San Francisco benevolent organizations founded by the French, Germans, labor organizations, Odd Fellow and Masonic lodges, and YMCA, the author includes brief mention of societies established by Protestant, Catholic, and Jewish women. In 1851, Protestant women formed the San Francisco Ladies' Orphan Asylum Society to establish and maintain an orphanage, "the first charitable institution of its kind in the state" of California. In 1853, Protestant women created the San Francisco Ladies' Protection and Relief Society to search out conditions of poor, sick, and needy women and children to provide them with aid. Jewish women founded a Hebrew Ladies' Benevolent Society. The author is unclear about the extent to which Catholic women participated in the shaping of the Catholic benevolent societies he describes in early San Francisco.

374 *s,z LUNARDINI, CHRISTINE A. *From Equal Suffrage to Equal Rights: Alice Paul and the National Woman's Party, 1910-1928.* New

York: New York University Press, 1986. xx, 230 pp. Notes, bib., indexes.

In a strong, serious, and clearly written historical study, Lunardini focuses on the charismatic Alice Paul, her contribution to the women's suffrage movement of 1910-20 and to the equal rights amendment drive launched in the 1920s. The author briefly surveys Paul's upbringing and the influence of British suffragists in shaping her political activity. Paul's leading role in the National American Woman Suffrage Association, her split with it to preserve her Congressional Union, and her formation of the militant National Woman's party is explored. The author provides sound portraits of the other women suffrage leaders, with whom Paul created an organization to pressure for a federal suffrage amendment to the Constitution, and those moderates whose tactics and strategies she challenged. While there is praise for Paul's political savvy, the author is unafraid to lodge criticism of Paul's shortcomings. Here is an important and scholarly contribution to a subject of great interest to feminists and academics.

375 *m LYND, ROBERT S., and HELEN MERRELL LYND. *Middletown: A Study in American Culture.* New York: Harcourt Brace Jovanovich, 1929. xi, 550 pp. Notes, indexes, appendixes with 24 tables.

In January 1924, a team of sociologists surveyed the town of Muncie, Indiana, to determine its patterns in private life, working experiences, and recreational, educational, and volunteer involvement. The study that resulted devotes pages 279-98 to formal clubs in Muncie—civic, literary, and culture clubs for women only, men only, and men and women together. The sections on women's clubs are detailed in describing topics discussed and providing excerpts from papers delivered by the membership.

376 *m -----. *Middletown in Transition.* New York: Harcourt, Brace and Co., 1937. xviii, 604 pp. Indexes, appendixes with 3 tables.

In 1935, the sociologists returned to Muncie, Indiana, to survey the changes that had taken place in the town within the decade. The effects of the Great Depression were noteworthy in women's clubs, and the study provides rich detail on the changing programs at the Women's Christian Temperance Union, women's literary clubs, civic clubs, and organizations for young women.

377 *b MacARTHUR, BURKE. *United Littles: The Story of the Needlework Guild of America.* New York: Coward-McCann, 1955. 127 pp.

In 1883, Lady Giana Wolverton founded a needlework guild in Dorsetshire, England, to provide clothing for the needy. The members were Christian women, but their work was not affiliated with a church. Two years later, the idea came to the United States with Laura Safford (later Mrs. John Wood Stewart). She founded the Needlework Guild of America and organized the first branch in Philadelphia. The organization, designed "to make useful garments and distribute them to the sick and the needy through Children's Aid Societies, Children's Hospitals, and Children's Homes," grew to include one million women, all over the United States. The earliest branches formed were in the Northeast, but a black women's branch opened in Washington, D.C., in 1890 and California formed five branches. Each member made or purchased two articles of clothing each year to donate to charitable enterprises. Miss Rosamond K. Bender served as the full-time executive secretary at the national headquarters in Philadelphia from 1903 to 1941. The author provides a list of the towns and groups in which organizational branches could be found.

378   *r MacCARTHY, ESTHER. "Catholic Women and the War: The National Council of Catholic Women, 1919-1946." *Peace and Change* 5 (1978): 23-32. Notes.

As an outgrowth of widespread relief activity during World War I, the National Council of Catholic Women was founded in 1920. Because five thousand parish and Catholic humane organizations had united for volunteer work in the war, the network remained intact for postwar relief work and the sponsorship of orphanages, lodgings, and classes in Europe. During the Great Depression, the organization passed peace resolutions, formed study departments, dealt with social services, immigrants, religious education, the welfare of girls, Parent-Teacher associations, and industrial problems. During World War II, the members again engaged in patriotic efforts. They acted as hostesses in recreational activities for soldiers, did service for the Red Cross, conserved food, and sent religious objects to those serving in the armed forces. Churchmen, however, steered the women away from questioning the ethics of war and urged them to confine themselves to prayer, study, and "healing the wounds" of war.

379   *f MacDONALD, JESSICA NORTH. *History of Alpha Delta Pi*. Ames, Iowa: Powers Press, 1930. xix, 395 pp. Illus.: 50 of founders, recent officers, and clubhouses.

Alpha Delta Pi was founded in 1851 at the Wesleyan Female College in Macon, Georgia. The history of the sorority is divided here into four sections, the first describing the beginnings, expansion, standardization, and centralization of the group. Part 2 consists of fifty-three chapter histories, rich with detail on the names of officers, activities, pledging and rushing practices, parties, and scholarships won by members. MacDonald includes a section of documents, such as the minutes of annual conventions, and closes with statistics about the organization, the lyrics of the official song, and a rendering of their flag.

380   *m MADSEN, CAROL CORNWALL.   "Emmeline B. Wells: 'Am I Not a Woman and a Sister?'" *Brigham Young University Studies* 22 (Spring 1982): 161-78. Notes, illus.: 1 of Emmeline B. Wells.

Although the beliefs rather than the clubwork of Mormon Emmeline B. Wells are featured here, the author informs us of her attendance at the National American Woman Suffrage Association convention in February 1895, where she reported on suffrage for women in the territory of Utah and forecast passage of statehood suffrage the following month.   For thirty-seven years, she edited *Woman's Exponent*, the publication of the Young Woman's Mutual Improvement Association, a relief society for Mormon women.   In 1910, at the age of eighty-two, she was appointed general president of the Woman's Relief Society, the highest ecclesiastical post available to Mormon women.

381   *r -----.   "Mormon Women and the Struggle for Definition." *Dialogue* 14 (Winter 1981): 40-47. Notes.

The organization in 1842 of the Mormon Woman's Relief Society marked the beginning of a specified collective role for women in the church, different from ladies aid and benevolent societies, although it certainly performed those functions as well. Formed "after the pattern of the priesthood," the members organized according to the "law of heaven." Eliza R. Snow directed the organization and shaped it to include economic, community, education, and religious dimensions. Joseph Smith authorized the women to participate in such rituals as the laying on of hands to heal the sick.

382   *s MAHONEY, JOSEPH F.   "Woman Suffrage and the Urban Masses." *New Jersey History* 87 (1969): 151-72. Notes, tables, illus.: suffrage booth at the Newark Industrial Exposition in 1913; three *Newark Evening News* political cartoons about woman suffrage, 1915 and one from the *Atlantic City Review*; suffragist Mrs. Michael O'Shaughnessy campaigning; women preparing a mailing at the Women's Political Union headquarters; Women's Political Union paraders on foot; six Women's Political Union campaigners in automobiles; costumed women at the 1916 Suffrage Ball.

Mahoney describes the work of the New Jersey Woman Suffrage Association, the Woman's Political Union, and the Men's League for Woman Suffrage in the general election of 1915, in which a woman suffrage referendum was defeated. The supporters argued that sexual discrimination at the ballot box was unjust and undemocratic and that votes for women would improve society by getting rid of crooked bosses. Although the suffragists blamed their loss on the political bosses, forty-two tables here reveal that immigrant neighborhoods, where ward bosses were powerful, did not come out strongly opposed to suffrage. Instead, organized labor and the New Jersey Federation of German Catholic Societies, which opposed prohibition and feared that the enfranchised women would bring in temperance, echoed the sentiments of the antisuffragist organizations. Opponents claimed that women did not really want to vote and that enfranchisement would destroy women's special role in the home.

383   *s MAMBRETTI, CATHERINE COLE. "The Battle against the Ballot: Illinois Woman Antisuffragists." *Chicago History* (Fall, 1980): 168-77. Bib., illus.: 4 of leaders; political cartoon satirizing antisuffragists.

Following the lead of antisuffragists in New York and Boston, Illinois women of 1886 founded Women Remonstrants of the State of Illinois to conduct a ladylike campaign against the passage of woman suffrage. Despite their efforts, Illinois legislators supported women's right to vote for school elections. Mambretti examines the backgrounds and strategies of the antisuffragists who were married to men of means. They avoided speaking on public platforms, preferred to correspond with their legislators, feared socialism and the end of traditional marriage, and revered motherhood. In Illinois the organization folded in 1913, defeated by full woman suffrage, but the national organization carried on.

384   *c MARKHAM, ANNE CATHERINE. *Julia Pauline Leavens, Founder of the New York Browning Society.* New York: New York Browning Society, 1924. 64 pp.

Markham wrote a memorial to Julia Pauline Leavens, founder of the New York Browning Society, ten years after her death. Leavens was a teacher and pioneer leader of extension classes in literature. There is a great deal of detail about her pedigree and early life and education. In 1907, at the age of sixty-one, she met with nine women in New York City, where they decided to meet the second Wednesday of every month to discuss literature, art, ethics, and music. Although they called themselves the Browning Society, they did not confine their studies to his works alone. In the winter of 1909, a conference was held, to which other Browning Societies in New York, Boston, and Philadelphia were invited to hear lectures by professors from Wellesley College and Columbia University. A later president said of Leavens, "It is for helping them to find and express themselves as well as for leading them to inform their minds that the women of the Browning Society today arise and call her blessed." She resigned from the presidency of the club in 1912 and died on 12 December 1916, the anniversary of Browning's death. The essay lists the names of the women members who gave a eulogy at her memorial service and excerpts complimentary remarks by her friends.

385   *w   -----. "On the Evolution of Women's Medical Societies." *Bulletin of the History of Medicine* 53 (Fall 1979): 434-48. Notes.

The author documents the interest of the General Federation of Women's Clubs on health issues in the 1890s. She asserts that members' activity to solve medical problems through civic reform techniques absolved clubs of women physicians in each city from taking leadership roles in public health issues through their own special interest alliances.

386   *c,z,w   MARTI, DONALD B. "Sisters of the Grange: Rural Feminism in the Late Nineteenth Century." *Agricultural History* 58 (July 1984): 247-61. Notes.

Begun as an organization merely to "uplift farm women," the Grange of the Order of the Patrons of Husbandry moved to support woman suffrage. Male and female members struggled with the question from the 1870s on, with debate in the New York State Grange. In 1881 and 1882, the Indiana State Grange adopted equal suffrage resolutions. The national organization considered it in 1879 and approved it in 1885. The success was undone in 1886 and more debate occurred in 1893 and 1914. In 1915, the endorsement was renewed, capping a long history of women's involvement with ritual, as officers, as speakers, and as contributors to Grange publications, throughout its history.

387   *c,z,w   -----. "Woman's Work in the Grange: Mary Ann Mayo of Michigan, 1882-1903." *Agricultural History* 56 (April 1982): 439-52. Notes.

Mary Ann Mayo was a leader of Michigan's rural women, articulating their needs in the Chautauqua Literary and Scientific Study circles and lecturing widely at Farmer's institutes. She spent twenty years participating in the Grange, leading the Michigan Committee for

Women's Work in the Order of the Patrons of Husbandry. She called for relief from drudgery, more reading, and gracious homes in her speeches and her articles in *Grange Visitor*. Among the projects she supported were a Children's Day, temperance Fresh Air holidays for Detroit working girls, and "Making Housework Easier."

388   *z MARTIN, DORRIS B. "A Congressional Wife in Wartime Washington." *Palimpsest* 64 (March-April 1983): 34-44. Illus.: author and husband.

In 1938, Thomas E. Martin won a seat in Congress from the first district in Iowa. With her two sons, Dorris B. Martin moved to Washington, D.C. Here, she explains her involvement with the Women's Congressional Club, incorporated in 1908 to unite the wives and daughters of members of Congress, the Cabinet, and the Supreme Court. She provides an insider's view of the organization, built for social interaction, which required members to call on every wife in government circles whose husband outranked that of the new member. Monday was Supreme Court Day. On Tuesday, House members' wives stayed home to await visits. Wednesday was Cabinet Day, Thursday, Senate Day, and Friday, Diplomatic Day. In fact, members seldom "received" on their official day and visitors who found no one at home could leave a calling card and be absolved of her responsibilities. In 1912, a clubhouse was built for the organization at the corner of New Hampshire Avenue and Sixteenth Street, on land given by a senator's widow, Mrs. Henderson of Missouri. No alcohol was served there until 1962. The group's projects were self-supporting through their sale of cookbooks. They held classes in public speaking, foreign languages, flower arranging, health and exercise, and hatmaking, sponsored hobby shows and art shows, and took trips to New York City and Panama. According to club etiquette, "coffee outranks tea," meaning that the wives who poured were seated by rank. If two held the same rank, determined by their husbands' status, the coffee was poured by the woman whose husband's state was admitted to the Union earlier in history.

389   *p MARTIN, LAWRENCE. "Women Fought at Bunker Hill." *New England Quarterly* 8 (December 1935): 467-79.

In June of 1775 the famous Battle of Bunker Hill was fought in Massachusetts. Fifty-five years later, women laid a cornerstone for a 220-foot obelisk to mark the event. The drive for the monument was led by Sarah Josepha Hale, who elicited enthusiasm through the periodical she edited, *Ladies' Magazine*. In it, she publicized a subscription society for women. Two individuals offered ten thousand dollars each if thirty-five thousand more was raised. At a Ladies' Fair lasting one week in September of 1840, women contributed cash and sundries to sell. Their efforts were successful and the monument was completed in July 1842.

390 *n MASSA, ANN. "Black Women in the 'White' City." *Journal of American Studies* 8 (December 1974): 319-37. Notes.

With great detail, Massa exposes the racism and conflict that occurred between white and black women planning the exhibits for the World's Columbia Exposition in Chicago between 1890 and 1893. Mrs. Lettie A. Ternt spoke for the black women at the first board meeting in 1890, asking that "colored women be designated by the Commission and legally authorized to be placed in charge of an exhibit of colored people." Instead, the white women on the Board of Lady Managers picked three white women with interest in black issues. The black women were divided on how to participate in the exhibitions and how to win influence among white organizers and administrators. Hallie Quinn Brown, a teacher, elocutionist, and lecturer, urged Mrs. Potter Palmer, head of the Board of Lady Managers, to create a Solicitor of Exhibits among the Colored People for the Columbia Exposition. Fannie Barrier Williams was appointed an unsalaried worker, but this solution was opposed by militant blacks, who published Ida B. Wells's essay, "The Reason Why the Colored American Is Not in the Columbia Exposition."

391 *c MASSACHUSETTS STATE FEDERATION OF WOMEN'S CLUBS. *Progress and Achievement: History of the Massachusetts State Federation of Women's Clubs, 1893-1962.* Lexington, Mass.: Lexington Press, 1962. xv, 288 pp. Appendixes, illus.: 28 portraits of president; Julia Ward Howe room at General Federation of Women's Clubs headquarters; bas-relief of Julia Ward Howe.

This history of the Massachusetts State Federation of Women's Clubs, founded in 1893, is divided into five sections. The first one details the history of the earliest women's clubs in the state, including the Salem Female Charitable Society founded in 1801 and the Ladies' Physiological Institute of 1848. Part 2 discusses the thirty administrations, and points out the great influence Massachusetts club leaders had on the General Federation of Women's Clubs. Part 3 documents the work of the departments and divisions, surveying the accomplishments of committees devoted to war relief, motion pictures, American home, community services, education, fine arts, international affairs, public affairs, federal forests, and junior clubs. The collection includes eulogies and biographies of deceased leaders in a memorials section and closes with appendixes that include a list of the presidents, a chronology of important events in the federation's history, and a copy of the state federation song.

392   *p MASSEY, MARY ELIZABETH. *Bonnet Brigades*. New York: Alfred A. Knopf, 1966. xxi, 371 pp. Notes, bib., index, illus.: 20 engravings, one of a meeting of New York City women at Cooper Union in April 1861, where the New York Central Association of Relief was organized with Louisa Lee Schuyler as president.

    Within two weeks after the outbreak of the Civil War, twenty thousand soldiers' aid societies were formed by women in the Union and the Confederacy. While Massey devotes most of her study to other contributions of women, she mentions the accomplishments of the Sanitary Commission, National Woman Suffrage Association, Dress Reform League, Women's Rescue League to oppose the wearing of bicycle costumes, United Daughters of the Confederacy, Ladies of the Grand Army of the Republic, Sorosis, New England Woman's Club, Association of Collegiate Alumnae (later American Association of University Women), and the Grange.

393   *m -----. "The Making of a Feminist." *Journal of Southern History* 39 (February 1973): 3-22.

    Here is a biography of Ella Gertrude Clanton Thomas (1834-1907) of Georgia, a woman active in the Women's Christian Temperance Union, Georgia Woman Suffrage Association, Daughters of the Confederacy, and Augusta Ladies Memorial Association, an organization devoted to observing Confederate Memorial Day. She kept a diary for forty-one years, from the age of fourteen, and confides there her support for integration in the South.

394   *w MAUPIN, JOYCE. *Working Women and Their Organizations —150 Years of Struggle*. Berkeley: Union WAGE Educational Committee, 1974. 37 pp. Bib., illus.: 13 of women working.

    This pamphlet, written by an activist in working women's associations, traces the history of women's labor since colonial times. Among the women's organizations she discusses, quoting leaders on the goals of the memberships, are the Women's Department of the Knights of Labor, Lowell Female Labor Reform Association, Women's Typographical Union, and Women's Trade Union League. This is a chronological treatment of American history, moving past 1960 to discuss the contemporary women's movement and the Coalition of Labor Union Women.

395 *c MAYO, EDITH P. "Women's History and Public History: The Museum Connection." *Public Historian* 5 (Spring 1983): 63-73. Notes.

This article deals with the concern women's organizations have held for public historical buildings. In 1858, Ann Pamela Cunningham of South Carolina purchased George Washington's home, Mount Vernon, and formed the Mt. Vernon Ladies' Association to raise funds to buy and maintain the estate. The association still holds title to the property. It also served as a model for other women's organizations, which purchased important historic sites for preservation: Thomas Jefferson's estate, Monticello, Andrew Jackson's Hermitage in Tennessee, and Sulgave Manor, Washington's ancestral home in England, which was purchased by the National Society of Colonial Dames of America. In 1900, a black women's group was formed to create the Frederick Douglass Memorial and Historical Association, preserving his Cedar Hill home in Anacostia, Washington, D.C. The effort was spearheaded by Helen Pitts Douglass, the second wife of Frederick Douglass. The National Association of Colored Women's Clubs became involved in fund-raising to maintain the home. Atlanta's Chapter of the United Daughters of the Confederacy conceived and developed the idea for Stone Mountain Memorial, a Confederate Mt. Rushmore in Georgia. The Uncle Remus Memorial Association bought Wren's Nest, Joel Chandler Harris's home, in 1913 and still runs the facility for public exhibition.

396 *r,n McAFEE, SARA JANE. *History of the Women's Missionary Society in the Colored Methodist Episcopal Church.* Jackson, Tennessee: Publishing House of CME Church, 1934, 1945. 203 pp. Illus.: author; husband; Bishop R.A. Carter; parents; officers in groups or as individuals; Mrs. Peggy Leruse; Mrs. Polly Hudson; Mrs. M.J. Dinkins; Mrs. Harriett Holsey; Mrs. Mary Shields; Mrs. Helena Brown Cobb.

The author, daughter and wife of ministers in the Colored Methodist Episcopal Church, was a missionary worker for thirty-eight years and served as president of the Georgia Missionary Women. She provides sample meeting outlines, with readings of Scripture, and reports on programs undertaken like Health Week and membership campaigns. As early as 1849, black women formed a Women's Missionary Society in Ft. Valley, Georgia. In 1883, Paine College in Augusta served as the site of summer classes for women in missionary societies who sought to learn skills to enable them to establish their own scholarships, vacation Bible schools, and youth services for young people at home and abroad. Separate essays by participating members illuminate the history of black women's missionary societies in Alabama, California, Florida, Kansas, Missouri, North Carolina, Mississippi, Southwest Georgia, Southeast Missouri, Illinois, and western Kentucky. For each, the authors detail the founding of the chapter, its officers, members, budget, programs for the needy, and churches it built. Additionally, the general conferences of 1902, 1904, and 1906 are documented, surveying the addresses heard, prayers offered, and music provided.

397   *t McCLARY, ANDREW. "The WCTU Discovers Science." *Michigan History* 68 (January-February 1984): 16-23. Illus.: Mary H. Hunt; temperance songs; ads for textbooks.

    Mary H. Hunt pioneered in the development of sophisticated effective political action for the Women's Christian Temperance Union fight against alcohol. She used scientific ideas to advance the cause of temperance as early as the 1870s. Her work in Michigan impressed the national WCTU leadership and inspired them to call for scientific temperance education. The WCTU of the nineteenth century successfully pressured state legislators to require temperance instruction in the classrooms. At the turn of the century, twenty-two million American children used twenty scientific temperance textbooks in school, and the organization battled with physicians who prescribed alcohol as medication.

398   *m McDONALD, JEANNE GRAY. *The Power of Belonging: Why 80 Million Women Can't Be Wrong.* Dallas: Handel and Sons, 1978. 203 pp.

    The author lists multitudes of women's organizations devoted to social philanthropy and observes what it is like for the membership to participate. She articulates the ways the groups raise money and which leadership qualities they acquire and nurture. The categories of clubs she discusses are service, business, professions, volunteer, civic education, politics, sororities, patriotic, religious, armed forces, and arts groups.

399   *r McDOWELL, JOHN PATRICK. *The Social Gospel in the South: The Woman's Home Mission Movement in the Methodist Episcopal Church, South, 1886-1939.* Baton Rouge: Louisiana State University Press, 1982. x, 167 pp. Notes, bib., indexes.

    The Woman's Home Mission Movement in the Methodist Episcopal Church, South, was a large one. When its home and foreign mission societies merged in 1910, the organization boasted 60,000 women members, and in 1940, there were 300,000 thousand members.

McDowell turns to its beginnings in 1886 in Richmond, Virginia, dispelling the notion that southern religion manifested little or no concern for social reform. He documents early projects for immigrants, native poor whites, blacks, children, and prohibition. Although he admits that condescending behavior sometimes occurred, he stresses the consistency of support for education, medical care, improved living conditions, and other social improvements. There is careful documentation of the city mission work, club emphasis on the Christian home, female and child labor reform issues supported, and attitudes toward blacks' and immigrants' efforts for peace, and a discussion, narrative rather than analytical, of the status of women in the church. He quotes Belle Bennett and Lily Hammond, opponents of racial prejudice. Chapter 2 dwells on members' efforts to solve problems at home and work; chapter three on immigrants and on peace; four on eight social settlement centers for blacks established in Southern cities before 1940; and five on women, observing that early suffragists and women legislators were among the leaders of this church organization.

400 *p McDUFFEE, ALICE LOUISE. "Early History of the National Society Daughters of the American Revolution." *DAR Magazine* 70 (April 1936): 283-89. Illus.: Continental Hall, the first home of the organization.

McDuffee discusses the early formative period in the history of the Daughters of the American Revolution. In April of 1890, members of the Sons of the American Revolution voted down a motion to admit women to the organization, and in July, Mrs. Mary Smith Lockwood published a *Washington Post* article asserting the importance of Hannah Arnett's contributions to the war effort, as if to remind the public that women's work was also worth respecting. In August of that year, three women formed the DAR: Miss Eugenia Washington, Miss Mary Desha, and Mrs. Ellin Hardin Walworth. They selected as their president general Mrs. Benjamin Harrison. By publicizing their new organization, they attracted sufficient numbers by autumn to adopt a constitution and articulate their desire to promote patriotism and Americanism, observe historic anniversaries, educate the public in history, erect monuments, and preserve documents and relics. They voted to build a monument to the mother of George Washington and to finance a Paris monument to Washington. Upon incorporation in 1891, the DAR had already attracted 818 charter members.

401 *c McGINNIS, RALPH J. "The Wimodausians." *Farm Quarterly* 6 (Summer 1951): 46-47, 121-25. Illus.: Dora Fleming; 4 group photos.

The farming community of Carlisle, Ohio, founded a literary club for the women of the town in 1901. Dora Fleming invited her friends to participate, despite the hostility and ridicule of the men in the community. The object of the group was to "stimulate intellectual and moral development and promote good fellowship." At each meeting three hostesses supplied three dishes for refreshments, and three papers were presented. Every member of the group took a turn at the presidency. The group supported woman suffrage. McGinnis provides rich detail on the meetings the members held.

402 *m McGLASHAN, ZENA BETH. "Club 'Ladies' and Working 'Girls': Rheta Childe Dorr and the New York Evening Post." *Journalism History* 8 (Spring 1981): 7-13.

The author credits journalist Rheta Childe Dorr with great influence in pushing middle-class members of the General Federation of Women's Clubs to create an Industrial Committee and work for improved working conditions for working women. She spoke widely at women's club conventions on behalf of striking workers. Her articles in the *New York Post* covered the work of the New York State Federation of Women's Clubs, the Consumers' League, and suffrage groups. She also exposed the poor working conditions under which black hospital nurses and Italian and Irish women spinners and weavers worked. Dorr moved to the Rivington Street Settlement in 1903 and joined the Women's Trade Union League in 1905.

403 *z McGOVERN, JAMES R. "Helen Hunt West: Florida's Pioneer for ERA." *Florida Historical Quarterly* 39 (July 1978): 39-52. Illus.: Helen Hunt West.

Here is a biography of Helen Hunt West of Jacksonville, Florida, a leading member of the National Woman's party in her state during World War I. She was a journalist, the society editor of the *Florida Times-Union* and editor of the *Southern Club Woman*. She was active in the 1920s, when few others were, in supporting the equal rights amendment and opposing protective legislation for women. As a member of the Duval County Democratic Women's Club, she became a key lobbyist for a bill to amend the state's election laws to guarantee women be placed in equal numbers with men on executive committees of political parties. In 1935, the governor signed a bill requiring participation by women at all levels of state party organizations and establishing equal opportunities for women to be elected as chair or vice-chair on state and county political committees. If the chair were a man, a woman would automatically serve as vice chair, and vice versa.

404 *s,z McKELVEY, BLAKE. "Women's Rights in Rochester: A Century of Progress, 1848-1948." *Rochester History* 10 (July 1948): 1-24. Notes.

One hundred years after the cities of Seneca Falls and Rochester, New York, housed the first women's rights conventions in America (July and August of 1848), McKelvey provided a chronological survey of the women's organizations that convened or began in Rochester. He draws distinctions between the women who attended the two early conferences, citing the Rochester meeting as attracting greater numbers of working class-women. He documents the founding of the Woman's Protection Union, under the presidency of Mrs. Ruth Roberts, to campaign in the late 1840s for increased wages for working girls. He discusses the goals of the Daughters of Temperance, which politicized Susan B. Anthony, Rochester's adopted daughter. The New York State Temperance Society and National Dress Reform Association both held well-attended meetings in Rochester. In 1873, the Women Taxpayers' Association was created around the issue of Anthony's hundred-dollar fine for attempting to vote in a local election. Rochester was the site of the Ladies' Hospital Relief Association, Ignorance Club (1881), Women's Political Club (later Political Equality Club), Ethical Club, Women's Educational and Industrial Union, Council of Women (1899), which pressed for the admission of women to the University of Rochester, Women's Christian Temperance Union, Monroe County Woman Suffrage Party, League of Women Voters, and Women's City Club. The National Woman's Studies Association held its 1878 convention in Rochester. The New York State Woman's Suffrage Association met there in the 1880s.

405 *m McMASTER, ELIZABETH WARING. *The Girls of the Sixties*. Columbia, S.C.: the author, 1937. 175 pp. Illus.: President Clark and 53 members of the club.

In 1917, fifty-three women in Columbia, South Carolina, formed a social and literary club under the presidency of Mrs. Clark Waring called Girls of the Sixties. These women wrote papers relating to their Confederate War experiences and participated in the National League for Women's Service to knit articles of clothing for the soldiers of World War I. They adopted two French orphans, bought and sold Liberty Bonds, contributed to a war memorial, and presented a silk state flag to the Young Men's Christian Association at Camp Jackson. This volume contains 110 essays by women who are reminiscing about the Civil War. For the detail it provides on the domestic sphere in the 1860s, this history is a gold mine.

406 *r MECKEL, RICHARD A. "Educating a Ministry of Mothers: Evangelical Maternal Associations, 1815-1860." *Journal of the Early Republic* 2 (Spring 1982): 403-23. Notes.

Presbyterian, Congregationalist, and Baptist maternal associations published journals for women who were members of mothers' clubs in antebellum America. Examining the advice about child raising in *Mother's Magazine, Mother's Journal,* and *Mother's Assistant and Young Ladies' Friend,* the author determines the serious attention to religious training that mothers brought from their clubs to their homes.

407 *r MEEKER, RUTH ESTHER. *Six Decades of Service, 1880-1940: A History of the Woman's Home Missionary Society of the Methodist Episcopal Church.* N.p.: the organization, 1969. 405 pp. Brief index plus full index (separate pamphlet attached), illus.: author; list of founding officers on 1880 plaque in Cincinnati; 7 of founding officers; 38 of 1940 Board of Trustees; 1 group photo of 1934 Girl's Golden Year Revue; Mercy Center in Chicago; Pheiffer Chapel of Bennett College in Greensboro, North Carolina; James Hall, Ethel Harpst Home in Cedartown, Georgia.

This one-hundred-year history of the Woman's Home Missionary Society of the Methodist Episcopal church surveys the members' accomplishments in three ways. Part 1 narrates the developments of each decade, quoting documents, citing leaders, and measuring growth. Part 2 enumerates projects undertaken by the association: deaconess work, educational work, social welfare, city missions, community work, medical work, special projects like deaconess work at navy yards, and outpost missions in Alabama, Puerto Rico, Santo Domingo, and Hawaii. The final section catalogs methods of work and considers its departments of young people, publications and publicity, promotional work, mite boxes, Lenten offerings, money, summer schools of missions, education, student work, evangelicalism, spiritual life, and christian citizenship.

408 *b MELDER, KEITH. "Ladies Bountiful: Organized Women's Benevolence in Early Nineteenth Century America." *New York History* 48 (July 1967): 231-54.

Melder catalogs the many women's voluntary activities inspired by the antebellum revival of Christianity and its attendant benevolent impact. Among the organizational work he examines is the Sunday school movement, missionary movements, female Bible societies, and clubs to assist the poor and the suffering, to found voluntary relief associations, to bring about moral reform of prostitutes, and to support the antislavery movement. The clergy, in calling for women's charitable compassion, unintentionally enlarged women's sphere and encouraged their "insubordination," for they took charge of their own clubs and treasuries.

409   *p MELLICKER, BETTY. *Fifty Years of Service: 1914-1964, Ladies Auxiliary to the Veterans of Foreign Wars of the United States.* Kansas City, Mo.: National Headquarters of the Ladies Auxiliary to the Veterans of Foreign Wars, 1964. iv, 159 pp. Illus.: 68 of officers; conventions; members participating in projects.

On its fiftieth anniversary, this organization sponsored a history for its 335,000 members, who were "wives, widows, sisters, mothers, daughters and granddaughters of campaign medal service veterans and women who have themselves served overseas." This group, organized in Pittsburgh in 1914, had been raising $3 million a year for health, research, education, and social welfare programs. Some of its gifts went to top graduates of the U.S. Military, Naval, Air Force and Coast Guard academies, to high school essay contest winners, to a Boy Scout scholarship, to the Martha Washington Building at Valley Forge, and, after 1936, to an annual birthday party for the Statue of Liberty. The eight chapters of the history are organized chronologically, from the forerunners of this association in the Civil War assistance that women provided through the "organizational struggles," World War I, the twenties, depression, World War II, the modern auxiliary, and continuing programs, especially home, hospital work, Americanism, rehabilitation, youth activities, cancer aid and research, community service, and civil defense. Using records from annual national conventions, this history emphasizes administrative angles rather than the work of local branches. Lists are provided of national presidents, from 1914-63, of national officers, 1914-63, and of important auxiliary dates between 1862 and 1963.

410   *z MERK, LOIS BANNISTER. "The Early Career of Maud Wood Park." *Radcliffe Quarterly* 32 (May 1948): 10-17. Informational notes, illus.: Maud Wood Park in 1898.

Maud Wood, of Albany, New York, entered Radcliffe College in 1895. Although the college administration and faculty opposed woman suffrage, she and her friend Inez Haynes invited Alice Stone Blackwell to speak in support of suffrage at the Emmanuel Club. Soon

Maud was active in the New England Suffrage Association. Her marriage to Charles Park did nothing to diminish her career as a suffragist. She spoke at women's clubs and suffrage leagues and joined the Massachusetts Woman Suffrage Association, revitalizing it as its executive director in 1900. In the same year, she and Inez formed the College Equal Suffrage League and encouraged colleges throughout the nation to enlist young women in the cause of suffrage. Although Radcliffe College opposed the establishment of a branch in 1913, the organization was successful in politicizing college women. In 1901, Maud Wood Park founded and served as executive secretary of the Boston Equal Suffrage Association for Good Government, an organization devoted both to woman suffrage and to the improvement of government. The society held New Voters' Festivals, held civics classes for women, and cooperated with the Women's Educational and Industrial Union and the Massachusetts Federation of Women's Clubs on legislative reforms the women supported. In 1908, Maud Wood Park toured the United States, founding College Equal Suffrage Leagues as she traveled. When the federal suffrage amendment was finally ratified in 1920, she served as the president of the League of Women Voters, developed from the National American Woman Suffrage Association.

411   *p MERKLEY, G. *Monument to Courage: A History of Beaver County*. Milford, Utah: Beaver Press, 1948.
      See Daughters of Utah Pioneers. [Beaver County Chapter].

412   *p METTLACH, MRS. FRANK R. *History of the California State Society Daughters of the American Revolution; 1938-1968*. San Diego: Neyenesch, 1968.
      See Daughters of the American Revolution, [California].

413   *c MICHELS, EILEEN MANNING. "Alice O'Brien: Volunteer and Philanthropist." In *Women of Minnesota: Selected Biographical Essays*, edited by Barbara Stuhler and Gretchen Kreuter, 136-54, 360-62. St. Paul: Minnesota Historical Society Press, 1977. Notes, illus.: Alice O'Brien.
      Alice O'Brien, was an active clubwoman in St. Paul, Minnesota, founded in 1920 the St. Paul's Women's City Club "to provide for women a center for organized work and for social and intellectual intercourse." The author of this essay traces the club's movement from literary study to civic reform and documents its World War I relief projects, its fund-raising through support of arts events, and its invitations to lecturers T.S. Eliot, Gertrude Stein, and Amelia

Earhart. The club peaked in size in the 1950s, with fifteen hundred members. The clubhouse costing $265,000, opened in 1931 for club activities and was sold in 1972.

414 *i MILLER, FRANCESCA. "The International Relations of Women of the Americas, 1890-1928." *The Americas* 43 (October 1986): 171-82. Notes.

Although no women delegates attended the first International Conference of American States in 1889, women later participated in Pan-Americanism. They attended subsequent conferences of ICAS, and Eleanor Foster Lansing planned the first Pan-American Women's Auxiliary Conference where the Pan-American International Council for Women was proposed. In 1922, under the sponsorship of the League of Women Voters, Baltimore hosted the Council's conference for the exchange of views by women of the Western Hemisphere.

415 *n MILLER, KATHLEEN ATKINSON. "The Ladies and the Lynchers: A Look at the Association of Southern Women for the Prevention of Lynching." *Southern Studies* 17 (Fall 1978): 221-40.

Praising its effort to overcome racial and sexual prejudice, Miller analyzes the work of the Association of Southern Women for the Prevention of Lynching, founded in 1930 by Jessie Daniel Ames, who was director of women's work for the Commission in Inter-racial Cooperation, a suffragist League of Woman Voters member, a delegate to the Democratic National Conventions of 1920, 1924 and 1928, and an organizer of the Texas American Association of University Women. She converted a loosely organized ladies auxiliary for interracial cooperation into a concerted attack upon lynching. In Atlanta, twenty-six women representing a variety of civic and religious organizations repudiated the idea that lynching defined and protected southern white women. They collected antilynching pledges, especially from sheriffs and governors, disseminated facts and statistics about the growing prevalence of lynching black women, exposed ambivalence about lynching in newspapers, especially in editorials, and enjoyed success in creating pressure to diminish the problem.

416 *z MILLER, SALLY M. "Other Socialists: Native-Born and Immigrant Women in the Socialist Party of America, 1901-1917." *Labor History* 24 (Winter 1983): 84-102.

In 1908, the Socialist party of America organized the Woman's National Committee, which represented a membership of 5 percent of the total organization. By 1912, women made up 10 percent of the total membership, and in 1914, 17 percent. Women were ignored or not recognized as potential party talent, and so they clustered in an auxiliary, engaging in separate activities. They were excluded from party policy-making, fiscal matters, and meetings to devise strategy. They served instead as a clearinghouse and focus for women's socialist activities and built a hierarchy parallel to the men's system. Most women members of the Socialist party were native-born middle-class Americans plus a few foreign-born working-class individuals. Its members, such as Kate Richards O'Hare, May Wood Simons, Lena Morrow Lewis, Theresa Serber Malkiel, Meta Stern Lilienthal, and Antoinette F. Konikow, prodded their party to an awareness of the diversity of the American work force.

417 MILLETT, EMILY, CAROLINE TICKNOR, and ELEANOR W. ALLEN. comps. *Saturday Morning Club*. Boston: the organization, 1931. 104 pp.

On its sixtieth birthday, in 1931, the Saturday Morning Club of Boston celebrated by commissioning its history to be written. Julia Ward Howe started the club for her daughters and their friends. This compilation includes reminiscences of early members of their social activities, literary study, civic awareness, and wartime relief efforts. The volume gives the members, officers, lectures, constitution, and bylaws.

418 *c MINTZ, LEONORA FERGUSON. "Reading Club of 1906 Becomes the Woman's Club in 1913." *Georgia Life*, Spring 1978, 44-45. Illus.: Mrs. W.B. Everett, first president in 1906; Mrs. B.T. Morgan, first president of the Rockmart Club in 1913; Rockmart Woman's Clubhouse in 1922.

In 1906, women of Rockmart, Georgia, organized the Reading Club. The name was changed to the Woman's Club in 1913, when the group joined the Georgia Federation of Women's Clubs. The author describes efforts of black and white women to beautify the town. She also outlines fund-raising efforts to build a clubhouse. By 1922, the members had raised eight hundred dollars through the sale of sandwiches and by holding silver teas. In 1922, the fifty-three women opened a clubhouse of 1,320 square feet, and paid off their five-thousand-dollar debt through rummage sales, plays, and meals provided to other organizations.

419 *z MITCHELL, BONNIE. "The League of Women Voters Marks Fifty Years." *Wisconsin Then and Now* 16 (September 1969): 1-3. Illus.: banner, "Wisconsin—First State to Have Equal Rights," held by 4 women, Carrie Chapman Catt, Jessie Jack Hooper, the state

league founder; telegram urging opposition to equal rights amendment.

Wisconsin feminist Carrie Chapman Catt led the National American Woman Suffrage Association to victory with the passage of the federal amendment granting women the vote in 1920. She rechanneled the energy of the membership into a League of Women Voters. In the state of Wisconsin, Jessie Jack Hooper founded the state counterpart. On the fiftieth anniversary of the Wisconsin group, its membership numbered 3,200 women in thirty-nine cities, part of a national membership of 156,000. Mitchell reviews the league's major battles in Wisconsin and documents a successful alliance with the National Woman's party in 1921 for a state equal rights bill.

420   *r   MITCHELL, NORMA TAYLOR. "From Social to Radical Feminism: A Survey of Emerging Diversity in Methodist Women's Organization, 1869-1974." *Methodist History* 13 (April 1975): 21-44. Notes.

In order to argue that there has been an interaction between feminism and Methodism for over a hundred years, the author focuses on the period before the 1939 unification of women's organizations in the Methodist Episcopal Church and Methodist Episcopal Church, South. The 1848 Seneca Falls Women's Rights Convention was held in a Wesleyan Methodist church. Nevertheless, feminists early on observed the patriarchal patterns in the church, and laymen and clergy alike were ambivalent toward the members of Methodist women's organizations. Mitchell uses the history of inequality within the church to explain the radicalism that erupted in Methodism in the 1960s.

421   *c   MOORE, CLARA. "Ladies' Education Society of Jacksonville, Illinois, Founded October 4, 1833." *Illinois State Historical Society Journal* 18 (April 1925): 196-200.

The oldest independent woman's society in America, claims Moore, was founded in 1833 in Jacksonville, Illinois. The Ladies' Education Society accepted donations from liberal friends in the northeastern part of the United States and built a treasury to assist in the education of girls. In its first year, it aided 5 girls on a budget of $246. By its third year of operation, members had collected $983 to assist 45 girls. In the first ten years, 180 young women were aided at a cost of $3,000. On its twentieth anniversary it counted 532 pupils at a cost of $7,531.

422   *c MOORE, DOROTHEA.   "Work of Women's Clubs in California." *Annals of the American Academy of Political and Social Science* 28 (September 1906): 257-60.

Although the author claims, wrongly, that the earliest woman's club in California was founded in 1876 in San Francisco, she provides little-known details about the history of the Outdoor Art League (1903) and a list of Los Angeles clubs and their projects.

423   *p MOORE, FRANK. *Women of the War: Their Heroism and Self-Sacrifice.* Hartford, Conn.: S.S. Scranton and Co., 1866. xvi, 596 pp. Illus.: 10 engravings.

Although much of this volume consists of biographies of individual women who nursed soldiers and aided the war effort, there is mention of their volunteer efforts in hospitals, charities, and fairs sprinkled throughout. The final chapter, "Sanitary Laborers," alone documents the history of women's wartime voluntary associations with coherence. Moore examines the contributions of the Woman's Central Relief Association, Sanitary commissions, Sanitary fairs, Soldiers' Aid societies, Pennsylvania Relief Association, New England Women's Auxiliary Association, and Soldiers' Homes and Rests.

424   *c MOORE, MARGARET KING. "The Ladies Association for Educating Females, 1833-1937." *Illinois State Historical Society Journal* 31 (June 1938): 166-87.

Margaret Moore here embellishes the history of the Ladies Association for Educating Females of Jacksonville, Illinois, which was documented in 1925 in the same publication by Clara Moore. This work details the early years and credits Celeste Ellis, the wife of a Presbyterian missionary, with founding the organization. Another charter member was Mrs. Edward Beecher, wife of the president of the Illinois College. The object of the organization was to find girls who might be educated as teachers and collect funds for their tuition. The author has collected minutes, reports, and members' accounts to flesh out the story of the members' work.

425   *p MORLEY, MRS. WALTER S., comp. *History of the California State Society, Daughters of the American Revolution, 1891-1938.* Berkeley, Calif.: Lederer, Street, and Zeus Co., 1938. 621 pp. Indexes, illus.: 17 of state regents.

Morley provides brief biographies of the seventeen women who served as state regents in the California Daughters of the American Revolution between its founding in 1891 and 1937. She has also written a history of the organization and its committees, with a long list of historical spots and old trails that were marked by DAR plaques. Another list details the papers circulated to California branches for study. The bulk of the text (pp. 189-480), however, consists of ninety chapter histories, each rich with names of officers and projects undertaken. Most are strongest on the most recent plans initiated by each group. A roster of members, pp. 481-619, rounds out the volume.

426 *b MORRIS, ANN J. "The History of the St. Louis Protestant Orphan Asylum." *Missouri Historical Society Bulletin* 36 (January 1980): 80-91. Notes, illus.: first home of St. Louis Association for the Relief of Orphan Children; Edgewood Children's Center.

For the most part, the author stresses the history of the institution rather than the women members of the association that funded the St. Louis Protestant Orphan Asylum. Brief attention is paid, however, to the sixteen women who adopted a constitution in 1834 to create the St. Louis Association of Ladies for the Relief of Orphan Children. The board of directors included four Protestant ministers, but the women were the backbone of fund-raisers, through one-dollar subscriptions, for the orphanage.

427 *s MORTON, KATHARINE A. "A Historical Review of Woman Suffrage." *Wyoming Annals* 12 (January 1940): 21-34. Illus.: Esther Hobart Morris; sketch of Wyoming Territory.

Morton provides a biography of Esther Hobart Morris, of Oswego, New York, as the individual responsible for woman suffrage in Wyoming Territory in 1869. As a widow, she moved west with her baby and settled in Wyoming. On 2 September 1869, she invited twenty friends to dinner, including the candidates for the legislature. At that time, W.H. Bright, president of the Council, or upper house, promised to introduce a woman suffrage bill to his colleagues. He did so in November 1869, and the house passed it and Governor Campbell signed it into law. Woman suffrage was not secure, however, for the Democrats tried to repeal the act in 1871. They failed, but woman suffrage remained controversial at the time of Wyoming's statehood in 1889. Morton articulates the arguments used unsuccessfully against women's enfranchisement.

428 *t MORTON, MARIAN J. "Temperance, Benevolence, and the City: The Cleveland Non-Partisan WCTU, 1874-1900." *Ohio History* 91 (1982): 58-73. Notes, illus.: 1 of women pickets in "prayer booth" during Ohio Temperance Crusade; 2 of *Harper's Weekly* report of "Women's Crusade against Intemperance" and Thomas Nast

cartoon, "The Good and Bad Spirits of War"—women crusaders as Joan of Arc.

In March of 1874, fifty Cleveland women formed a Women's Temperance league, to combat the use of alcohol. In 1885, however, they distinguished themselves from the Women's Christian Temperance Union by calling themselves the Non-Partisan Woman's Christian Temperance Union and disassociating themselves from the larger WCTU which planned to endorse a political party, the Prohibition party. The Cleveland women sought instead to combine benevolent work with evangelism and steer clear of politics. Concerning themselves chiefly with needy women and children who were victims of male inebriation, the membership founded Open Door, a home for friendless women and unwed mothers. It served the public from 1878 to 1890. In 1882, the members founded a Kitchen Garden. Divided about the issue of woman suffrage, the members refused to take a stand as the WCTU had. In 1913, the women joined the Cleveland Federation for Charity and Philanthropy. Except for its distancing from politics, its work resembled that of the WCTU closely.

429   *n MOSSELL, MRS. N.F. *The Work of the Afro-American Woman.* 2nd ed. Philadelphia: Ferguson Co., 1908. Facsimile. Ann Arbor: University Microfilms, 1973. 178 pp. Illus.: 3 black women.

This volume includes twenty-five pages of verse by the author and biographies of leading black women in the fields of education, literature, journalism, health, art, embalming, commerce, invention, and composition. There is also attention to the work of black women's organizations. Mossell discusses the Women's Christian Temperance Union, which was headed by Mrs. Frances Ellen Watkins Harper, who was also a member of the National Council of Women, Association for the Advancement of Women, and the Colored Authors and Educators Association. She surveys the antislavery, temperance, and suffrage activities of Sojourner Truth. Misses Fanny and Alma Somerville of Philadelphia supported Working Girls clubs. The Woman's Loyal Union of Brooklyn and New York honored Ida B. Wells. The Colored Women's League of Washington, D.C., also receives consideration in this volume.

430   *b,r MUDGE, FLORENCE A. "History of the Benevolent Society of the First Baptist Church." *Danvers* (Mass.) *Historical Society Collection* 23 (1935): 33-40.

This article features the history of the Ladies Benevolent Society of the First Church of Danvers which was founded in 1832, but recognizes that earlier women's charitable societies had existed: the Charitable Female Century Society in Danvers and Middleton (1816), the South Danvers Female Benevolent Society (1812), and the Salem Female Charitable Society (1801), which still functioned at the time this study was written. Mudge lists the names of the women officers in the Benevolent Society of the First Church, and the active and honorary (over forty years old) members who made and distributed garments for the needy or sold garments to raise money for charitable causes. In its first twenty years, the organization's members produced 3,634 articles of clothing. In its one hundred years, 549 women and 26 men spent fifteen thousand to help the needy, repair the parsonage, and restore graveyards. They made money by sponsoring quilting parties, husking bees, bazaars, suppers, picnics, blueberrying events, and concerts. The first of its thirty-four presidents, Mrs. Mary Parker Barman, wife of a pastor, served as leader from 1832 to 54. Her biography is provided. Descriptions of the fiftieth and seventy-fifth anniversary parties are provided.

431 *f MULLINS, MARION DAY. *The History of Kappa Delta Sorority, 1897-1937.* 2 vols. Menasha, Wis.: the organization, 1937. 352 pp. Indexes, illus.: vol. 2 is entirely pictorial, offering hundreds of photographs of groups of sorority sisters between the years 1897 and 1937; portraits of officers; interiors and exteriors of chapter houses.

Kappa Delta sorority formed in Virginia in 1897, at the State Female Normal School in Farmville. Mullins documents the national officers and accomplishments of council meetings each year. For every convention, she details the place, publications, speeches, social events, and delegates who attended. A list of the colleges with chapters is provided.

432 *m NATHAN, MAUD. *The Story of an Epoch-Making Movement.* Garden City, N.Y.: Doubleday, Page and Co., 1926. xxi, 245 pp. Index, appendixes, illus.: statue by Daniel Chester French, *The Spirit of Life*, which appeared on all Consumers' League leaflets.

In seven chapters, the founder of the National Consumers' League documents its founding in 1891 in New York City and its growth and development as an organization devoted to identifying and ameliorating working conditions of saleswomen and children employed in retail mercantile houses. Its middle-class members patronized department stores that agreed to the "Standards of a Fair House" which the league prepared and publicized, thereby encouraging establishments to improve wages, hours, and physical conditions of labor as well as other humanitarian conditions. Nathan lists the stores on the league's approved White List, prints the standards in full, and elaborates on the acceptance of her goals through support by the Russell Sage Foundation and the General Federation of Women's Clubs and the formation of branch leagues throughout the United States and abroad. She credits the Working Women's Society and Alice Woodbridge with the initial study of department store conditions in 1889-90 and the inspiration to found the National Consumers' League. Her study, unlike many of the detailed encyclopedias about women's association history, is readable and instructive, providing multitudes of anecdotes and examples about specific workers, stores, and tactics to alter unfair working conditions. Appendixes include documents pertinent to the history of the organization, with reports of all state consumers' leagues.

433   *s   NATIONAL AMERICAN WOMAN SUFFRAGE ASSOCIATION. *Victory, How Women Won It: A Centennial Symposium, 1840-1940.* New York: H.W. Wilson Co., 1940. 174 pp. Bib., appendixes, illus.: 8 including Lucretia Mott; Lucy Stone; Elizabeth Cady Stanton; Susan B. Anthony; Anna Howard Shaw; Carrie Chapman Catt; Speaker Gillett of House of Representatives signing suffrage bill on 5 June 1919.

Eleven activists prominent in the suffrage struggle wrote one chapter each about the movement and their experiences in an accessible, breezy style. Mary Foulke Morrison's "Preliminary Agitation" is a history of the woman's movement from 1776 to 1848; Mary Gray Peck's "First Organized Action" describes the 1848 Seneca Falls Conference; Mildred Adams's "Rampant Women" documents the women's rights conventions of 1850-60; Mary Foulke Morrison's "That Word Male" explains the debate about the civil rights amendment enfranchising black men rather than all men and all women; Carrie Chapman Catt's and Nettie Rogers Shuler's "Wyoming: The First Surrender" praises the first state to grant women suffrage; Maud Wood Park's "Campaigning State by State" catalogs efforts against antisuffragists from 1869 to 1915; Gertrude Foster Brown's "The Opposition Breaks" explores the significance of Illinois granting women the vote in 1913; Penelope P.B. Huse's "Appeals to Congress" explores lobbying efforts before federal legislators in the late nineteenth and early twentieth century; Gertrude Foster Brown's "A Decisive Victory Won" tells of stunts and parades employed by New York suffragists in 1915; Maud Wood Park's "The Winning Plan" bares the final push by suffragists to attain their goal; Mary Gray Peck's "The Secretary Has Signed the Proclamation" recounts Carrie Chapman Catt's ratification campaign in the states, once Congress had passed the suffrage amendment to the Constitution. Nine appendixes include lists of 1940 officers of National American Woman Suffrage Association, important dates in the history of the woman's movement, and notes on contributors.

434　*s　NEU, CHARLES E. "Olympia Brown and the Woman's Suffrage Movement." *Wisconsin Magazine of History* 43 (Summer 1960): 277-87. Illus.: Olympia Brown; Elizabeth Cady Stanton; Susan B. Anthony; Lucy Stone; 1917 White House pickets.

　　　　A thoughtful piece, which reflects on Olympia Brown's political positions, this article gives her biography and describes her long involvement with the woman suffrage struggle. In 1866 she met Susan B. Anthony and became an ardent suffragist. In 1876, she toured Kansas on behalf of the woman suffrage amendment. She was a charter member of the American Equal Rights Association to advance the cause of black and female enfranchisement. She stayed aloof of the American Woman Suffrage and the National Woman Suffrage associations for the most part, but held the presidency in the 1880s of Wisconsin's State Suffrage Association. In 1890, she signed the call for a Woman's National Liberal Union and spoke at its Washington, D.C., convention. In 1892, finding the newly merged National American Woman Suffrage Association uncongenial, she founded the Federal Suffrage Association in Chicago, insisting on a federal Constitution amendment rather than state campaigns. In 1902, with Clara Colby, she reshaped it into the Federal Woman's Equality Association, and the two lobbied Congress annually on its behalf. In 1912, when Wisconsin voted on the suffrage amendment, Brown's young rivals formed the flamboyant Political Equality League. When legislators failed to pass the amendment, Brown resigned from the presidency of the Woman's Suffrage Association in Wisconsin. Still, she remained active, supporting the National Woman's party at the age of seventy-eight in 1913. She picketed the White House in 1917 and 1918 and picketed the Republican National Convention in 1920. Almost until her death in 1926, she remained visible in the suffrage struggle.

435　*c,n　NEVERDON-MORTON, CYNTHIA. "Self-Help Programs as Educative Activities of Black Women in the South, 1895-1925: Focus on Four Key Areas." *Journal of Negro Education* 51 (Summer 1982): 254-65.

Arguing that black women strived to effect changes and develop programs that would offer stability and advancement for black communities, this historian outlines four women's organizations at the turn of the century, in Tuskegee, Alabama; Hampton, Virginia; Atlanta, Georgia; and Baltimore, Maryland. Mrs. Mary M. Washington, wife of Booker T. Washington, founded the Tuskegee Woman's Club and served as its first president. In 1897, the group opened a settlement house at Russell Plantation. By 1910 they had a full night school with such classes as cooking and Negro history, a Mother's Club, and a publication the *Messenger*. In Hampton, girls' clubs were initiated by extension agents for the purpose of self-betterment, housekeeping instruction, handicrafts, patriotism, and outdoor activities. In Atlanta, women opened the Neighborhood Union in 1907, which sponsored the Anti-Tuberculosis Association's health program. In 1904, the Baltimore Colored Empty Stocking and Fresh Air Circle brought sunshine and joy to Baltimore's dependent children. They established a junior circle as well, which gave gifts through the churches. In 1905, the circle bought a ten-and-a-half-acre farm fourteen miles from Baltimore and ran a camp there until August 1912, when they ran out of funds.

436 *p NEWTON, CATHERINE A. "History of Daughters of the American Revolution Museum When in Memorial Continental Hall, 1910-1950." *DAR Magazine* 84 (February 1950): 101-2.

This traces the history of the museum sponsored by the Daughters of the American Revolution in Washington, D.C., from its origins in 1890 through the building of Memorial Continental Hall in 1910 to the completion of Constitution Hall in 1930. Current plans were to add additional galleries to hold the historical artifacts donated by state chapters.

437 *c NICHOLS, MAY ELLIS. *A History of the Cambridge Club*. N.p.: the organization, 1911. 46 pp. Illus.: 1 of Julia Arnold Kempshall.

Julia Arnold Kempshall founded the Cambridge, Massachusetts, reading circle in 1890. This brief and chatty discussion about the club's social and intellectual development also contains a list of all its members in its first twenty years.

438 *p NOBLE, LUCY SEWARD. "National Society of the U.S. Daughters of 1812, State of Michigan." *Michigan History Magazine* 3 (July 1919): 361-66.

Succinctly, Noble surveys the history of the national society, the Michigan branch, and its General Isaac Shelby Chapter. The national was founded in 1892 by Flora Adams Darling to commemorate military engagements between the United States and Great Britain between 1812 and-1815. It was determined "to carry on patriotic and historical enterprises and to further educational and benevolent undertakings . . . not ancestor worship, but to preserve ancient landmarks, honor the graves of valiant soldiers with appropriate markers, carry on projects for the preservation, continuance and uplift of coming generations." The first national president was Mrs. William Gerry Slade of New York, who enlisted the support of 75 members. By 1919, 4,092 members had joined from thirty-five states. The women raised $1,250 for a six-paneled window in Dartmoore, England's St. Michael's Church to honor 218 American prisoners detained in Dartmoore War Prison in 1813-16. The men had helped build the church and died in the town. The women also presented five vases to George Washington Memorial Chapel in Valley Forge in 1917. A Michigan organization was first organized in 1896 and grew to have 139 members, although there were 74 on the rolls at the time of this article's preparation. Officers are listed. These women raised $12,000 for a monument to Major-General Alexander Macomb. The General Isaac Shelby Chapter was organized in 1917. Its members allied with the Red Cross, National League of Women's Service, and the Society for French Wounded. They held drives, knit surgical dressings, raised $50 for a hospital and $125 for an ambulance, adopted orphans, and bought Liberty Bonds.

439 *p NONWEILER, MARY H. "Sibley House Association of the Minnesota D.A.R." *DAR Magazine* 83 (January 1949): 37-38.

In 1835, the Sibley House was built by Henry Hastings Sibley, the first governor of Minnesota. In 1837, two neighboring houses were constructed by the Faribaults and DePuises. In 1910, these historical sites were taken over by the Minnesota DAR. In 1935, the federal WPA program undertook to restore the homes and turned them over to the DAR for completion. They opened a tea house, which paid for expenses, and furnished the places with mid-nineteenth-century artifacts and Indian relics. Ten thousand visitors toured the facilities in the summer of 1948.

440 *n NORDYKE, LEWIS T. "Ladies and Lynching." In *The Changing Character of Lynching*, by Jessie Daniel Ames, 63-68. Atlanta: Commission on Inter-racial Cooperation, 1942. (First published in *Survey Graphic*, November 1939.)

In 1930, Jessie Daniel Ames founded the Association of Southern Women for the Prevention of Lynching and remained its executive director. The author estimates a membership of forty thousand southern women, backed by two million members of southern social, civic, and religious associations. The number of lynchings fell dramatically after this group began to prevent mobs from forming by writing letters, circulating leaflets, and seeking pledges from sheriffs to avoid confrontation. The success of the effort destroys the myth that white men lynched in women's names, for these women would not condone the mob violence of lynchers. Education to eradicate the horror of lynching was the goal of the organization.

441   *r NORTH, LOUISE McCOY. *The Story of the New York Branch of the Woman's Foreign Missionary Society of the Methodist Episcopal Church.* New York: the organization, 1926. 340 pp. Indexes, illus.: 22 of officers and founders.

This history is generous with quotations from correspondence of individuals involved with the organization. Forerunners of this association organized in April 1819 as the New York City Missionary and Bible Society of the Methodist Episcopal church. In July of that same year, they reorganized the Female Missionary Society of New York, an auxiliary to the Missionary and Bible Society. The first director, Mary W. Mason, served for forty years. Her addresses, journals, and letters are used. Most of the founders had died by the 1860s and the group folded, but in 1869, in Boston, the Woman's Foreign Missionary Society of the Methodist Episcopal church was revived. It sent Isabella Thorburn to India as a missionary. The New York branch hosted the first annual meeting, in 1870. Their first task was to establish an orphanage in India. Early auxiliary branches of the New York chapter grew up in Brooklyn, New Jersey, and upstate New York. Biographical accounts are provided on officers, who tended to be involved in the group's work for decades. In the chapter "Service," these topics are surveyed: *Heathen Woman's Friend*, the newspaper; study missions for reading; leaflets; mite boxes; headquarters at 805 Broadway in New York City; student work among college and seminary girls; adopting missionaries; organizing auxiliaries; children's work; public meetings; prayer, Thanksgiving offering; library service; and travel. The final chapter describes the women missionaries sent abroad, who passed on Christian attitudes about women. In 1871, they refused to teach Chinese girls who had bound feet to encourage the end of the custom. They opposed marriage of children as well. Lists are provided of the forty-five women missionaries to Africa, China, Europe, Japan, Korea, Malaysia, Mexico, and South America; of delegates from the New York branch to the General Executive Committee between

1870 and 1925; and annual meetings of the New York branch, place, president, secretary, and receipts from 1871 to 1925.

442   *m NORTHRUP, FLORA L. *The Record of a Century, 1834-1934.* New York: American Female Guardian Society and Home for the Friendless, 1934.   110 pp.   Illus.: 32 including Home for the Friendless, 936 Woody Crest Ave. (erected in 1902); children at play in the facilities.

This history was commissioned to celebrate the centennial of the American Female Guardian Society and Home for the Friendless. Its work was inspired by the Great Awakening of the 1830s in which the Reverend Charles Finney was a leading preacher.   John R. McDowall assisted in mobilizing religious fervor for good works and formed the New York Female Benevolent Society in 1833.   Its first director was Reverend Finney's wife, Mrs. Charles Finney.   In 1837, the group formed an employment aid committee for women.   Members visited slums, jails, and houses of ill-refute with religious tracts and rented a house to serve as an asylum for "reclaimed women," or reformed prostitutes.   Auxiliaries of this society quickly formed throughout New York State and New England.   In 1839, a national society formed, the American Female Moral Reform Society, which expanded membership still further and bought land to build homes for the friendless.   In 1847, the name of the organization was changed to the American Female Reform and Guardian Society, and now the women moved to petition legislators to pass laws taking neglected children or vagrants from their parents.   This society opened an Industrial School, built a chapel, and during the Civil War, cared for children left destitute by drafted soldiers.   Members bought sewing machines and let women buy them on time to earn a living through sewing.   In 1885, they established the Oceanport branch for country vacations for needy city-dwellers.   The author examines the progress of the organization by summarizing the work of each president.   Great love and admiration for the officers is reflected in descriptions of their efforts.   The last chapter contains a list of the boys and girls, among the 6,452 served, who "made good," or entered professions.   There is a list of the women managers of the institutions created by the association from 1834 to 1934 and a roster of present staff members and managers.

443   *p   NORTON, MARY BETH.   *Liberty's Daughters: The Revolutionary Experience of American Women, 1750-1800.*   Boston: Little, Brown and Co., 1980. xvi, 384 pp. Notes, bib., indexes, illus.: 21 portraits of colonial women.

Norton documents the efforts of the Ladies Association, which was founded in Philadelphia in 1780 by Esther De Berdt Reed, to raise money for the war effort. The women members raised a substantial sum for the revolutionary cause, but insisted on guiding George Washington as to how they wanted it spent. Women in Trenton, New Jersey, and in the state of Virginia copied the plan and raised funds as well. The bulk of the study, however, deals not with women's organizations but with their attitudes toward their private lives and the growth of their political opinions during the American Revolution.

444. *p -----. "The Philadelphia Ladies' Association." *American Heritage* 31 (April-May 1980): 102-7. Illus.: Color portraits of Esther De Berdt Reed by Charles Wilson Peale; Sarah Franklin Bache, Ben Franklin's daughter; Sarah Armitage McKean and daughter, Sophia Dorothea, by Charles Wilson Peale.

Adapted from Norton's book, *Liberty's Daughters*, this article examines the woman's relief society, formed in 1780, the Philadelphia Ladies Association. Esther De Berdt Reed, its president, published a broadside, *The Sentiments of an American Woman*, in which she argued that women's activity in the public sphere was not improper but appropriate activity for good citizens in wartime. She urged women readers to renounce "vain ornaments" and donate money to the American Revolution. She created an organization in which each county of her region was assigned a "treasuress" and this was a position of status. The wife of the Pennsylvania governor became the "treasuress-general." Philadelphia was divided into ten districts, with two to five women traveling in each, in pairs, to canvass every woman and girl to donate money. In a short time, members raised $300,000 from 1,600 people. With inflation, its purchase power was really $7,500, but the women saw their work as a symbol of their true patriotism. Women in Trenton, New Jersey, copied the model and raised $15,500 in currency, and Maryland women raised $16,000. Women made sure that the money was spent as they saw fit—on two thousand shirts identified with the names of the female sponsors.

445 *s NOUN, LOUISE R. *Strong-Minded Women: The Emergence of Woman Suffrage in Iowa.* Ames: Iowa State University Press, 1969. xv, 322 pp. Informational notes, appendixes, bib., indexes, illus.: 76 including Iowa officers; 1889 group photo of Iowa Women's Suffrage Association; Iowa news cartoons.

This author is careful to provide a national context for the Iowa material she collected. She is aware of the national suffrage figures and issues surrounding and explaining the efforts of Iowa women. In ten chapters, she moves from biographies of Elizabeth Cady Stanton, Lucy Stone, and Amelia Bloomer, founders of the suffrage movement in the East, through the Civil War Sanitary Commission which had an Iowa branch. The woman suffrage debate broke out in Iowa in 1866, with discussion over the implementation of a Negro suffrage amendment to the U.S. Constitution. Noun describes the lectures suffragist Anna Dickenson gave in Iowa and quotes legislators and newspapermen. In 1869, the Northern Iowa Woman Suffrage Association formed. Eight biographies of leaders and excerpts from speeches are included. In 1870, the Iowa Woman Suffrage Association formed and again Noun provides biographies of prominent leaders. She documents internal friction among the members which dissolved the organization in 1871. Suffragists who campaigned for suffrage were unsuccessful in 1872. The final section of the work consists of a biography of Carrie Chapman Catt, who lived in Iowa as a girl and developed her political savvy organizing suffragists there. In 1900, she became the president of the National American Woman Suffrage Association. Eleven biographies of Iowa women active in the national suffrage scene between 1872 and 1920 rounds out the collection. Appendixes include the Women's Declaration of Independence, 1848, and a report of the 1870 women's suffrage convention at Mount Pleasant.

446   *m O'CONNER, LILLIAN. *Pioneer Women Orators: Rhetoric in the Ante-Bellum Reform Movement.* New York: Columbia University Press, 1954. xvii, 246 pp. Notes, bib., indexes.

To analyze the style of rhetoric employed by activist women in New England, New York State, Ohio, Indiana, and Minnesota, O'Connor examined the speeches given at suffrage, temperance, and abolitionist meetings of women by twenty-eight individuals. They include Lucy Stone, Lucretia Mott, Paulina Wright Davis, Emma Robinson Coe, Elizabeth Cady Stanton, Susan B. Anthony, Mary Grew, Abby Kelley, Jane Grey Swisshelm, Sojourner Truth, Angelina Grimké, Ernestine Rose, and Antoinette Brown Blackwell.

447   *b ODELL, MRS. JONATHAN, et al, comps. *Origin and History of the Orphan Society in the City of New York, 1806-1896.* 2 vols. New York: Bonnell, Silver and Co., 1896. Vol. 1, iv, 1-352, illus.: 1 of the exterior of the building. Vol. 2, iv, 353-744.

Much of this work is a compilation of primary sources, rather than an analysis of the organization's history, but an introduction by Dr. George W. Bethune narrates his mother's founding of the Society for the Relief of Widows with Small Children in 1797. In 1806, Mrs.

Joanna Bethune called a public meeting of ladies to organize another society, devoted to establishing an orphan asylum. Officers were elected and a treasury created to provide shelter and lessons for the children. A cornerstone, in 1807, was laid for a building to house two hundred children. The bulk of the book consists of annual reports full of rich detail for the researcher. Volume 1 contains reports 3-51, and volume 2 contains reports 52-89.

448   *c OHIO FEDERATION OF WOMEN'S CLUBS. *The History of the Ohio Federation of Women's Clubs, 1924-1954.* Vol. 2. N.p.: the organization, 1954. 360 pp. Illus.: 14 of officers.

The work begins with a brief history of the federation from its birth in 1912, and then launches into a detailed account of each presidential administration from 1924-26 through 1954-56. Such information as the names of officers and committee members, types of civic, social service, arts, educational and wartime relief work projects initiated, and winners of theatrical competitions is lovingly and painstakingly provided.

See Annie Laws for volume 1.

449   *s,z O'NEILL, WILLIAM L. *Everyone Was Brave: A History of Feminism in America.* Chicago: Quadrangle Books, 1969. xi, 379 pp. Notes, indexes.

Defining social feminists as women who subordinated their belief in women's rights to a program of broad social reforms they thought more urgent, O'Neill examines their efforts in the late nineteenth and early twentieth century. He begins with a survey of suffrage and temperance organizations of the mid-nineteenth century and moves on to catalog the formation of other special interest organizations. For the period 1890-1920, he examines the reform programs of the Association of Collegiate Alumnae, General Federation of Women's Clubs, the National Federation of Settlements, the National Consumers' League and the National Women's Trade Union League. He then focuses on the biographies of these leading clubwomen: Josephine Shaw Lowell, Mrs. Carey Thomas, Margaret Dreier Robins, Jane Addams, Anna Howard Shaw, Carrie Chapman Catt, Alice Paul, Charlotte Perkins Gilman, Florence Kelley, and Vida Scudder. O'Neill examines feminism in the Progressive Era, the generous patriotic activity of most clubwomen during World War I via the Woman's Committee of the Council of National Defense, the dissent from the Woman's Peace party, the postwar club work of the Women's International League for Peace and Freedom, the political work of women's organizations after they had won the suffrage amendment to the Constitution, and the limits of social feminism on the advancement of women's status.

450 *m OTTO, KATHRYN. "Dakota Resources: The Jane Breeden Papers at the South Dakota Historical Resource Center." *South Dakota History* 10 (Summer 1980): 241-244. Illus.: Women in Pierre Dickens Club, Pierre, South Dakota, in 1911 at a costume party.

Here is a biography and a survey of primary sources on Jane Rooker Smith Breeden, a temperance, literary, and suffrage club leader in South Dakota.

451 *p PAINTER, MRS. W.R. "Achievements of the Missouri D.A.R." *Missouri Historical Review* 20 (April 1926): 382-87.

In 1890, eighteen women in Washington, D.C., founded the Daughters of the American Revolution and by 1926, it had 150,000 members. Missouri established a branch in 1897 and grew to have five thousand members. Its first state conference was held in St. Louis in 1899, and the group was active in aiding Spanish-American war soldiers. In addition, they took on these projects: sponsored a bill, which became law in 1903, to prevent desecration of the flag; dedicated a boulder to the Unknown Soldier in the National Cemetery at Jefferson Barracks, Missouri; gave $650 in scholarship money to the Ozark School; located and marked the Old Santa Fe Trail and El Camino Real; created a state flag of Missouri in 1913; established a monument at the starting point of the Pony Express; funded a Thomas Hart Benton Memorial; dedicated a bronze tablet to 280 Revolutionary War soldiers buried in Missouri; pledged service to World War I relief efforts; passed a resolution opposing the teaching of the German language in all schools under grade eight in 1918; supported a loan fund for rehabilitating 1,307 disabled soldiers; published a volume on pioneer women of Missouri; and purchased Arrow Rock Tavern and restored it.

452 *w PALIMPSEST. *The History of the Iowa Branch, National Federation of Business and Professional Women's Clubs, 1919-1970,* [Special Issue] 52 (March 1971): 129-58. Illus.: emblem; charter members; early and recent members and officers of the Iowa BPW; clubroom in 1920; minutes of 1919 meeting; "Golden Key" lyrics and music.

In 1919, at the Young Women's Christian Association in Des Moines, a handful of Iowa business and professional women formed a branch of the new organization the National Federation of Business and Professional Women's Clubs. Four of the women attended the national convention in St. Louis and returned to hold the first Iowa convention, in 1920. This issue of *Palimpsest* examines the issues undertaken by delegates to the annual Iowa conventions. The women addressed community service in the 1920s, the economy in the 1930s, war service in the 1940s, and international cooperation in the postwar era. Henrietta Zagel, "BPW in Retrospect" (pp. 155-58), stresses community projects members sponsored. Support of the Red Cross, Heart Fund, Cancer Fund, Easter Seals, local history projects including restoration of old buildings, scholarships, and a Woman's Exchange for the sale of goods made by housebound women are among the projects the author documents. Helen Vanderburg, in "Thread of Legislation," (146-50), details the early support for the Sheppard-Towner Maternity Act which the membership offered. The group stood behind the equal rights amendment as early as the 1920s, and also launched lobbying efforts for child labor laws, American participation in the World Court, a federal Department of Education, and a uniform marriage and divorce bill. Doris Reed, "Iowa Business Women" (151-54), discusses the mechanics of producing a newsletter and chronicles the cost and distribution techniques of the Iowa BPW publication, the *Bulletin*, throughout its history. R. Flak, "District History" (143-45), articulates the organizational and structural changes within the organization. In 1927, four districts were created in Iowa to produce regional alliances. Quickly, however, nine districts were needed and created. The issue includes lists of state presidents, annual conventions, clubs belonging to the federaion, and the dates they joined.

453   *t PAPACHRISTOU, JUDITH. "WCTU: They Were Fighting More than Demon Rum." *Ms.* 4 (June 1976): 73-76, 105. Illus.: Frances Willard; 2 sketches of the Woman's Crusade Pray-in; 1891 convention.

Although the Woman's Christian Temperance Union has been ridiculed as a group of puritanical militants, Papachristou argues that it was a serious mass movement that confronted the critical social problem of alcoholism with sophisticated political techniques. Included here are excerpts from the author's collection, *Women Together: A History in Documents*: an account of the Woman's Crusade from the *Fayette County Herald* in Washington Courthouse, Ohio; Annie Wittenmyer's presidential address of 1877; Frances Willard's 1883 address; and Alice Stone Blackwell's report of a WCTU conference to the *Woman's Journal*.

454   *r PAPAGEORGE, LINDA MADSON. "'The Hand That Rocks the Cradle Rules the World': Laura Asken Haygood and Methodist

Education in China, 1884-1899." *Proceedings and Papers of the Georgia Association of History* (1982): 123-32. Notes.

Although the focus of this article is on the missionary work of Laura Askew Haygood in China, the author also addresses the contribution of the Women's Missionary Society of the Methodist Episcopal Church, South, which was authorized to form in 1878. The organization directed its missionary activities to China, funding especially programs for Chinese women and female children. The volunteers required that its representatives be unmarried women, between the ages of twenty-two and thirty-five, who would remain in China for five years of missionary effort.

455   *s PARK, MAUD WOOD. *Front Door Lobby.* Edited by Edna Lamprey Stantial. Boston: Beacon Press, 1960. 278 pp. Notes, illus.: Carrie Chapman Catt; Maud Wood Park; 2 of women at signing of suffrage amendment in House of Representatives and Senate.

As chair of the Congressional Committee of the National American Woman Suffrage Association in its final years of 1917-20, the author was a key lobbyist for the federal suffrage amendment. She was also the first president of the League of Women Voters. She died in 1955, and this manuscript, which limits itself to the final five years of the suffrage struggle, was completed by Edna Lamprey Stantial. Park speaks warmly of the talents of NAWSA president Carrie Chapman Catt, with whom Park worked easily. Park defends NAWSA from the attacks it wrongly suffered when "militant antics" perpetrated by the National Woman's party shocked the public. Provided are generous excerpts from NAWSA documents, like "Directions for Lobbyists." Besides offering accounts of Park's lobbying efforts with Democrats and Republicans, and her lists of suffrage votes by each legislator, the study succeeds in painting a vivid portrait of suffragist strategies and great persistence in the final and difficult period which delivered suffrage to American women.

456   *n,f PARKER, MARJORIE H. *Alpha Kappa Alpha Sorority, 1908-1958.* Washington, D.C.: the organization, 1958. iii, 140 pp. Appendixes.

Here is a fifty-year history of "the oldest Greek-letter sorority in America established by Negro Women." Founded in 1908 at Howard University by Ethel Hedgeman, it grew to inspire branches which convened in 1918. The work of the national conventions, or boules, are summarized alongside biographies of the key founding figures. Among resolutions passed by the membership were those concerned with the eradication of lynching (1934), and the establishment of a health clinic (1934), a summer school for rural teachers, and a nutrition clinic (1940). In the early 1930s the sorority cooperated with the National Association for the Advancement of Colored People and lobbied against racial discrimination. War service during World War II, postwar reconstruction, international relations, and integration and nondiscrimination efforts are cataloged here, along with biographies of leaders and membership figures. In 1942, for example, the sorority had 3,128 members and the figure rose to 8,862 in 1956. The appendixes offer lists of officers, conventions, and undergraduate and graduate chapters.

457   *c PARSONS, KATHERINE BARRETTE. *History of Fifty Years: Ladies' Literary Club, Salt Lake City, Utah, 1877-1927.* N.p.: Arrow Press, 1927. 167 pp. Illus.: 8 of leaders; membership list.

     Beginning with the genesis of the woman's club movement and the beginning of the Ladies' Literary Club, this work traces the development of the sections within the Salt Lake City society. Early departments were devoted to the study of history, tourism, art, current events, Shakespeare, music, Browning, drama, parliamentary law, arts and crafts, and literature. Parsons evaluates the relationship of the club to the General Federation of Women's Clubs and describes daily club life in both the first and second clubhouses which members built.

458   *s PATTON, E.E. "The First Suffrage Convention." *DAR Magazine* 82 (August 1948): 591-92 (First published in the *Knoxville Journal*, Knoxville, Tennessee.)

     Reprinted on the occasion of the hundredth anniversary of the Seneca Falls Woman's Rights Convention of 1848, this history catalogs the progress of women's political clout. Beginning in New Jersey, where 1790 and 1797 laws granting propertied women the vote were not repealed until 1807, the piece traces the creation of the first Boston woman's club in 1818, the Seneca Falls meeting of 1848, Tennessee's ratification of the federal suffrage amendment in 1919, the founding of the Daughters of the American Revolution in 1890, and the founding in 1894 of the United Daughters of the Confederacy in Nashville.

459   *s,t PAULSON, ROSS EVANS. *Women's Suffrage and Prohibition: A Comparative Study of Equality and Social Control.* Glenview, Ill.: Scott, Foresman and Co., 1973. iv, 21 pp. Notes, indexes.

     Temperance and suffrage are the focus of this study, which compares both issues internationally. The nations Paulson examines are the United States, England, Australia, New Zealand, Scandinavian countries, modern India, France, Russia, and republican Turkey. Chapter 1 examines the history of the woman's rights movement in the United States and England in the 1830s and 1840s. Chapter 2 compares France and the United States in the 1848 Seneca Falls era. Chapter 3 looks at questions of prohibition of alcohol in the United States, England, Norway, and Sweden. The fourth chapter compares suffrage in the United States, England, and Scandinavia, and the fifth, alliances of suffragists and temperance advocates in the United States and Scandinavia. The franchise on the frontier in the United States, Australian, and New Zealand is the topic of chapter 6. Questions of national and social control through temperance and suffrage in the years 1906-18, internationally, are summarized in the conclusion.

460   *s,i PECK, MARY GRAY. *Carrie Chapman Catt: A Biography*. New York: H.W. Wilson, 1944. 495 pp. Indexes, illus.: 45 of Carrie Chapman Catt; suffragists at conferences in the United States and abroad.

In a hyperbolic fashion, Peck presents Catt as the first international leader of the political phase of the feminist movement, who visited every continent of the globe to bring the women of all races into a common front via the International Woman Suffrage Alliance. Profoundly shocked when the United States failed to enter the League of Nations, she grew determined, at the age of sixty-five, to organize eleven American women's organizations into the Conference on the Cause and Cure of War. She waged a fifteen-year educational campaign to broaden her government's isolationist policy. Despite her emphasis on Catt's international commitments, Peck also provides background on her ancestors, childhood, education, school superintendency in Mason City, Iowa, marriage to Leo Chapman, and participation in the 1887 Iowa woman suffrage campaign. Catt became a state suffrage organizer and officer, learned strategy from the suffrage defeat in Iowa, and went on to participate in Colorado's victorious suffrage campaign of 1893. An examination of Catt's leadership in the National American Woman Suffrage Association, as successor to Susan B. Anthony, from 1900 to 1904, and again after 1915, and her role in international suffrage, accompanies the discussions of her postwar peace and disarmament efforts.

461   *n,c PEEBLES, ROBIN S. "Detroit's Black Women's Clubs." *Michigan History* 70 (January-February 1986): 48. Illus.: Mary McCoy and Detroit Association Clubhouse.

Peebles regards Mary McCoy, wife of inventor Elijah McCoy and an 1890s member of In As Much Circle of the International Order of King's Daughters and Sons Club, as a key figure in the federation of black women's clubs in Detroit. "The Mother of Clubs" was a founder of the Phyllis Wheatley Home for the Aged, McCoy Home for Colored Children, Lydian Association of Detroit, Guiding Star Chapter of the Order of Eastern Star, and Willing Workers. She was the only black charter member, in 1894, of the Twentieth Century Club. In 1898, there was an effort among black women's clubs of Michigan to organize at the National Association of Colored Women conference in Chicago. The first state president for Michigan's black women's clubs was Lucy Thurman, a Women's Christian Temperance Union lecturer. The subsequent leaders of the Michigan federation are listed. By 1920, Detroit had eight black women's clubs. In 1921, the city's clubwomen created the Detroit Association of Colored Women's Clubs. In 1941, the year of its incorporation, the federation was given a colonial revival home to serve as its clubhouse, by President Rosa Gragg. The house was located on an exclusively white street, and white residents, objecting to integration, and required that an entrance to the establishment be constructed on a side street, attended by an address change. The building was included in the 1984 State Register of Historical Sites. The peak of club membership occurred in 1945, with seventy-three clubs and three thousand members. In 1984, there were twenty-eight clubs and five hundred women.

462   *w PEISS, KATHY. *Cheap Amusements: Working Women and Leisure in Turn-of-the-Century New York.* Philadelphia: Temple University Press, 1986. xi, 244 pp. Notes, indexes, illus.: didactic talk at 38th St. Working Girls' Club.

Peiss's examination of working girls' clubs asserts that they exemplified the recreation reform movement at the turn of the century and the cultural conflicts it engendered. In New York City, a wealthy young philanthropist, Grace Hoadley Dodge, became a moving spirit behind the clubs. She moved from church lectures for young working women in her parish in 1884 to the establishment of the 38th St. Working Girls' Society, an idea that spread throughout New York City in the 1880s and 1890s. Paying twenty-five cents dues each month, girls enjoyed the use of clubrooms with a library, classes, entertainment, and services of a physician. By 1885, similar clubs in other cities federated with New York City clubs to establish an Association of Working Girls' Societies. This served as a mutual benefit society, published *Far and Near*, and held annual conventions. By 1894, nineteen clubs with 2,200 members existed in New York City alone. Peiss explains that the leadership was middle and upper class, much as it was in the larger woman's culture club movement, but meetings were held in the evening for the working girls it served. The clubs stressed solidarity among women and their advancement, individual self-improvement, service, and social interaction. The bylaws defined self-support as the goal of the association. Many fund-raising activities were held to supplement philanthropic gifts for an employment bureau, mutual aid society, and vocational training program. Instruction in women's traditional household and family roles was provided.

Most working women were indifferent to the clubs. Antagonism existed between the ladies and working girls. Condescending and unresponsive leadership led some factory girls to split off and modify their club goals. Some girls' political and economic awareness in the 1890s inspired them to stress trade unionism and support labor associations like the Working Women's Society. Other groups of members emphasized social pleasures at their meetings, such as receptions with music and refreshments, fancy dress balls, fairs, ice-cream and card parties, theatrical entertainments, bowling, summer picnics, trolley rides, and excursions. Once or twice a month, men were invited to club dances. By 1900, however, a drop in membership was observable. In 1902, only 1,267 women belonged to New York clubs, and some branches had closed down. Dodge resigned as director in 1896. In all, the emphasis had been on American-born workers at the expense of the foreign-born. Working girls could move on to new alternatives, associations like the Women's Trade Union League, or to commercial amusements. Finally, working women were not tolerant of the domestic ideology that leaders had brought to the groups.

463   *r PENFIELD, JANET HARBISON. "Women in the Presbyterian Church: An Historical Overview." *Journal of Presbyterian History* 55 (1977): 107-23. Notes, illus.: Frances Haines, officer in Women's Executive Committee for Home Missions societies.

Penfield addresses the rise and development of Women's Cent societies or Praying societies in the first quarter of the nineteenth century on the eastern seaboard. She looks at the early Newark, New Jersey, Female Charitable Society founded in 1803 and the fifty branches of the Female Missionary Society in the Synod of Albany, New York, in the 1820s. Regional and ultimately national women's boards of home and foreign missions developed in the 1870s and consolidated in 1923, with the male-dominated Presbyterian church hierarchy.

464   *m P.E.O. SISTERHOOD. *The History of the P.E.O. Sisterhood.* Davenport, Iowa: the organization, 1903. 271 pp. Illus.: 40 individual photos of officers.

A committee of P.E.O. members created this compilation of biographies, autobiographies, and factual summaries of the first thirty years of this woman's organization. Seven college women formed the society in 1869 at Iowa Wesleyan College. One of the founders, Mrs. Alice Babb, has provided her reminiscence of the birth of the sorority. This account lays out the order of the branches' forming, and includes biographies of the founders and histories of the chapters. The history of the Supreme Grant chapter is rich in detail about the officers, conventions, treasurers' reports, committees, and speeches at programs. A 1892-93 program focuses on the history of women from biblical times to the present, including artists, writers, and leaders in nations all over the world. The account provides a summary of the growth of the *P.E.O. Record*, the group's publication, and biographies of its editors. Lengthy chapters follow on the most active states (Nebraska, Illinois, Kansas, Missouri, and Iowa) including reports of state conventions and presidential administrations. Names of officers are included. The charitable work of the chapters is well documented.

465 *r PERRINE, MRS. MABEL. *History of the Woman's Home and Foreign Missionary Society: Michigan Conference, Wesleyan Methodist Church of America, 1890-1940*. Grand Rapids, Mich.: Zondervan Publishing House, 1940. 121 pp. Illus.: Mrs. Mabel Perrine; presidents; first committee; annual conference song of 1890; pioneer women; Masumbo School for Girls in Africa; dormitory; Dr. Helen S. Barnard, medical missionary; Michigan Memorial Hospital in Africa; male and female missionaries; Kunso Cemetery in Sierra Leone; 1907 Executive Board; Susan McCarty.

In 1890, this Michigan group formed as an auxiliary to the General Conference of the Women's Home and Foreign Missionary Society "to meet the imperative need for missionary work." The constitution, bylaws, and lists of original officers and charter members are printed here. Michigan societies and bands raised money and made quilts to sell for mission work. In 1905, they also formed a Young Missionary Workers' Band, so youth could assist in fund-raising efforts. A list of local societies and their dates of organization, from 1890 to 1940, are provided. Narrations about society projects cover adoptions of African children, funding a dispensary, supplying books to needy ministry students, and paying medical missionary Dr. Helen Paine. Perrine details the financial history of the society and provides biographies of men and women missionaries it supported and of male and female general officials. Memoirs of some key women in the organization are included, notably that of Mary Paine Manwell (1859-1932), first president of the WH&FM Society. At the conclusion are several lists of all officers in the history of the society, life members, honored dead, and honorary members.

466   *f   PLUMB, MILDRED.   *History of Tau Beta.*   Detroit: the organization, 1938.   181 pp.   Illus.: 4 founders; 25 group photos; 2 of camps; a few of buildings.

In 1901, four young women in Detroit, aged fifteen and sixteen, formed a club that soon attracted other members from all over the city. Tau beta's initiation and pledging procedures are reviewed and lyrics to sorority songs are cataloged.   The parties, dances, and entertainments from the first decade are recorded in a chatty, detailed narrative.   In 1905, Tau Beta Alumnae Association formed for the purpose of maintaining interest in the sorority and increasing its charitable work. Such endeavors included a Friendly Visitors program to the needy, cooperation with a settlement house and the Anti-Tuberculosis Association, and war service in the form of weekly dances for soldiers during World War I.   Members also supported Hamtramck Neighborhood Settlement House, with a salaried resident, cooking and sewing classes, picnics, a community garden, and a music program.   In 1922, they built a second cottage, moving their own clubrooms and children's nursery into the old structure.   By 1928, they could support Community House with the YWCA, Woman's Hospital, and Florence Crittenton House.   The Great Depression of the 1930s made it impossible for the members to realize their dream of buying their own summer camp for neighborhood children.

467   *p   POPPENHEIM, MARY BARNETT.   *The History of the United Daughters of the Confederacy.*   Richmond, Va.: Garrett and Massie, 1938. xi, 226 pp. Notes, illus.: 28 including officers and monuments they erected in Richmond, Virginia, Fairview, Kentucky, and Shiloh.

This history is fashioned into eight parts by eight authors who were members of the United Daughters of the Confederacy. Mrs. C.M. Goodlet was the founder and first president in 1894.   Early work, including the definition of goals, formation of branches, and initiation of projects, is outlined, documented generously with quotations from convention proceedings and resolutions.   Monuments and memorials celebrating Confederate accomplishments were funded by the group, including portraits, stained-glass windows, and a memorial highway named for military and political leaders.   Emphasis on minutiae, including a list of all prizes and scholarships given between 1907 and 1929 to students of history, make this study a treasure trove for researchers, but a frustration for scholars seeking analysis.   The historical work of members, cataloged here, is varied-study courses, evenings with pageants on the history of the Confederacy, costume parties, awards to outstanding departments of history in educational institutions, presentation of state flags. Official badges, medals, ribbons, and banners are described, as is the *Confederate Veteran,* the official publication from 1893 on, the Confederate Museum in Richmond, the Children of the Confederacy organization begun in 1897, and the program to place materials on the Confederacy in home and foreign libraries. The final section records the extensive war relief effort this group engaged in during World War I, particularly through Red Cross activities.

468   *s PORTER, MELBA D. "Madeline McDowell Breckinridge: Her Role in the Kentucky Woman Suffrage Movement, 1908-1920." *Register of the Kentucky Historical Society* 72 (October 1974): 342-63. Notes.

The Kentucky Equal Rights Association was formed in 1888 by Laura Clay, who presided over it for twenty-four years. In 1912, however, Madeline McDowell Breckinridge assumed the presidency, a post she held for eight years until women were enfranchised. Breckinridge was a skilled civic reformer, embarking on educational, health, and charitable programs. As a supporter of legislation to enfranchise Kentucky women in school elections, she served as legislative committee chairman in the Kentucky Federation of Women's Clubs in their unsuccessful lobbying campaigns of 1908 and 1909. By 1915, she had managed to win for the Kentucky Equal Rights Association the endorsement of the Grange, WCTU, American Federation of Labor, Socialist party, Progressive party and Republican party. Only the Democrats remained outside the fold. Unlike some southerners, such as Laura Clay, she did not limit her suffrage campaigning to the state level. She also supported a federal amendment that would not exclude black women from voting, as state amendments might. To be sure, she held "the racism of her time" but also felt that black women were too few in number to topple any white votes.

469   *c POTTER, FANNIE C., ed. *History of the Texas Federation of Women's Clubs, 1918-1938.* Vol.2. Denton, Texas: the organization, 1938. 403 pp. Illus.: Texas headquarters; Washington, D.C., headquarters; officers.

Here is a compendium of detail about the years 1918 to 1938 in the Texas Federation of Women's Clubs. The federation was founded in 1897, and the volume contains biographies of the pioneers in the group, portraits of charter clubs, and "Pearls from Presidents." But the emphasis is on ten two-year presidential administrations from 1917 to 1939, the resolutions passed at conventions, and projects initiated there. A headquarters for the federation was established in 1923, when the officers received free space in the building of the Woman's Club of Fort Worth. In 1929, however, the members began to plan a permanent headquarters for themselves. The structure was paid for in 1939. Generous quotations from convention speeches provide a vivid sense of the humor and seriousness of the clubwomen. The work contains several lists: past presidents, conventions held, life members, honorary members, and donors to the endowment honor roll for 1897-1938.

470 *r PRATT, NORMA FAIN. "Transitions in Judaism: The Jewish American Woman through the 1930s." *American Quarterly* 30 (Winter 1978): 681-702. Notes.

Although Pratt deals with many roles of Jewish American women, she includes a substantial amount of material about their organizations. The great number of clubs, she asserts about the 1920s and 1930s, "testified to the vitality of Jewish women and to their interest in religion and community affairs, as well as to the strength of the separatist tradition." Although they met for some of the same reasons as non-Jewish women in America, they also met for the guardianship of their faith and opposition to anti-Semitism. Pratt details the work of the Junior Hadassah (founded in 1921), Conference Committee of National Jewish Women's Organizations (1923), Women's Branch of the Union of Orthodox Jewish Congregations of America (1924), Women's Division of the Communist Workers' Order (1924), Women's Organization of the Pioneer Women of Palestine (1925), Women's American ORT (1927), Women's League for Palestine (1927), American Beth Jacob Committee (1928), Mizrach Women's Organization of America (1930), Menorah League (1935), and three older groups: National Congress of Jewish Women (1893), National Federation of Temple Sisterhoods (1913), and Women's League of the United Synagogues of America (1918).

471 *s,n PRESTON, L.E. "Speakers for Women's Rights in Pennsylvania." *Western Pennsylvania Magazine* 54 (July 1971): 245-63.

In four areas of women's rights—education, journalism, suffrage, and antislavery—Pennsylvania women made significant contributions. The material here that will most interest researchers of women's organizational efforts deals with Lucretia Mott and the Grimké sisters' activity in the American Anti-Slavery Society, which was organized in Philadelphia in 1833, and the Philadelphia Female Anti-

Slavery Society, founded in the same year. Quaker Mary Grew presided over the Pennsylvania Woman Suffrage Association from 1869 until 1892, when she resigned at the age of eighty. Alice Paul earned a Ph.D. at the University of Pennsylvania and held her first open-air meetings for suffrage in July 1911 in Philadelphia. Her activity forecast her program of lively suffrage campaign strategies at the Congressional Union and National Woman's party.

472   *z PRINCE, VINTON M., Jr. "Will Women Turn the Tide? Mississippi Women and the 1922 United States Senate Race." *Journal of Mississippi History* 42 (August 1980): 212-20.
        Prince relates an account of a Mississippi Senate race in 1922 in which the League of Women Voters and the Mississippi Federation of Women's Clubs were influential. One of the four Democratic candidates, James K. Vardaman expected support from the women. The league, however, endorsed Belle Kearney, a veteran activist who had not previously been taken seriously. Vardaman did win the primary, but he effectively courted the women by endorsing suffrage, prohibition, child labor laws, and education.

473   *i RAINBOLT, ROSEMARY. "Women and War in the United States: The Case of Dorothy Detzer, National Secretary of the Women's International League for Peace and Freedom." *Peace and Change* 4 (1977): 18-22. Notes.
        This biography of Dorothy Detzer includes considerable material on her involvement with the Women's International League for Peace and Freedom. She joined the organization in 1924 and devoted herself to lobbying among legislators for total and universal disarmament in the 1920s and 1930s. WILPF did not support the equal rights amendment at this time, and favoring special protective legislation instead. One tangible gain of the era was winning a place for a woman representative, Mary E. Woolley, at the 1932 Geneva Disarmament Conference.

474   *c RAINEY, LURETTA. *History of the Oklahoma State Federation of Women's Clubs.* Guthrie, Oka.: Cooperative Publishing Co., 1939. xi, 341 pp. Illus.: 63, mostly of officers in the Oklahoma Federation; Ponca City Library, sponsored by Ponca City's Twentieth Century Club; Pioneer Club Building, Atoka; group photo of Marshall Women's Club; Shakespeare Garden in Guthrie, established by the Guthrie Shakespeare Club; Waurika Library, created and maintained by Sorosis

The Oklahoma Federation of Women's Clubs was founded in 1897 and the women's clubs in the Indian Territories federated in 1904. This comprehensive study begins with the early work of the federation on libraries, its educational loan fund, endowment fund, war victory commission which raised money to send young women overseas for Red Cross work, a Community House at the State Industrial School for Girls in Tecumseh, suffrage support, official publications, and contributions to the Oklahoma Historical Building and to the Oklahoma Club Room at the General Federation of Women's Club headquarters in Washington, D.C. Junior clubs, Epsilon Sigma Omicron—the honorary society of the GFWC (founded 1928)—a Memory Rose Garden dedicated in 1932 and rededicated in 1939, and the State Pioneer Club are also projects that receive the author's attention. Biographies of the club activity, but not the private lives, of twenty-two federation presidents are provided. The largest portion of the text, pp. 83-301, contains details on each club in the nine districts of the state, with a history of the accomplishments, purpose, dates of founding, and names of charter members, plus an account of the founding, priorities, officers, and size of each district.

475   *i RANDALL, MERCEDES M. *Improper Boston: Emily Greene Balch.* New York: Twayne Publishers, 1964.   475 pp.   Notes, indexes, illus.: 5, of Mary Kingsburg Simkovitch, Emily Greene Balch, and other members of the women's peace community.

This nineteen-chapter biography of the 1946 Nobel Peace Prize winner includes a descriptive chapter of the 1915 International Congress of Women at The Hague.   Throughout the story, which stresses Balch's peacemaking efforts, is mention of the Woman's Peace party and its successor, the Women's International League for Peace and Freedom.   Narration and quotations illustrate that Balch attended many of the national congresses and served as honorary head of WILPF during World War II.

476   *b RAUCH, JULIA B. "Women in Social Work: Friendly Visitors in Philadelphia, 1880." *Social Service Review* 49 (June 1975): 241-59.

Rauch documents the history of the Philadelphia Society for Organizing Charitable Relief and Repressing Mendicancy from 1879 to 1909. "Its founding marked the expansion of women's participation in Philadelphia's formally organized charitable system and a weakening of role constraints which limited women's charitable activities." The typical "Friendly Visitors" who participated to counsel the poor were older, native-born white women from Philadelphia's upper socioeconomic strata, single women or married ones with grown children propelled by feminist impulses to become active in public life. Rauch characterizes the membership as active clubwomen, many of whom belonged to the New Century Club, a literary society founded in 1877. Many also supported the women's rights movement, like Lucretia Blankenburg, the Pennsylvania Woman Suffrage Association president from 1892 to 1908, Fannie Baker Ames, who attended the founding convention of the American Woman Suffrage Association, and Mary E. Mumford, General Federation of Women's Clubs board member in the 1890s.

477   *c RAUSCH, STELLA J., and CARRIE B. ROBINSON, comps. *Our First Twenty Years, 1912-1932: The Women's Art Club of Cleveland.* Cleveland: Central Publishing House, 1933. 111 pp. Illus.: 26 reproductions of work by members including sculpture, block-printed Christmas cards, jewelry, silver bowl, batik hanging, oil painting, watercolor landscapes, portraits, still lifes; Wade Lodge; Robinwood Studio; all 13 presidents.

Rausch provides a wealth of detail about a little-documented phenomenon, the woman's art club. In 1912, the Woman's Art Club of Cleveland was formed, the first art organization in the city to be composed solely of women. Members worked in oil and watercolor. They were muralists, sculptors, illustrators, designers, silversmiths, jewelers, ceramic, and textile craftswomen. They were determined to assist each other and serve the city by educating its public about art. At first, they met in Gage Gallery, the studio of Miss Belle Hoffman, the treasurer of the organization. Rausch's account summarizes the work of each year, the meeting places, names of officers, dues, parties, music, and Saturday teas. She catalogs the topics they considered: rhythm, composition, and color, flowers, summer, storms, and light. She enumerates the assignments they gave each other: design a purse, tea set, bookplate, box, lamp base, flag, Christmas card. Speakers gave papers on art as well as on woman suffrage. Members put their work on exhibition. In 1918, they incorporated on the occasion of establishing their own clubhouse, Robinwood, a residence donated by a member, Mrs. Robinson. In 1921, they joined the Ohio Federation of Women's Clubs. They held an annual exhibition at the Cleveland Art School. In 1924, they enjoyed a progressive luncheon, each course served at the studio of a different member. In 1925, they formed a nonvoting auxiliary, giving a role for art enthusiasts to play.

478   *r,b REBER, AUDRIE E. *Women United for Mission: A History of the Women's Society of World Service of the Evangelical United Brethren Church, 1946-1968.* Dayton, Ohio: Otterbein Press, 1969.

134 pp. Notes, bib., indexes, illus.: group and individual photos of officers; documents.

The author was a missionary in South China and president of a local Women's Society of World Service at the First Evangelical United Brethren Church in Dayton, Ohio. She traces the origins of women's missionary work to a Boston society in 1800. In 1839, the first Evangelical Church Women's Society began in Philadelphia. In 1872, the United Brethren Women began their first women's society. It was in 1884 that the the General Board of Missions ratified the constitution, providing for a Woman's Missionary Society of Evangelical Associations to "make Christ known throughout the world." In 1946, there was a merger of the United Brethren Women and Evangelical Church Women. This work is the story of the organization after the merger and an account of the programs developed for the following twenty-two years: prayer, educational programs, Christian social action (through interchurch fellowship, brotherhood, citizenship, and family living), local church responsibility for missions, children's education, fund-raising, overseas women's societies with an emphasis on their leaders, and new trends after 1963 to strengthen the roles of the 115,000 members and other women in the church. The volume contains statistical charts on size of membership, number of societies, participants in the reading course, profile of subscribers to *World Evangel*, and the number of societies using the new program packets.

479 *m REED, DORIS. "BPW." *Palimpsest* 52 (1971).
     See *Palimpsest*.

480 *f REEVES, WINONA EVANS. *The Story of P.E.O.* N.p.: the organization, 1923. 159 pp. Illus.: 89 of officers of chapters.

To celebrate its fiftieth anniversary, this secret society collected its history. It was organized in 1869 at Iowa Wesleyan College with "a determination to do all we can at all times and under all circumstances to promote each other's interest. To care for each other in trouble, to sympathize in affection and to console in grief." Included are biographies of founders, discussion of the growth of branches, description of the first convention in 1883, a list of charter members and all members prior to 1887, a commendation of the literary contributions by 33-year *P.E.O. Record* editor Miss Mary Osmond, and details about the Educational Loan Fund, Philanthropic Fund, and World War I relief work. Reeves also collected biographical material on the presidents of the Supreme Chapter and details on the histories of the state chapters.

481 *c REISHTEIN, ELEANOR FEIN. "Minutes of the West Grove Housekeepers Association as Source Material for Folklife Studies." *Pennsylvania Folklife* 21 (1971): 16-25. Illus.: engravings of the town; sample records of the organization.

The West Grove Farmers and Gardeners Association formed in Pennsylvania in 1860. Three years later, the women split off to form the West Grove Housekeepers Association. It would operate independently until 1931, when it returned once again to the original organization. West Grove was a Quaker community, thirty miles west of Philadelphia, and its members kept careful records and minutes for 1863 to 1869, which Reishtein has examined. The group limited its size to eighteen members, preferring wives of the farmers and gardeners in the West Grove Farmers and Gardeners Association. They discussed household economy, especially food, clothing, and homemaking. An essay was prepared by a member for each meeting. The author demonstrates that the detailed club records are an important source of information about dairy chores, poultry raising, kitchen gardens, preservation of foods, recipes, new products women adopted for cleaning and sewing, and child-care ideas.

482 *w,y REITANO, JOANNE. "Working Girls Unite." *American Quarterly* 36 (Spring 1984): 112-34. Notes.

In the last two decades of the nineteenth century, American working class-women supported a network of clubs and used them "to forge a middle road between independence and domesticity." The clubs met the needs of thousands of unmarried females struggling for survival in the city, especially by acknowledging the validity of their ordinary problems. The first club, the New York Working Girls' Society, formed in a Manhattan silk factory to provide companionship and self-improvement. By 1885, eleven clubs could form an Association of Working Girls' Clubs. In 1897, a National League of Women Workers had drawn in young single women seeking immediate and practical ways to improve their work and personal lives. The majority of working girls were factory workers, but dressmakers, saleswomen, telegraph operators, stenographers, and teachers also joined. A national convention was held in New York in 1890, in Boston in 1894, in Philadelphia in 1897, and annually from 1897 through 1914. Branches developed in Philadelphia, Brooklyn, Rhode Island, Maryland, Illinois, Ohio, and New Jersey. By 1914, there were one hundred clubs with fourteen thousand women meeting in modestly furnished apartments in poorer sections of the city, to talk, read, sing, sew, exercise, and attend lectures. Club facilities were sponsored by middle-class women under the direction of Grace Hoadley Dodge, a prominent New York philanthropist. The clubs made an effort to cut across class lines without denying their existence. Reitano finds it difficult to evaluate the balance of power between the two groups in club government, and points to examples of firm friendships forming between members of different classes and also of real antagonism. In 1891, an employment bureau was formed, supplementing such projects as lunch programs, the pressuring of employers for improved working conditions, initiating cooperative housekeeping experiments, and also peddling the 3 Ps: Purity, Perseverance, and Pleasantness.

483   *s RHODE ISLAND WOMAN SUFFRAGE ASSOCIATION. *A Brief History of the Rhode Island Woman Suffrage Association, 1868-1893*. Providence: E.L. Freeman, 1893. 20 pp. This study is available as no. A2371 in the Gerritson Collection.

This brief history traces the roots of the woman suffrage struggle to colonial times, when early women called for liberty for all. It also observes the importance of the abolitionist movement in alerting women to social inequities. Like most suffrage histories, it points to the 1848 Seneca Falls Women's Rights convention as the starting point for the suffrage campaign. Twenty-years later, in 1868, two Rhode Island women, Paulina Wright Davis and Elizabeth B. Chace, represented their state at the Boston meeting to organize the New England Woman Suffrage Association. They called Rhode Islanders to a December 1868 meeting to form a Rhode Island Woman Suffrage Association. Davis was elected its first president and she served for two years. Chace succeeded her and served from 1870 through the date of this pamphlet's publication, 1893. In 1870, the group allied with the American Woman Suffrage Association. In 1891, it joined the National American Woman Suffrage Association. This account documents the efforts of the Rhode Island suffragists to achieve a state constitutional amendment, through annual conventions, petitions, lobbying of legislators, participating in hearings, pressuring for women to serve on juries and on state social service institution boards. The study surveys a variety of women's achievements during the years 1868-1893, including the admission of women at Brown University and the creation "of the first scholarship which ever bore a woman's name." Among the primary documents included are the "Call" to form a state association, from the 5 December 1868 *Providence Journal*, the 1892 act of incorporation, a list of executive officers and executive committee members for 1892-93, and the names of auxiliary leagues in Anthony; Washington; Carolina; Little Compton; Pawtucket; Providence; and Valley Falls, Rhode Island.

484 *y RICE, ANNA V. *A History of the World's Young Women's Christian Association.* New York: Woman's Press, 1947. viii, 299 pp. Notes, appendixes, indexes, illus.: 40 photos of officers.

Published in observance of a half century of the world's Young Women's Christian Association, this carefully researched volume surveys the growth of the organization from its founding in 1894 to the post-World War II era. Women of the United States, along with those in Great Britain, Norway, and Sweden, founded it to accomplish Christian projects and facilities for girls all over the world. Biographies are provided for American and other presidents and general secretaries. Chapter 3 describes the pre-1984 YWCA work in the United States and Canada. Basically, the study is top-heavy, concentrating on leadership, administrative details, policies regarding growth and expansion, and positions on social issues and ecumenical questions. Rice does not attempt to provide a feeling for the members who supported and enjoyed the services of the organization. Eight appendixes give lists of meetings, presidents, general secretaries, member nations, date each nation joined, and countries with YWCA projects.

485 *c RICHARDS, LAURA E., and MAUD HOWE ELLIOT. *Julia Ward Howe, 1819-1910.* Boston: Houghton Mifflin Co., 1916. 434 pp. Indexes, illus.: 11 of Julia Ward Howe and family.

Julia Ward Howe's two daughters wrote this biography using excerpts from their mother's diaries. Throughout the story is reference to Howe's role in the New England Woman's Club and Women's Educational and Industrial Union. Howe's fondness for the friends she met in women's clubs and for the work of the clubs is also woven throughout the text.

486 *c RICHMOND, REBECCA L. *A Woman of Texas: Mrs. Percy V. Pennybacker.* San Antonio: Naylor Co., 1941. viii, 367 pp. Bib., indexes, illus.: 7 including 2 of Anna J. Hardwicke Pennybacker, her mother, father, husband, and maternal grandmother.

This chatty biography, thoroughly researched and rich with detail, focuses on the life of clubwoman Anna Hardwicke Pennybacker (1861-1938). While Richmond collected considerable material on her personal life, the work conveys much about the work of turn-of-the-century club life for women. When Anna Harwicke married a Texas school superintendent, Percy V. Pennybacker, she joined the Palestine Magazine Club (later called the Self-Culture Club). Her husband died, leaving her with three children to raise, and she moved to Austin. There, she joined the American History Club and attended conventions of the Texas Federation of Women's Clubs, which formed in 1897. By 1901, she was elected president of the Texas Federation, steering three thousand members into volunteer work in libraries, a traveling art gallery, and educational programs. She traveled throughout Texas, visiting clubs and encouraging their development. She also got involved at the national level of the federated club movement, attending the Los Angeles biennial of the General Federation of Women's Clubs in 1902. She became treasurer under President Sarah Platt Decker and headed the Program Committee for the Boston biennial in 1906-8. She was elected to the presidency of the General Federation of Women's Clubs in 1912 and served for four years. Afterward, she went on to participate in club life as the president of the Chautauqua Woman's Club network in 1917, as a member of the Texas Food Administration during World War I, as a leader of the YWCA, and in suffrage work with the Democratic party in 1919-20. In 1921, under the General Federation presidency of Alice Ames Winter, she chaired the new American Citizenship Department and served as a conferee at the Conference on the Cause and Cure of War. She visited Geneva in 1925, 1927, and 1929 to observe the work of the League of Nations, and wrote articles in support of it. Even in the last decade of her life, she remained active in public affairs, working for such women's issues as child labor laws. She enjoyed great esteem from women's organizations for her contributions to club life and to women's reform issues.

487 *s,c,n RIEGEL, ROBERT E. *American Feminists*. Lawrence: University Press of Kansas, 1963. xiii, 223 pp. Notes, bib., indexes.

Although Riegel emphasizes biographies of women active in voluntary associations of nineteenth-century America, he mentions the work of antislavery societies in his accounts of Lucretia Mott, Martha Coffin Pelham, the Grimké sisters, and Abby Kelley Foster. Suffrage associations are treated in his remarks on Elizabeth Cady Stanton, Susan B. Anthony, and Lucy Stone. In treating women in the professions, he includes material on literary associations, the New England Woman's Club among them.

488 *p ROBINSON, EMMA B. *History 1884-1934 Department of Iowa Woman's Relief Corps Auxiliary to the Grand Army of the Republic*. N.p.: the organization, 1934. 64 pp. Illus.: department president elected in convention; departmental commanders, 1884-1934; war memorials dedicated by women.

Although this volume contains more primary documents than narration, the researcher can piece together the story of Iowa's

Woman's Relief Corps Auxiliary to the Grand Army of the Republic from its founding in 1884 until 1934. Robinson provides a list of officers elected at each convention, a list of financial and patriotic assistance provided by 178 corps during World War I, and a summary of projects including their erecting a Soldiers' Home in 1886. She includes memorial poetry to veterans and patriotic essays. The Iowa group peaked in size in 1895, with 258 branch organizations. In 1934, there were 168 active groups. In all, 393 corps formed in Iowa, including those that ultimately disbanded.

489 *s,c,n ROBINSON, HARRIET. *Massachusetts in the Woman Suffrage Movement*. Boston: Roberts Brothers, 1881. xi, 265 pp. Indexes, appendixes:

In six chapters, Robinson surveys the history of the woman suffrage movement in which she was a participant. Among the early influences of the Massachusetts efforts, she credits the Boston Female Anti-Slavery Society. She also cites "Ten Great Conventions (1850-1860)" of abolitionists and suffragists in Worcester, Syracuse, Cleveland, Boston, and New York City. Robinson discusses the machinery of conventions, from 1860 to 1881, covering the 1866 meeting of the American Equal Rights Association in Boston and the New England Woman Suffrage Association of 1868. These later became the rival National Woman Suffrage Association and American Woman Suffrage Association. In her chapter on political history from 1870 to 1880, she studies the Woman Suffrage State Central Committee, which agitated within the Republican party and urged women to form political clubs. Robinson's legal and legislative history collects laws addressing women in her state. Finally, in "Results of Thirty Years of Agitation," she lists accomplishments of women in public life, including the founding of the New England Woman's Club in 1868. Fourteen appendixes include these documents: the call for the First National Woman's Rights Convention in Worcester, Massachusetts, in 1850; three Middlesex County convention announcements of 1875; Malden, Melrose, and Concord conference resolutions; and legislative hearings and court decisions on suffrage in Massachusetts.

490 *m ROMANOFSKY, PETER. "The Public Is Aroused: Missouri Children's Code Commission, 1915-1919." *Missouri Historical Review* 68 (January 1974): 204-22. Notes, illus.: Lucille B. Lowenstein, executive secretary of the commission.

In 1915, the Missouri governor appointed twenty-four volunteers to the first Missouri Children's Code Commission. Among the supporters for the commission's creation were women's organizations, including the Women's Christian Temperance Union, Missouri Federation of Women's Clubs, the Missouri Women's Committee of the National Defense Council and the Equal Suffrage Club. Commission suggestions included abolition of child labor, compulsory school attendance for children under the age of sixteen, cleaner rural schools, improved public health programs, and free medical exams in the schools. Under pressure from the Missouri Federation of Women's Clubs and the Rotary Club, the model code established by the Commission was enacted by the state legislature.

491 *t ROOT, GRACE C. *Women and Repeal: The Story of the Women's Organization for National Prohibition Reform.* New York: Harper and Row, 1934. 217 pp. Indexes, illus.: officers.

The Women's Organization for National Prohibition Reform was founded in 1929 and disbanded in 1933. Pauline Morton Sabin resigned from her efforts with the Women's National Republican Club to assume the national chairmanship of the effort to work against the Prohibition Amendment to the United States Constitution. Housewives, teachers, nurses, stenographers, secretaries, and manual workers joined to support the repeal of the unenforceable law. Membership was highest in Massachusetts (26,710), California (20,643), Ohio (12,000), and New York (71,000), where such women's groups as the League of Women Voters, Republican Women, federated clubs, patriotic societies, and college alumnae associations gave a forum to discussion about the failure of Prohibition laws. Root's study outlines the committees formed, the work at the four national conventions, and the support of the leadership, which grew to 1,326,862 in April of 1933. An appendix reprints the group's Delcaration of Principles, By-laws, and Executive Committee and Official Resolutions.

492 *r ROSENBERG, CARROLL SMITH. *Religion and the Rise of the American City: The New York City Mission Movement, 1812-1870.* Ithaca, N.Y.: Cornell University Press, 1971.
See Carrol Smith-Rosenberg.

493 *m ROSENTHAL, NAOMI. "Social Movements and Network Analysis: A Case Study of Nineteenth Century Women's Reform in New York State." *American Journal of Sociology* 90 (March 1985): 1022-54. Notes, bib.

The authors examine organizational affiliations of nineteenth-century women reform leaders in New York State and uncover the primacy of suffrage and women's rights organizations for women reform activists from 1840 to 1914. Most particularly, their memberships in the Women's Trade Union League, Sorosis literary club, and Garrisonian abolitionist organizations stand out among reformers' interests. The authors chart 202 reform women with memberships in one thousand organizations. By tabulating the fifty most popular associations among them, the authors determine that charitable work was insignificant among feminists. They reject the idea that the WCTU was central to women in reform, and they assert that the Women's Trade Union League and National Woman's Party members did not perceive themselves as rivals.

494   *m ROTHMAN, SHEILA M. *Woman's Proper Place: A History of Changing Ideals and Practices, 1870 to the Present.* New York: Basic Books, 1978. xiv, 322 pp. Notes, indexes, illus.: 25 including George Eliot Club, Smith College, 1880; New York City meeting of the General Federation of Women's Clubs in 1900.

In her chapter on the Protestant nun, Rothman discusses the nineteenth-century women to whom organizational activity was important as a vehicle to a public life. Moral elevation and female fellowship are among the impulses she cites as crucial to the club members. Societies discussed include Sorosis, General Federation of Women's Clubs, Women's Christian Temperance Union, Charity Organization Society, Civil War Sanitary Commission, Young Women's Christian Association, working girls' clubs, Florence Crittenton missions, National Congress of Mothers, and National American Woman Suffrage Association. In another chapter, "The Politics of Protection," clubwomen are not prominent in the discussion on the Sheppard-Towner Act, but the rivalry between the National Woman's party and clubs opposed to the equal rights amendment in the 1920s is surveyed.

495   *y ROTHSCHILD, MARY AICKIN. "To Scout or to Guide? Girl Scout-Boy Scout Controversy, 1912-1941." *Frontiers* 6 (Fall 1981): 115-21. Notes.

This historian explores the origins of the Girl Scouts and observes that the organization wove together elements of domesticity and feminism for its youthful members. Training in physical fitness, survival skills, camping, citizenship, and career preparation moved members away from traditional social roles for women. Juliette Gordon Lowe founded the organization, inspired by Sir Robert Baden-Powell's Boy Scouts in England. His sister, Agnes Baden-Powell, had formed the Girl Guides there. In 1912, Lowe brought the Girl Scouts to Savannah, Georgia. The Boy Scouts, feeling the use of the term "scouts" by females "sissified" the masculine endeavor, called for a name change. In 1918, a meeting was held to discuss a change, but the American Girl Scouts retained their original name. In 1913, Lowe moved Girl Scout headquarters to Washington, D.C. By 1915, it incorporated, with 5,000 members. In 1920, there were 50,000 members, and by 1930, 275,000. The leaders of troops tended to be upper-middle-class and upper-class, Protestant well-educated women, leisured or social workers. The girls tended to be white and middle class, but there were also multiracial, multicultural, and handicapped members. The dilemma of the society was to challenge prevailing ideas of proper behavior and enlarge girls' sphere, especially in the areas of physical fitness and outdoor survival, without weakening the ultimate fundamental goal of guiding girls to grow up to be wives and mothers. Their solution was to define their goal as forming "up-to-date traditional women." Thus, merit badges the girls could earn included cooking for invalids and hospital nursing alongside electrician, flyer, telegraphist, and camper.

496 *b ROUSMANIERE, JOHN P. "Cultural Hybrid in the Slums: The College Woman and the Settlement House, 1889-1894." *American Quarterly* 22 (Spring 1970): 45-66.

In an effort to determine which young women volunteered to work in urban settlement houses, Rousmaniere dissects the membership of the College Settlement Association, which was founded in 1890. Although not all settlement house residents he located were college women, three-fifths of the ninety-two residents between the years 1889 and 1896 had attended college. Three women's schools were highly represented—Vassar, Smith, and Wellesley. Members welcomed the family and home aspects of settlement life while they sought to be useful and active in social work activity, which included the founding of community clubs.

497 *c,p,t RUCKMAN, JO ANN. "Knit, Knit and Then Knit: The Women of Pocatello and the War Effort of 1917-1918." *Idaho Yesterdays* 26 (Spring 1982): 26-32. Notes, illus.: Pocatello in World War I; Dr. Minnie Howard; Dr. William Howard; officers at Fort Lewis.

Six key women's organizations in the Pocatello City Federation of Women's Clubs united for patriotic service during World War I under Dr. Minnie Howard, president of the local Red Cross unit. They were the Women's Civic Club, Women's Study League, Art Club, Thursday Music Club, Women's Christian Temperance Union, and Daughters of the American Revolution. In 1917, members devoted themselves wholeheartedly to knitting, sewing, and sponsoring a bazaar where they sold dainty articles to raise money for the war. The women were excluded from leadership among the men's fund-raising drives. In sponsoring a swimming and gymnastics program for women through a Woman's Auxiliary to the Young Men's Christian Association, in the absence of any Young Women's Christian Association, they engendered criticism for diverting attention from war relief. The energetic women were frustrated by the unsatisfactory outlets for their talents.

498   *y -----. "Pocatello in Its Middle Years: View from the YWCA." *Rendezvous* 18 (Spring 1983): 18-27.

Using notes taken by field representatives for the national headquarters of the Young Women's Christian Association, Ruckman provides an honest report on the Pocatello YWCA, with its blemishes as well as its achievements. Organized in 1920, it was able to buy its own home in 1924. Financial irregularities ensued, but the club undertook a variety of projects for young women. The low salaries offered failed to attract and retain capable leadership, however. In the 1930s the YWCA allied with the Community Chest for financial support. The existence of strong Mormon youth organizations attracting Mormon girls weakened the pool of resources for the YWCA.

499   *c RUDDY, ELLA GILES. *The Mother of Clubs: Caroline M. Seymour Severance: An Estimate and an Appreciation.* Los Angeles: Baumgardt Publishing Co., 1906. 191 pp. Illus.: Caroline M. Seymour Severance; Mrs. Severance with Ella Ruddy; Mrs. Severance with Rebecca Spring and Susan B. Anthony; Mrs. Severance's home.

Relying heavily on a broad range of documents, Ruddy provides a biography of Caroline Severance, founder and first president of "the first woman's club in the United States—the New England Woman's Club of Boston." The chapter on the genesis and purpose of the club idea includes whole papers written and delivered by Madame Severance and a reminiscence about the forces she recognized as contributing to the development of the Boston club. There is description of the early years of the club, the topics considered and the members involved. In 1875, Severance moved from Boston to Los Angeles, where she founded the Friday Morning Club and served as its first president, in 1891. She continued to visit the Boston club on visits east and her 1881 and 1886 speeches are reprinted here. Chapter 3, on the history of the Friday Morning Club, contains six excerpts from her six presidential addresses there. Severance's letters and addresses to the Association for the Advancement of Women between 1873 and 1897, to the Woman's Parliament of Southern California (1894), and to the General Federation of Women's Clubs in 1902 provide a solid sense of late nineteenth-century club leaders' goals and zeal. Her papers on peace, mothers, the ideal home, kindergartens, Christian socialism, the beauties of Los Angeles, and new Italy are included, alongside reminiscences of John Greenleaf Whittier, Ralph Waldo Emerson, the William Lloyd Garrison family, the Lyman Beecher family, Julia Ward Howe, and Jane Cunningham Croly, as well as extracts from her letters from Susan B. Anthony, Lucy Stone, Elizabeth Cady Stanton, and leading clubwomen of New England. Her ancestry and private life at her estate, El Nido, in California are also covered.

500 *r,b,t,n RUETHER, ROSEMARY RADFORD, and ROSEMARY SKINNER KELLER, eds. *Women and Religion in America*. Vol. 1, *Nineteenth Century*. San Francisco: Harper and Row, 1981. xiv, 353 pp. Notes, indexes, illus.: 46 of women active in church life.

Seven articles by seven authors explore women in revivalism, utopian movements, nuns in immigrant Catholicism, Jewish women's encounters with American culture, the struggle for the Right to preach, lay women in the Protestant tradition, and women in social reform movements. Throughout, there is brief reference to such women's organizations as the women's missionary societies, Women's Christian Temperance Union, Moral Reform societies, and Council of Jewish Women.

501 *p,c,w RUPP, LEILA, and VERTA TAYLOR. *Surviving the Doldrums: Femininism in America, 1945-1960*. New York: Oxford University Press, 1987. ix, 284 pp. Notes, bib., indexes.

Rupp, historian, and Taylor, a sociologist, combine archival research and fifty interviews to provide a reading of the history of the woman's movement and a sociology of social movements in an era of conservatism. Although the period between World War II and the modern woman's movement is usually presumed to have been an era of domesticity and conformity for American women, rather than years of discontent and protest, the authors have traced feminists and their organizations that survived through the period to provide mobilizable resources for the later round of feminist activism. When they examine the activities, goals, and strategies of existing organizations (National Woman's party, National Federation of Business and Professional Women's Clubs, National Association of Women Lawyers, American Medical Women's Association) and emergent ones (Connecticut and

Massachusetts committees for the ERA, Lucy Stone League, Women's Joint Legislative Committee, Industrial Women's League for Equality, St. Joan Society), they see three basic goals emerging. The women sought to pass the ERA, to place women in policy-making positions, and to recognize women's history. The study lovingly documents the endurance and wisdom and the conflict among early feminists.

502 *m RYAN, MARY P. *Cradle of the Middle Class: The Family in Oneida County, New York, 1790-1865.* New York: Cambridge University Press, 1981. xiv, 321 pp. Notes, appendixes, bib., indexes, illus.: 5, of Oneida, New York, in this era; map of Oneida.

In a monograph of five chapters, Ryan devotes chapter 3 to the "Era of Associations: Between Family and Society, 1825-1845." This historian notes that a third of the groups formed in this era of organizational fervor were created exclusively for females. She scrutinizes the evangelicalism, abolitionism, female moral reform, and temperance movements in Oneida, and determines that significant alliances developed between families and associations. Forty tables in the appendixes give the family and social characteristics of members of the associations described.

503 *b -----. "The Power of Women's Networks: A Case Study of Female Moral Reform in Antebellum America." *Feminist Studies* 5 (Spring 1979): 66-85. Notes.

Ryan examines the Female Moral Reform Society of Utica, New York, founded in 1837. It was one of four hundred chapters established in New England and the Middle Atlantic states in the 1830s and 1840s. Their goal was to reform standards of sexual morality and regulate sexual behavior in their communities. The members expressed special concern about the sexual behavior of the young and unmarried in Utica and demanded stricter purity from both their sons and their daughters. Ryan points to a contradiction in their efforts to attack the double standard and yet to celebrate the domestic feminine stereotype. In the end, "they used their social power to create a moral code which exacted particularly stringent sexual repression from their own sex." Theirs was not a covert and privatized use of power, but leverage—for a few active, organized, and well-situated women—beyond the world of their households.

504　*r -----. "A Woman's Awakening: Evangelical Religion and the
Families of Utica, New York, 1800-1840." *American Quarterly* 30
(Winter 1978): 602-23. Notes, tables.

　　　Ryan treats the work of two women's voluntary associations in
Utica, New York, in the early part of the nineteenth century. The
Female Missionary Society, formed in 1806, evolved into the Female
Missionary Society of the Western District in 1824, with seventy
auxiliaries which raised twelve hundred dollars each year for eleven
male missionaries on the New York frontier. Wives of businessmen,
the members used a businessman's style, electing officers formally,
holding formal meetings, and keeping accounts scrupulously. In 1827,
they were absorbed into the Western Domestic Missionary Society.
Ryan also studies the Maternal Association, which was founded in 1824
to contribute financially to the education of missionaries. Members
prayed for children daily, attended meetings every other Wednesday,
and read Christian literature on child raising. This group developed no
formal organizational structure. Ryan determines that the mothers
supplanted the ministers as the agents of religious conversion and the
Christian socialization of children. The revivalism of the Great
Awakening, then, did not stop with the women's own conversion but
created a maternal role and image for their sex as well.

505　*r SAFFORD, MRS. HENRY G. *The Golden Jubilee, Woman's
American Baptist Foreign Mission Society, 1871-1921.* New York: the
organization, 1922. xii, 263 pp. Illus.: 34 of officers; facilities for
girls abroad; schoolchildren using schools; hospitals; sewing class;
kindergarten; and college nurses.

　　　The preface insists that the founders of the Woman's
American Baptist Foreign Mission Society were not feminists and were
not college women, but rather were Christians who grew determined
after the Civil War to attempt relief work around the world. They
sought advice from the men in the American Baptist Foreign Mission
Society and received valuable assistance in methods for "teaching and
preaching" for the development of Oriental women "who are to make a
new world possible." In five chapters, each devoted to one decade of
growth and expansion of mission work, we see the impressive results of
thousands of American circles of adult and children's bands raising
money for girls' schools, kindergartens, colleges, hospitals, and Bible
study groups in Asia, Europe, and Africa. Although Baptist women
had hoped to send single women abroad even in the antebellum period,
it was not until after the Civil War, in 1871, that the Baptist church gave
permission for Boston women to establish a woman's society for the

purpose of sending American women abroad to work with foreign girls and women. Quickly, Chicago, St. Louis, and San Francisco women formed regional branches, and local societies sprung up in churches throughout America. The emphasis of the history is less on the steady efforts of the fund-raisers at home than on the institutions and services their money provided.

506   *y SAXTON, MARTHA. "Best Girl Scout of Them All." *American Heritage* 33 (June-July 1982): 38-47. Illus.: Juliette Low at age 17; 1920s Girl Scout postcards; scenes from a 1918 Girl Scout film; 1930 campers; 1924 Norman Rockwell cover of *Life* Magazine.

This biography illuminates the life of the founder of the Girl Scouts, Juliette "Daisy" Gordon Low, a Savannah divorcée from elite circles. In 1912, eight girls joined her organization; by 1915 there were five thousand members and by 1920, forty-two hundred. The latter number contradicts historian Mary A. Rothschild's membership figure. Low was not a suffragist, but she did found and develop a society geared to strengthening resourcefulness in young women. Low died in 1927.

507   *c SCARGLE, RUSS. "Music and Men's Minds: A World War II Vignette." *Pacific Historian* 16 (1972): 28-35. Illus.: "Tune Timers" playing in hospital; ward patients playing musical instruments in hospital.

The author, a neighbor of one of the six women who founded the "Tune Timers" during World War II, tells the story of six Oakland, California, women who formed a group to cheer up hospitalized veterans. For five years, Helen Shutes, Genevieve Wood, Mary Jacobus, Eleanor Price, Dorothy Pearson Chapman, and Leila Timpson traveled to California hospitals to play and use music to uplift the spirits of veterans. Music clubs donated money to the group, and the members took a class in music therapy offered by the Federation of Music Clubs of America. To ensure their admission to hospitals, the women qualified as Red Cross Grey Ladies.

508   *s SCHAFFER, RONALD. "The Montana Woman Suffrage Campaign, 1911-1914." *Pacific Northwest Quarterly* 55 (January 1964): 9-15. Notes, illus.: cover portrait of Jeannette Rankin; page from *Votes for Women*, (Seattle; (July 1910) identifying distinguished people who declared themselves for women's suffrage.

Focusing on the biography of Jeannette Rankin, the first American woman to hold a seat in Congress, Schaffer describes Rankin's political development in Washington State's 1908-9 suffrage campaign. She returned to her home state of Montana to become vice president of the Missoula Political Equality Club. The obstacles suffragists faced included immigrant opposition, antisuffragist feeling, and antagonism by brewers and saloon keepers, owing to Women's Christian Temperance Union goals. In 1913, Rankin headed the state suffrage association and directed a variety of tactics to persuade Montana voters to grant women enfranchisement. Demonstrations, speeches, state fair parades, and lobbying for the support of women's groups, Granges, and unions educated the public sufficiently to win the vote in 1914. Montana suffrage societies transformed themselves into the League of Good Government clubs and, in the 1920s, the League of Women Voters.

509   *s -----. "The Problem of Consciousness in the Woman Suffrage Movement: A California Perspective." *Pacific Historical Review* 44 (November 1976): 469-493. Notes.

Schaffer provides tables about thirty-seven leaders of the California suffrage campaigns between 1897 and 1911. Sex, age, place of birth, education, religion, and marital status are collected. He traces the arguments leaders used to try to stir up the apathetic women who might become suffrage supporters. They recruited in women's clubs, cooperated with socialists and wage-earning women, and insisted that the vote could bring reform-minded women new clout to achieve regulations correcting such problems as unclean milk for babies. Leaders minimized the militancy, holding only one foot parade, and limited their public speaking on the street. They appealed to women's egos, urging them to "be a person." Success was limited in organizing rural women.

510   *z,w SCHARF, LOIS. "The Forgotten Woman: Working Women, The New Deal, and Woman's Organizations." In *Decades of Discontent: The Woman's Movement, 1920-1940*, edited by Lois Scharf and Joan Jensen, 243-59. Westport, Conn.: Greenwood Press, 1983. Notes.

Scharf exposes the bitter rift over the equal rights amendment which women's organizations suffered in the 1930s, deriving from issues of working women. The Woman's Bureau, League of Women Voters, and National Federation of Business and Professional Women's Clubs supported special legislation for working women. Only the National Woman's party supported the ERA. Yet clubs of reformers, including the General Federation of Women's Clubs, Young Women's Christian Association, and Women's Trade Union League, objected to President

Franklin Roosevelt's NIRA and later NRA codes which endorsed a wage differential by sex.

511   *m   SCHARF, LOIS, and JOAN JENSEN, eds. *Decades of Discontent: The Woman's Movement, 1920-1940.* Contributions in Women's Studies, no. 28. Westport, Conn. Greenwood Press, 1983. 313 pp.

Part 4 is entitled "Organizational and Ideological Struggles" and contains three pertinent articles.

See entries by Joan M. Jensen, Susan Becker, and Lois Scharf.

512   *p   SCHNELL, CHRISTOPHER J. "Mary Livermore and the Great Northwestern Fair." *Chicago History* 4 (Spring 1975): 34-43. Illus.: poster; McVicker's Theatre when it housed the Chicago Sanitary Commission; Jane Hoge; wagons carrying army supplies under Sanitary Commission flag; Abraham Lincoln letter to the Sanitary Commission auctioned at the fair; list of 6 months of supplies shipped; Sanitary Commission fair speaker Anna Dickinson; Mary Livermore.

In 1861, Abraham Lincoln authorized the establishment of the U.S. Sanitary Commission, a civilian volunteer organization that provided the Union army with nurses, hospital supplies, and other services, like food and bedding, necessary to maintain adequate sanitary conditions in army camps. Mary Livermore and Jane Hoge managed the Chicago branch, creating a newsletter to communicate with four thousand ladies' aid societies. Livermore, whose biography is provided, inspected battlefronts, depots, camps, and hospitals. She planned the Great Northwestern Sanitary Fair for two weeks in October of 1863. Eighty-five thousand people attended, buying donated souvenirs, viewing exhibits, dining, listening to lectures, watching tableaux, and spending huge sums. The eighty-six-thousand-dollar profit inspired other cities to support the war effort in a similar way. After the Civil War, Livermore organized the 1868 Chicago suffrage convention. In 1869, she edited the *Agitator*, a suffrage and temperance newspaper, which merged with the *Woman's Journal* the following year.

513   *i   SCHOTT, LINDA. "Woman's Peace Party and the Moral Basis for Women's Pacifism." *Frontiers* 8, no. 2, (1985): 18-24. Notes.

This historian recounts the development of a separate women's peace movement by examining the January 1915 meeting in Washington, D.C., of three thousand women from the International Woman Suffrage Alliance. The women's associations that sent delegates were the National American Woman Suffrage Association,

General Federation of Women's Clubs, National Council of Jewish Women, National Conference of Catholic Charities, Women's Trade Union League, International Congress of Farm Women, the National League of Teachers, National Federation of Settlement Workers, League of American Pen Women, Women's Christian Temperance Union, National Association of Colored Women, DAR, and Spanish-American War Nurses. The Woman's Peace party which they formed (later becoming the Women's International League for Peace and Freedom) tended to attract white, middle-class, college-educated working women, especially teachers and social workers. It was a moral opposition to war that united them. Believing women possess distinctive values from men, they wanted to humanize society by integrating women and their values into the male-dominated public sphere to decrease violence. Even as World War I continued, they stressed that women must remain united with their common "love of justice, civilization and beauty which are all destroyed by war." Their antiwar activities and work for racial equality addressed their belief in an improved quality of life for each individual. Schott asserts that the strength of the organization came from women's identification with their own sex.

514   *y   SCHULTZ, GLADYS DENNY, and DAISY GORDON LAWRENCE. *Lady from Savannah: The Life of Juliette Low.* Philadelphia: J.B. Lippincott Co., 1958. 383 pp. Illus.: 14, of Low and her relatives, headquarters of the first American Girl Guides in Savannah, Ga., and Low at the first National Girl Scout headquarters in New York City.

This is a richly detailed biography of Juliette Gordon Low, the founder of the Girl Scouts, but it includes little material on the organization itself. Nevertheless, Schultz includes some information on the sixteen girls who registered formally in March 1912 to create the first two troops in America. She remarks on the development of the uniforms and badges. An account is provided of the 1920 national convention at which Juliette Low resigned from the presidency of the organization. Low's house has become the headquarters of Georgia's branch of the National Society of Colonial Dames, but it remains a mecca for the millions of girls who joined the organization. From 1912 to 1927, 12 million girls were involved with the organization. In 1927 alone, 167,900 American girls belonged. By 1958, the date of this publication, 2.8 million girls had participated in Girl Scouting.

515   *z   SCHWARTZ, JUDITH. *Radical Feminists of Heterodoxy: Greenwich Village, 1912-1940.* Lebanon, Vt.: New Victoria

Publishers, 1982. 110 pp. Notes, appendixes, bib., indexes, illus.: 29 of members.

Greenwich Village in New York City saw the association of unorthodox women in 1912, when Jennie Howe united women leaders of social activism in a club called Heterodoxy. Meeting every other week until the early 1940s, the members shared their ideas and encouraged each other to continue to make contributions to the arts, politics, and social reform. The author provides biographies of the members' public and private lives and excerpts from their writings and their club records.

516   *z SCOTT, ANNE FIROR. "After Suffrage: Southern Women in the 1920s." *Journal of Southern History* 30 (1963): 298-318. Notes.

Far from abandoning politics in 1920, when women finally succeeded in their seventy-two-year battle for the vote, southern activists began with new vigor to press, as voters, for a broad range of legislation. This essay surveys the spectrum of issues addressed by a wide variety of women's voluntary organizations, to document the firmness of women's expectations that their new vote would grant them greater clout on the political scene.

517   *m -----. *Making the Invisible Woman Visible*. Urbana: University of Illinois Press, 1984. xxvii, 387 pp. Notes, indexes.

This collection of essays includes "After Suffrage: Southern Women in the 1920s" (see separate entry above) and "Women, Religion and Social Change in the South, 1830-1930," an adaptation of a chapter from *The Southern Lady* (see entry below) addressing women's voluntary associations in the churches and for temperance. Part 3 of this volume, "Voluntary Associations," contains two essays of interest to researchers on women's organizational history. "As Easily as They Breathe" (pp. 261-78) surveys the work of several late eighteenth- and early nineteenth-century women's benevolent societies. These include the Society for the Relief of Poor Widows with Small Children in New York, the Hopkinton, New Hampshire, Chesterfield Female Benevolent Society, the Morristown, New Jersey, Presbyterian Women's Benevolent Society, and the Shrewsbury, Massachusetts, Woman's Benevolent Society. An essay entitled "Women's Voluntary Associations in the Forming of American Society" (279-94) argues that women's associations brought social justice issues to the wider public. Women's impulse to be good Christians propelled them to challenge alcohol consumption, and their interest in building good citizenship inspired their charitable societies, missionary movements, and community improvement programs.

518   *m -----.   "On Seeing and Not Seeing: A Case of Historical Invisibility." *Journal of American History* 71 (June 1984): 7-21. Notes, bib.

Scott asserts that American scholars have neglected the importance of women's voluntary associations to history.   The organizations helped women to train for new roles in society and also led to profound social changes. She provides an overview of women's voluntary efforts from the early national period to the present, provides a sound bibliography of dissertations and published histories of women's organizations, and calls for serious attention to their significance in American history. Scott outlines the associations women developed in the 1830s—for temperance, moral reform, education, benevolence, health reform, physical education, antislavery, and working women. The Civil War gave occasion for the establishment of soldiers' aid societies. After 1865, a new explosion of associations erupted, when urban women investigated and attempted to solve new urban problems, and created dense webs linking their efforts to community federations. This cooperative work trained some women for public roles of other kinds in the professions and politics.

519   *z -----.   *The Southern Lady: From Pedestal to Politics, 1830-1930.* Chicago: University of Chicago Press, 1970. xv, 247 pp. Notes, indexes, bib.

Part 1 of this study, on the antebellum lady, emphasizes life in the domestic sphere and roles in the Civil War. Part 2 on "The New Woman" uncovers an impressive array of factual and analytical findings about southern women's public record. Certainly there is attention, in this survey, to women as educators, writers, journalists, and factory laborers, but there is also valuable material on the work of women's voluntary associations. Among the groups investigated are Woman's Social and Industrial Association of New Orleans (founded in 1881), which encouraged and helped working women; New Orleans Woman's Club (1885), which ran an employment bureau; church societies such as the Woman's Board of Foreign Missions of the Methodists, Baptists, and Presbyterians; the Civic Improvement League of Augusta, Georgia (1911); Women's Christian Temperance Union; literary clubs, which created federations like the North Carolina Federation of Women's Clubs, propelling member clubs from the study of books to the solving of civic problems; suffrage associations; YWCA; League of Women Voters; Consumers' League; unions; and race relations organizations. Scott argues persuasively that the work of these societies gave women a strong public voice and influence in the South.

520   *s SCOTT, MARY SEMPLE, ed. "History of the Woman Suffrage
      Movement in Missouri." *Missouri Historical Review* 14 (April 1920):
      281-384.   Illus.: governor and women signing the Montana
      ratification of the federal suffrage amendment in 1919.
          Several suffrage activists of Missouri wrote sections of this
      issue, providing great density of detail. "Early Beginnings" deals with
      the formation of the St. Louis Suffrage Association, which formed in
      1867 and claimed to be the first group in the world whose sole object
      was the political enfranchisement of women.   By 1870, its members
      were petitioning legislators for a woman suffrage amendment to the
      Constitution.   The chapter entitled "Middle Ages" deals with the
      founding of the St. Louis Equal Suffrage League in 1910. The group's
      part in relief work of World War I is described.   Other topics covered
      include the part played by the Kansas City League, creating suffrage
      sentiment in Missouri through tours of speakers, the presidential
      suffrage bill, state work in 1916, ratification, League of Women Voters'
      citizenship schools, congressional work, news coverage in mainstream
      and women's publications, Kansas City's Susan B. Anthony League,
      Warrensburg League (founded 1911), Columbia League (1912), and St.
      Louis Business Women's League (1912).

521   *c SCOULLER, MILDRED MARSHALL. *Women Who Man Our
      Clubs*. Chicago: John C. Winston Co., 1934. x, 221 pp. Illus.: 51
      including Mrs. Grace Morrison Poole; Mrs. Robert J. Burdette; Mrs.
      Lucretia L. Blankenburg; Miss Alice Lakey; Mrs. Charles S. Morris;
      Mrs. Thomas M. Land; Mrs. William R. Alvord; other women
      described.
          This book comprises fifty-one biographies of women leaders in
      the General Federation of Women's Clubs, quoting from their own
      accounts of their club accomplishments in civics and the arts.   It
      illuminates the volunteer work of six pioneer founders, four past
      presidents, the president at the time of publication, Grace Morrison
      Poole, three leaders in the Junior Club movement, and other mid-
      twentieth-century powerhouses in the federation from all regions of
      America.

522   *t SCOVELL, BESSIE LATHE, comp. *A Brief History of the
      Minnesota Woman's Christian Temperance Union from Its
      Organization, September 6, 1877 to 1939*. St. Paul: Bruce Publishing
      Co., 1939. 264 pp. Illus.: Frances E. Willard, state president of the
      Women's Christian Temperance Union, and other officers; guest
      speakers; editors of *Minnesota White Ribbon*; formal groups at
      conferences; state superintendents of departments.

The narrative is overshadowed by lists, documents, and speeches. Scovell does provide summaries of the work accomplished at Minnesota annual temperance conventions from 1877 to 1937, but this history's strongest contribution lies in its collection of lyrics to state hymns; pledges of 1879, 1927, 1933; location lists for state conventions and speakers; key dates in the histories of the thirty-three districts; reports of the state superintendent of scientific instruction; and addresses of the presidents.

523 *z SEALANDER, JUDITH. "Feminists against Feminism: The First Phase of the Equal Rights Amendment Debate, 1923-1963." *South Atlantic Quarterly* 81 (Spring 1982): 147-61. Notes.

In 1922, the National Woman's party wrote the equal rights amendment and pressured Congress to grant men and women equality under the law. Opposition was fierce, even among women's groups, who refused to support the abolition of protective legislation they had worked long and hard to institute. Not until the 1960s did interest in the ERA reawaken, leading to congressional endorsement of it in 1972. In the interim, a few women's groups reconsidered their antagonism to it. The National Federation of Business and Professional Women's Clubs endorsed it in 1937, but discussed repealing their support in 1963. During World War II, the General Federation of Women's Clubs came around and the Democratic and Republican platforms supported it.

524 *c SEARLE, NEWELL. "Minnesota National Forest: Politics of Compromise, 1898-1908." *Minnesota History* 42 (Fall 1971): 242-57. Notes, illus.: Florence Bramhall, chairman of the Forest Reserve Commission of the Minnesota Federation of Women's Clubs.

Members of the Minnesota Federation of Women's Clubs played the largest role in securing a forest reserve (later known as the Minnesota National Forest and still later, the Chippewa National Forest) by negotiating with opponents to the plan. They prompted an investigation of reservation logging in 1898 and again in 1901, and pressed to discover whether Indians really enjoyed all the benefits from timber harvesting to which the Nelson Law entitled them. In 1899, asking for 489,000 acres of park, they settled for 225,000 acres.

525 *b SEE, ANNA PHILLIPS. "A Grandmother among Women's Clubs." *DAR Magazine* 54 (May 1920): 285-92. Illus.: home of Judge Lee where the group organized; home of the 1919 president; Mrs. "Tempe" Lee, first hostess; Mrs. Sally Sayword Wood, presidentess, 1805-1810.

In 1805, a handful of women in Maine formed the Female Charitable Society of Wiscasset. Thirty members paid dues for charitable purposes to "respectable, indigent women." At the time of this essay's publication, the group still met, once annually, as it had for 115 years. The tone of the article is anecdotal, and researchers will be frustrated by the absence of notes.

526 *m SELAVAN, IDA COHEN. "The Founding of Columbian Council." *American Jewish Archives* 30 (April 1978): 24-42. Notes.

At the Chicago World's Fair of 1893, Jewish women formed a National Council of Jewish Women. Branches were quickly established in Chicago, Quincy, Baltimore, and Allegheny-Pittsburgh, where it was called the Columbian Council. Predating the 1894 organization in Pittsburgh was the Ladies Auxiliary to the Hebrew Benevolent Society for Jewish relief founded in 1856. The members of the Columbian Council were American-born, middle-class women, and included a high percentage of college graduates. The members engaged in "preventive philanthropy," teaching English and civics to immigrants, skills that were to assist them in self-sufficiency. Immediately, the women established a free kindergarten. In 1895, they created study circles to examine the Bible and Jewish history, but this program was unsuccessful and disbanded in 1899. Members preferred guest lectures. Thirty-five women, in a "sisterhood of Personal Service," began to visit impoverished families, helping them to become self-sufficient: they ordered needlework from the women and paid them for it; they tutored the women in English at their homes; and they established a religious school for the children. In 1901, the Columbian Council hired a trained nurse to survey health conditions in the public schools. Their findings shocked the community into making great improvements in sanitary conditions. In 1904, the members opened public evening schools, seeing a need for classes for working people. Selavan's study is a loving portrait of the good works performed during the early years of the Pittsburgh branch of the National Council of Jewish Women.

527 *m SEWELL, MAY WRIGHT, comp. *Genesis of the International Council of Women and the Story of Its Growth: 1888-1893*. Indianapolis, Ind.: the organization, 1914. iii, 75 pp. Illus.: 2 medals and 1 scroll from the Chicago Exposition.

Compiled from official organizational records, from its founding in 1888 through the meetings at the Chicago Exposition in 1893, this history clarifies the emergence of the International Council of Women from the National Council of Women. To celebrate the fortieth anniversary of the 1848 Seneca Falls Women's Rights

Convention, Sewall called representatives from both American and foreign groups to Washington, D.C., to cooperate to win the suffrage "to conserve the highest good of the family and state." Sewall's correspondence and the constitutions of her National Council of Women and International Council are printed. She also lists the American women's organizations involved in international work for women's rights around the globe.

528 *m -----. *The World's Congress of Representative Women*. 2 vols. Chicago: Rand McNally and Co., 1894. Vol. 1, xxiv, 1-448, illus.: 60, including women officers of the World's Congress of Representative Women and women speakers. Vol. 2, 451-952, indexes for both vols.

    Here is a two-volume collection of women's speeches delivered at the 1893 Chicago Exposition, many of which deal with the histories of the women's organizations they represented. Volume 1 contains details on the women's organizational efforts to guide the World's Congress of Representative Women. Charlotte Emerson Brown, first president of the General Federation of Women's Clubs, refers to the brief history of her group in "Organization as a Means of Literary Culture." Mary E. Richmond's speech, "Organization among Women Considered with Respect to Philanthropy," and Clara C. Hoffman's presentation of the Women's Christian Temperance Union provide generalities rather than specifics about the histories of their groups. Mary Lowe Dickinson's remarks on "Organization among Women as an Instrument in Promoting Religion" provides more detail on the WCTU. Generalities also pervade clubwoman Julia Ward Howe's "The Moral Initiative as Related to Women" and Maud Ballington Booth's "Organization as an Instrument in Promoting Moral Reform." Elizabeth Wheeler Andrew spoke on "The Development of the World's Women's Christian Temperance Union after 1883."

    In volume 2, Susan B. Anthony lists all kinds of women's clubs in "Organization among Women as an Instrument in Promoting the Interests of Political Liberty." Mary A. Flint discusses organizational goals in "The Value of Eastern Star." Mrs. William E. Burke founded the Women's National Indian Association in 1880 and reviews her group's efforts to gain more just congressional legislation for Indians. Sarah J. Early spoke on "Organized Efforts of the Colored Women of the South to Improve Their Condition," drawing heavily on church work, and Hallie Q. Brown emphasized black women's roles in the King's Daughters, YWCA, and WCTU. Marion Talbot spoke on the "History, Aims and Methods of the Association of Collegiate Alumnae." Lucilia W. Learned spoke on "Results of Club Life among Women upon the Home." Belle Grant Armstrong spoke on the New

England Woman's Press Association, a new organization at the time. Mary Joseph Onahan addressed "Catholic Women's Part in Philanthropy." Other entries of interest to researchers on voluntary associations of women include Alice May Scudder, "Women's Work in the Society of Christian Endeavor"; Mrs. William Boyd, "Young Women's Christian Association"; Clara C. Hoffman, "Bird's Eye View of the National WCTU"; Elizabeth B. Grannis, "National Christian League for the Promotion of Social Purity"; Mrs. John Wood Stewart, "Needlework Guild of America"; Kate Brownlee Sherwood, "Past, Present and Future of the Woman's Relief Corps"; Mary C. Snedden, "Eastern Star"; and Rachel Foster Avery, "Organization and Its Relation to the International and National Councils of Women." The women's club movement, on the verge of an explosion of activity in this era, is well described by its founders in this collection. Foreign clubs, especially among European women, are also surveyed in this volume.

529   *b   SEXTON, RICHARD D.   "San Diego Woman's Home Association: A Volunteer Charity Organization." *Journal of San Diego History* 29 (Winter 1983): 41-53. Notes, illus.: a membership leaflet; Dr. Charlotte Baker, M.D., and Kate Sessions, horticulturist.

Supporters of the San Diego Woman's Home Association drew on funds from the Methodist church women's WCTU and the Flower Festival Association to build a home for indigent, unfortunate, aged, helpless or working women in 1887. They leased a building that could lodge four women and then created a day-care facility and woman's exchange to sell commodities made by housebound women. Sexton lists the prominent members who volunteered to administer the home, which still exists as the San Diego Center for Children. She exposes conflicts over fund-raising and expenditures.

530   *b   SEYMOUR, CAPTAIN JACK M.   *Ships, Sailors and Samaritans: The Woman's Seaman's Friend Society of Connecticut, 1859-1976.* New Haven: the organization, 1976. x, 157 pp. Notes, indexes, illus.: 12 including scenes from the covers of the annual report, concert, cookbook of the Woman's Seaman's Friend Society; 3 of homes and chapel.

Chapter 1 surveys the history of the seaport of New Haven, and chapter 2 traces the history of agencies designed to assist destitute and derelict seamen and to benefit sailors' "temporal and spiritual interests." Seymour observes that the Connecticut governor called for an agent to handle seamen's relief as early as 1776. In Boston, a society formed in 1812, and in New York City, the Society for Promoting the Gospel among Seamen formed in 1819. It was in 1817 that New

Haven's gentlemen founded the Seamen's Friend and Marine Bible Society of New Haven. This group was reorganized in 1843 as the Ladies' Seamen's Friend Society of New Haven. It obtained a charter from the city of New Haven in 1860, modified its name, and remained a member of the American Seamen's Friend Society, but nevertheless remained independent and operated on its own. Chapter 3 details the efforts of the Woman's Seamen's Friend Society from 1859 through 1976, providing a list of its fifteen presidents, listing its officers during the 1973-76 administration, and printing its constitution and bylaws. The group began to raise funds by holding a fair. The members cleared $880 in 1860 and used it to buy a $2,000 "home away from home," which provided seamen with a reading room, foreign-language papers for non-English-speaking sailors, mail service, chapel, boarding house, Christmas festivities such as refreshments, music, gifts, and decorations, medical care, games, free stationery, charity clothing and lodging for the shipwrecked, free passage to home ports, and a cemetery plot for thirty-six "worthy sailors," a granite monument, and scholarships for their children. Women served as the presidents, officers, members, and managers of this association. The history catalogs their teas, concerts, amateur dramatic productions, and fruitcake sales to raise money for the establishment and maintenance of the three homes (1894-1903, 1904-54, 1955-71), and chapel of 1905.

531   no entry

532   *b SHANKMAN, ARNOLD. "The South Carolina Council for the Common Good." *Proceedings of the South Carolina Historical Association* (1982): 90-99. Notes.

In 1935, Mrs. C. Fred Laurence, president of the South Carolina Federation of Women's Clubs, founded a new organization for South Carolina women, the Women's Council for the Common Good. The object of the organization was to improve living conditions in the state, especially through home life, highway safety, temperance, and better schools for children. The membership also worked for adult education, a bigger state library budget, free textbooks for schoolchildren, a college degree for every teacher, and better conditions for women in penitentiaries. Although it saw much success, it made no progress in the realm of marriage reform and federal aid to education. Members persuaded legislators to repeal the margarine tax. They provided relief work in World War II. They supported the equal rights amendment throughout their history. No black women, however, were admitted to the membership, and the group supported literacy tests for voters, which often served to exclude black voters from political participation.

533   *s   SHAW, ANNA HOWARD. *The Story of a Pioneer*. New York: Harper and Brothers, 1915. 338 pp. Illus.: 30, of Anna Howard Shaw; her family; her friends who advocated women's rights.

       Anna Howard Shaw (1847-1919) was born in England, but her autobiography surveys her early life in the United States, her college experience in Albion, Michigan, and her pioneering roles as an early woman physician and minister. In 1885, she began to lecture and organize for the Massachusetts Woman Suffrage Association and the American Woman Suffrage Association, but moved her allegiance, after meeting Susan B. Anthony, to Anthony's rival organization, the National Woman Suffrage Association. From 1886 to 1892, Shaw also served as superintendent of the Franchise Department of the Women's Christian Temperance Union. Her story is rich in anecdotes about her experiences with suffrage and temperance. In 1890, the National and the American Woman Suffrage associations merged, and she served as vice president of the new National American Woman Suffrage Association from 1892 to 1904. In 1904, she became the organization's president, serving until 1915. The story of her life after the 1880s is the story of the fight for women's enfranchisement in the West while she toured and spoke, at the conventions she attended between 1887 and 1914, and as a representative at the International Council of Women and the International Suffrage Alliance.

534   *m   SHAW, EASDALE. *The History of the North Carolina Branch of the International Order of the King's Daughters and Sons*. Raleigh, N.C.: Capitol Printing Co. 1929. 30 pp.

       As club historian, Easdale Shaw provides us with an account of the founding of "a sisterhood of service," the International Order of the King's Daughters in New York City in 1886. The name was changed the following year when members decided to admit men to the organization, but men did not enter in large numbers. In 1886, Wilmington, North Carolina, women formed the Whatsoever Circle at the First Baptist Church under the leadership of Mrs. Emma G. Williams. Members raised money to buy a cemetery plot for the worthy poor. In 1907, the group severed its special ties with the Baptist church and opened membership to women of all churches. Shaw traces the founding of other circles in North Carolina, numbering twenty-two by 1929, with a membership of one thousand women. These groups built homes for aged and infirm women, established a day nursery in Charlotte, and raised money for the Stonewall Jackson Manual

Training and Industrial School for Boys. Considerable correspondence from the latter project is quoted in the text. The author provides a list of state presidents from 1890 to 1930, with Mrs. W.H.S. Burgwyn serving for much of the group's history, from 1901 to 1924. All state circles are named with dates of founding.

535 *c SHELTON, BRENDA K. "Organized Mother Love: The Buffalo Woman's Educational and Industrial Union, 1885-1915." *New York History* 67 (April 1986): 155-76. Notes, illus.: Women's Educational and Industrial Union headquarters, 1897-1915; Harriet Townsend.

Harriet Townsend founded the Buffalo Women's Educational and Industrial Union in 1884 and served as its president until 1905. For ten years, until its dissolution, she served as the group's honorary president. The article provides biographical detail as well as the story of the club's social dimensions, its inclusion of a few Jewish members, and its projects designed to address the needs of all women in Buffalo, not just those of the women of privilege among the membership. The organization established an employment bureau, skills training, domestic education, kitchen garden, kindergarten, physical culture classes, and legal aid. In 1915, when the members felt their work had been taken up by other organizations, they disbanded, giving their building to the University of Buffalo, to be named Townsend Hall. Shelton argues that like many progressive reformers of the day, the club women were successful at articulating specific social problems and solving them. Among the achievements of the Women's Educational and Industrial Union in Buffalo was the appointment of police matrons in city government, legal protection for domestic workers, and vocational education for girls.

536 *c SHEPARD, MRS. FREDERICK, comp. "The Women's Educational and Industrial Union of Buffalo." *Buffalo Historical Society Publication* 22 (1918): 147-200. Illus.: WEIU clubhouse, interior and exterior; twenty-two-year president, Mrs. George Townsend.

In 1884, the president of Boston's Women's Educational and Industrial Union came to Buffalo, New York, to speak with clubwomen and encourage them to form a new club of the kind she represented. They did so, electing Mrs. George Townsend their president, a position she would hold for twenty-two years. Protestant, Catholic, and Jewish women were invited, and the membership reached 794 in the first year. Soon the group had sufficient funds to buy a building, replace it with a larger facility, and establish an impressive variety of programs for members and for other women of the city, a kitchen garden, coteries where members delivered papers, noon rest, domestic training classes, a lecture series, receptions for visiting celebrities, girls' Union Circle, a civic club to inform members of current events, charitable projects, facilities for conventions of the National Association of Colored Women, the International Conference of Nurses, and National Home Economics Association, first aid instruction, a gymnasium, literary and musical entertainments, a collection and display of women's art, legal aid, and employment bureau. The organization dissolved in 1915, believing other agencies in Buffalo were handling the projects they had developed. Their building was donated to the University of Buffalo, and named in Mrs. Townsend's honor. The history includes a detailed list of generous donors to the club's projects and a reprint of their articles of incorporation.

537   *c SHERMAN, MRS. JOHN DICKINSON. "Women's Clubs in the Middle Western States." *Annals of the American Academy of Political and Social Science* 28 (September 1906): 227-47.

Sherman asserts that thirteen hundred clubs with seventy-five thousand women members thrived in Illinois, Indiana, Iowa, Michigan, Missouri, and Ohio in the year of this publication. She outlines the work of the early clubs and provides the dates on which each state federated its local clubs. She categorizes the history of club development into three stages: the earliest era devoted to intellectual betterment of its members, the next for the benefit of the local community, and finally the cultivation of power in municipal, state, and national affairs. Providing specific examples from midwestern club projects, she details accomplishments in the areas of education, libraries, compulsory education, vacation schools, domestic arts, aid to working women, juvenile courts, child labor laws, arts, city improvement, and civil service.

538   *r SHERMAN, MARGARET MARSTON. *True to Their Heritage: A Brief History of the Woman's Auxiliary, 1871-1958.* New York: National Council of Episcopal Church Center, 1958. 43 pp. Indexes, appendixes.

Sherman's study divides the history of the women's auxiliaries of the Episcopal church from 1871 to 1958 into five eras: "Prehistoric Days, 1821-1871"; "Organization and Early Years of the Woman's Auxiliary from 1871-1900"; "Enlarging the Association, 1900-1921"; "Breaking Old Patterns, 1922-1940"; and "Advancing toward New Relationships, 1940-1958". In the earliest period, eleven women's auxiliaries existed, many of which were missionary societies. In 1871, the dioceses' auxiliaries united for mission work and initiated new programs, like children's auxiliaries. The alliance grew so fully and rapidly that major reorganization was implemented in 1919. During the 1920s, however, the women developed broader programs, which yielded tension with the church. In 1927, an organizational redefinition was imposed and the women lost their separate status and autonomy. In the final era under study, the women took stances on new social issues, in addition to their missionary work. They passed resolutions, for example, on child labor, peace, and the United Nations. In 1943, the black and white women's groups, heretofore separate, integrated. Three appendixes list members of the staff from 1871 to 1958, executive board members from 1919 to 1958, and the elected presiding officers of the triennial meetings from 1928 to 1958.

539   *p SIMKINS, FRANCIS B., and JAMES W. PATTON. "The Work of Southern Women among the Sick and Wounded of the Confederate Armies." *Journal of Southern History* 1 (November 1935): 476-96. Notes.

The northern women of the Civil War are renowned for their relief work through the U.S. Sanitary Commission. Here, Confederate women get their due, for they too formed hospital relief societies for their soldiers. In fact, the Southern Mothers' Society in Memphis founded the Southern Mothers' Hospital, and the Ladies' Hospital Society of Montgomery formed the Soldiers' Home in Alabama. Simkins includes biographies of pioneering hospital matrons. Roman Catholic sisterhoods also engaged in relief work. In many communities, women organized wayside homes, small hospitals, or restrooms at railroad junctions for soldiers. In March of 1872, the Columbia, South Carolina, Young Ladies' Hospital Association created a Soldiers' Rest. A committee of women in Anderson, South Carolina, met every train with food, medicine, buttermilk, and whiskey. Some women took disabled soldiers into their homes for a period of convalescence.

540   *m SIMMS, L. MOODY, Jr. "A Horror of Hoops." *Southwestern Historical Quarterly* 72 (July 1968): 88-92. Notes.

In the notes and documents section of this publication, Simms recounts the work of the Anti-Crinoline League of Brenham, Texas, which housewives and professional women formed in March of 1893 for the purpose of satirizing women's dress in local newspapers. Teacher Ethel Hutson's article, from the Brenham Herald, is reprinted here in full.

541   *y,r SIMS, MARY SOPHIA. *The First Twenty-Five Years: A Summary of the Work of the YWCA of the U.S. of A., 1906-1931.* New York: Woman's Press, 1932. 82 pp. Appendixes.

Sims's history begins in 1906 on the date of the merging of two Young Women's Christian Association boards, the international and the American, whereupon a new executive board of thirty people unified the YWCA work of 608 affiliated American associations (with 186,000 women and girl members), 469 American student associations with 41,688 members, and members in China, India, Argentina, and Japan. The first president of the national board, Grace Dodge, established a headquarters in New York City in 1912 at 600 Lexington Avenue. This study documents the work of the War Work Council of the National Board of the YWCA, which operated from 1917 to 1921 to deal with special World War I and postwar problems. The council trained officers for leadership in American recreation centers, hostess houses, health clinics, war bride programs, and overseas nursing. It created recreational facilities for "colored girls and women" and aided foreign families in an era of intense nationalism. A chapter on "Return to Normalcy" in the 1920s explores peace and international relations initiatives of the organization and documents its funding problems. During the Great Depression of the 1930s, the forces moved more fully toward relief and unemployment programs and opposition to racial discrimination. A concluding section asserts that the YWCA will continue to offer satisfactory leadership experiences to women along with a spiritual power from its Christian emphasis. Sims reminds readers that the YWCA nurtured the founding of the National Federation of Business and Professional Women's Clubs, the Summer School for Women Workers in Industry at Bryn Mawr College, Travelers' Aid program, and the International Migration Service. The appendixes include the constitution; "Social Ideals of the Churches," report of the 1920 sixth national YWCA convention; list of important dates in YWCA history from 1855 to 1932; membership figures for 1906, 1916, 1921, 1926, and 1931; and summer conference figures from 1906 to 1931 including the number of conferences and attendance figures.

542   *y,r -----. *The Natural History of a Social Institution—The Young Women's Christian Association.* New York: Woman's Press, 1936. 251 pp. Notes, index.

This is a strong and serious history of the YWCA in America between the years of its founding in New York City in 1858 through 1934. Its solid research and generous quotations make it a useful survey for researchers. Sims outlines the general history of the organization in her first three chapters, dividing the story into 1855-71, 1871-1906, and 1906-34. In the following eight chapters, she examines themes and issues. In addressing the relationship of the YWCA to the woman's movement, Sims documents early classes in vocational training for women, support for health programs, and classes teaching responsible citizenship. The work articulates the role of religion in the organization. Although she is careful not to imply any organizational relationship to a particular church, the author observes a sagging religious commitment after World War I and praises a renewal of social Christianity in the postwar period. Foreign programs began to be promoted in the late nineteenth century, yielding numerous overseas centers. By 1920, thirty-two branches in the Orient and South America and fifty-nine European and Near Eastern centers required administration by 118 staff women. Sims devotes a chapter to "Pioneering," or creating unique and lasting women's programs. She describes the Woman's Exchange, day nursery, kindergarten, and several philanthropies that became independent: Travelers' Aid, National Federation of Business and Professional Women's Clubs, summer schools and scholarships for industrial workers, the International Migration Service, and National Institute of Immigrant Welfare. Under a section entitled "Strains and Stresses," Sims exposes controversial issues on which the Y has taken a stand. Internationalism, during unpopular eras of 1915 and the 1920s; improved race relations through black women's Y branches, beginning in 1893 in Dayton, Ohio, and, after 1906, the creation of "open" branches that were not strictly segregated; and efforts to influence public opinion on issues of concern to liberal Protestantism are among the topics Sims treats most fully. A chapter on the "YWCA in Crisis" documents World War I relief work, including the establishment of hostess houses at home and abroad for soldiers' recreation, lectures on social morality, care of war brides, education against hatred of the foreign-born, and in times of depression, relief programs and employment projects. "Breaking Down Barriers" catalogs efforts to cooperate with black women, working women, foreign-born, and business and professional women. Appendexes include a chronological table of important events in Y history from 1855 through 1934; the 1934 constitution of the organization, and policy statements on "Christian Bases for Determining Eligibility to Affiliation with the National Organization," the original and the 1920, 1926, 1928, and 1934 revisions.

543   *y,r -----. *The YWCA: An Unfolding Purpose.* New York: Woman's Press, 1950. xv, 157 pp. Index, bib.

Nearing the hundred-year mark, the YWCA produced this short overview of the history of the organization. It is an introduction to its goals and work and is not laden with encyclopedic details on its branches, officers, and budget. Instead, it quickly surveys its development from 1855 to 1949 and then moves to thematic chapters on its Christian emphasis, student involvement, diversity of members served including immigrants and working girls, work for social ideals like desegregation and legislation to protect workers, its international focus, its development of women leaders, its treasury and membership. This is a quick and concise record of YWCA accomplishments for young women.

544   *m SINCLAIR, ANDREW. *The Emancipation of the American Woman*. New York: Harper and Row, 1965. xxix, 401 pp. Notes, index.

Although this author is not concerned with women's organizations, how they function, or their importance in women's lives, he sprinkles mention of several important associations in this good and broad survey of women's history: Boston Female Anti-Slavery Society, women's rights conventions of the antebellum era, Equal Rights Association, National American Woman Suffrage Association, Women's Christian Temperance Union, General Federation of Women's Clubs, National Consumers' League, and National Woman's Party.

545   *t SMITH, BECKY. "Prohibition in Alaska." *Alaska Journal* 3 (Summer 1973): 170-79. Notes, illus.: saloons; legislators; 2 editorials.

Although most of this article deals with legislators and the press, Smith includes useful material on the Women's Christian Temperance Union in Alaska. Although the organization was founded in 1874, it was not until Mrs. S.E. Shorthill of Skagway was appointed an Alaska representative in 1899 that branches began to form. By 1913, the WCTU formed an Alaska federation, its first president being Mrs. Cornelia Templeton Jewett Hatcher, who had served as managing editor of the *Union Signal* in Evanston, Illinois, before she married a prospector and moved north in 1909.

546   *p SMITH, ESSIE WADE BUTLER (MRS. CABELL). *Forty Years with the Virginia Division, United Daughters of the Confederacy*. N.p.: the author, 1935. 22 pp.

In May 1894, women of Charlottesville, Virginia, formed an auxiliary to the Grand Camp of Confederate Veterans and called themselves the Grand Division of Virginia. By 1903, several Virginia women's groups, devoted to honoring the war dead of the Confederacy and preserving history, united to form the United Daughters of the Confederacy. The history recounts the growth, officers, evolution of internal administration, and special projects such as relief, scholarships, monuments, World War I service, and the presentation of the Virginia Historical Pageant in 1920 in Richmond.

547   *c SMITH, HENRY LADD. "The Beauteous Jennie June: Pioneer Woman Journalist." *Journalism Quarterly* 40 (Spring 1963): 169-74. Notes.

While the author emphasizes the biography of Jane Cunningham Croly and her writing for newspapers, he includes some detail about her founding of three important women's organizations: Sorosis in 1868, a literary club for New York City career women and reformers, the Woman's Parliament of 1869, a public forum in which forward-looking women addressed women's rights issues in New York City, and the General Federation of Women's Clubs in 1890, a unification of literary clubs nationwide. Smith excerpts material from Croly's huge 1898 *History of the Woman's Club Movement in America*.

548   *y,r SMITH, JAMES RAVENEL. "YWCA." *Chautauquan* 59 (June 1910): 135-41.

See *Chautauquan*.

549   *s SMITH, WILDA M. "A Half-century of Struggle: Gaining Woman Suffrage in Kansas." *Kansas History* 4 (Summer 1981): 74-95. Notes, illus.: 15, including 2 cars of women in suffrage parade; Clarina I.H. Nichols; Lilla Day Monroe; Lucy Johnston; Sarah A. Brown; Laura Johns; Annie L. Diggs.

Smith surveys the suffrage struggle in Kansas from 1859, when Clarina I.H. Nichols and other suffragists appeared at the constitutional convention to demand women suffrage, until 1912, when male voters adopted woman suffrage. She examines the school election campaign of 1861, the municipal election campaign of 1861, and three statewide suffrage campaigns in 1867, 1894, and 1911-12. The factors she isolates as important to understanding the Kansas fight include the apathy or timidity of Kansas women, the suffragist link with temperance, fund-raising efforts, suffrage as a political issue, tactics that antagonized men, preautomobile difficulties in transportation, disagreement among leaders about tactics, and big egos among the leaders.

550   *b,r SMITH-ROSENBERG, CARROLL. "Beauty, the Beast and
the Militant Woman: A Case Study in Sex Roles and Social Stress in
Jacksonian America." *American Quarterly* 23 (October 1971): 562-
84. Notes. Reprinted in *A Heritage of Her Own: Toward a New
Social History of American Women*, edited by Nancy F. Cott and
Elizabeth H. Pleck, 197-221. New York: Simon and Schuster, 1979.
     This historian analyzes the work of the New York Female
Moral Reform Society, which formed in 1834 in Manhattan's Third
Presbyterian Church. Its members sought to convert New York City's
prostitutes to evangelical Protestantism and close the brothels. In
addition, however, a larger significance of the society lay in its nurturing
of the budding woman's movement. The "self-assertive women hoped
as well to confront the larger and more fundamental abuse, the double
standard, and the male sexual license it condoned."

551   *b,r -----. *Religion and the Rise of the American City: The New York
City Mission Movement, 1812-1870*. Ithaca, N.Y.: Cornell University
Press, 1971. 300 pp. Notes, bibliographic essay, index.
     Evangelical Protestants of 1830-60, converts of Charles
Finney's revival efforts, changed city mission activities in New England
and New York State. The American Female Guardian Society formed
with an urban middle-class membership, in part because their growing
affluence freed women from some of the pressures of domestic labor.
The author devotes Chapter 4, pp. 97-124, to the examination of the
New York Female Moral Reform Society, which was founded in 1835
and had become part of a network of 445 female auxiliaries by 1839.
The focus of activity was against New York City's houses of
prostitution, especially through Sunday morning visits to brothels, with
Bibles, prayers, and hymns. The members also offered temporary
lodgings in homes of refuge to reformed prostitutes.

552   *p SMYTHE, AUGUSTINE T. "History of the United
Daughters." *Confederate Veteran* 19 (February 1911): 61-62.
     In 1894, Mrs. L.H. Raines of Savannah secured a charter to
transform the Ladies' Auxiliary of the Confederate Soldiers' Home in
Nashville into the United Daughters of the Confederacy. In September
of that year, she invited women through Confederate organizations to
Nashville to form the United Daughters of the Confederacy to preserve
and collect relics, history, and data of all kinds relating to the struggle
for southern independence. At the 1894 Charleston convention, the
author of this article was elected president. She recounts the history of
the organization's meetings in the District of Columbia and Atlanta in
November 1895, in Nashville and Baltimore in November 1896, its

growth in membership, and its plans to erect a monument to Jefferson Davis.

553 *s SNAPP, MEREDITH D.   "Defeat the Democrats: The Congressional Union for Woman Suffrage in Arizona, 1914 and 1916." *Journal of the West* 14 (October 1975): 131-39. Notes.

The Congressional Union, spearheaded by Alice Paul and Lucy Burns, embarked on a 1914 campaign in the nine western states that had enfranchised women. They sought to scare Congress into immediate support for the federal woman suffrage amendment by encouraging their supporters to vote out all Democrats running for national office. In Arizona, women had won the vote in 1912 and would vote for the first time in the 1914 election. The union distributed news releases and sent well-known feminists on speaking tours to sway the labor vote and anti-Democratic vote. Newspapers, however, did not publicize their events, and their banners disappeared from public sites. The two Democratic congressmen were returned to office, indicating that the women's plan was unsuccessful. In 1916, the women targeted President Woodrow Wilson, as he ran for reelection, but they were unsuccessful again.

554 *r SOCHEN, JUNE.   "Some Observations on the Role of American Jewish Women in Communist Activities." *American Jewish History* 70 (September 1980): 23-34. Notes, illus.: Sadie American, executive secretary of the National Council of Jewish Women; volunteers at open-air-school.

The author asserts that Jewish women have always been public-spirited, using women's voluntary associations to make their stamp on American life. She outlines two basic types of members: the middle-aged woman who joins after her children are grown, enjoying leisure from her husband's income, and the single woman who volunteers before marriage, but stays active if she does not marry. In 1893, at the Chicago Exposition, the National Council of Jewish Women formed for religious, philanthropic, and educational purposes. Membership encouraged women to leave their home responsibilities for a few hours a week, to make important decisions about club programs, and to raise their self-esteem. Hannah Solomon organized the Chicago chapter, which established a workroom for needy women and a woman's home society for new Russian Jewish girls and women in America. They cooperated with the settlement houses to provide social services for immigrants. They founded a program of Sabbath schools for girls, visited delinquent children, and lobbied for juvenile courts. In 1912, Hadassah was founded by Henrietta Szold, to send public health nurses to Palestine. The tradition of club work gave women practice in speaking publicly and organizing. The movement reflected elements of Jewish culture, American culture, and a Jewish-American fusion of both.

555   *m SOKOLOW, JAYNE A., and MARY ANN LAMANNA. "Women and Utopia: The Woman's Commonwealth of Belton, Texas." *Southwestern Historical Quarterly* 84 (April 1984): 371-92. Illus.: Martha White McWhirter, founder; Central Hotel.

This non-Catholic utopian community, owned and operated by women, formed in 1879 when the Sanctified Sisters began a communal venture in Belton, Texas. Based on a radical variant of Methodist perfectionism, the community advocated celibacy, the abolition of patriarchy, and the pooling of economic resources. The fifty women enjoyed financial independence by the mid-1880s, running a hotel and three farms and buying a steam laundry. They grew to occupy eight buildings. By 1891, the community declined in size to thirty-two members and included boys and men. All rotated work assignments, women doing traditional men's jobs. In the 1890s, the women formed the Women's Wednesday Club devoted to the study of literature, art, science, and current events. Their collection of 350 books became Belton's first public library. In 1899, the members sold their property and moved to the more stimulating environment of Washington, D.C. A biography of the charismatic director, Martha White McWhirter (1827-1904), is included.

556   *m SOLOMON, HANNAH. *Fabric of My Life*. New York: Bloch Publishing Co., 1946. 277 pp. Illus.: 11 of the author, including her seated at a dinner at the International Council of Women conference, with Jane Addams at Solomon's 75th birthday, and at a banquet of a 1938 meeting of the National Council of Jewish Women's Council Tribunal.

Although she is modest about her role in the development of Jewish women's organizational life, Hannah Greenebaum Solomon's memoirs provide a wealth of details about the National Council of Jewish Women, which she founded in 1894 in the aftermath of the Congress of Jewish Women held at the 1893 Chicago Exposition. Her reminiscences from birth in 1858 through her eighty-fifth year include anecdotes about early family life, the Sanitary Commission Fair, piano instruction, singing with the Beethoven Society, the Zion Literary Society for young folks which her father organized in 1877, her admission with her sister Henriette to the Chicago Woman's Club—the first two Jews to be admitted to the organization—her 1892 paper on

"Our Debt to Judaism" which was published in the Unitarian church magazine *Unity*, and her marriage and travels. Part 2 emphasizes her efforts to bring Jewish women to the Chicago fair for a Jewish Women's Congress. She provides reports on the papers given there by the women and on the organization the following year of the National Council of Jewish Women. As first president, she guided committees on religion and philanthropy, urged a program of friendly visiting, and affiliated in 1894 with the National Council of Women. She refused to join the General Federation of Women's Clubs, seeing it as a Protestant body. Solomon reports on her European tour en route to the International Council of Women meetings, at which she represented the National Council of Jewish Women. She also describes the work of the Chicago Woman's Club and the Book and Play Club. The last chapter of the biography (pp. 264-77) contains a brief account of issues undertaken by the National Council of Jewish Women, appended by the council for this edition.

557   *r SORRILL, BOBBIE. "The History of the Week of Prayer for Foreign Missions." *Baptist History and Heritage* 15 (1980): 28-35. Notes.

The author, Education Division director of the Women's Missionary Union, Southern Baptist church, in Birmingham, Alabama, asserts that the Woman's Missionary Union led the Week of Prayer to undergird its foreign mission work. In 1888, Lottie Moon, a missionary to China, urged women to initiate a week of prayers and offerings for world missions. They did so just before Christmas and collected considerable sums for missions. Sorrill discusses the changes in the fund-raising endeavor over the years. Young people were included in special programs after 1903. By 1920, the Woman's Missionary Union had earned $40,000 for missions. By 1929, they had collected $200,000.

558   *p SOUTH CAROLINA DAUGHTERS OF THE AMERICAN REVOLUTION. *History of the South Carolina Daughters of the American Revolution, 1936-1946.* N.p.: the organization, 1946. 92 pp.

This compendium of forty-four chapter histories collects the projects of a decade. The branches of the South Carolina Daughters of the American Revolution took on such projects as sending money to the Red Cross, restoring old buildings, raising a contribution for the chimes at Valley Forge, giving scholarships, buying War Bonds, supporting Tamassee—a mountain school founded in 1919 to teach American citizenship, homemaking, handicrafts, and midwifery—collecting and recording tombstone inscriptions, donating flags to high schools, sending boxes of clothing to Indians and Ellis Island immigrants, giving Christmas gifts to servicemen, buying lunches for schoolchildren, revitalizing the Children of the American Revolution organization, locating graves of Revolutionary War soldiers, awarding silver dollars for the best essays on national defense, and providing equipment to high school home economics classes. Reports of state regents for the decade are included, as are a list of officers and a list of six disbanded chapters.

559   *c SPANGLER, D.W. "Mary Stewart, Educator, Author, and Club Woman." *Colorado Magazine* 27 (July 1950): 218-25.

This biography of Miss Mary Stewart (1876-1943), a high school principal and writer, also includes material on her life in clubs. She was born in Ohio, but her family moved to Colorado, where she earned a B.A., and became a teacher and then a school administrator. She joined several women's clubs affiliated with the General Federation of Women's Clubs including the Longmont Fortnightly Club and a Chautauqua Circle. In 1904, she wrote the Collect, a prayer for clubwomen, which English Farm Women's Institutes adopted as their official prayer. Stewart served as a dean of women at the University of Montana and then moved to Washington, D.C., where she became a charter member of the Women's Joint Congressional Committee. For eight years, she served as the legislative representative of the National Federation of Business and Professional Women's Clubs, which she helped organize in 1919. She worked at the Department of Labor, the Office of Indian Affairs, and the Department of Education.

560   *c SPRAGUE, JULIA. *History of the New England Woman's Club from 1868 to 1893*. Boston: Lee and Shepard, 1894. 99 pp.

Julia A. Sprague, club historian in Boston's New England Woman's Club, assembed sixty pages of history and a thirty-page appendix of documents to summarize the work of the first twenty-five years of the organization. She quotes from 1868 correspondence to outline the efforts of Caroline Severance, Julia Ward Howe, Ednah Dow Cheney, and Dr. Harriet K. Hunt to found one of the earliest literary clubs in America. The women rented rooms at Tremont Place and held their first public meeting there in November of 1868, attracting 118 women. Sprague outlines the work of the committees devoted to art and literature, education, and discussion. She surveys the projects members supported, sponsoring a table at a 1871 fair to raise money for the New England Hospital for Women and Children and funding scholarships for women at Boston University. She describes the Monday guest speakers, the teas, receptions, and picnics.

Her appendix lists the 1893 officers, all the Monday guest speakers and their topics, all members and any topics on which they spoke, a necrology with dates of deceased members, poems about the club, and memorials to deceased members.

561   *z SQUIRE, BELLE. *The Woman Movement in America: A Short Account of the Struggle for Equal Rights*. Chicago: A.C. McClurg and Co., 1911. 286 pp. Illus.: sketches of individuals.

    Squire stresses the contributions of individuals in American women's history, rather than of women's organizations, but she mentions the Philadelphia Female Anti-Slavery Society, American Equal Rights Society, National and American Woman Suffrage Associations, and credits the Women's Christian Temperance Union for its bold stance on a variety of issues, including suffrage. The General Federation of Women's Clubs, she observes, made public life attractive to women who had been afraid to fight for suffrage before they joined its affiliated clubs. The first six chapters of this volume were originally written for the *Chicago Sunday Tribune* as her introduction to the story of suffrage in Illinois. She begins with portraits of adventurous women in the colonial and revolutionary periods, moves to antebellum America, the post-Civil War suffrage struggle, and the militant faction in the National American Woman Suffrage Association.

562   *s STANTON, ELIZABETH, SUSAN B. ANTHONY, and MATILDA JOSLYN GAGE. *The History of Woman Suffrage*. Vol. 1, *1848-1861*, Rochester, N.Y.: N.p., 1881, 1887, 878 pp., appendixes for each chapter, illus.: 12 engravings of Frances Wright, Ernestine Rose, Frances Gage, Clarina Nichols, Pauline Wright Davis, Lucretia Mott, Antoinette Brown, Amelia Bloomer, Susan B. Anthony, Martha C. Wright, Elizabeth Cady Stanton, Matilda J. Gage. Vol. 2, *1861-1876*, New York: Fowler and Wells, 1882 (reprint, New York: Arno Press and the New York Times, Co., 1969), vii, 952 pp., appendix, illus.: Anna Dickinson, Clara Barton, Dr. Clemence Sophia Lozier, Olympia Brown, Jane G. Jones, Virginia L. Minor, Isabella Beecher Hooker, Belva A. Lockwood, Ellen Clark Sargent, Myra Bradwell, Julia Ward Howe, Mary A. Livermore. Vol.3, *1876-1885*, Rochester, N.Y.: N.p., 1886, xix, 1013 pp., notes, index, appendixes for each chapter, illus.: 22 engravings including Abigal Scott Duniway, Harriet H. Robinson, Clare Bewick Colby, M. Taylor.

    Volume 1 outlines the earliest struggles by American women for equality from colonial times to the Civil War. Using quotations liberally from speeches, correspondence, and conference resolutions, fifteen chapters discuss preceding causes for the women's rights struggle (from the sixteenth century on); women in journalism; the 1840 World's Anti-Slavery Convention; the Seneca Falls, New York, Women's Rights Convention of 1848; Mrs. Collins's, reminiscences; Ohio; Clarina Nichols's reminiscences; Massachusetts; Indiana and Wisconsin; Pennsylvania; Lucretia Mott; New Jersey; Mrs. Stanton's reminiscences; New York; Woman, Church, and State.

Volume 2, covering the years 1861-76, and written by participants in the movement, examines women's patriotism in the Civil War through their service on the Sanitary Commission, the work of the Women's National Loyal League, the national conventions of the National Woman Suffrage Association, the Kansas campaign of 1867, the Equal Rights Association, the New York State constitutional convention, and the debate over the Fourteenth Amendment. A brief chapter discusses the rival organization to the National Woman Suffrage Association, the Boston-based American Woman Suffrage Association. An appendix includes primary source documents, such as correspondence, reports, and lists of donors.

Volume 3 picks up the story from 1876 to 1885. It surveys the work of the Centennial Year of 1876; National conventions, hearings, and reports, 1877-79; congressional reports and conventions, 1880-81; congressional reports and conventions, 1882-83; Massachusetts efforts; Connecticut; Rhode Island; Maine; New Hampshire; Vermont; New York, 1860-85; Pennsylvania; New Jersey; Ohio; Michigan; Indiana; Illinois; Missouri; Iowa; Wisconsin; Minnesota; the Dakotas; Nebraska; Kansas; Colorado; Wyoming; California; and the Pacific Northwest. Chapter 50 contains miscellaneous materials on Louisiana, Texas, Arkansas, Mississippi, District of Columbia, Maryland, Florida, and Canada. Following that are chapters on the suffragists' work in Great Britain and Continental Europe, and finally, reminiscences by Elizabeth Cady Stanton.

See also Susan B. Anthony and Ida Husted Harper for volume 4, and Ida Husted Harper for volumes 5-6 of this account.

563 *t,s,c, STEFANCO, CAROLYN. "Networking on the Frontier: The Colorado Women's Suffrage Movement, 1876-1893." In *The Women's West*, edited by Susan Armitage and Elizabeth Jameson, 265-76. Norman: University of Oklahoma Press, 1987. Notes, illus.: Woman at Denver polling place.

Pointing to the difficulty of the suffrage struggle, which involved many groups of women for decades, Stefanco traces the Colorado fight from 1876 to 1893. She articulates the arguments used by woman suffrage advocates, including those of social justice, economic need, and genteel morality. Denver was the focal point for suffrage activity in Colorado and served as headquarters for the state battle. The first territorial suffrage society was founded there in January 1877 in order to lobby for woman suffrage at the February territorial constitutional convention. Women won suffrage in school elections only, but won the right to stage a referendum for a state suffrage amendment in October of 1877. At the polls, the women lost again. Stefanco features individual women who took the initiative in maintaining the suffrage struggle as well as women's organizations who supported suffrage, including the Women's Christian Temperance Union, literary clubs like the Denver Fortnightly Club and women in labor organizations and union politics.

564 *p STEINSON, BARBARA J. *American Women's Activism in World War I.* New York: Garland Publishing Co., 1982. ix, 440 pp. Notes, bib., index.

This is a strong and thorough work on women's relationship to war issues during World War I. Steinson divides her subject into eight chapters: "The Beginning of the Woman's Peace Party"; "Women's Mediation Efforts at Home and Abroad"; "the Woman's Peace Party, American Union against Militarism versus the Preparedness Movement;" "Relief for Europe and Defense for America;" "The Peace Movement Faces War;" "The Woman's Peace Movement during War"; "Woman's Relief, Preparedness and Suffragists Go to war"; "Female Activists in the Postwar Period." While the author scrutinizes the unpopular pacifists (especially the New York City and Massachusetts branches of the Woman's Peace party, and after the war, Women's International League for Peace and Freedom), she reveals that an unprecedented number of women became engaged in voluntary activities devoted to the war and relief during the years 1914-19. She examines the thirty-two women's groups that cooperated under the Woman's Committee of the Council of National Defense, including the General Federation of Women's Clubs, International Council of Women, National Woman's party, Woman's Liberty Loan Committee, Woman's Department of National Civic Federations, and Daughters of the American Revolution. Here is a sophisticated analysis of the tensions between pacifist women and war supporters, between male-dominated state councils for defense and their female counterparts.

565 *c STEPHENS, JANE. "May Wright Sewall: An Indiana Reformer." *Indiana Magazine of History* 78 (December 1982): 273-95. Notes, illus.: May Wright Sewall.

Although May Wright Sewall spent her early life in the Midwest as an educator, she took a step in 1888 at the age of forty-four that catapulted her to international importance in the world of women's organizations. She founded the National Council of Women and the International Council of Women, an alliance of women's groups to marshall unique strength for the issues of human rights, peace, and woman suffrage. By 1907, the International was the largest of all organizations of women in the world, uniting twenty sizable organizations representing 8 million women. Sewall was a suffrage activist at home in Indiana, although she supported the National Woman Suffrage Association while most of her state supported the American Woman Suffrage Association. She organized the Indianapolis Equal Suffrage Association in the 1870s and remained steady in the fight for women's rights. As chair of the Committee on Peace and Arbitration in her International Council of Women, she organized and chaired an International Conference of Women Workers to Promote Peace at the Panama-Pacific International Exposition in 1915 in San Francisco.

566   *c   STEPHENSON, WILLIAM. "How Sallie Southall Cotten Brought North Carolina to the Chicago World's Fair of 1893." *North Carolina Historical Review* 58 (Autumn 1981): 364-83. Notes, illus.: Florence Hill Kidder; General Federation of Women's Clubs; marble statue of Virginia Dare in North Carolina.

Sallie Southall Cotten (1846-1929) of North Carolina was active in the National Congress of Mothers and the General Federation of Women's Clubs. With Mary Roberts Price and Florence Hill Kidder, she was selected to organize participation by her state in the World's Columbia Exposition of 1893 in Chicago. Needing ten thousand dollars to erect a North Carolina building at the fair, she administered the raising of four thousand dollars by women of her state. The men, however, failed to raise their six thousand dollars. The women, then, did not see their dream realized in the form of a North Carolina building, but they did secure space for a North Carolina Women's Room at the international exposition.

567   *c   STEPHENSON, WILLIAM. *Sallie Southall Cotten, a Woman's Life in North Carolina.* Greenville, N.C.: Pamlico Press, 1987. ix, 197 pp. Notes, index. Illus: Sallie Southall Cotten.

Expanding on his article about the same subject, Stephenson relates the biography of Progressive-era leader Sallie Southall Cotten of North Carolina. Her family provided her with a solid education for her time. She taught briefly before she married at the age of nineteen and raised a family of nine children, six of whom lived to adulthood. She found time to write for *Demorest's Monthly* as well. Not until the governor appointed her to serve as a Lady Manager to the 1893 Chicago World's Fair did she embark on a public career, of almost four decades. She became an officer in the Greenville End of the Century Club, the North Carolina Federation of Women's Clubs, and the National Congress of Mothers. The author traces her involvement with educational reform, school-board suffrage for women, and World War I relief. The study is brief and uses an unconventional form for footnoting, but is a useful foundation for the study of volumtarism in one woman's life.

568   *b,r STERN, NORTON B. "Charitable Jewish Ladies of San Bernardino and Their Woman of Valor, Henrietta Ancker." *Western States Jewish Historical Quarterly* 13 (July 1981): 369-76. Notes, illus.: Henrietta Ancker; her husband.

    Henrietta Ancker organized twenty-five Jewish families in San Bernardino, California, in 1886 to form a Ladies' Hebrew Benevolent Society. The members carried on charitable activities, raising funds at social affairs to support several projects. They built a fence around a Jewish cemetery, contributed to a camp for tuberculosis sufferers, cared for Jewish transients and local families in need, and sent funds to the consumptive hospital, City of Hope. Ancker died in 1890, and on the first anniversary of her death, the membership renamed the club in her honor, calling themselves the Henrietta Hebrew Benevolent Society.

569   *s STEVENS, DORIS. *Jailed for Freedom*. New York: Boni and Liveright, 1920. Reprints. New York: Schocken, 1976. xxxii, 388 pp. Appendixes, illus.: 36, of National Woman's party members.

    Following an introduction by Janice Law Trecker, which sets the suffrage activity of the National Woman's party in the context of the general suffrage struggle, Doris Stevens shares her firsthand knowledge of the militant campaign for the Nineteenth Amendment. As a founder of the National Woman's party and impatient with the moderate tactics used by the rival National American Woman Suffrage Association, she narrates the story of the five hundred National Woman's party members who were arrested between June 1917 and spring 1919 while demonstrating for the vote. The bulk of her autobiography, twenty-seven chapters, describes the pickets at the White House, the arrests, hunger strikes in jail, and other strategies used by the militant membership to win public support for the suffrage amendment to the U.S. Constitution. Six appendixes offer supporting documents.

570 *t STEVENS, LILLIAN M.N. "The Work of the National Women's Christian Temperance Union." *Annals of the American Academy of Political and Social Science* 32 (November 1908): 508-12.

Here is a succinct overview of Women's Christian Temperance Union history. In 1873, in a Woman's Temperance Crusade, women banded together "for the abolition of the liquor traffic, the protection of the home, and the triumph of Christ's Golden Rule in custom and law." The WCTU formed in 1874, the lineal descendant of the 250-town Crusade and issued a declaration of principles calling for the Crusade and total abstinence from alcohol, prohibition, antisaloons, antidistilleries, and antibreweries. Ten thousand local unions formed in the late nineteenth century, and Stevens summarizes the projects undertaken and the conventions held. In 1883, a World's WCTU was organized, with fifty-two nations and half a million women. They petitioned, lobbied, and organized their children to eradicate the evils of alcohol.

571 *r STEVENS, THELMA. "A Place of Their Own." *Southern Exposure* 4, no. 3, (1976): 54-58. Illus.: 3 women at Jordan's Chapel.

The Methodist Mississippi-born author served as president of the Women's Division of Christian Service when it was established in 1939 upon the merger of the Methodist Episcopal Church, South, the Methodist Episcopal Church, North, and the Methodist Protestant Church. She remained active in it until she retired in the early 1970s. Her memoir excerpted here was created when Prof. Jacquelyn Hall of the Southern Oral History Program interviewed her. It relays more information than simply an analysis of her experiences. In 1941, the organization demanded that union labor prepare all its printed material and took a stance urging Social Security benefits for domestic workers. In 1939, the group called for women to secure full rights to become clergy, which they attained in 1956. Having created a Commission of Race Relations, at the instigation of Belle H. Bennett, in 1920, it became active in the 1930s in the Association of Southern Women for the Prevention of Lynching. In the 1940s, it provided demobilization workshops to transform defense industries, supported the Fellowship of the Concerned for justice in the courts and school desegregation, opposed McCarthyism in the 1950s and in 1951, collated an eight-hundred-page document collecting state laws on race and color.

572 *f STEVENSON, FRANCIS, BARBARA CARVILL, and MARY ANN DALTON SHEPARD, eds. *A History of Delta Gamma Since*

1873 Presented by the Anchora: Winter 1973. N.p.: the organization, 1973. 320 pp. Index, illus.: hundreds of founders and documents.

In order to celebrate the sorority's one hundredth anniversary, Delta Gamma members compiled an encyclopedia of detail about the its growth and development. Each convention is summarized, with names of officers elected and lists of resolutions passed. Each campus branch has provided a history, rich with photographs of members. Rituals and badges are cataloged.

573 *t STEVENSON, KATHERINE LENT. *A Brief History of the Women's Christian Temperance Union.* Evanston, Ill.: Union Signal, 1907. 117 pp. Bib., index.

Designed as a study guide for Women's Christian Temperance Union chapters, with discussion questions at the back for members to explore, this work excerpts convention resolutions to outline the history of the Woman's Crusade of 1873, the formation of the organization in 1874, the early development from 1875 to 79, the organization of state unions, the evolution of departments between 1874 and 1880 (such as evangelistic, juvenile, young women's branch, unfermented wine at sacrament, press, legislative, Sabbath schools, penal and reformatory, literature), evolution of departments between 1880 to 1883 (such as textbooks, drawing room meetings, work among blacks, foreigners, Indians, labor and railroad workers), evolution of the World's WCTU, formal organization of the World's WCTU and the "Polyglot Petition," seven conventions of the World's WCTU (in America: Boston, 1891; Chicago, 1893; Boston, 1906), departments of the work in the World's WCTU, and important events of the last decade.

574 *t -----. "Organization and Accomplishments of the Women's Christian Temperance Union in Massachusetts." *Annals of the American Academy of Political and Social Science* 32 (November 1908): 514-18.

Beginning with a portrait of the earliest supporters of the Women's Christian Temperance Union in 1874, including Susan S. Gifford, a Quaker from Worcester, and Mary A. Livermore, this article lauds ten thousand Massachusetts members for support for temperance issues. She lists officers, projects undertaken, including the Frances E. Willard Settlement House in Boston's West End, the 1906 hosting of the World's WCTU convention, and successful passage of laws raising the age of consent and teaching about the dangers of alcohol and other narcotics in the schools.

575 *s STEVENSON, LOUISE L. "Women Anti-Suffragists in the 1915 Massachusetts Campaign." *New England Quarterly* 52 (March 1979): 80-93.

In 1895, the Massachusetts Association Opposed to the Further Extension of the Suffrage to Women was founded to help defeat the state referendum on whether women should vote in municipal elections. In 1915, it mobilized against a proposed amendment to the state constitution to permit women to vote in all elections. The women cooperated with the Massachusetts Anti-Suffrage Committee, appointed George Conroy to handle their publicity, and hired a man to edit their newspaper, the *Remonstrance*. Determined not to act boldly, as they felt the suffragists did, the women conducted their campaign in a ladylike fashion, refusing to speak on the streets and establishing a homey headquarters. They argued that the sanctity of the home would be destroyed by the passage of woman suffrage.

576 *p STEWART, JANE A.   "National Patriotic Societies." *Chautauquan* 59 (June 1910): 142-146.

See *Chautauquan*.

577 *w -----. "National Woman's Trade Union League." *Chautauquan* 59 (June 1910): 116-20.

See *Chautauquan*.

578 no entry

579 *p STRAYER, MARTHA.   *The DAR: An Informal History.* Washington, D.C.: Public Affairs Press, 1958. vi, 262 pp. Index.

With a journalist's eye for controversy, Strayer exploits the conflict in the history of the Daughters of the American Revolution. She exposes the debate over the actual founder of the organization: Flora Darling and Mary Desha are the contenders. She illuminates the 1924 DAR attack on the "Communist Menace," resulting in the 1927 targeting of many leading clubwomen. She also relates the sensational story of the 1929 convention, at which Helen Bailie was denied a hearing regarding her expulsion by the president, Mrs. Alfred Brousseau, over Bailie's publicization of a secret black list of radical speakers unwelcome at meetings. The author reminds readers of the organization's refusal to permit black singer Marian Anderson to perform in their Washington, D.C., headquarters auditorium. Strayer also narrates more sober activities: historical projects to preserve cemeteries, graves, monuments, and buildings; sponsorship of schools for mountain children; Americanization classes to teach English to foreign-born women; prizes for patriotic school essays; the building of a grand headquarters in the state capitol; creating a "juniors" department in 1936 for women aged eighteen to thirty-five; establishing an organization for the Children of the American Revolution in 1895; and the collection of a massive library for genealogical research for the purpose of determining the eligibility of members. To belong, any woman (white only until recent years) of eighteen years or older must prove "descendance from a man or woman who with unfailing loyalty to the cause of American independence, served as a sailor, a soldier or a civil officer in one of the several colonies or States; or in the United Colonies or States, or as a recognized patriot."

580   *y STRICKLAND, CHARLES E. "Juliette Low, The Girl Scouts and the Role of American Women." *In Woman's Being, Woman's Place*, edited by Mary Kelley, 252-64. Boston: G.K. Hall and Co., 1979. Notes.

This historian points to military conflict abroad during World War I and agitation for sexual equality at home as providing the context within which the movement for female Scouting arose. Girl Scouts provided founder Juliette Low with a cause and an opportunity to resolve a crisis of personal identity. Her conservative stance on female roles did not prevent the organization from breaking conventions by encouraging sports, hiking, careers, and military marching drills.

581   *s STROM, SHARON H. "Leadership and Tactics in the American Woman Suffrage Movement: A New Perspective from Massachusetts." *Journal of American History* 62 (September 1975): 296-315. Notes.

Although Boston suffragists are generally characterized as conservative in comparison to the New Yorkers, Strom argues that Boston women, in the fight to win a woman suffrage amendment in Massachusetts in 1919, devised an equally rich source of tactics and workers for the final battle. She outlines the history of the suffrage struggle in Massachusetts from 1879 and identifies three groups as especially significant in the post-1900 era: the Massachusetts Woman Suffrage Association, the College Equal Suffrage League, and the smallest, the Boston Equal Suffrage Association for Good Government in which Pauline Agassiz Shaw, Mary Hutcheson Page, and Maud Wood Park were especially prominent. The groups worked with clubs like the Women's Trade Union League, and drew on the ideas of the English militant suffragists. In 1908, for example, a successful open-air meeting, endorsed by Henry Blackwell and his daughter Alice Stone

Blackwell, was held.   Boston warmly welcomed a visit from Mrs. Pankhurst as well.   On balance, the author asserts that the Massachusetts groups were extremely inventive in their efforts to win public support for woman suffrage.

582   *f STROUT, SHIRLEY KREASAN. *The History of Zeta Tau Alpha, 1898-1948.* Menasha, Wis.: the organization, 1956. xxi, 913 pp. Notes, bib., illus.: 232 of individual leaders or groups and interiors of facilities.

Here is a giant encyclopedia of five decades of sorority work, from 1898. Five young women in Virginia founded the organization in 1898, and the branches grew solely in the South for many years. Through a loving assemblage of documents, constitutions, speeches, correspondence, and even menus of food served at conventions and names of people who proposed the toasts, the author provides a careful history. Dividing the history into five eras, Strout explains the founding; the history of each convention starting with the first in 1903 at State Normal School in Farmville, Virginia; biographies of the founders; portraits of each chapter; and descriptions of projects, elections, scholarships, war relief, and philanthropy.

583   *m STUHLER, BARBARA. "Fanny Brin: Woman of Peace." In *Women of Minnesota: Selected Biographical Essays*, edited by Barbara Stuhler and Gretchen Kreuter, 284-330, 378-86. St. Paul: Minnesota Historical Society Press, 1977. Notes, illus.: 1 of Fanny Brin.

Fanny Brin was a Minneapolis activist within the National Council of Jewish Women for world peace and disarmament. She served as president of the Minneapolis NCJW in 1924 after directing the Minneapolis Woman's Committee for World Disarmament. She urged cooperation among peace organizations. She chaired the NCJW Committee on Peace and Arbitration and became the organization's ninth national president, 1932-38.   After 1935, she supported unrestricted immigration of Jews into Palestine. She supported relief and refugees throughout World War II and worked for peace in the 1950s. She died in 1961.

584   *m STUHLER, BARBARA, and GRETCHEN KREUTER, eds. *Women of Minnesota: Selected Biographical Essays*.   St. Paul: Minnesota Historical Society, 1977. 402 pp. Notes, index, illus.: 1 each of the 24 individuals examined.

Seventeen essays by different authors—scholars, writers, librarians, and activists—deal with women's clubs in some capacity, but club work is featured only in two essays: "Alice O'Brien: Volunteer and Philanthropist," by Eileen Manning Michels, and "Fanny Brin: Woman of Peace," by Barbara Stuhler.

See Eileen Manning Michels; Barbara Stuhler.

585　*y STURDEVANT, LYNDA M. "Girl Scouting in Stillwater, Oklahoma: A Case Study in Local History." *Chronicles of Oklahoma* 57 (1979): 34-48. Notes, illus.: 9 women in the 1938 Stillwater Girl Scout Council; Girl Scouts planting trees at the courthouse; flag ceremony during World War II at the high school; the 1954 cornerstone at Kinaani, a lodge at camp; the Oklahoma State University president buying a box of cookies.

In 1922, a short-lived troop of Girl Scouts was sponsored in Stillwater, Oklahoma, by the Business and Professional Women's Club. In 1927, the Girl Scouts was founded again, this time with greater success. Miss Flora May Ellis, director of health, physical education, and recreation for women at Oklahoma State University, initiated leadership training for the organization. Membership drives yielded young members; girls made cookies and sold calendars to secure camping facilities and equipment for their organization. At first, they used the high school for games, arts, crafts, archery, folk dance, drama, and nature lore. Later they rented Camp Redlands for overnight excursions. There, they practiced swimming, riding horseback, handicrafts, cooking, building fires, and outdoor survival. In the 1950s, they obtained their own camp for members, Camp Sylvia Stapley. In 1938, the organization built an office, using $500 donated from the Women's Club and $150 from the Business and Professional Women's Club. Unions provided free labor to erect the structure. During the 1940s, Girl Scouts served the community, making cookies for servicemen and selling tulips to raise money for the blood plasma fund. In the 1950s, international relief issues concerned members. Although the organization resisted a merger with other girls' organizations in the 1960s, it was forced to unite and hand over its facilities to the larger network.

586　no entry

587　*z SWENSON, MARY E. "To Uplift a State and Nation: The Formative Years of the Alabama League of Women Voters, 1920-1921." *Alabama Historical Quarterly* 37 (Summer 1975): 115-35. Notes.

The League of Women Voters was founded on the idea that women working in a nonpartisan organization could contribute to the success of a democracy by laying the foundations for a politically educated voting population. The first Alabama suffrage club was formed in Decatur in 1892. In 1902, a second formed in Huntsville, which joined the National American Woman Suffrage Association. In 1910, the Selma Suffrage Association formed, and the following year, the Equal Suffrage League of Birmingham. After women founded the League of Woman Voters in St. Louis in 1919, the Alabama branch quickly started to work for child welfare reform. As branches did throughout the nation, the Alabama League opposed the equal rights amendment as proposed by the National Woman's party. The organization had problems attracting rural members. Swenson exposes internal conflicts among the membership and disagreements with national headquarters.

588 *s TABER, RONALD W. "Sacajawea and the Suffragettes." *Pacific Northwest Quarterly* 58 (January 1967): 7-13. Notes, illus.: Eva Emery Dye.

Eva Emery Dye was an activist in the woman's movement at the turn of the century in Oregon. She supported the cause of woman suffrage, chairing the Oregon Equal Suffrage Association in Clackamas County, Oregon. In addition, she was an author and published in 1902 a historical novel, *The Conquest: The True Story of Lewis and Clark*, which identified the Native American woman and guide, Sacajawea, as a contributor to the success of the western exploration. Dye presided over a Sacajawea Statue Association, formed by the Portland Woman's Club, and raised seven thousand dollars between 1902 and 1905 to commission Alice Cooper of Denver to create a statue of Sacajawea. The piece was unveiled on 6 July 1905 at the Lewis and Clark Centennial Exposition in Portland, serving as a symbol for suffragists of women's vital importance to society.

589 *c TALBOT, MARION, and LOIS KIMBALL MATHEWS ROSENBERRY. *The History of the American Association of University Women, 1881-1931.* Boston: Houghton Mifflin, 1931. viii, 479 pp. Informational notes, index, appendixes, illus.: American Association of University Women headquarters in Washington, D.C.

Talbot commemorates a half century of women's organizational life devoted to the cause of women's education by detailing the history of the work and cooperation of the Association of Collegiate Alumnae, Western Association of Collegiate Alumnae, the Southern Association of College Women, the American Association of University Women, and the International Federation of University Women. The Association of Collegiate Alumnae, the forerunner of the other organizations, was founded in 1881 in Boston by Marion Talbot, the author of this volume. Printing many documents in full, Talbot documents her "Call" to educated women and the constitution they formed. She recounts details about the first years, including the earliest topics the women discussed at their meetings, the rise of branches, the amendments to the constitution, and reorganization in 1912. She provides a history of the Southern Association of College Women, founded in 1903 in Knoxville, and the merger of the two organizations in 1921. She traces the development of the Western Association of Collegiate Alumnae, formed in Chicago in 1883, through 1889. Enumerating the institutions and clubs that joined, Talbot provides short histories of the chapters in Washington, D.C., New York, Philadelphia, Boston, central New York, Minnesota, Chicago, Detroit, Indiana, and Cleveland. The first research project the organization undertook, in 1882, evaluated the health of and physical education offerings available to women students. The group also evaluated postgraduate study at home and abroad, child study and euthenics, college and university administrative policies that effected women students and women faculty, legislation on education, and new vocations for women. Talbot provides material on scholarships the group awarded, a 1919 headquarters built in Washington, D.C., at Lafayette Square, and World War I aid to the Red Cross, Liberty Loan drives, food conservation movement, YWCA, YMCA, and war savings stamp campaign. In the interests of a growing international relations concern, the organization assisted in founding an International Federation of University Women in 1918. AAUW branches formed in Manila, Honolulu, Tokyo, Peking, Paris, Tunisia, Shanghai, Puerto Rico, and Madrid. The relationships among organizations are documented. For example, the ACA declined to cooperate with the National Council of Women in 1890 and 1894, joined in 1915, and withdrew in 1929. The local branches worked with their local civic clubs, Parent-Teacher Associations, General Federation of Women's Clubs, and YWCAs on the arts and library issues. Details about publications and printed records, educational policies, sectional conferences and state divisions, and adult education, make this a valuable resource for researchers of educational club activity. Seven appendixes list past presidents, original members, the approved list of universities and colleges in 1930, a list of AAUW branches in 1930, a list of fellowships awarded between 1890 and 1931, officers for 1930-31, and the chairs of standing and special committees in 1930-31.

590　*r TATUM, NOREEN DUNN. *A Crown of Service: A Story of Woman's Work in the Methodist Episcopal Church, South, from 1878-*

1940. Nashville: Parthenon Press, 1960. 418 pp. Bib., index, illus.: founding officers; 4 of missionaries; group of first deaconesses, 1903; officers of the Woman's Board of Home Missions.

In 1939, when three branches of Methodism in the United States merged, a new Woman's Division of Christian Service, Board of Missions, formed. In order to preserve the story of its origins, the women in the Methodist Episcopal Church, South, sponsored a history of its long labors. In 1882, the women formed a Woman's Board of Home Missions and in 1890, the Woman's Board of Foreign Missions. The two boards united in 1910, and this account details their oaths, membership, literary and educational endeavors, and organizational methods. Considerable material, including generous quotation from original documents, enumerates their establishment of schools, colleges, Bible teacher training classes, kindergartens, hospitals, nurses' training, medical schools for women, and urban and rural evangelistic work by women missionaries in China, Korea, Japan, Brazil, Mexico, Cuba, Africa, Manchuria, Poland, and at home. Christian schools were sponsored in Kentucky, Florida, Georgia, Louisiana, Oklahoma, and Texas, and city missions were formed in Alabama, Florida, Georgia, Louisiana, Mississippi, Missouri, South Carolina, North Carolina, Oklahoma, Tennessee, Texas, and Virginia. Portraits of several institutions are provided. Additional programs, like cooperative homes for working girls, Scarritt College, and aid to Indian tribes on the western frontier are described. Between 1878 and 1940, the women's missionary societies raised and spent over $34 million.

591   *s TAYLOR, ANTOINETTE ELIZABETH. "The Origin of the Woman Suffrage Movement in Georgia." *Georgia Historical Quarterly* 28 (June 1944): 63-79. Notes.

Using lengthy excerpts from addresses by Georgia suffragists, Taylor documents the origins and development of the Georgia Woman Suffrage Association. It was founded in Columbus, Georgia, by Miss H. Augusta Howard and by 1894, had twenty members from five counties. It hosted the national conference of the National American Woman Suffrage Association in Atlanta in 1895; ninety-three delegates from twenty-eight states attended. The Georgia women sought to educate the public and to support woman suffrage by arguing that women suffered responsibilities of citizenship, through taxation, but did not enjoy its benefits, through enfranchisement. Members publicized the names of prominent Georgia men who supported woman suffrage in order to sway public opinion.

592 *s -----. "A Short History of the Woman Suffrage Movement in Tennessee." *Tennessee Historical Quarterly* 2 (September 1943): 195-215. Notes.

In 1889, Mrs. Lide A. Meriwether organized the first Tennessee woman suffrage society with forty-five members. By 1897, ten organizations had formed. As president of the Tennessee Woman's Christian Temperance Union, Meriwether had occasion to travel throughout her state, speaking about women's issues and encouraging new organizations to form. After the turn of the century, the nationally experienced "doldrums" slowed Tennessee suffrage agitation, leaving only one league in Memphis during the years 1906-10. However, in 1911, rapid progress resumed, with many clubs and larger memberships working for woman suffrage. Taylor provides the names of national speakers who came to speak in Tennessee. She describes three May Day demonstrations that took place in 1914-16. She catalogs the fairs, debates, entertainments, classes in parliamentary law, and literature printed to win support for their cause. The National American Woman Suffrage Association held its 1914 convention in Nashville. Two years later, the Congressional Union formed a chapter in Knoxville, although its national president, Alice Paul, was not largely supported by Tennessee suffragists who opposed her militant tactics. In 1916, a branch of the National Association Opposed to Woman Suffrage opened in Tennessee. Efforts to win legislators' support were successful, in that Tennessee legislators' positive vote enabled the federal suffrage amendment to be ratified.

593 *s -----. "South Carolina and the Enfranchisement of Women: The Later Years." *South Carolina Historical Magazine* 77 (1976): 115-26; 80 (1979): 298-310. Notes.

Although South Carolina women had created an Equal Rights Association in the 1890s, it was defunct by the time the woman suffrage struggle heated up again in 1912. However, the brand new Spartanburg society, the New Era Club, grew active in women's rights issues immediately. For example, the thirty members sponsored a special edition of the *Spartanburg Herald*, which included much material on the burgeoning women's movement. Basically, the club functioned as a study group until January 1914, when it transformed itself into the state's only suffrage club. With two newer women's clubs it created the South Carolina Equal Suffrage League, dropping prosuffrage pamphlets out of a plane in Aiken, sending speakers to public forums, and building a float for the state fair parade. While most of the members were loyal to the National American Woman Suffrage

Association, some organized the South Carolina division of the National Woman's party.

594 *s -----. "The Woman Suffrage Movement in Mississippi, 1890-1920." *Journal of Mississippi History* 30 (February 1968): 1-34. Notes.

    Until 1890, Mississippi had no woman suffrage movement. It was men who founded it in order to minimize the effect of black male voters. During an effort to rewrite the state constitution, a resolution was introduced to enfranchise all women whose husbands owned three hundred dollars worth of Mississippi real estate. These women were to authorize male electors to cast their ballots. No officeholding for women was suggested. The Committee on the Elective Franchise failed to recommend this resolution, "unwilling to send her adrift on the uncertain sea of modern politics" and "drag her from the shrine on which she sits enthroned in the heart of every pure Southern man." Soon, however, suffragists from other parts of the country lectured in Mississippi in the hopes of generating women's support for a suffrage movement. The National American Woman Suffrage Association sent a speaker in 1893, and the Massachusetts Women's Christian Temperance Union, in 1895. In 1897, on the heels of a WCTU conference, a state suffrage association formed. Gradually clubs, members, and conference delegates grew in number, publishing pamphlets on "The Legal Status of Women under the Laws of Mississippi" and "Woman's Place under the Gospel." The group fell apart at the turn of the century, holding no meetings in 1901 or 1902, but it revived in 1903 and enjoyed a revitalization with Belle Kearney's founding in 1906 of the Southern Woman Suffrage Conference. Kearney toured and lectured, organizing clubs as she traveled. The new clubs distributed woman suffrage literature, opened a booth at the state fair, gave speeches, approached the state legislators in 1914 and were rebuffed, and participated in the state fair parade. In 1915, when Anna Howard Shaw came to Mississippi, five hundred listeners attended her speech. In 1917, however, the National Woman's party found insufficient support to found a Mississippi branch. In 1919, the suffrage supporters allied with the Mississippi State Federation of Women's Clubs, and when the federal amendment was passed in 1920, the suffrage association formed a League of Women Voters.

595 *s -----. *The Woman Suffrage Movement in Tennessee.* New York: Bookman Associates, 1957. 150 pp. Notes, bib., index.

Taylor surveys the history of the woman suffrage movement in Tennessee, tracing its origins to the Woman's Christian Temperance Union convention of 1887 in Nashville, where cautious support was first offered. In 1889, the first woman suffrage league in Tennessee was founded in Memphis and gradually other leagues formed, uniting into a statewide organization. Dormancy stalled the movement at the turn of the century, but the 1906 formation of the Southern Woman Suffrage Conference, led by Laura Clay of Kentucky, generated new enthusiasm. Taylor summarizes newspaper accounts of the annual conventions held, listing the names of towns and colleges with clubs that sent delegates and enumerating strategies to court public opinion. Club members set up booths at local fairs, held a parade in 1916, gave speeches, planted newspaper articles, sponsored social activities, and engaged in patriotic relief work during World War I. Suffragists were not immune to conflict in this era. The Tennessee Equal Suffrage Association, founded in 1906, split into two groups in 1914, the Tennessee Equal Suffrage Association and the Tennessee Equal Suffrage Association, Inc. Both affiliated with the National American Woman Suffrage Association. In 1918, they united again to form the Tennessee Woman Suffrage Association. A Tennessee chapter of the Congressional Union for Woman Suffrage also formed, itself facing internal conflict over strategy. Antisuffragists united in 1912, forming a chapter of the National Association Opposed to Woman Suffrage in Tennessee, when the national president, Mrs. Arthur M. Dodge, came to speak in 1916. While their campaign was low key, the Tennessee suffragists spent a great deal of time refuting their arguments that suffrage would unsex women, that political participation was contrary to nature. Suffragists had first introduced a bill to the Tennessee Senate in 1883, but their first real gain occurred in 1917 when women were granted enfranchisement in municipal elections in Lookout Mountain. In order to win ratification of the federal amendment, Carrie Chapman Catt and other nationally known suffragists came to Tennessee to lobby. Opponents also surfaced, including representatives of the Tennessee division of the Southern Woman's League for the Rejection of the Susan B. Anthony Amendment. Nevertheless, Tennessee ratification of the amendment added woman suffrage to the U.S. Constitution.

596 *s -----. "The Woman Suffrage Movement in Texas." *Journal of Southern History* 17 (May 1951): 194-215. Notes.

As she has for other southern states, Taylor surveys the history of woman suffrage in Texas, drawing on newspaper accounts to document organizational progress. Woman suffrage was proposed as early as 1868 in anticipation of a constitutional convention, but when it was held the following year, the idea was rejected. In 1875, when another constitutional convention was held, woman suffrage was ignored altogether. In 1887, the WCTU endorsed it, however, and by 1893 a Texas Equal Rights Association formed and allied with the National American Woman Suffrage Association. In addition to listing speakers, topics, and convention resolutions, Taylor reviews two newspapers to evaluate coverage of the issue, the *Dallas Morning News* and the *San Antonio Express*. The Texas Association split in 1894, dividing over issues of strategy. In 1913, a Texas Woman Suffrage Association formed and performed relief work in wartime, bent on demonstrating women's competence in public life. In 1916, the National Woman's party founded a Texas branch with one hundred members. The previous year, a branch of the National Association Opposed to Woman Suffrage had formed. Not until 1915 did the Texas legislature first discuss woman suffrage. When Governor Ferguson was impeached in 1917, the suffragists were delighted, for he had been an important opponent of their cause. Lieutenant Governor Hobby, in 1918, essentially enfranchised women by granting them participation in the primary election. In a one-party state, this gave women new clout. Texas became the first southern state to ratify the federal suffrage amendment.

597   *c TAYLOR, DAVID. "Ladies of the Club: An Arkansas Story." *Wilson Library Bulletin* 59 (January 1985): 324-27. Illus.: 4 of facilities established by the club.

This article demonstrates the importance of women's literary clubs to the establishment of public libraries in Arkansas. In Helena, women formed the Pacaha Club in 1888. They began to work to establish a permanent library in their town, forty members forming a Woman's Library Association. The women collected books and secured a room in the Grand Opera House. In 1891, they had secured support for a town library and paid off the mortgage by renting its rooms to civic groups for meetings. In 1929, they added a museum wing to the structure. Other branches formed—in Marvell, when the Mothers' Club ran a library from 1924 to 1950; in West Helena, when Mrs. E.G. Nelson donated a facility; and in Elaine, when clubwomen established a board in 1974 and renovated a café to create a public library.

598   *c TAYLOR, MARY D. "A Farmers' Wives' Society in Pioneer Days." *Annals of Iowa* 13 (July 1921): 22-31.

In 1872, the first woman's club in Harrison County, Iowa, was formed "by a group of New England women who were denied the privileges enjoyed by town ladies, yet possessed all their social qualities, talents, and culture." Desiring relief from routine and monotony, they met once every two weeks for social intercourse. "Every lady," said the constitution, "shall bring from her store of eatables whatever she may think most convenient; the lady of the house where said society meets providing the tea, butter, biscuits, and condiments." The women agreed to "wear a plain home dress" and pay a fine for "speaking disparagingly for another." Even storms did not keep members away from the meetings, which provided friendly sociability and information exchange on home duties. The women sent quilts to a Christian Home in Council Bluffs and held an annual picnic for all their family members. With engaging prose, Taylor draws on twenty-five years of minutes of meetings to describe the association's work and play. A list of all 129 members of the club is included.

599   *r TELLEEN, JANE. "Yours in the Master's Service: Emmy Evald and the Woman's Missionary Society of the Augustana Lutheran Church, 1892-1942." *Swedish Pioneer Historical Quarterly* 30 (July 1979): 183-95. Illus.: Emmy Carlsson Evald, founder and president of Woman's Missionary Society; 1908 Woman's Missionary Conference in Chicago; group by the Emmy Evald Training School for Girls in Husuchang, Honan Province, in China.

In 1892, Emmy Carlsson Evald, daughter and wife of Swedish-American ministers in the Augustana Lutheran Church, attended a conference of the synod. There she founded and became president of its Woman's Missionary Society, designed to raise money for missions abroad. The association grew in membership and the treasury expanded as well, enabling the women to support medical care and educational programs at home and abroad. In 1903, they paid the salaries of women missionary doctors, sent women to medical school, published a magazine, supported a hospital for women and children in India, and made up the deficit in the men's mission society. The society grew large and efficient, with an executive board and fifteen regional conferences, a myriad of committees and national publications. In 1907, the women won church permission to control their own efforts entirely after raising twelve thousand dollars for a hospital in Rajahmundry, India. The women controlled their association, including the finances, which amounted to hundreds of thousands of dollars each year which they invested in securities and property. The society's strength diminished in 1921, when a the $121,000 women's dorm was proposed for Augustana College in Rock Island, Illinois. The women were denied the right to decide on the site, layout, and cost despite their impressive fund-raising efforts. When the structure was dedicated in 1927, one the members deemed unsuitable, no official of the Woman's Missionary Society attended. In 1935, Evald stepped down from the presidency and women's autonomy shrank still further. Evald was a suffragist, who attended the 1898 National American Woman Suffrage Association conference in Washington, D.C., but Telleen suggests Evald kept her political interests separate from her religious work.

600   *m   TENNESSEE STATE FEDERATION OF WOMEN'S CLUBS. *Woman's Work in Tennessee*. Memphis: Jones-Briggs Co., 1916. 317 pp. Index, illus.: officers of the Tennessee Federation of Women's Clubs; leaders.

Several clubwomen cooperated to survey the history of the accomplishments of organized women in Tennessee. Essays include "Twenty Years of the Tennessee Federation of Women's Clubs," by Mrs. William Stewart Harkness; "History of Mountain Settlement Work of the Tennessee Federation of Women's Clubs," by Mrs. Charles A. Perkins; others describing department work of the Federation of Legislation, civil service reform, industrial conditions, the Home for Incurables, public health, home economics, civics, public schools, traveling libraries, and literature; "Tennessee Branch of the International Order of the King's Daughters and Sons," by Elizabeth M. Norvell; "The Tennessee Music Clubs and Musicians," by Mrs. Henry Lupton; "Aims of the Art Department," by Miss L. Pearl Saunders; "Conservation Department," by Lalla Block Armstein; "Prison Reform"; "Juvenile Courts"; "Tennessee's Congress of Mothers"; "Visiting Nurses Association"; "Playground Association"; "Ladies Hermitage Association" to restore and preserve the home of Gen. Andrew Jackson; "The Daughters of the American Revolution"; "United Daughters of the Confederacy"; "Girls Friendly Society"; "Nineteenth Century Club of Memphis, Nashville Section"; "Council of Jewish Women"; "Women's Christian Temperance Union"; and "Chattanooga Woman's Club." Memorial biographies of twelve active clubwomen round out the volume.

601   *n,s   TERBOR-PENN, ROSALYN. "Nineteenth Century Black Women and Woman Suffrage." *Potomac Review* 7 (Spring-Summer 1977): 13-24. Notes.

Terbor-Penn examines the commitment of black women to woman's suffrage organizations in the nineteenth century, determining a steady level of participation and a rationale for involvement that included expectations that suffrage would be a partial solution to the racial problems in America. The author describes the work of

Sojourner Truth in the early suffrage campaign and the efforts of Harriet Forten Purvis and her sister, Margaritta Forten, who were pioneers in the Philadelphia Female Anti-Slavery Society, which laid the groundwork for the Philadelphia National Woman's Rights Convention in 1854. Black women were involved in the American Equal Rights Association, which formed in 1866 in New York City. Harriet Purvis and Frances Harper served as officers and board members. When the women's suffrage movement split, divided over the granting of black male suffrage in the Constitution, these black women joined the American Woman Suffrage Association: Frances Harper, Caroline Remond Putman, Josephine St. Pierre Ruffin, and Lottie Rollin. Mary Ann Shadd Cary joined the National Woman Suffrage Association, and in 1880, she organized the Colored Women's Progressive Franchise Association in Washington, D.C. Harriet Purvis was active in the Pennsylvania Woman's Suffrage Association and from 1883 to 1900, the National Woman Suffrage Association and then the National American Woman Suffrage Association. Frances Harper in 1887 became superintendent of Work Among Colored People at the Women's Christian Temperance Union. Ruffin served on the Board of Officers in the Massachusetts Woman Suffrage Association. In 1895, in Boston, Ruffin and Harper organized the National Federation of Afro-American Women. In the following year, it merged with the National Colored Women's Association to create the National Association of Colored Women, with Mary Church Terrell presiding. The author also catalogs the work of the Tuskegee Woman's Club of Alabama, St. Louis Suffrage Club of Missouri, Woman's Era Club of Boston, Colored Woman's Suffrage Club of Los Angeles, and Women's Loyal Union of Charleston, Philadelphia, Memphis, and Brooklyn.

602 *n TERRELL, MARY CHURCH. *A Colored Woman in a White World*. Washington, D.C.: Ransdell, 1940. Reprint. New York: Arno Press, 1980. viii, 437 pp. Index, illus.: Mary Church Terrell.

Mary Church Terrell's memoirs provide a veritable index to women's organizations at the turn of the century. The associations she discusses include the National American Woman Suffrage Association, War Relief in World War I, Woman's Peace party, Colored Woman's League, Boston's Federation of Afro-American Women, the National Association of Colored Women over which she presided, Baptist Woman's Home Missionary Society, Calhoun Club in Boston, College Alumnae Club, Delta Sigma Theta sorority, Eastern Division of Colored Women in the Harding-Coolidge political campaign, National Council of Women, International Congress of Women, Women's International League for Peace and Freedom, National Society for

Women's Service, Musical Union at Oberlin College, Mu-So-Lit Club in Washington, D.C., Ohio State Federation of Colored Women's Clubs, Women's Republican League in Washington, D.C., Woman's Club in Washington, D.C., Woman's Club in Fall River, Massachusetts, Woman's Congress of Missions in San Francisco, and Women's Henry George League in New York City.

603 *s THATCHER, LINDA. " 'I Care Nothing for Politics': Ruth May Fox, Forgotten Suffragist." *Utah Historical Society* 49 (Summer 1981): 239-53. Illus.: Ruth May Fox.

Ruth May Fox was born in England, but her parents became Mormons when she was five months old and they moved to the United States while she was a young girl. She grew up in Philadelphia and Utah, married at the age of 19, raised twelve children, and lived to be 104. This biography discusses her participation in several Utah clubs, including the Utah Woman's Press Club, Utah Woman Suffrage Association, Reaper's Club for writers, Salt Lake County Republican Committee, Deseret Agricultural and Manufacturing Society, Travelers' Aid Society, and Young Ladies' Mutual Improvement Association. The excerpts from her diary include attention to women's clubs during the year 1894-95.

604 *p THOMPSON, MRS. ALBERT LEE, et al. *The History of the United Daughters of the Confederacy*. Vol. 2, *1930-1955*. Raleigh, N.C.: Edwards and Broughton Co., 1956. 391 pp. Notes, index, illus.: 20 of officers.

A sequel to Ruth Jennings Lawton's history of the UDC, this volume covers the years 1930-55. It briefly surveys the territory from 1894 to 1929, but it also features the accomplishments of more recent decades. A long list appears of scholarship winners from 1930 to 1956. A compilation of memorials and markers to Jefferson Davis, Robert E. Lee, and other generals of the Confederacy is provided, including a memorial to three thousand soldiers who died at the Confederate prison in Elmira, New York. One chapter details the insignia and ribbons of the organization. The patriotic service offered during World War II, such as nursing through the Red Cross, is documented. Thompson discusses the Daughters' contributions to the Confederate Museum in Virginia, the publications of the organization, and their gifts of southern literature for home and foreign libraries. Committee reports are provided and figures on the growth of membership in Children of the Confederacy.

See Ruth Jennings Lawton for volume 1 of this work.

605 *n THOMPSON, CAROL L. "Women in the Antislavery Movement." *Current History* 70 (May 1976): 198-201.

In 1832, Boston women founded the Female Anti-Slavery Society under the leadership of Maria Weston Chapman. The following year, when four women who attended the Philadelphia meeting of the American Anti-Slavery Society were not seated, they adjourned to found the Philadelphia Female Anti-Slavery Society. In May 1863, the National Woman's Loyal League was founded by Elizabeth Cady Stanton, Susan B. Anthony, and Lucy Stone to free the slaves in the Union who were not emancipated by President Lincoln's Emancipation Proclamation. The author also examines the efforts of individual women in the anti-slavery movement, including the speeches of Sarah and Angelina Grimké and the daring of women in the underground railroad.

606 *f THOMSON, RUTH SANDERS. *History of the Alpha Phi Fraternity from the Founding in 1872 through the Year 1902.* Vol. 1. Norwood, Mass.: Alpha Phi International Fraternity, 1943. xii, 334 pp. Bib., index, illus.: 70 of officers; interior and exterior of houses.

This thirty-year history of a sorority is divided into three parts. The first decade, 1872-82, begins with a history of higher education for women. Thomson describes the ten women who founded Alpha Phi at Syracuse University in 1872, including Clara Bradley, who later became an influential clubwoman in the General Federation of Women's Clubs. Sections two and three document the spread of chapters and the activities initiated at the general conventions. Details on the treasury and the leadership provide a solid overview of the work of the organization.

607 *c THORPE, ELIZABETH J. "The Owls of Newcastle." *Montana: Magazine of Western History* 19 (April 1969): 71-73. Illus.: 1 group photo.

In June 1894, fifteen women in Newcastle, Wyoming, met in Ellen Horton's kitchen to form "The Owls," an organization devoted to the study of culture. The members pursued the BayView Course and the Delphian Course for literary study. In 1909, they became the first Wyoming women's club to federate with the General Federation of Women's Clubs. At that time, they changed their name to the Twentieth Century Club.

608 *w THROCKMORTON, H. BRUCE. "The First Woman's Bank in Tennessee, 1919-1926." *Tennessee Historical Quarterly* 35 (Winter 1976): 389-92.

The history of the first bank in the United States organized and operated by women articulates the importance of clubwomen in initiating new institutions. The Clarksville, Tennessee, First Woman's Bank, founded in October 1919, was incorporated by Mrs. F.J. Runyan, president of the Federated Clubs and chair of the Red Cross of Clarksville and Montgomery County, and by Mrs. W. Bailey Winn, former president of the United Daughters of the Confederacy of Kentucky. The bank closed in June 1926.

609 *f TOOMEY, MRS. JOSEPH M. *History of the Department of Georgia/The American Legion Auxiliary.* Macon, Ga.: J.W. Burke Co., 1936. Illus.: officers alone and in groups.

Toomey traces the history of fourteen administrations, from 1921 to 1935, in Georgia's American Legion Auxiliary. She reprints the constitution and bylaws, which reserve membership to mothers, wives, daughters, and sisters of members of the American Legion and of men and women in the military or naval service of the United States between 6 April 1917 and 11 November 1918 and died in line of duty or after honorable discharge. In 1920, 1,342 local units had formed in forty-five states, uniting eleven thousand dues-paying members. Their object, like that of the American Legion itself, was a patriotic one, to preserve memories of the Great War. The Georgia Department story is generous with details and names of officers and members. Conferences are summarized and descriptions are provided of parades in which members participated, Christmas dinners to which disabled men were invited, and resolutions passed by the membership. The study is disappointing in terms of its analysis of issues addressed.

610 *r TORBET, ROBERT G. *Venture of Faith: Story of the American Baptist Foreign Mission Society and Woman's American Baptist Foreign Mission Society 1814-1954.* Philadelphia: Judson Press, 1955. 634 pp. Notes, bib., index.

Chapters 11 and 25 detail the contribution church women made to the growth and development of programs for missions abroad. While there is some attention to the officers, guilds, and members raising money at home, there is also material on the foreign schools and hospitals for women established by the support in the United States.

611 *p TOWNER, MRS. HORACE M. "The Mt. Vernon Ladies Association of the Union." *Annals of Iowa* 12 (July 1920): 359-65.

The author, vice-regent for the Iowa branch of the Mt. Vernon Ladies Association of the Union, emphasizes the honor and responsibility of restoring, preserving, and caring for the home and tomb of George Washington. The two-hundred-acre property in Virginia was purchased for $200,000 in 1856 by women representatives from twenty-two states, at which time the government declined to buy it from a descendant. Although vice-regents had been appointed in Iowa during the early 1870s, no subsequent representatives had organized support in Iowa until the author was appointed in 1913.

612 *w TRACY, LENA HARVEY. *How My Heart Sang: The Story of Pioneer Industrial Welfare Work.* New York: Richard P. Smith, 1950. 192 pp. Illus.: 22 including 2 of Lena Harvey Tracy on her 80th birthday; at age 10; Mrs. Charles Henrotin addressing Century Club; boys' and girls' club members; House of Usefulness, clubhouse.

This memoir traces the life and work of the first welfare director of the National Cash Register Company in Dayton, Ohio, during the years 1897-1901. Although details of her early life in Pennsylvania and Ohio are rich, it is her efforts in forming boys' and girls' clubs that will interest researchers of women's organizations. She spoke at the third National Working Girls' Convention in Philadelphia in April 1897, describing her work establishing clubs for young people in Dayton. She also inspired the founding of the South Park Improvement Association, the Century Club, for neighborhood women, which federated with the General Federation of Women's Clubs, and the Young People's Club. Her employment ended when the company's employees went on strike in 1901.

613 *s TRECKER, JANICE LAW. "The Suffrage Prisoners." *American Scholar* 41 (Summer 1972): 409-23.

Members of the National Woman's party were arrested for obstructing traffic in 1917, as they picketed the White House in support of a woman suffrage amendment. The group, under the leadership of Alice Paul, was borrowing the techniques of British militants. The author catalogs the prison's poor treatment of the activists, discussing their food, living conditions, attacks by the guards, lack of medical care, and forced baths in tubs with syphilitics.

614 *b TREUDLEY, MARY BOSWORTH. " 'Benevolent Fair': A Study of Charitable Organizations among American Women in the First Third of the Nineteenth Century." *Social Service Review* 14 (September 1940): 509-22. Notes.

As early as the late eighteenth century, women founded charities to assist the poor. Taking her examples from Philadelphia, New York, Boston, and Newark charitable societies, the author examines the early nineteenth-century growth of the phenomenon by documenting the volunteers' facilitation of work relief in the needle trades and laundries.

615   *n   TRIGG, EULA S.   "Washington, D.C., Chapter LINKS, Incorporated: Friendship and Service." *Negro History Bulletin* 39 (May 1976): 584-89. Illus.: 6 of members; 7 of documents of the organization.

In 1946 in Philadelphia, Links, Incorporated, was created for social, charitable and intercultural activities by two black women, Margaret Hawkins and Sarah Scott. By 1951, it had grown enormously, with 144 chapters in thirty-three states and the District of Columbia. Thirty-five hundred women looked to headquarters in Trenton, New Jersey, which directed large contributions to the National Association for the Advancement of Colored People, the Urban League, and the United Negro College Fund. In addition, the women took on programs for youth, the arts, and international relations, providing live theater for children, awards for high school essays on Afro-American life and history, a loan fund at Howard University, and a tour of Black Heritage for the Bicentennial in 1976. Biographies of current chapter members in the fields of journalism, dentistry, community endeavor, education and administration, government and politics, medicine and social services, and religion and human rights are included.

616   *s   TROUT, GRACE WILBUR. "Side Lights on Illinois Suffrage History." *Illinois Historical Society Journal* 13 (July 1920): 145-79.

This chatty memoir describes Trout's activity in the last decade of the Illinois woman suffrage struggle. From 1910 to 1912, she served as president of the Chicago Political Equality League, increasing its membership from 143 to 390. Her administration undertook flamboyant techniques to shape public opinion on suffrage, including the creation of a suffrage float for Chicago's Fourth of July parade and an auto tour of the state to raise money and publicize the issue. She remembers lobbying efforts and thanks, by name, the newspapermen of Chicago who assisted the suffragists. As president of the Illinois Equal Suffrage Association from 1912 to 1919, she encountered many hard-working women and supportive legislators, whom she lists in her article. Her account of the 1919 celebration of the passage of the federal amendment is joyful.

617   *c   TRYON, RUTH W. *The AAUW 1881-1949.* Washington, D.C.: the organization, 1950. 53 pp.

In a small space, Tryon manages to outline a surprising number of projects initiated by the American Association of University Women, from its founding in Boston 1881 as the Association of Collegiate Alumnae, to its merger in 1921 with the Southern Association of College Women to the post-World War II era. By 1931, the AAUW consisted of 521 branches with 36,800 members. By 1948, it had grown to 1,097 branches with 108,000 members. In 1949, it abandoned its policy of racial discrimination. In the nineteenth century, the association undertook research projects pertinent to college women. It began a program of fellowships in 1890. Civic reform attracted the attention of the organization's members. In the 1920s, childhood education, international relations, and the economic and legal status of women became priorities. In 1924, a Committee on Fine Arts was established, supporting local artists and children's art, theater, crafts, and writing. Legislative efforts were launched on behalf of the Children's Bureau, abolition of child labor, a federal Department of Education, civil service, League of Nations, Woman's Bureau, and world disarmament. In 1925, they opened study of the equal rights amendment, but they opposed it formally in 1939 for jeopardizing desirable protective legislation. During World War I, members engaged in war relief projects. After the war, they helped university women who were refugees, supported the United Nations, provided reconstruction aid for women who had suffered from the war, and resumed their older interests in education, arts, international relations, and the status of women.

618 *c TUBBS, STEPHANIE AMBROSE. "Montana Women's Clubs at the Turn of the Century." *Montana: The Magazine of Western History* (Winter 1986): 26-30. Notes, illus.: 1917 group at the Montana Women's Christian Temperance Union convention; 1932 group of the Current Topics Club of Helena; group from a turn-of-the-century literary club in Anaconda.

When early settlers to Montana might have suffered isolation, women's clubs provided cultural and intellectual self-expression and enabled civic reform activity to flourish. The first club in Montana formed in 1889, the Deer Lodge Women's Club. Those that followed included Bozeman's State Housekeepers Society (1894), As You Like It Club in Missoula (1891), Current Topics Club in Helena (1892), the Helena Improvement Society (1898), and relief societies and several branches of the Women's Christian Temperance Union. Tubbs surveys the work of many clubs, some of which joined the General Federation of Women's Clubs. Sanitation, education, and child welfare were among the causes for which the women cooperated.

619 *t TYLER, HELEN E. *Where Prayer and Purpose Meet: WCTU Story, 1873-1949.* Evanston, Ill.: Signal Press, 1949. x, 311 pp. Notes, index, illus.: 97, including statue of Frances Willard in U.S. Capitol Building; Rest Cottage, Frances Willard's home in Evanston; officers in states and around the world; Little Cold Water Girl Fountain at 1893 Chicago Exposition; interior and exterior of National Women's Christian Temperance Union Administration Building in Evanston, Illinois.

  As a former editor of the Women's Christian Temperance Union publication, the *Union Signal*, Tyler is in a unique position to provide a comprehensive picture of the work of the organization. Hers is a laudatory account, praising "the broad vision, farsightedness and single purposefulness" of the temperance campaign. She includes official documents like the Declaration of Principles and the Pledge. She quotes generously from resolutions passed at the early conferences regarding the establishment of juvenile temperance organizations, the support of coffee rooms over saloons, and the building of drinking fountains. Much attention is given to the long presidency of Frances Willard, from 1879 to 1898; her "Home Protection" and "Do Everything" policy is examined for its support for woman suffrage, labor, free silver, Mother's Day, peace, and many other issues. The first World WCTU Convention in Boston in 1891 is described, as is the WCTU exhibit at the Columbia Exposition in 1893. Tyler includes details about war relief work in both World War I and World War II, the members' fight against repeal of Prohibition, and its jubilee celebration in 1923.

620 *t TYRRELL, IAN R. "Women and Temperance in Antebellum America, 1830-1860." *Civil War History* 28 (June 1982): 128-52.

  With extensive examples and rich footnoting, Tyrrell argues that large numbers of women exerted their influence against alcohol by forming such women's temperance organizations as the Martha Washington Societies, Daughters of Temperance, and Lady Franklin Society. Their work politicized them for women's rights activism, but they reinforced sexual stereotypes limiting women's place in society by basing their arguments on the era's widelyheld respect for women's moral superiority.

621 *m UNDERWOOD, JUNE O. "Civilizing Kansas: Women's Organizations, 1880-1920." *Kansas History* 7 (Winter 1984-85): 291-306. Illus.: members of Woman's Hesperian Library Club at their library, 1884; delegates to Woman's Relief Corps conference in 1895; members of Ladies' Aid Society of Elmdale; Meade Methodist

Ladies' Aid in 1912, selling hay to raise money for their church; woman suffragists with Governor Arthur Copper in 1916; Lucy Browne Johnson, clubwoman.

Underwood argues that frontier women brought to the West the same nurturing responsibilities that eastern women cultivated, reforming their world through a wide variety of charitable and civic clubs. She discusses the Woman's Relief Corps, American Association of University Women, National Association of Colored Women, Parent-Teachers Association, Altrusa, Daughters of the American Revolution, League of Women Voters, National Federation of Business and Professional Women's club, Grange, P.E.O, Women's Christian Temperance Union, and Kansas Federation of Women's Clubs. Members' "Municipal Housekeeping" efforts created libraries, educational institutions, legislation, and vital support for numerous progressive reform issues.

622 *r,b VAIL, ALBERT L. *Mary Webb and the Mother Society*. Philadelphia: American Baptist Publication Society, 1914. 110 pp.

"To rescue from oblivion a woman of rare character and great practical benevolence . . . of humble means and a helpless cripple," Albert Vail records the philanthropic work of Mary Webb. In 1800, when Congregationalist and Baptist women in Boston formed the first woman's missionary society, the Massachusetts Baptist Missionary Society, Mary Webb addressed the members of the new organization. She had been born in 1779, disabled by sickness, and unable to walk for the rest of her seventy-seven years, but she pressed for the formation of a number of women's benevolent organizations: the Female Cent Society in Boston (1804), Children's Cent Society (1810), Sunday School (1816), Corban Society (1811) to aid candidates for gospel ministry, Penitent Females' Refuge (1818), Fragment Society (1812) to clothe the destitute, Fatherless and Widows Society, Children's Friend Society (1833) to care for babies of working women, Missions to the Jews, and the Boston Female Society for Missionary Purposes. For the latter, Webb probably co-authored the constitution in 1800 with Thomas Baldwin, pastor. The account quotes from Mary Webb's public addresses and her correspondence with other American female mission and mite society workers. When Baptists and Congregationalists split in 1829, Webb worked with the Baptists. The study, then, does not describe the work of Congregationalist women but confines itself to the Baptists' projects to preach among Negroes, and at Females' Refuge, Marine Hospital of Seamen, and the House of Corrections.

623   *t   VAN METER, HARRIET F. *First Quarter Century of the Women's Christian Temperance Union.*   Salem, N.J.: the organization, 1909. 129 pp.

     Succinctly, the author surveys the work of the Salem, New Jersey, Women's Christian Temperance Union, from its origins in the 1884 ladies' prayer circle at the Broadway Methodist Episcopal Church. Six years later, the women formed a branch of the WCTU, electing officers, charging dues, holding meetings, and initiating projects. Their pledge is included plus descriptions of their celebrations of national president Frances Willard's birthday, lists of songs, guests, and members, and accounts of reports, papers delivered, and projects. The latter include the dedication of a water fountain, a rummage sale, and committee work on the flower mission, scientific temperance instruction, prisons, social meetings, literature at the railroad station and workplaces, Sabbath observance, Sunday schools, relation of intemperance to capital and labor, state and county fairs, outreach to the German population, unfermented wine, evangelistic work, good health and heredity, soldiers and sailors, social purity, literature and periodicals, outreach among colored people, woman suffrage, anti-narcotics, peace and arbitration, and kitchen gardens.

624   *y,r   VANCE, CATHERINE S. *The Girl Reserve Movement of the YWCA.* New York: Bureau of Publications, Teacher's College, Columbia University, 1937. ix, 184 pp. Notes, bib.

     Providing more theory than detail, Vance discusses the Girl Reserve Movement at the Young Women's Christian Association, founded in 1918. By 1934, it had grown in membership to include 325,000 girls, making it larger than the Girl Scouts and Brownies (288,290 members) and Camp Fire Girls and Bluebirds (134,851). Determined to build character in a Christian organization, the group, Vance says, considered itself to provide more opportunities for democratic participation than did the Camp Fire Girls and to be less competitive, in terms of external rewards and badges, than were the Girl Scouts. The Girl Reserve stressed social idealism from religious commitment. Among the projects it encouraged was wartime relief work for patriotic purposes. Beginning in 1881, the YWCA established rooms for girls' association, with games, reading tables, halls for entertainments and calisthenics, equipment for sewing and cooking, music, and formal classes for high school and college-age girls. By 1920, the groups pressed to encourage social responsibility in its membership. In the period 1926-34, greater flexibility was seen in the program, based on the interests and needs of the girls and stimulated by adult leaders trained in Adult Guidance Councils. Religion remained prominent in the work of the organization. The author is highly skilled at examining change over time in the material she analyzes.

625   *c   VANCE, LINDA D. "May Mann Jennings and the Royal Palm State Park." *Florida Historical Quarterly* 55 (July 1976): 1-17. Notes, illus.: May Mann Jennings; Royal Palm State Park; Royal Palm State Park Board dedication of the Everglades in 1918.

      This biography of May Mann Jennings outlines a clubwoman's thirty-three-year career as an activist for public reforms. To her efforts is credited the establishment of Florida's Royal Palm State Park, dedicated as a national park in 1947. Jennings worked through the Jacksonville Woman's Club, Dade County Federation of Women's Clubs, and Florida Federation of Women's Clubs. She took an active role in all the women's organizations to which she belonged, and served as president of the Florida federation in 1904.

626   *c   -----. *May Mann Jennings: Florida's Genteel Activist.* Gainesville: University Presses of Florida, 1985. viii, 200 pp. Notes, bib., appendixes, index, illus.: 15, mostly of May Mann Jennings.

      This biography of a Florida clubwoman from the Progressive Era catalogs the dedicated activism typical in women of the day. The daughter of a Florida legislator and the wife of a Florida governor, May Mann Jennings learned political lessons at home that she would use to reform the state, once her husband retired from government. A perusal of her six-page resumé (included in the appendix) alerts us to the range of organizations and issues she initiated or supported between 1890 and 1966. The list resembles that of other women of her generation: leadership in the state Federation of Women's Clubs, YWCA, Daughters of the American Revolution, Prohibition League, World War I's National Defense Council, Democratic party, and Friday Musicale Chorus. This activity yielded action in support of Florida conservation, beautification, woman suffrage, temperance, health, child labor and compulsory school attendance laws, antituberculosis campaigns, and improved conditions for Seminole Indians. Although respectful of her subject's efforts, the author is willing to reveal such shortcomings of May Mann Jennings and her peers in women's clubs as their refusal to use Beethoven's music while America was at war with Germany and the limits of their cooperation with black clubwomen in Florida. Appendix give her senior essay of 1889; presidents of the Florida Federation of Women's Clubs; locations of conventions from 1885 to 1919; an essay on the "old-girl" network among her influential women friends in clubs and their interests and connections; campaign song for her presidential campaign in the General Federation of Women's Clubs in 1924; women appointed by her to organize Democratic Women's Clubs in Florida counties in 1920; members of the Beautification Committee in 1934; the Florida State Chamber of Commerce; and a list of her achievements and awards.

627   *z VANDENBURG, HELEN. "Thread of Legislation." *Palimpsest* 52 (1971): 146-50.
       See *Palimpsest*.

628   *p VETERANS OF FOREIGN WARS OF THE UNITED STATES, LADIES AUXILIARY TO. *Record of the First Twenty-Five Years, Silver Jubilee, Ladies Auxiliary to the Veterans of Foreign Wars of the United States, 1914-1939*. N.p.: the organization, 1939.
       See Ladies Auxiliary to the Veterans of Foreign Wars.

629   *f VROMAN, MARY ELIZABETH. *Shaped to Its Purpose: Delta Sigma Theta, The First Fifty Years*. New York: Random House, 1965.   xi, 213 pp.   Index, appendix, illus.: 1 of Mary Elizabeth Vroman.
       The author was the first black woman to be given membership in the Screen Writers Guild. As an honorary member of Delta Sigma Theta, she writes a laudatory account of the black sorority's origins and fifty years of development. Twenty-two college women founded the association in 1913, splitting off from the first black sorority at Howard University, Alpha Kappa Alpha. The group pledged itself to assist the underprivileged and needy, and did so by working with local Parent-Teacher Associations, black hospitals, and agencies working for social justice and allying with the National Association for the Advancement of Colored People, the Young Women's Christian Association, Red Cross, National Urban League, CARE, and UNESCO. Among the projects that the members undertook included traveling libraries, working for fair employment practices and job training, international relations, mental health, and voluntarism in community service. In 1953, the women purchased a headquarters for all its branches in the District of Columbia at 1814 M Street NW. By 1963, it had thirty thousand members, "sustained by the bonds of sisterhood" to improve society. The appendix lists the following: twenty-two founders; twenty-one living honorary members and twenty-three deceased members; twelve national presidents, 1919-63; national conventions, 1919-63; 163 alumnae chapters, 90 undergraduate chapters, and 26 mixed chapters.

630 *p WAIT, CLARA HADLEY (MRS. WILLIAM HENRY). "Report of the War Work of the D.A.R. of Michigan from April, 1915 to April, 1919." *Michigan History Magazine* 4 (January 1920): 193-242.

After providing a brief history of the Daughters of the American Revolution, the author catalogs with great care the wartime work of its Michigan members. Pages of lists document the donors and gifts of individuals to World War I relief projects. The names of twelve Michigan DAR members who served in the war are provided, along with names of eleven members who went abroad to serve the soldiers. All chapters in the association with dates of founding are included, as are the names of fifty-seven clubs of Children of the American Revolution and Sons of the Republic. The group provided scholarships "for a Comanche Indian in Kansas, a Negro at Wilberforce University, a Philippino," and aided the Blind Babies Home and Berea's Fireside Industries. Members adopted a ship, the USS *Paul Jones*, supplying the crew with knitted garments and comfort bags. They made hot chocolate for aviators, provided films for soldiers, and did sewing for French children. In addition, the group continued its regular patriotic work, placing flags in courtrooms, researching genealogies, studying art and literature, listing historic sites, and marking Revolutionary War soldiers' graves and old national trails.

631 *p WARD, GRACE LOUISE CADMUS (MRS. HENRY CARR), comp. *State History of the New Jersey Daughters of the American Revolution*. Sea Isle City, N.J: Atlantic Printing and Publishing Co., 1929. 367 pp. Index to ancestors of members, illus.: 62 individual portraits of officers; group of officers at 1928 Trenton conference; 5 of furnishings placed in the New Jersey Room of Memorial Continental Hall; 1 monument erected in 1928 by the group; 5 of historical sites; 6 of historical buildings serving as chapter houses.

Although the author provides a history of the New Jersey Daughters of the American Revolution from 1891 to 1928, including lists of the state regents, their biographies, and the 62 chapters and the dates of their founding, the bulk of the text consists of histories of each chapter. Ward includes the date the chapter was organized, the names of its organizers, a history of the historical figure for whom the chapter was named, and biographies of the early (and sometimes every) regent in the group's history. The emphasis is on the individuals rather than the achievements of the entire membership, and considerable credit is given to the administrator who initiated projects. Brief mention is made of the size of the treasury and the membership.

632 *c WARD, MAY ALDEN. "The Influence of Women's Clubs in New England and in the Middle Eastern States." *Annals of the American Academy of Political and Social Science* 28 (September 1906): 205-26.

Ward surveys the accomplishments of northeastern U.S. women's clubs, which began to develop in 1868. She outlines club projects that touched the home (domestic science), the school (kindergartens, manual training, reform schools, decoration of classrooms, the problems of college women, legislation for blind students), the community (public health, civic work, playgrounds, philanthropy), and the state (forestry, pure food, industrial conditions, legislation, civil service reform).

633 *r WASSON, MARGARET. "Texas Methodism's Other Half." *Methodist History* 19 (July 1981): 206-23. Notes.

This work is devoted more to the formal structure of women's organizations than to the good works they initiated. The earliest women's groups in Texas Methodism were parsonage societies, formed to ensure that the preacher and his family had a decent place to live. Soon Ladies' Aid societies also developed, to raise money for the building of the First Methodist Church. In Dallas and in Fort Worth, they formed in 1874; in Beaumont, 1877. The formal organization of missionary societies in Southern Methodist churches began in 1880. However, two years later, the West Texas Conference Missionary Society in Seguin expressed concern about local unfortunates. Therefore, by 1886, the Woman's Department of Church Extension reorganized into the Woman's Home Missionary Society. In 1910, the foreign and home missionary organizations merged. Among its projects was the formation, in black neighborhoods, of Bethlehem Centers. In recent times, the Texas Methodist women reorganized again, renaming their effort the Woman's Society for Christian Service. Today, it is called United Methodist Women, with a membership of 1.5 million.

634 WEBSTER, IRENE. *Seventy-Five Years of Service: A History of the National Society of the Daughters of the American Revolution of North Carolina*. New Bern: Owen G. Dunn Co., 1975.

635 *m WEIMANN, JEANNE MADELINE. *The Fair Women: The Story of the Woman's Building, World's Columbian Exposition, Chicago 1893*. Chicago: Academy, 1981. ix, 611 pp. Notes, bib., index, illus.: hundreds of photos of exhibits and women who participated in the fair.

The author begins by surveying the early work of the Chicago Woman's Club, the Civil War Sanitary Commission, and the WCTU. The primary goal of this study is to document women's participation in the 1893 Chicago fair. It provides a great deal of detail about women's organizations. Early chapters document the organization and development of the Board of Lady Managers, which administered the women's events and the Woman's Building at the exposition. Chapter 19 is devoted to the cooperation and dissent among women's groups for display space. The YWCA, Order of the Eastern Star, Travelers' Aid, National American Woman Suffrage Association, National Council of Women, Women's Christian Temperance Union, Woman's National Indian Association, General Federation of Women's Clubs, Daughters of the American Revolution, Association of Collegiate Alumnae, Working Girls' Clubs, and educational and business organizations are studied. Weimann explores black women's grievances about their exclusion from the planning. Chapter 20, on the Congresses of Women, surveys the speeches presented on topics of interest to women, including many by women's club leaders, dealing with issues to which the clubwomen were devoted.

636 *b,w,r WEINER, LYNN. "Our Sister's Keepers: The Minneapolis Woman's Christian Association and Housing for Working Women." *Minnesota History* 46 (Spring 1979): 189-200. Notes, illus.: matron chatting with 2 guests in Woman's Hotel; exterior of the hotel; parlor of the hotel; exterior of Mahala Fisk Pillsbury Club with members; Woman's Boarding Home in 1940 including 1908 annex; Kate Dunwoody Hall's Garden Court in 1965; 5 girls and a matron at a piano in the Woman's Christian Association's Transient Home for Girls; food preparation in a Woman's Christian Association kitchen; lunchroom; listening to the Victrola; girl paying matron; a girl's room in Woman's Christian Association club; 2 girls and 2 gentlemen callers in a parlor.

In 1866, the Minneapolis Woman's Christian Association formed by churchwomen interested in providing charity for working women. By 1874, it was providing safe lodging for workers and transients. At that time, over nine thousand Minneapolis women, or almost half the female labor force, lived apart from their families. Sixty percent were native-born and 40 percent immigrant. Most worked as domestic servants or waitresses, but almost 20 percent worked in the sewing trades. Their low wages required inexpensive lodgings in a respectable locale, for prostitution lurked as a constant danger unless a domestic influence could instill values of self-reliance, economy, and thrift. In the absence of a YWCA, which was not formed until 1891, it fell to the MWCA to provide a network of homes, under the supervision of a matron or substitute parent, who structured leisure hours with classes and athletics, strictly regulated the institution, and expelled residents for infringement of rules. By the end of World War I, six homes housed one thousand of the city's eighteen thousand female boarders. Gifts from local businessmen enabled the treasury to support the homes. In the twenties, the need for services declined, and vacancies grew increasingly available, owing to the growing sophistication and independence of working women.

637　*n,c WELLS, IDA B. *Crusade for Justice: The Autobiography of Ida B. Wells*. Edited by Alfreda M. Duster. Chicago: University of Chicago Press, 1970. Index, illus.: 6 of Ida B. Wells.

This black leader was born in 1862, a slave in Holly Springs, Mississippi. Her parents and brother died in an 1878 yellow fever epidemic, but she became a teacher in the Memphis city schools and a writer for church and city newspapers. She was fired in 1891 for her critical opinions. In 1884, when a railroad employee told her to move from the white car to the smoking car, she refused and sued the railroad, winning five hundred dollars in damages but then seeing a higher court reverse the decision. By 1892, she took on the cause of lynchings and toured Britain to lecture on the subject. She married Ferdinand L. Barnett and had four children, staying at home until her baby turned eight. She joined a variety of women's clubs, including the American Rose Art Club and the Chicago, Northern District, and State Federations of Black Women's Clubs. She was also active in the Cook County Federation of Clubwomen, an organization that included black and white members. She organized the Alpha Suffrage Club and a neighborhood club that was later named for her. In 1924, she ran against Mary McLeod Bethune for the presidency of the National Association of Colored Women but lost. Among the women's organizations that she describes in her memoirs are the Chicago Woman's Club for black women, the Chicago City Federation of Colored Women's Clubs, the Douglass Center Women's Club, Equal Rights League, General Federation of Women's Clubs, the Chicago Board of Lady Managers in 1893, the National Association of Colored Women's Clubs, the National Women's Civic League conference in the District of Columbia in 1896, the State Federation of Illinois which did not admit black women, the Woman's Suffrage Association, and the Women's Christian Temperance Union.

638　*c WELLS, MILDRED WHITE. *Unity in Diversity: The History of the General Federation of Women's Clubs*. Washington, D.C.: the organization, 1953. xii, 525 pp. Index, appendixes, illus.: 1952-54 president, Mrs. Oscar A. Ahlgren; pins; flags; interior and exterior of headquarters; volunteers in WW I and WW II; all the presidents and founders.

This clubwoman and long-time historian of the General Federation of Women's Clubs wrote a history of the organization's development which includes a survey of the woman's club movement before the GFWC formed in 1890, a description of the organizational meeting, a series of three-page portraits of each president between 1890 and 1953, a history of each committee, and an account of the juniors—a vehicle for attracting younger women to the organization with special clubs and different projects. Wells documents the establishment of a national headquarters at 1734 N Street N.W. in Washington, D.C., to which the leadership moved in 1922. She summarizes the work of the GFWC periodicals and argues their value in communicating club goals and projects. A chapter on organizational details spells out the administrative hierarchy of trustees, board of directors, and membership, discusses the financial structure of the GFWC, and summarizes the debate over exclusion of black participation in 1902. Each biennial convention is discussed, the largest having taken place in Los Angeles in 1924, attracting 7,372 women, 2,407 of whom were club delegates. Wells also includes a paragraph on each state federation in the GFWC, cataloging its size and special strengths. The appendixes offer a list of officers, the 1953 constitution and bylaws, and locations of conventions.

639 *c -----. *Unity in Diversity: The History of the General Federation of Women's Clubs*. Diamond Jubilee Ed. Washington, D.C.: the organization, 1965. 152 pp. Illus.: 26 of officers.

In the seventy-fifth year of the GFWC, Wells updated her 1953 history of the organization, covering the twelve years and six presidential administrations, the programs, and the projects tackled in recent history. She amplified the history she had provided in the previous volume, acknowledging more fully the work of particular nineteenth- and twentieth-century leaders in the organization.

640 *c -----. *Unity in Diversity: The History of the General Federation of Women's Clubs*. Vol. 2. Washington, D.C.: the organization, 1975. xiii, 254 pp. Index, appendix, illus.: 39 of officers; exterior and interior of Washington, D.C., headquarters.

In six chapters, Wells surveys the eighty-five-year history of the General Federation of Women's Clubs from 1890. Although she discusses the clubwomen who shaped the movement even before the federation was formed, the bulk of her text is devoted to the leadership, particularly during the period 1952-75. She also catalogs the achievements, projects, and programs of the membership, as she did in her two earlier histories. Insofar as the pre-1952 sections are brief, this material will best serve researchers of the modern period.

641 *w,c WELTMAN, JANIE GORDON. *Our First Fifty Years: The New England Woman's Press Association, 1885-1935.* Malden, Mass.: Maplewood Press, 1936, 82 pp. Illus.: past and present officers, 1885-1935; group photo at 1936 banquet.

Written by the New England Woman's Press Association president in 1933, this study provides a detailed account of each month of her administration. Beginning in October of 1933 and moving to May 1936, Weltman catalogs the resignations from the club, the forty-ninth birthday party with senior members, names of new members, speakers such as member Mrs. Frances A. Blanchard who edited the woman's page of the *Boston Herald*, singers who entertained at the meetings, members who poured tea at social events, names and affiliations of guests received by the club, details on the annual meetings and elections, reminiscences of members' summer holidays, a speech on women and journalism, Antoinette Brown Blackwell's ideas on "The Progress of Women," problems of a woman drama critic, a fiftieth-anniversary poem, a revision of the bylaws, the president's message, an account of the fiftieth celebration attended by Helen Winslow, the last living member of the six founders and marked with a speech by Congresswoman Edith Nourse Rogers, and notes on the establishment of an International Relations Committee in 1936.

642 *c,n WESLEY, CHARLES HARRIS. *The History of the National Association of Colored Women's Clubs: A Legacy of Service.* Washington, D.C., 1984. viii, 562 pp. Bib., indexes, illus.: hundreds of officers at the national and state levels.

Wesley's history surveys the origins and development of the National Association of Colored Women's Clubs, beginning with the biographies of black women of the nineteenth century active in public reform who assisted in founding the organization in 1896. He examines twentieth-century activities, including war relief in two world wars, the preservation of the Frederick Douglass House in Washington, D.C., and scholarships awarded through 1984. The bulk of the text consists of summaries of club work accomplished at the state and local levels. These vary in length and detail, some summarizing convention resolutions over the years and others featuring the work of a single influential club in the region. Convention meeting places, fund-raising projects, civic programs, clubhouses erected, cooperation with other groups, social service institutions supported, are among the topics considered for the North Eastern Federation, South Eastern Federation, South Western Federation, Central Association, and North Western Federation of the organization.

643   *c WEST, DECCA LAMAR. "Achievements of Three Decades of the Texas Federation of Woman's Clubs." *Southern Magazine* 2 (1935): 30-31, 47.

Praising the "unselfish women who give brains, time and money to help solve social, economic, and educational problems in Texas," West documents the work of the Texas Federation of Women's Clubs. It formed in 1897, with nineteen women's clubs. Twenty years later, it represented sixty thousand women in six hundred clubs. The author details thirty years of presidential administrations, featuring the projects undertaken by each leader. She explores the following issues: organization, library, education, juvenile courts, prison reform, endowment of the organization, Girls Training School, reorganization and compulsory education, World War I relief, educational and cultural programs of the 1920s, Americanization, and the building of a state headquarters in Austin during the 1930s.

644   *s WHEELER, ADADE MITCHELL. "Conflict in the Illinois Woman Suffrage Movement of 1913." *Journal of the Illinois State Historical Society* 76 (Summer 1983): 95-114. Notes, illus.: 1910 suffrage float; Catherine Howard Chandler Christy; Waugh McCulloch; Ella Stewart; 2 of Grace Wilbur Trout; illustration from Brand Whitlock novel, *Her Infinite Variety*; Chicago suffragist greeting Illinois legislators.

This careful and detailed study documents the history of the Illinois woman suffrage struggle. In 1913, Illinois became the first state east of the Mississippi River to give women the right to vote for presidential electors. The author asserts that this was a turning point for the national woman suffrage movement, in providing a precedent and leading a force toward ratification of the federal suffrage amendment. The fight was long and hard, however, the women working for the vote as early as 1869, through the Illinois Woman Suffrage Association. Wheeler traces the conflicts, splits, and changes within the suffrage ranks and enumerates their attempts to change the law. Biographies of Grace Wilbur Trout, physician Anna Ellsworth Blount, Ella Stewart, clubwoman Elizabeth Know Booth, lawyer Antoinette Leland Funk, and Ruth Hanna McCormick, the daughter of Republican kingmaker Mark Hanna, contrast quiet and ladylike methods of persuasion with the more flamboyant techniques of Waugh McCulloch.

645   *w,b,c WHEELER, CANDACE. *Yesterdays in a Busy Life*. New York: Harper and Brothers, 1918. 428 pp. Illus.: 9, of author and friends.

This biography includes the history of the Society of Decorative Art, formed by Candace Wheeler in New York City, in the late 1860s. She wanted to provide a vehicle for respectable women to earn a living and hoped that the production of small pictures, embroidery, and handiwork for affluent women would provide support for impoverished artistic women. The society was formed in the home of Mrs. Benjamin Arnold, because her daughter Charlotte Arnold supported Wheeler's idea. An office on Madison Avenue was secured, and a female Board of Managers and male Advisory Council were selected from prominent New Yorkers. The society stated its objectives: "to encourage profitable industries among women who possess artistic talent, to furnish a standard of excellence and a market for their work," "to accumulate and distribute information on art industries," "to secure rooms to exhibit and sell paintings, wood-carvings, paintings upon slate, porcelain and pottery, lace-work, art and ecclesiastical needlework, tapestries, and hangings by women," "to form auxiliary committees in American cities to receive work for consignment in New York," "to obtain orders from dealers," and to "induce each worker to master a variety of decorative arts and make a reputation of commercial value." Auxiliaries formed in Boston and Chicago and thirty societies of decorative arts supported this organization. For ten years, Wheeler cooperated with the organization and then split off to form a different society with Mrs. William Choate, a Woman's Exchange, which endorsed culinary talents as well and was less stringent in its artistic standards for women.

646   *t WHITAKER, FRANCES M. "Ohio WCTU and the Prohibition Amendment 1883." *Ohio History* 83 (Spring 1974): 84-102. Notes, illus.: Mrs. Harriet McCabe; Mrs. Mary A. Woodbridge; group photo of 5 women including Esther Pugh, Lillian Stevens, Caroline Buell, Frances Willard, Mary Woodbridge.

This article sets out to expose the conflict within the Ohio Women's Christian Temperance Union over the endorsement of the prohibition amendment. Whitaker examines a wide variety of unsuccessful efforts to pressure Ohio legislators and the public to support a prohibition amendment in 1883, undertaken by the organization's leader, Mary Woodbridge. Disgruntled members replaced her with a new leader from Cleveland, Ellen J. Phinney. Tensions continued, as the prohibitionists in the Ohio WCTU voted in 1885 to endorse the Prohibition party, as national president Frances Willard had urged. Woodbridge then returned to the Ohio state WCTU presidency. The Cleveland women, in anger, dissolved their connection with both the national and state WCTU organizations, working alone for temperance goals.

647 *c WHITCOMB, CARRIE NILES. *Reminiscences of the Springfield Women's Club, 1884-1924.* Springfield, Mass.: the organization, 1924. 218 pp. Illus.: 13 of officers.

This history is divided by its clubwoman author into twelve sections, one for each administration. Loving details of the projects undertaken, topics discussed, and social events enjoyed have been collected. In addition, the volume contains a complete list of members and twenty-three pages of poems by the members of the club.

648 *m WHITE, DANA F., and TIMOTHY J. CRIMMINS. "Urban Structure, Atlanta." *Journal of Urban History* 2 (February 1976): 231-52. Notes, tables.

As part of a larger study of Atlanta city development, Dana White has examined residential patterns of black and white clubwomen in 1920 and 1940. She compares membership lists of the three most prestigious black women's organizations, the Chautauqua Circle, Inquirers, and Junior Matrons, with those of the white women in Colonial Dames. The housing patterns that emerge are illuminated by several charts detailing the figures analyzed.

649 *z,r WHITE, WILLIAM GRIFFIN, Jr. "The Feminist Campaign for the Exclusion of Brigham Henry Roberts from the Fifty-Sixth Congress." *Journal of the West* 17 (January 1978): 45-52. Notes, illus.: William Griffin White and Susan B. Anthony.

In 1900, women's groups allied to unseat a polygamous Mormon from Utah who served as a congressman in the U.S. House of Representatives. After an investigation by the Woman's Board of Home Missions of the Presbyterian church, women from other organizations joined in the cry to exclude Brigham Henry Roberts from Congress on the grounds that polygamy was unlawful. Baptist women, Congregationalist women, members of the National Congress of Mothers, and the American Female Guardian Society petitioned to unseat the lawbreaker. The New York State Federation of Women's Clubs and National Council of Jewish Women refused to cooperate in the campaign, which was successful. Members of the House voted to exclude Roberts.

650   no entry

651   *s WILHITE, ANN L. WIEGMAN. "Sixty-five Years till Victory: A History of Woman Suffrage in Nebraska." *Nebraska History* 49 (Summer 1968): 144-63.   Notes, illus.: Mrs. Lucy Correll; contributions to her husband's paper, *Western Woman's Journal*; suffrage banners.

The author has collected the steps that Nebraska women took to gain their legislators' ratification of the federal amendment for women suffrage in August of 1919. She begins in 1855, with Amelia Bloomer's first speech in the state on the topic of woman suffrage. Wilhite examines bills rejected by the Nebraska Territorial legislators, women's school suffrage campaigns, 1881 referendum before the public, songs written by women for their meetings, and opposition by liquor interests, leading business and professional women, women who were antisuffragists, and working women, foreign-born, and German-Americans who sided with brewers.

652   *t WILLARD, FRANCES E. *Glimpses of Fifty Years*. Boston: George M. Smith and Co., 1889. xvi, 704 pp. Illus.: 77 pen and ink sketches of individuals, and groups from WCTU meetings.

Almost a compendium of primary sources, Frances Willard, long-time president of the Women's Christian Temperance Union, includes multitudes of documents, dates, and names of supporters in her account of her life's work. She also prints papers she delivered on "Mother," "Father," "The National Council of Women," and "People I Have Met." While early sections of the volume are devoted to her growing-up years, her teaching experiences, and travels, the meat of the book (pp. 331-74) consists of her account of her labors as a temperance advocate. Also of value to researchers is her chapter on women in politics, surveying her work with the World Women's Christian Temperance Union.

653   *c WILLIAMS, ISABELLA H. *A History of the Brighthelmstone Club of Brighton and Allston*. Cambridge, Mass.: Harvard University Press, 1923. 165 pp. Illus.: clubhouse; founders; officers; children enjoying the club's vacation school.

Founded in 1897, the Brighthelmstone Club quickly became an active association devoted to literary study by its membership and civic reform in the suburbs of Boston. Each administration is examined, detailing the names of its officers and the projects undertaken. A calendar of topics studied and projects initiated, including names of visiting speakers and music performed by artists, is provided. In 1902, the club joined the General Federation of Women's Clubs. In 1901, however, it withdrew, in protest of the GFWC's failure to recognize admission of the New Era Club of Colored Women in Boston, at its biennial convention. This is one of only two clubs to protest this capitulation to southern segregated white women's clubs. In 1908, the club reentered the GFWC.

654 *s WILLIS, GWENDOLEN B., ed. and comp. "Olympia Brown: An Autobiography." *Journal of the Universalist Historical Society* 4 (1963): 1-77. Informational notes, illus.: 2 of Olympia Brown.

The daughter of suffragist Olympia Brown (1835-1926) has edited her mother's memoirs, which were written at the age of eighty-five. Drawing heavily from Brown's published memoir, *Acquaintances, Old and New, among Reformers*, Willis provides ample detail about Brown's twenty-eight-year presidency of the Wisconsin Woman Suffrage Association. In addition, there is material on Brown's earliest women's club activity, membership in the Literary Society at Cedar Park Seminary in Michigan. Brown's work with the American Woman Suffrage Association and the National Woman Suffrage Association, at congresses and conventions of suffragists, is plentiful and richly described.

655 *f WILSON, CAROL GREEN. *We Who Wear Kites: The Story of Kappa Alpha Theta, 1870-1956*. Menasha, Wis.: George Banta Co., 1956. xi, 268 pp. Index, appendix, illus.: 37 of members.

Here is a veritable encyclopedia of material on this sorority's eighty-six-year history, which supplements *Sixty Years in Kappa Alpha Theta*, written by Estelle Riddle Dodge and edited by L. Pearle Green (1930). Part one is succinct, crediting Bettie McReynolds Locke, the first woman student at the Methodist College of Indiana Asbury College (known as DePauw since 1884), with founding the sorority in 1869. The growth of chapters between 1870 and 1955 is surveyed. Special attention is given to the facilities of the fifty-three chapters with their own houses (out of a total of eighty chapters). The author devotes separate chapters to the sorority's emphasis good grades and on good works. The bulk of the text catalogs the "Mature Alumnae" by providing hundreds of brief biographies of alumnae distinguished in a wide variety of endeavors. Larger biographies are collected on alumnae with particular devotion to the work of their sorority's alumnae chapters or clubs. A final, brief section documents the wartime service of the alumnae members and provides a detailed list of the eighty alumnae chapters and clubs, their size, their most successful methods of making money in 1954 and the amounts earned. The appendix lists officers and district presidents, date of charter for each chapter, state chairs, and district conventions.

656　*c　WILSON, CARRIE B. *History of the Carolina State Division of the American Association of University Women, 1927-1947.* Greensboro, N.C.: Riser Printing Co., 1948. vi, 77 pp.

In 1927, the North Carolina State Division of the American Association of University Women formed, electing officers, holding conferences, and initiating collective projects for state branches of the organization. Although education was the focus of the work, women interpreted it broadly and took on programs involving international relations, fellowships, war relief work in World War II, arts, legal and economic status of women, social studies, and the situations of recent graduates. The study provides statistics and lists on dates of branches that formed in North Carolina, names of first branch presidents, and officers of the state organization between 1927 and 1947. Fifteen histories of the branches, totaling one thousand members, survey local projects, especially those undertaken in the 1940s. These include Christmas toy exhibits with safety guides for parents, public nutrition clinics, volunteer activity in war service, relief for the British, art exhibitions, adding equipment to the schools, scholarships, sending books and games to hospitals, organizing Girl Scout troops, studying "North Carolina folklore and pottery," "The Negro in Literature," "Drama," and "Juvenile Delinquency."

657　*y,r　WILSON, ELIZABETH. *Fifty Years of Association Work among Young Women, 1866-1916: A History of YWCAs in the U.S.* New York: National Board of the YWCAs of the U.S., 1916. 402 pp. Bib., index, appendix, illus.: 27 of founders and early officers; classes at YWCA buildings; buildings where the YWCA met; group photo of 1913's fourth biennial convention in Richmond, Virginia; auditorium of Asilomar, California.

This detailed history of the Young Women's Christian Association divides the story into three eras, pre-1866, 1866-1906, and 1906-16. The first section examines the first English Prayer Unions, which began in 1859 and helped inspire U.S. societies to form. In 1858, however, Mrs. Marshall O. Roberts became first directress of New York's Ladies' Christian Association. Its constitution is printed here. The organization held prayer meetings in a Manhattan skirt factory, and soon after it supported a boardinghouse for twenty-one working girls. The second section of this study devotes close attention to the growth of branches and projects, classes for workers, vacation cottages for working girls, entertainments for fund-raising for libraries, boardinghouses, cooking schools, and sewing rooms. Wilson narrates the story of the four early colleges in the Midwest to establish Y branches. The author then moves to the national and international story, enumerating the resolutions passed at annual conferences. The third and last section examines YWCA work thematically, evaluating positively its work with students, city girls, girls in industry, country girls, young girls, foreign girls in the United States, and girls abroad. The appendix gives a chronology of important events from 1844 to 1915 in Young Women's Christian Association history.

658   *r -----. *Mulberry Leaves: The Story of the First Sixty-Five Years of the Women's Foreign Missionary Society of the Methodist Episcopal Church, Wisconsin Conference, 1869-1934.* Appleton, Wis.: the organization, 1934. 56 pp. Illus.: 13 of volunteers at conferences; individual women.

This study celebrates the sixty-fifth anniversary of the 1869 formation of the Women's Foreign Missionary Society from older Boston and Wisconsin women's groups. Wilson traces the origins of the two strains, articulates the course of systematic study on missionary subjects which the WFMS of the Methodist Episcopal church followed in their regular meetings, and documents the women's contributions to the Girls' Orphanage in India. She reprints addresses delivered by returning women missionaries from abroad, hymns and anthems sung by church choirs, and a play, *Mulberry Leaves*, performed throughout the organization's history to inform audiences of their good works. She reports financial figures of the organization and lists officers and women missionaries to Mexico, China, Japan, India, and Malaysia, supported by the fund-raising efforts of this organization's membership.

659   *f WILSON, ESTHER BARNEY. *History of Alpha Chi Omega Fraternity, 1885-1928.* Menasha, Wis.: George Banta Publishing Co., 1929. xii, 404 pp. Index, appendix, illus.: 66 of chapter houses, founders, leaders; maps of chapter locations.

This sorority was founded in 1885 by the dean of the music school at DePauw University in Indiana. All seven young women who founded it were music students, but they decided to admit liberal arts majors as well. Still, an enthusiasm for music has remained steady throughout the years. This eighteen-chapter history is generous with quotations from minutes, the constitution, and reports. It contains personal sketches of the seven founders and fifteen other leaders. It summarizes the work of its twenty-five National Council meetings, 1891-1928, and of twenty national Panhellenic Congresses, 1902-28. A list of twenty-one alumnae clubs and their histories is included, as is a list of fifty campus chapters and their histories. Thirty-two chapter houses are photographed and described. The *Lyre*, the publication, is described. Scholarships for needy children and support for MacDowell Colony, a summer haven for creative artists are among the projects funded. The appendix lists council officers, province presidents, and honorary members.

660   *z WILSON, JOAN HOFF. *Rights of Passage: The Past and Future of ERA*.
       See Joan Hoff-Wilson.

661   *b,y WILSON, OTTO. *Fifty Years Work with Girls, 1883-1933: A Story of the Florence Crittenton Homes*. Alexandria, Va.: National Florence Crittenton Mission, 1933. 513 pp. Index, illus.: homes; Dr. K.W. Barrett; Florence Crittenton; forty-nineth banquet; Detroit superintendents and committee members.

       Here is a comprehensive overview of the National Florence Crittenton Mission work, a network of sixty-five homes for unwed mothers created and supported in the late nineteenth- and early twentieth-century by volunteer women. Sixty-one brief histories of specific homes around the nation are included and sixty-five annual reports for 1932. Five of the homes were supported not by Florence Crittenton Boards but by local Women's Christian Temperance Unions. The first home was established in New York City in 1883. In 1895, the individual homes united to form a national Florence Crittenton Mission and extended their influence by joining the National Council of Women. This volume also includes a biography of businessman Charles Nelson Crittenton, who was inspired to initiate this program upon the death of his young daughter, Florence. In addition, the life of Dr. Kate Waller Barrett, president of the National Florence Crittenton Mission after 1909, is included. Her experience also benefited a number of other women's organizations, including Liberty Bond and Red Cross campaigns during World War I, soldier's rehabilitation programs, and the Virginia Daughters of the American Revolution, for whom she served as state regent.

662   *r WINGFIELD, MRS. MARSHALL. "Church Women United in Memphis and Shelby County." *West Tennessee Historical Society Papers* 25 (1971): 135-37.

In October of 1937, the Council of Church Women was formed by Memphis women who met to observe a World Day of Prayer. The group united representatives of ten churches, the Salvation Army, the Young Women's Christian Association, and one black woman for three purposes: to celebrate the World Day of Prayer, May Fellowship Day, and World Community Day. They aspired to encourage full cooperation between black and white Christians and in 1946 accepted nine black churches into the membership. The organization took on many causes, including assisting servicemen and providing charity for the underprivileged. They donated money to a milk fund and held a white elephant sale to contribute funds to a black nursery. In 1966 the Roman Catholics joined. A member of the Memphis group was elected to the National Board of Church Women United, an organization with 2,400 chapters representing 15 million women. In 1967, the name was changed to Church Women United. In 1969, the women separated from the National Council of Churches and became autonomous as Church Women United. In that year, its first black woman president was elected, Mrs. W.B. Brooks. The author lists the Memphis/Shelby County presidents from 1937 to 1969.

663   *c WINSLOW, HELEN M. "The Story of the Woman's Club Movement, Part 1." *New England Magazine* 38 (July 1908): 543-57. Illus.: president, Sarah Platt Decker; vice president, Eva Perry Moore; auditor, Mrs. Percy Pennybacker; vice president, Mrs. May Allen Ward; Mrs. Ione Cowles; Mrs. John D. Sherman; Mrs. Denison; Miss Georgia Bacon; Mrs. Caroline Severance in Los Angeles; Charlotte Wilbour, Sorosis; Ellen Henrotin; Jane Croly.

Anticipating the findings in her volume on the history of the General Federation of Women's Clubs, Winslow lists the earliest women's club in each state in the United States. She asserts the magnitude of enthusiasm and results by surveying the many committees and issues in art, civics, civil service, education, household economics, pure food, forestry, industrial and child labor, legislation, and library extension that were supported by clubwomen. She bares the rivalry between Sorosis and the New England Woman's Club over which group was earliest in 1868 to initiate the women's club movement, and suggests it was neither, but the Jacksonville Ladies Education Association, founded in 1833. She lists other examples of early clubs and also features the contributions of many early clubwomen.

664   *c -----. "The Story of the Woman's Club Movement, Part II." *New England Magazine* 39 (October 1908): 214-22. Illus.: Mrs. Cornelius Stevens, president of the Philadelphia Civics Club; Mrs. Lilian C.

Streeter, Concord, New Hampshire, Federation founder; Mrs. William Tod Helmuth, president of the Pioneers; Miss Louise B. Poppenheim, Charleston, first president of the South Carolina Federation; Mrs. C.B. Buchwalter, Springfield, Ohio State Federation of Women's Clubs; Mrs. Mary Wood, Portsmouth, New Hampshire, manager of the Board of Information.

This article describes the founding of the General Federation of Women's Clubs in 1890, from an 1889 conference attended by representatives of sixty-one women's organizations called together to celebrate the twenty-first birthday of a New York City women's club, Sorosis. She accuses Boston women of sour grapes, for refusing to participate. She credits the women of Portland, Maine for inventing the idea of local federations and praises the states of Maine, Iowa, Utah, Massachusetts, and Kentucky for quickly federating their local clubs into unified state federations, devoted to the consolidation of energy and resources to facilitate the success of their civic projects.

665 *t WITTENMYER, MRS. ANNIE. *History of the Woman's Temperance Crusade*. Philadelphia: Women's Christian Temperance Union, 1878. 781 pp. Illus.: Mrs. Annie Wittenmyer; sketch of a Crusade scene; leaders of the Crusade.

Perhaps to assert her importance as the first Women's Christian Temperance Union leader, despite Frances Willard's usurpation of her presidency, Wittenmyer spares no detail to write a giant history of the early years of the organization. She provides portraits of Women's Crusades in specific Ohio towns in the winter of 1873-74 and then reviews the first projects, officers, opponents, court cases, and antagonistic judges encountered by temperance advocates in Indiana, Illinois, West Virginia, District of Columbia, Pennsylvania, New York, Vermont, New Hampshire, Rhode Island, Massachusetts, Maine, Michigan, Wisconsin, Minnesota, Iowa, Missouri, California, Oregon, New Jersey, Maryland, Connecticut, and Delaware.

666 *s WITTMAYER, CECILIA. "The 1889-1890 Woman Suffrage Campaign: A Need oo Organize." *South Dakota History* 11 (Summer 1981): 199-225. Notes, illus.: Alice Pickler; Emma Smith DeVoe.

South Dakota women had not formed a woman suffrage association in 1889, so it was Women's Christian Temperance Union members who brought petitions to the legislators who framed the constitution for statehood. Outsiders came to speak on behalf of women's enfranchisement, including Matilda Joslyn Gage and later Carrie Chapman Catt, Anna Howard Shaw, and Susan B. Anthony.

The population, widely dispersed, was difficult to organize, and brewers encouraged the foreign population to vote against woman suffrage. Although the Farmers Alliance supported the women, the other political parties did not, and women were not successful until 1918 in winning the vote.

667　*z　WOLFE, ALLIS ROSENBERG. "Women, Consumerism and the National Consumers' League in the Progressive Era, 1900-1923." *Labor History* 16 (Summer 1975): 378-92. Notes.

Many middle- and upper-class women who wished to participate in the progressive reform movement, turned to the National Consumers' League to exert influence as consumers to improve working conditions for women and children workers. Under the leadership of Maud Nathan and Florence Kelley, the organization grew from New York City's Working Women's Society, active in the 1890s. In New York, the league developed tactics and goals later adopted by other local branches and the national leadership. They worked for protective legislation limiting workers' hours and improving the conditions under which they worked. They also pressed for ethical control of consumption, preparing a White List of employers who paid fair wages and provided decent conditions for workers. The list could guide shoppers to give their business to decent merchants and manufacturers. In 1904, the National Consumers' League and the International Ladies Garment Workers Union clashed over their common use of labels to identify their association with a product. Hurt by Red baiting in the 1920s, the organization weakened, having enjoyed only minimal success in its heyday in the first two decades of the twentieth century.

668　no entry

669　*c　WOOD, MARY I. *The History of the General Federation of Women's Clubs for the First Twenty-Two Years*. New York: History Department, General Federation of Women's Clubs, 1912. x, 445 pp. Index, illus.: 14 portraits of early officers.

To provide one of the basic reference works for understanding the programs of the General Federation of Women's Clubs, this member and director of their Bureau of Information reviews pre-1890 women's literary clubs, surveys accomplishments at the biennial conventions held between 1890 and 1912, recounts federation ideals, and prints eighteen documents: the constitution, original bylaws, modified bylaws of 1896, 1902 and 1910, incorporation documents, list of first organizations, and founding date of each state federation.

Whereas Jane Cunningham Croly's 1898 study stressed the work of local clubs, this history emphasizes the leadership in national positions and justifies their turn-of-the-century attention to civic reform at the expense of literary study.

669a   *c WOODY, THOMAS. "Woman's Club Movement." In *A History of Women's Education in the United States.* Vol. 2. New York: Science Press, 1929, pp. 453-68. Notes, bib., index, illus.: Jennie C. Croly.

670   *c -----. "Woman's Club Movement." *Chatauquan* 59 (June 1910): 13-64.
       See *Chautauquan.*

671   *c WORRELL, DOROTHY. *The Women's Municipal League of Boston: A History of Thirty-five Years of Civic Endeavor, 1908-1943.* Boston: the organization, 1943. xvi, 224 pp.
       Bent on establishing a program of "Municipal Housekeeping," or urban reform projects devoted to public improvement and sanitation, education, and social welfare, Mrs. T. James Bowlker, "a sister of President Lawrence Lowell of Harvard," founded the Women's Municipal League of Boston in 1908. In the thirty-five years that this study surveys, only three other presidents joined Bowlker in directing the association (Mrs. R.T. Paine, the second; Mrs. Frederick T. Lord, and Mrs. Henry D. Tudor). The object—"to educate and organize among the women of Boston and the surrounding communities an intelligent, representative public opinion which will exert its influence in the public service"—was thoroughly met. Extensive quotations from club surveys and reports prove that the women carried out their mandate. Among the projects they took on were the creation of public gardens, playgrounds, organizing schoolchildren into Junior Municipal Leagues to work for a better and cleaner city, recreation centers open in the evening with classes, clubs, a library, needlework, naturalization help, well-baby clinics, prenatal care clinics, classes in English for the foreign-born woman, an open-air school for "Anemic and Otherwise Delicate Children," inspection of streets and alleys, anti-fly and rat campaigns, household nurses, war work, and canning kitchens. A tight chronological list of programs is provided at the back of the text.

672   *s WRIGHT, JAMES R., Jr. "The Assiduous Wedge: Woman Suffrage and the Oklahoma Constitutional Convention." *Chronicles*

of Oklahoma 51 (Winter 1973-74): 421-43. Notes, illus.: William H. Murray, suffrage opponent, and Henry Asp, prosuffrage figure.

In September 1907, the Oklahoma Constitution was said to be one of the most progressive ever enacted by any state, but it restricted woman suffrage to school elections. Wright documents women's efforts to achieve enfranchisement in the seventeen years before the ratification of the new constitution. As early as 1890, suffragist and temperance advocate Mrs. Margaret O. Rhodes rallied supporters to pressure for suffrage in Oklahoma. The first Oklahoma Territorial Legislature rejected woman suffrage, however, in that year. At the turn of the century, suffrage organizations, allied with the National American Woman Suffrage Association, formed in the state and attempted to win suffrage again. They failed. Dr. Anna Howard Shaw, from national headquarters, came to stir up support in the Indian Territories in 1904. Wright lavishes care on articulating the opposition of male delegates in government. He suggests that women's lack of success came from white women's failure to work for woman's vote, for fear that black women would deliver electoral power to the black population, and because the issue was perceived by some as socialistic.

672a *m WULFEKAMMER, VERNA MARY. *Ella Victoria Dobbs: a Portrait Biography.* N.p.: Pi Lambda Theta, 1961. xi, 235 pp. Bib., index, illus.: 6 of Ella Victoria Dobbs.

This biography of Ella Victoria Dobbs (1866-1952) was authorized by Pi Lambda Theta, a national honorary education fraternity for women, which she helped to found in 1910. Dobbs served as national president from 1921 to 1925 and edited its *Pi Lambda Theta Journal* from 1921 to 1933. The book narrates her life of teaching and her philosophy of participatory education in the arts for elementary school children and details her activity in voluntary associations. Among those described are early suffrage associations in Missouri, League of Women Voters (president, 1923-24), American Association of University Women (1928 State Education Chair), Tuesday Club, Delta Phi Delta, a national honorary art fraternity, Art Lovers Guild, Faculty Women's Club, Business and Professional Women's Club (for which she taught parlimentary law in 1925), Fortnightly Club, Columbia Weavers Guild, Mothers Club of Columbia, Parent-Teachers Association, Missouri Federation of Women's Clubs, Missouri State Teachers Association, Missouri Art Education Association, Association for Childhood Education International.

673   *s YOUMANS, THEODORA W. "How Wisconsin Women Won the Ballot." *Wisconsin Magazine of History* 5 (September 1921): 3-32. Notes.

The author participated in the 1912 campaign for woman suffrage in Wisconsin, and she provides a vivid memoir of the final decade of activism in her state. The Political Equality League to which she belonged created stunts, auto tours, and airplane spectacles to catch the attention of the public. Youmans also researched the earlier efforts to attain enfranchisement for women, however, beginning her story in 1849, when a local newspaper insisted, "Women are confessedly angels and angels do not vote." Suffragists began to lecture and organize in the 1850s and held a state convention for universal suffrage in 1867. It was in 1881 that their bill was defeated by popular referendum. In 1912, they lost again, 227,000 to 135,000. Youmans argues that women's fervent patriotic and relief work in World War I hastened their enfranchisement, which finally occurred after the war.

674   *z YOUNG, LOUISE M. "The Records of the League of Women Voters, 1920-1944." *Library of Congress Quarterly Journal* 8 (February 1951): 3-11.

In the process of describing the holdings of the League of Women Voters for the years 1920-44, which were acquired by the Library of Congress in 1950, the author surveys the projects and issues which the woman's organization addressed from its founding, on the eve of the woman suffrage amendment's ratification, through its activities in World War II.

675   *m -----. "Women's Place in American Politics: The Historical Perspective." *Journal of Politics* 38 (August 1976): 295-335. Notes.

Here is an overview of women's political activity from colonial times to the early twentieth century. Young discusses Puritan women, Quaker women, the early First Ladies, Frances Wright, the Grimké sisters, the Quaker women who founded the independent Female Anti-Slavery Society in 1833, the women who attended the 1840 World Anti-Slavery Conference, the Seneca Falls Women's Rights Convention organizers, the Civil War split of suffragists into the National and the American Woman Suffrage associations, Association for the Advancement of Women (1873-97), Women's Christian Temperance Union, National American Woman Suffrage Association, state suffrage campaigns, and settlement house reformers.

676   *w ZAGEL, HENRIETTA. "Business and Professional Women in Retrospect." *Palimpsest* 52 (1971): 155-58.
See *Palimpsest.*

677 *m ZIEBARTH, MARILYN. "Woman's Rights Movement."
Minnesota History 42 (Summer 1971): 225-30. Illus.: 1914 suffrage
rally; 7 women in literary society.

    With brevity, Ziebarth describes a suffrage rally held by seven
Minnesota women who had formed a literary society. She surveys
national women's history developments with examples of Minnesota
women's organizational activity, stressing suffrage, the Young Women's
Christian Association, and literary societies.

678 *y,c ZIMMERMAN, JOAN G. "Daughters of Main Street:
Culture and the Female Community at Grinnell, 1884-1917." In
*Woman's Being, Woman's Place: Identity and Vocation in American
History*, edited by Mary Kelley, 154-70. Boston: G.K. Hall and Co.,
1979. Notes.

    Zimmerman unfolds the development of women's
organizational life in Grinnell, Iowa. She examines the popularity of
Chautauqua Literary and Scientific circles throughout Iowa, with 99
branches in 1895, and 668 by 1919, comprising twenty thousand
members. In Dubuque, the Ladies Literary Association enjoyed
prestige. At Grinnell, campus organizations at the college attracted
young women. The Calocagathian Society, a literary club, had been
founded in 1863. The Young Women's Christian Association and other
clubs rounded out a broad range of societies to which college women
were attracted.

Index

References are to entry numbers.

The symbol (+) after an entry number designates that the item listed contains both text and illustration.

The symbol (■) after an entry number designates that the item listed contains only an illustration.

Coleman, Alice B., 318(■)
Collect, 559
College Alumnae Club, 602
College Equal Suffrage League,
 294, 410, 581
College Settlement Association,
 496
Colonial Dames of America. *See*
 National Society of Colonial
 Dames of America
Colonial Dames of the Seventeenth
 Century, 45a
Colony of New England Women,
 Minnesota, 191
Colorado Cottage Home, 69(+)
Colorado Equal Suffrage
 Association, 40a
Colored Authors and Educators
 Association, 429
Colored Circles, 238
Colored Girls' Council, Cincinnati,
 Ohio, 336(■)
Colored Ladies Legal Rights
 Association, Denver,
 Colorado, 155
Colored Methodist Episcopal
 Church, 396
Colored Social Settlement,
 Washington, D.C., 247
Colored Woman's Conference, 115
Colored Woman's League, 189,
 315, 602
 Washington, D.C., 104, 247, 335,
 363, 429
Colored women, 7, 141, 290, 304,
 528, 541, 623, 653. *See also*
 Black Women; Negroes;
 Race; and entries coded n
Colored Women's Progressive
 Franchise Association in
 Washington, D.C., 601
Colored Women's Republican
 Club, Denver, Colorado, 155

Colored Women's Suffrage Club,
 Louisiana, 601
Colored Young Women's Christian
 Association, Washington,
 D.C., 247
Colt, Henrietta, 292
Columbia League of Women
 Voters, 520
Columbia Maternal Association,
 Washington Territory, 160
Columbia Readers, Missouri, 672a
Columbia University, 384
Columbia Weavers Guild,
 Missouri, 672a
Columbian Council, Allegheny-
 Pittsburgh, 526
Commission for Relief, Belgium, 5
Commission in Inter-racial
 Cooperation, 32, 242, 415
Commission of Indian Affairs, 44
Commission of Race Relations, 571
Commission on Racial
 Relationships, 2
Committee for the ERA,
 Connecticut, 501,
Committee for the ERA,
 Massachusetts, 501
Committee on the Elective
 Franchise, Mississippi, 594
Community Chest, 498
Community House, 466
Community House, State Industrial
 School for Girls, Tecumseh,
 Oklahoma, 474
Companions of the Forest, 214
Concord Summer School of
 Philospophy, 284
Concordia Society of Swedish
 Hospital, Minnesota, 191
Confederacy, 16(+), 342, 353, 392,
 395, 467, 539, 546, 604
Confederate Museum, Virginia,
 467, 604

Daughters of the Sphinx, 214
Davis, David, 345(■)
Davis, Elizabeth, 146(■)
Davis, Jefferson, 353, 552, 604
Davis, Mrs. John, 277(■)
Davis, Pauline Wright, 446, 483,
  562(■)
Davis, Philip, 102
Davis Amendment, 1
Dawn Patrols, 124
Day care, 49, 124, 363, 529
Day nursery, 180, 247, 261, 279,
  335, 534, 542
De Zavala, Andina, 3(+)
Decker, Sarah Platt, 102(■), 486,
  663(■)
Declaration of Rights of Women,
  186. *See also* Seneca Falls
  Declaration of Sentiments
Deer Lodge Women's Club,
  Montana, 618
Degree of Honor, 72
Degree of Honor Protective
  Association, 214
Deloria, Ella, 44
Delphian Course, 607
Delta Gamma, 154, 572(+)
Delta Phi Delta, 672a
Delta Sigma Theta Sorority, 23,
  289(+), 602, 629
Delta Theta Tau, 316(+)
Democratic Party, 54, 96, 201, 223,
  271, 311, 361, 415, 455, 472,
  486, 523, 553, 626
Democratic Party, Women's
  Division, 235
Democratic Women's Club, Duval
  County, Florida 403
Democratic Women's Club,
  Florida, 626
Demorest's Monthly, 566
Denison, Dimies T.S., 102(■)
Denison, Mrs., 663(■)

Denny, Arthur A., 348
Denver Fortnightly Club, 563
Denver Ladies' Relief Society, 280
Department of Education, 559, 617
Department of Labor, 559
DePauw University, Indiana, 131,
  655, 659
Deseret Agricultural and
  Manufacturing Society, 603
Desha, Mary, 400, 579
DeSolmes, Madame Therese
  Blanc, 150(+)
Detroit Association of Colored
  Women's Clubs, 461
Detroit Literary Club, Minnesota,
  191
Detzer, Dorothy, 473
DeVoe, Emma Smith, 78, 345,
  346(+), 348(+), 349, 350,
  666(■)
Dickens Club, Pierre, South
  Dakota, 450(+)
Dickinson, Anna E., 40a(■), 445,
  512(+), 562,(■)
Dickinson, Mary Lowe, 528
Diggs, Annie L., 549(■)
Dinkins, Mrs. M.J., 396(■)
Disabled, 622
Disarmament, 1, 36, 89, 120, 312,
  368, 617
Discoverers Club, Findlay, Ohio,
  64(+)
District of Columbia Historical
  Society, 177
Dix, Mary Augusta, 160
Do Everything Policy, 61, 102, 169,
  175, 229, 619
Dobbs, Ella Victoria, 672a(+)
Dodd, Eva Webb, 154
Dodge, Mrs. Arthur M., 595
Dodge, Estelle Riddle, 655
Dodge, Grace H., 150, 228(+), 462,
  482, 541

102(■), 109, 114, 118, 122,
126, 145, 151, 158, 173, 182,
187,189, 198, 215, 219, 233,
235, 236, 245, 309, 312, 314,
317, 385, 391(+), 402, 432,
449, 457, 474, 476, 486,
494(■), 499, 512, 513, 521,
523, 528, 547, 556, 559, 561,
564, 567(■), 589, 606, 607,
612, 618, 626, 635, 637, 638,
639(+), 640(+), 653, 663,
664(+), 669(+)
General Sewing Circle Committee
of the Mennonite Board of
Missions, 330
Geneva, 486
Geneva Disarmament Conference,
36, 473
George Eliot Club, Massachusetts,
494(■)
George Washington Memorial
Chapel, Valley Forge, 438
Georgia Federation of Women's
Clubs, 418
Georgia Missionary Women, 396
Georgia Woman Suffrage
Association, 393, 591
Germany, 626
Gerritson Collection of Microfilms,
24, 483
Gifford, Susan S., 574
Gill, Laura Drake, 102(■)
Gillfield Baptist Church, 357
Gilman, Charlotte Perkins, 449
Girl Guides, 495
Girl Reserve Movement, 624
Girl Scouts, 219, 495, 506(+), 514,
580, 585(+), 624, 656
Minnesota, 191
Stillwater, Oklahoma, 585
Girl's Business Club, 180
Girls Friendly Society, 72
Tennessee, 600

Girls' Normal School, Boston,
Massachusetts, 206
"Girls of the Sixties," Columbia,
South Carolina, 405
Girls' Orphanage in India, 658
Girls Training School, 643
Girls' Union Circle, Buffalo, New
York, 536
Gold Star Mothers, Florida, 45a
Golden Gate Park, 152(■)
Goldman, Emma, 216
Good Citizenship League, 102(■)
Good Samaritan Sisters and
Female Building Society, 357
Goodlet, Mrs. C.M., 467
Gordon, Anna, 61
Gordon, Kate, 23, 314
Gould, Mrs. Harriet, 51
Graduates' Association of the
Buffalo Seminary, New York,
48
Gragg, Rosa, 461
Graham, Isabell, 211
Grand Army of the Republic, 5, 199
American South, 143
Grand Camp of Confederate
Veterans, 546
Grand International Auxiliary to
the Brotherhood of
Locomotive Engineers, 21a
Grand Traverse Herald, 81
Grange, 72, 392, 468
Indiana, 386
Kansas, 621
Michigan(Committee for
Women's Work), 387
Montana, 508
New York State, 386
Grange Visitor, 387
Grannis, Elizabeth B., 528
Gratz, Rebecca, 218
Gray, Mrs. Arthur S., 67a(■)

International Council of Women, 21a, 102(■), 153, 249, 251, 527, 528, 533, 556(■), 564, 565

International Council of Women, Committee on Peace and Arbitration, 565

International Council of Women of the Darker Races, 289

International Federation of University Women, 293, 589

International Kindergarten Union, 182

International Ladies Garment Workers Union, 217, 327, 362, 667

International Migration Service, 541, 542

International Order of the King's Daughters and Sons, 221, 238(+)
  Detroit,(In As Much Circle), 461
  New York City, 534
  Tennessee Branch, 600

International relations, 456

International Suffrage Alliance, 158, 533

International Sunshine Society, 21a, 102(■)

International Woman Suffrage Alliance, 251, 293, 460, 513

Inter-racial Council of the Federal Council of Church Women, 289

Iowa Wesleyan College, 107, 464, 480

Iowa Woman Suffrage Association, 101, 445

Irish women, 402

Italian women, 402

Italy, 29

Jackson, Andrew, 395, 600

Jackson, Kate, 61

Jacksonville Garden Club, Florida, 12

Jacksonville Ladies Education Association, 663

Jacksonville Woman's Club, Florida, 45a, 625(+)

Jacob Holt House, 128(+)

Jacobs, Frances, 280

Jacobus, Mary, 507

Jamaican women, 124

James, Ada, 231(+)

James, David, 231(+)

James, Hall, 407

Japan, 29, 83, 441, 541, 590, 658

Japanese-Americans, 124

Japanese Women's Home, Seattle, Washington, 318(+)

Jefferson Davis National Highway, 353

Jefferson, Thomas, 395

Jenkins, Therese A., 40a(■), 350(■)

Jennings, May Mann, 625(+), 626(+)

Jewish Culture Club, Indiana, 248

Jewish Home for the Aged, Rhode Island, 282, 283

Jewish Times and Observer, 58

Jewish women, 58,72, 194, 218, 227, 246, 280, 282, 283, 320, 327, 370, 373, 470, 500, 526, 535, 536, 554, 556, 568, 622

Jewish Women's Congress, Chicago, 218

Jim Crow, 259, 315

Joan of Arc, 5, 232, 428(■)

Job's Daughters, 214

Johns, Laura Mitchell, 28(■), 549(■)

Johns Hopkins University, 185

Johnson, Lucy Browne, 621(■)

Johnston, Lucy, 549(■)

Joint Committee of Representative Women's Organizations, 293

Missouri Federation of Women's
Clubs, 490, 672a
Missouri State Teachers
Association, 672a
Missouri Women's Committee of
the National Defense
Council, 490
Mitchell, Maria, 334
Mitchell, Rebecca, 349
Mitchner, Lillian May Early, 28(■)
Mizrach Women's Organization of
America, 470
Molly Pitcher Clubs, 342
Monday Class, Buffalo, New York,
48
Monday Club, Indiana, 248
Monday Club, Minnesota, 191
Monmouth College, 110, 128
Monroe, Lilla Day, 549(■)
Monroe County Woman Suffrage
Party, New York, 404
Montana Woman's Suffrage
Association, 346
Montefiore Lodge Ladies Hebrew
Benevolent Association,
Rhode Island, 283
Monticello, 395
Moon, Lottie, 557
Moore, Eva Perry, 102(■), 663(■)
Moore, Clara, 421, 424
Moral Reform Societies, 31, 67,
119, 213, 500, 502, 518
Morgan, Anne, 240(■), 304(■)
Morgan, Mrs. B.T., 418(■)
Morgan, Dr. Joseph Williams, 349
Mormon, 139, 158, 207, 260, 349,
380, 381, 498, 603, 649
Morning Bridge Club, Sapulpa,
Oklahoma, 301
Morris, Mrs. Charles S., 521(■)
Morris, Esther Hobart, 350, 427(+)
Morrison, Mary Foulke, 433

Morristown Female Charitable
Society, 329
Mother Bickerdyke, 5, 82(■)
Mother Cobb, 78
Mother Goose, 22
Mothers and Daughters Club
House, Plainfield, New
Hampshire, 102(■)
Mothers' Anti-High Price League,
194
*Mother's Assistant and Young
Ladies' Friend*, 406
Mothers Club, Columbia, 672a
Mothers' Club, Marvell, Montana,
597
Mother's Day, 619
Mother's Journal, 406
Mother's Magazine, 160, 406
Mott, Lucretia, 76, 77, 186(+),
251(■), 340(+), 433(■), 446,
471, 487, 562(+)
Mozart Club, Minnesota, 191
Mount Holyoke College, 206
Mount Holyoke Female Seminary,
365(■)
Mount Rushmore, 395
Mount Vernon, 395
Mount Vernon Ladies Association,
21a, 142, 395
Florida, 45a
Iowa, 611
Mrs. Simon Baruch University
Prize, 353
Mulberry Leaves, 658
Mumford, Jane, 139(■)
Mumford, Mary E., 476
Municipal Housekeepers, 47, 49,
621, 671
Murray, William H., 672(■)
Music, 4, 19, 36, 37, 49, 50, 67a, 68,
74, 131, 132, 136, 141, 147,
164, 172, 180, 230, 233, 245,
284, 316, 336, 354, 369(+),

Quincy Homestead, Massachusetts, 206
Quincy House, 206(■)
Quinton, Amelia S., 168

Race, 38, 95, 120, 124, 244, 261, 290, 350, 393, 495, 513, 519, 571. *See also* Colored women; Black women; Negroes; Race; and entries coded n
Racism, 2, 273, 337
Radcliffe College, 206, 410
Radical feminists, 219
Raines, Mrs. L.H., 552
Raleigh Fine Arts Society, North Carolina, 114
Raleigh Garden Club, North Carolina, 114
Raleigh Woman's Club, North Carolina , 99(■)
Ramsey County Republican Woman's Club, Minnesota, 191
Ramsey County Suffrage Club, Minnesota, 191
Randolph, Florence, 224
Rankin, Jeannette, 346(+), 508(+)
Rankin, Lochie, 286(■)
Reading Club, Rockmart, Georgia, 418
Reading Club, Sapulpa, Oklahoma, 301
Reaper's Club, Utah, 603
Rebekah Degrees, 111
Red Cross, 4, 5, 21a, 34(+), 73, 93, 109, 152, 157, 163, 180, 199, 241, 378
438, 452, 467, 474, 558, 589, 604, 629, 661
   Clarksville and Montgomery County, Tennessee, 608
   Idaho, 497

   Sapulpa, Oklahoma, 271
Red Cross Corey Ladies, 507
Red Scare, 209
Redwood Grove, 355(+)
Reed, Doris, 452
Reed, Esther de Berdt, 443, 444(+)
Reed, Rev. Myron, 280
Reed, Mrs. William, 185
Reform School for Girls and Women's Prison, Indiana, 248
Refreshment Saloons, 232
Reilley, Laura Holmes, 73
Remond, Sara Parker, 23
Remonstrance, 575
Repeal Week, 342
Republican Committee of Delaware, 289
Republican National Convention, 434
Republican National Committee, 104
Republican Party, 223, 224, 361, 368, 455, 468, 489, 523
Republican Party, Women's Division, 235
Research Club, 289
Revolution, 21, 158
Revolutionary War, 451, 558
Rhode Island Woman Suffrage Association, 483
Rhodes, Margaret O., 672
Richards, Emily S., 40a
Richardson, Mrs. John D., 51
Richmond, Mary E., 528
Rivington Street Settlement, 402
Robbins, Lena Anthony, 223
Roberts, Brigham Henry, 158, 649
Roberts, Margaret, 345(■)
Roberts, Mrs. Marshall O., 657
Robertson, Mrs. Lucy Owen, 73(■)
Robins, Margaret Dreier, 116(+), 159(+), 449
Robinson, Harriet H., 562(■)

Robinson, Mrs., 477
Robinson, Stuart, 237
Robinwood Studio, Ohio, 477
Rockmart Club, Georgia, 418(+)
Rockmart Woman's Clubhouse,
    Georgia, 418(+)
Rockwell, Norman, 506(■)
Roessing, Jennie Bradley, 356
Roger Williams Park, Rhode
    Island, 152
Rogers, Aurelia, 140
Rogers, Congresswoman Edith
    Nourse, 641
Rollin, Lottie, 601
Roman Catholic Church, 43, 92,
    325, 356, 370, 373, 378, 500,
    528, 536, 539, 555
Rookwood Pottery, 173
Roosevelt, Franklin, 359, 512
Rosa, Mrs. Charles D., 36
Rose, Ernestine L., 193, 446, 562(■)
Rotary Club, 364, 490
Rothschild, Mary A., 506
Royal Military College, Sandhurst,
    England, 353
Royal Palm State Park, Florida,
    625(+)
Ruddy, Ella, 499(+)
Ruffin, Josephine St. Pierre, 23,
    67a, 145, 335(+), 363, 601
Runyan, Mrs. F.J., 608
Rural women, 81, 179, 364, 456,
    490, 509, 587, 590. *See also*
    Farm women
Ruskin Art Club, Los Angeles, 288
Russell Plantation, 435
Russell Sage Foundation, 432
Russia, 34
Rust College, 259
Ruth, 5

Sabin, Mrs. Charles H., 100(+)
Sabin, Pauline Morton, 342, 491

Sacajawea, 588
Sacajawea Statue Association, 588
Safford, Laura, 377
Sailors Club in Philadelphia,
    Pennsylvania, 304(■)
St. Joan Society, 501
St. Louis Association for the Relief
    of Orphan Children, 426(+)
St. Louis Business Women's
    League, 520
St. Louis Children's Hospital,
    291(+)
St. Louis Equal Suffrage League,
    520
St. Louis' Ladies Union Aid
    Society, 75
St. Louis Protestant Orphan
    Asylum, 426
St. Louis Suffrage Association, 520
St. Louis Suffrage Club of Missouri,
    601
St. Michael's Church, 438
St. Paul Housewives League,
    Minnesota, 191
St. Paul's Women's City Club, 413
Salem Female Charitable Society,
    351, 430
    Massachusetts, 391
Salem(Ohio) Woman's Rights
    Convention of 1850, 1
Salt Lake County Republican
    Committee, 603
Salvation Army, 662
San Antonio Express, 596
San Diego Center for Children, 529
San Diego Woman's Home
    Association, 529
San Francisco Chronicle, 41(■)
Sanctified Sisters, 555
Sandburg, Carl, 240(■)
Sanders, Harriet P., 346(+)
Sanders, Sarepta, 346(■)